ANDY BENOIT'S
TOUCHDOWN
2005

Everything You Need to Know About the NFL This Year

BALLANTINE • NEW YORK

A Ballantine Books Trade Paperback Original

Published in the United States by Ballantine Books,
an imprint of The Random House Publishing Group,
a division of Random House, Inc., New York.

BALLANTINE and colophon are registered trademarks of
Random House, Inc.

This book has not been prepared, approved, licensed or endorsed
by the National Football League (NFL).

ISBN: 0-345-48432-0

Printed in the United States of America

www.ballantinebooks.com

9 8 7 6 5 4 3 2 1

The Game Plan

Team Reports

The Opening Kickoff

Dear NFL fan,

Well, well, well. It looks like the NFL season has finally arrived. If you are like me, then you ought to congratulate yourself for making it through another offseason without succumbing to drinking, gambling, or depression—or at least not in excess. Going seven months without football is never easy. Sure, there's always March Madness and the NBA playoffs, Major League Baseball, or the PGA Tour Majors, but nothing quite compares to the magic that is the National Football League.

We football fans take for granted the great league that we have—we don't stop often enough to appreciate the near perfection with which our sport is presented. We have a game that is *not* overrun by steroids, *not* controlled by a handful of superstar athletes, and *not* in a position to experience a lockout. Ponder for a moment just how great the NFL is—purely from a business standpoint. The league is managed by the best commissioner in sports (Paul Tagliabue), a players union that cares about the integrity of the game, and a collective bargaining agreement that, granted, soon needs to be extended but, nevertheless, is as close to perfect as a deal can get. Since the agreement went into effect in 1993, NFL franchises, on average, have quadrupled in value, while at the same time player salaries have doubled. Finally, and most significant from the perspective of us fans, is that the thrilling competitive balance among the 32 teams has been exquisite. The NFL is as healthy as a sports league can get.

And let's not forget the actual game itself. What, in this great country, compares to a sport like football? It requires athletic prowess, high intelligence, teamwork, leadership, and character. The game of football takes each of the finest qualities that shape America today and combines them into one amazing spectacle.

The NFL is destined for another great season in 2005. The parity achieved by the advancements of the game remains at full tilt; however, there is also the intrigue of teams trying to overthrow a powerful dynasty that stands in New England.

But the unexpected continues to highlight the game today. Even though the Patriots are in their own galaxy right now, who in the world can actually say *for sure* that they'll win Super Bowl XL? Nobody—not with the way this unpredictable league has panned out over the past six or seven years. When I write *Touchdown*, I cannot confidently wager my life on my predictions—instead, I have to almost accept the fact that preseason analysis and rankings are nothing more than *projections*. I, like everyone else, cannot *guarantee* how the 32 teams in the league are going to pan out in 2005. The only thing that I can do is break down how a club looks at the front of the year and form some kind of expectation for them. (Of course, I like to think my "expectations" are, in some way, prophecies—don't we all?)

But after that, as with every other fan, I can only sit back and watch the story unfold, possibly with an unforeseen, fairy-tale ending. Yes, it makes predicting the league hard, but who in the world wouldn't agree that it's a small price to pay for such incredible drama?

Life sure is great. The current days of intense summer heat are soon going to fade away. The sun will set over football fields across America and the evening sky will be illuminated in shades of burnt orange, scattered magenta, and cadet blue over the goalposts. The crickets will chirp, the warm breeze will rustle the trees, and the lush, green grass will begin to dampen. Then, one morning, we'll all wake up to a cooler, crisper air, filled with anticipation and excitement. The days will shorten, the leaves will turn, and the Sunday afternoons will unfold in sheer wonder. The 2005 NFL season will have arrived.

Thank you and enjoy *Touchdown 2005*.

Sincerely,

Andy Benoit

My Five Cents

With each passing day, America is becoming a more opinionated society. From American Idol to red states versus blue states, clear down to nugatory issues like paper or plastic, everybody has an opinion and wants to share it with as many people as possible. The world of sports serves as the headquarters for this growing phenomenon.

No sports league attracts more attention and, thus, more opinions, than the NFL. Being an American and an avid football fan, I am more than guilty of committing the "act of opinionating." In fact, I am so bad that I have even taken the cliché "my two cents" and patented the phrase "my five cents," in an effort to accurately portray the value of my opinions. So while the typical person is attacking issues by throwing in a couple of copper Lincolns, I'm tossing down a nickel Jefferson.

With that, I present a clearheaded and intelligent perspective on some of the key topics concerning the NFL.

New Television Deals

Television is one of the most significant components of the NFL's success. After all, as Pete Rozelle and Roone Arledge learned, most fans experience the game primarily—or even solely—by watching it on the tube. This is why the NFL's new television agreement with the Walt Disney Company—which will move Monday night telecasts to ESPN starting in 2006—is a potentially monumental shift.

I am a major believer in the old adage "If it ain't broke, don't fix it." For me, Monday Night Football on ABC was never broke. I like it just the way it is—I even wish they would bring back the giants smashing helmets in the intro. Being a purist, I fear change the way J.Lo fears commitment.

But granted, I'm not the one who was losing $150 million a year on the show. As a semi-intelligent American, I do realize that change is vital to the success of any business. Nevertheless, I can't help but worry about a few things.

- Is starting Monday night games 20 minutes earlier (8:40 P.M. ET) a smart idea, considering that people in California are still stuck in traffic at 5:40 P.M. on weekdays?
- Speaking of California, what will happen to the beloved Al Michaels and his partner John Madden?
- Does ESPN have the brass to—heaven forbid!—dump Hank Williams, Jr., and the MNF theme music that has captured the hearts of so many and become a staple of the game itself?
- And perhaps most important of all: Is that classic catchphrase going to remain? Am I still going to be asked every Monday if I am ready for some football?

With everything these days being "satellite" this and "high-tech" or "broadband" that, I'm sure the cable network ESPN will carry a strong enough viewership. Plus, the network that is the self-proclaimed "World Wide Leader in Sports" has been just that over the past decade, so ESPN's desire to broadcast MNF is not without merit.

Of course, I still don't understand why the NFL and ABC never dug too deeply into working out a flexible Monday night schedule for the second half of the NFL season in the first place. That could have helped boost ABC's ratings, saved some of that $150 million, and generated another broadcasting deal. After all, the popularity of football has not been subsiding one bit (witness the league's revenue, which has been growing year after year). But somehow the popularity of MNF has faded like that of bell-bottom pants and socks with sandals.

Gee, I wonder why that is. Perhaps it was being stuck with a slate of games in the second half of the 2004 season that featured teams like the 6-10 Dallas Cowboys (twice, I might add!), the 6-10 Kansas City Chiefs (twice!), the 5-11 Tennessee Titans, and the 3-13 Miami Dolphins. Oh, and let's not forget ABC's week 16 showdown between the St. Louis Rams and the "Thanks, but we already clinched homefield advantage" Philadelphia Eagles, who started half of the Central High School Lancers junior varsity squad that game.

It wasn't just 2004—late-season stink bombs have plagued ABC for the past four years. The reason for this, of course, is parity in the league, which has helped everyone in the NFL industry except the Monday night schedule makers.

There are many who will argue that it would be too difficult to reschedule games in the middle of the year, because teams and fans with tickets to the game would have to juggle their agendas on Sundays and Mondays. Please. I can only laugh at that notion. Many more will say that a flexible schedule is not so simple,

Los Angeles already proved itself a letdown when it had the Rams and the Raiders. Why should the city get a second chance now?

mainly because it wouldn't be fair for the league's other networks—FOX and CBS—to lose late-season quality matchups. Well, then how were Dick Ebersol and NBC able to talk the NFL into a flexible schedule for their newly acquired 2006 Sunday night telecasts?

Going Back to Cali?

Back in February, in his State of the League address, NFL commissioner Paul Tagliabue vowed to have a franchise back in the city of Los Angeles in the near future. My question is, "Why?"

I know, I know. It's foolish not to exploit the country's second largest media market, but let's keep a perspective on things and examine the past decade. L.A. *had* a team; in fact, they had *two!* They had the Rams (who, *I* admit, were terrible for a majority of their stay in town) and the Raiders (who, *you* must admit, are one of the most well-known organizations in all of sports). The fans in the city did nothing to keep those clubs there. In 1994, the Raiders' average attendance was 51,196, while the Rams averaged 42,312. Granted, the Rams were only 4-12 that year, but the Raiders were 9-7. Putting records aside, you're telling me that a city with a metropolitan population that hovered around 10 million at the time could not even come close to filling a football stadium? Forget it L.A.; you had your chance.

Needless to say, this rant is irrelevant because the NFL is going to take its blue-collar product to the white-collar citizens of Beverly Hills one way or another, but it would be an absolute tragedy if the league did so by adding a 33rd team. An expansion franchise would jumble the perfectly balanced 32-team league, it would decrease the overall level of play by allowing 53 more players to enter the league, and it would lead to the same problems that have plagued major league baseball and professional hockey. The NFL is already pushing the limit by having 32 teams; just 10 years ago there were only 28 teams. If we have to go back to Tinseltown, let's make a team like the Vikings or Colts pack up and relocate.

NFL Illegal Contact Rule

After all was said and done in 2004, NFL referees wound up calling 191 illegal contact penalties during the regular season, which was nearly 2½ times as many as the previous year's total of 79. However, when all was said and done, not too much had changed, either.

The NFL simply started enforcing a rule that had long been overlooked. Sure, scoring was up 1.3 points per game and passing yards increased by about 20 per game, but after the smoke had cleared, both teams that met atop the mountain and duked it out for the Lombardi Trophy were tied for second in scoring defense. Defense still prevailed.

All we know now is that the NFL's tighter regulations on defensive tactics are entering year two and we won't know for sure how "offensively oriented" the game has become until we have had at least four or five years to evaluate the situation. In the meantime, do not credit Peyton Manning's new single-season touchdown record to the rule adjustments, do not extol a cornerback for making an interception, and do not listen to ex-players whine about how easy it is to play offense these days.

NFL Referees

While we're on the issue of illegal contact, allow me to settle all officiating controversies once and for all by telling fans to shut up and quit blaming their team's troubles on the zebras. The officiating in the NFL is top-notch, especially considering the speed of the game, the number of players on the field, the number of infractions that can occur on any given play, and the number of fans criticizing the select few flag-tossers who are simply doing their job. All in all, the refereeing in the NFL is outstanding.

Occasionally you'll see a poorly judged pass interference call, an oversensitive personal foul, or a flag-happy umpire leave his mark on a game. However, one single play has never once in the history of football determined the outcome of a game. Therefore, a single penalty has never determined the outcome of a game. Instead, devout fans have developed an uncanny ability to make excuses for their team.

Let's break it down. In a hypothetical situation, let's say you're watching a Philadelphia-Dallas game. Eagles cornerback Lito Sheppard is called for pass interference on Cowboys receiver Keyshawn Johnson. It's a close play, so the officials gather together and discuss what they saw, before ultimately reaching the conclusion that a flag should indeed have been thrown. The call is outstanding news to some and an absolute scandal to others.

Work with me here and hypothetically suppose that, for some reason, your life is on the line. The only way that you, the reader, can save yourself is by choosing which side is most likely correct.

Let's take Tom Sifferman who, under head official Terry McAulay, was the field judge in Super Bowl XXXIX, working with the highest-rated crew in the country. As a team, the crew has 65 years of refereeing experience among them, including Sifferman, who alone has 18 years of experience, plus the honor of having worked three Super Bowls. He can truthfully claim that he has dedicated much of his life to the rules of football.

Sifferman saw Sheppard grab Johnson's shoulder while the ball was in the air, so he decided to throw some yellow laundry. He was a mere 15 feet from the players and had a perfect look at the

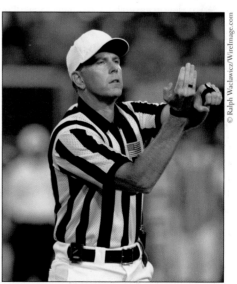

The outstanding officiating in the NFL is one of the most underrated elements of the game.

action. His knowledge and sense of the game told him to throw his flag, so he did.

Now let's look at Joe Fan. Fan is a resident of Philadelphia and has been an avid Eagles supporter for over 30 years. He saw the same play that Sifferman saw, except he was hundreds of feet away, sitting in the 14th row of section 240, which is angled between the goal line and the 10-yard line. He is absolutely sure that Sifferman is a dope and proves it by boisterously booing and screaming to nobody in particular that the ref "must be blind" and that he "isn't watching the same game."

This is where you have to make your decision. Sifferman or Fan? No, you can't look at the replay; that wouldn't be fair. Besides, Fan has already rambled out a slew of allegations claiming that even he could see right away that the play was obviously not pass interference. So whom do you side with? That's what I thought.

Now, just for fun, let's throw in a replay. Sifferman, of course, cannot look at the JumboTron at Lincoln Financial Field. He has to get ready to do his job all over again, not to mention that he's seen this time and again in the NFL; he knows what he called. Fan, on the other hand, has by now seen the play six times from four different angles, each time becoming more and more adamant that the field judge is a closet Cowboys supporter who is trying to throw the game.

Without looking at the replay yourself, who would you *now* say is most likely to be right? Before you side with Fan, let me remind you that your life *does* depend on this. Do you still think the "stupid" official with years of experience blew the call or are you maybe starting to see that perhaps Sheppard really did make a mistake? I'll let you ponder that one for a while . . .

Quick Hits

The NFL's decision to play a regular season game between the Cardinals and the 49ers in Mexico City is, at best, questionable. I am a very patriotic American who takes his football pure, so I can't help but roll my eyes just a little when I hear so much talk about tapping into the international market. Furthermore, why sacrifice a regular season game for Mexico? In the past, the league has played an exhibition game in front of our neighbors to the south. Do you really think the people in Mexico City will care that it's a real game? Also, if I'm a player for the Cardinals, and I see that one of my team's home games is exchanged for a "marketing opportunity," I can't help but question how much the organization really cares about winning. ■■■ The players union and owners are not stupid enough to dillydally on extending the collective bargaining agreement. They have about a year left to do so; otherwise, they'll **lose the salary cap for 2007**, which would send the league into a catastrophic hole. ■■■ Sorry St. Louis, but it's time to join the rest of the league in **throwing out the Astroturf** and replacing it with the safer, more attractive FieldTurf. Even *the Colts* are doing it this year. The league should step in and enforce this. ■■■ Everybody saw the **Terrell Owens and Nicolette Sheridan** controversy on Monday Night Football last year. Much like the Janet Jackson mishap, it was simply inappropriate. But I will say that ABC did do a good

How would you like to be Jerome Bettis and win the Levitra Play of the Year Award? He is recognized for performing *on the field,* right?

job of rectifying their mistake the next week, with an intro to the Chiefs-Patriots game that featured only one provocative question: "Are you ready for some football?" ■■■ Of course, how can league executives point fingers at stunts like ABC's when the NFL Shield has practically morphed into the Levitra logo? I can't even get up for a game anymore without seeing a few hundred ads for erectile dysfunction. ■■■ **Expanding the regular season to 18 games** and cutting the preseason to 2 games is the fastest way to see *more* injuries, *fewer* big games, and *less* young talent on the field. Not to mention that for everybody who was upset with Philadelphia's tank job during the final two weeks of the regular season (a decision that was entirely Andy Reid's prerogative), think about how often such things might occur with two extra weeks of games to play. ■■■ Any agent who allows his **rookie to hold out from training camp** ought to be fired. ■■■ I am sick and tired of hearing about how a player's comments in the media, particularly during the playoffs, can inspire another team, fire them up, and serve as **bulletin board material.** Look at the Patriots last year when Colts kicker Mike Vanderjagt said they were "ripe for the picking." The Indianapolis organization

How can the NFL complain about Janet Jackson and Nicolette Sheridan when the league's shield practically morphed into the Levitra logo?

went crazy because they didn't want to give the Pats any extra incentive to get psyched for the game. Honestly, come on. It's the *playoffs*; this is the *NFL*; these are *professionals*. Do you really think anything that a player says is going to make the other team play harder on Sunday? Let me repeat: It was already the *playoffs!* Season on the line? Everything you worked for coming down to this? Super Bowl in sight? They are going to play hard one way or another. ■■■ P.S.: Enough with teams having this "us against the world" mentality. The entire "nobody gives us a chance, we have nothing to lose, we're underdogs, blah, blah, blah" is way out of hand. Unless you are Ralph Nader, someone is giving you a chance. You're in the NFL—plenty of people believe in you. As far as having nothing to lose, well, I think a big football game or your season is something to lose, isn't it? But maybe that's just me. And John Elway. And Joe Montana. And Brett Favre. And Troy Aikman. And Tom Brady. And any other man who has ever won anything in his life.

Painting a New Picture

During the offseason, the NFL practically becomes its own private trading center, with officials from each team setting out with a list of needs that they hope to address in free agency. Soon-to-be rookies have their stock fluctuate by the day, as hot tips come in from scouts attending workouts and watching film. Even a few of the 32 major corporations that make up the NFL replace their CEO (i.e., their head coach) in hopes of a fresh start. By the time summer rolls around, the once clear and explicit portrait that was the NFL has gone from a fine piece of Gustave Courbet's mid-19th-century realism to Pablo Picasso's Cubism. Here is an artistic look at the major brushstrokes on the NFL canvas this year.

Head Coaches

Romeo Crennel, Cleveland Browns

After 24 years as an assistant coach in the NFL, 57-year-old Romeo Crennel has received his long-overdue invitation to the head coaching party. The former Browns defensive coordinator and, most recently, defensive conductor behind the three-time world champion New England Patriots, is taking over a team that is coming off of a 4-12 season and has won a league-low 30 games since 1999. The Browns gave Crennel a five-year deal, valued at $11 million.

Crennel's presence promises the utter overhaul of a poorly run organization. For starters, he intends to build his team around the same principles that he learned in New England, which prioritizes a player's character ahead of his skill. In fact, Crennel began working on that goal immediately, making it known as early as February that players like Gerard Warren would not be a part of his program in 2005. Crennel will also install his 3–4 defensive philosophy for the Orange and Brown, which should finally get Cleveland out of their dreadful defensive-lineman mind-set and shift the focus more toward their youthful linebackers.

Do not expect the Browns to be refurbished right away; Crennel will need at least two years to fully transform this team into his brand. However, with Romeo around, these Montagues stand a much better chance of finally overtaking the Capulets of the AFC North.

Nick Saban, Miami Dolphins

After last season, the Miami Dolphins needed a change in the worst of ways. With Dave Wannstedt "resigning" midway through and defensive coordinator Jim Bates not being invited back to serve as the head coach (despite an admirable showing under the "interim" label), Miami got serious. Dolphin owner Wayne Huizenga swam upstream, against the current, and convinced Nick Saban, one of the game's most coveted coaches, to leave the college ranks for the big-money world of the NFL. Huizenga is paying Saban,

53, around $5 million a season to help ensure that he won't have to watch his Dolphin team from South Beach slip even farther south and become canned tuna right before his eyes.

Saban, who won a national championship at LSU, is a Bill Belichick product. Although most of his coaching experience comes from the college ranks, he has been highly touted as an NFL guy since his days as Belichick's defensive coordinator in Cleveland (1991–94). Consequently, there has been some speculation that the Fins will install a 3–4 defense in 2005.

In the past, Saban has turned down many proposals to join the NFL, including offers from the Chicago Bears and the Atlanta Falcons as recently as a year ago. So why would he choose Miami now? It's simple: Huizenga gave him full control over player-personnel. Giving control over personnel to any coach leaving the college ranks for the pro game is risky (see Butch Davis in Cleveland). Whether Saban will become Andy Reid and masterfully manage a team both in the front office and on the sidelines, or become a Mike Holmgren (who had his GM duties stripped from him two years ago) is yet to be known.

However, a few things are for sure: He does not waste time and energy, he has won big games with less-than-powerhouse college programs, he is a defensive-minded man, and he has the Belichick factor working for him.

Mike Nolan, San Francisco 49ers

Of the three head-coaching changes in the NFL this year, it is more than fair to say that Mike Nolan to the San Francisco 49ers is the most unheralded move. Nolan, 45, has served as the defensive coordinator for the Baltimore Ravens for the past three years. Before that, he had the same job with the New York Giants, the Washington Redskins, and the New York Jets.

It is no secret that Pete Carroll of USC was the first choice of 49ers' owner John York. Following Carroll were unavailable names like Holmgren and Crennel. However, Nolan did beat out several other NFL offensive and defensive coordinators for the job. He proved that he can work well with young talent when he was able to maintain the Ravens' defensive dominance with several second- and third-year players over the past two seasons.

Furthermore, what head-coaching job could possibly carry less pressure than replacing Dennis Erickson and taking over a 2-14 team that is still stricken by an inflamed salary cap? Of course, the people in Marin and San Mateo counties, who remember the Super Bowl days of Montana and Rice, likely won't see things that way.

Painting a New Picture

Veteran Acquisitions

1. Randy Moss, WR, Oakland Raiders

Former Team: Minnesota Vikings
Experience: 8th year (28 years old)
How acquired: Traded for LB Napoleon Harris and 1st- and 7th-round draft picks
Contract: Four years left on eight-year, $75 million deal
2004 Resume: 49 rec., 767 yds., 13 td. (11 games)

It is no secret that Oakland traded for a superstar player who will often be a distracting team-chemistry buster. However, Al Davis's Raiders have never cared one iota about player character, which makes the Black Hole the perfect home for Moss. With Moss around, the Raiders have an offense that is guaranteed to stretch the field and go deep. Other Raiders—namely, receiver Jerry Porter and newly acquired running back LaMont Jordan—will also be more productive now that the league's most talented vertical threat is around.

2. Derrick Mason, WR, Baltimore Ravens

Former Team: Tennessee Titans
Experience: 9th year (31 years old)
How acquired: Released by Tennessee
Contract: Five years, $20 million ($7 million signing bonus)
2004 Resume: 96 rec., 1168 yds., 7 td.

The Ravens have obviously needed a dramatic upgrade in their passing game for some time now (league-worst 159.9 passing yards per game last year), and they could not have found one much better than Mason. For a team that has struggled with consistency (thanks to the youthfulness at quarterback, injuries at tight end, and a deficiency of talent at receiver), Mason offers a calm and collected approach, with guaranteed game-by-game production. He has the hands to make almost any catch, he runs great routes anywhere on the field, and he has just enough speed and quickness to turn a big play.

3. Patrick Surtain, CB, Kansas City Chiefs

Former Team: Miami Dolphins
Experience: 8th year (29 years old)
How acquired: Traded along with a 5th-round draft pick for 2nd- and 5th-round draft picks
Contract: Seven years, $50.8 million ($14 million guaranteed)
2004 Resume: 58 tkl., 4 int., 11 pd.

The Kansas City Chiefs ranked 32nd in pass defense a year ago, 24th in 2003, and 30th in 2002. This season, those numbers are sure to improve at least a few notches, now that Surtain is manning one side of the field. Often overlooked while playing with Sam Madison in Miami, Surtain is a skilled cover corner who is masterful at playing the ball and capitalizing on big-play opportunities (his total of 25 interceptions over the past three years is the most among all cornerbacks). While perhaps just shy of "shutdown corner" status, Surtain is certainly capable of taking any receiver out of a game on Sundays.

4. Fred Smoot, CB, Minnesota Vikings

Former Team: Washington Redskins
Experience: 5th year (26 years old)
How acquired: Signed as free agent
Contract: Six years, $34 million ($10.8 million in bonuses)
2004 Resume: 61 tkl., 3 int., 13 pd.

Last year, the Vikings were able to upgrade their secondary with the signing of cornerback Antoine Winfield. This season, the upgrades will continue with the addition of Smoot. Smoot's arrival gives Minnesota two first-rate cornerbacks with superb man-to-man cover skills. Even better is the fact that Smoot's style of play—which is predicated on athleticism, speed to cover the deep pass, and the confidence to have a playmaker mentality—will allow other Viking defensive backs more room to operate within what should be an aggressive defensive system in 2005.

5. Samari Rolle, CB, Baltimore Ravens

Former Team: Tennessee Titans
Experience: 8th year (28 years old)
How acquired: Released by Tennessee
Contract: Six years, $30.5 million ($11 million signing bonus)
2004 Resume: 28 tkl., 1 int., 7 pd. (10 games)

Rolle is one of the 10 best cornerbacks in the league. He has a natural feel for the game that allows him to overmatch most opponents. He is coming off an injury-plagued year in Tennessee and a legally trying offseason (Rolle is currently on probation for a domestic dispute with his wife back in February). However, a place like Baltimore has become somewhat of a haven for troubled veterans looking to right their ship. Expect Rolle to rebound just fine. What makes his addition such a home run for the Ravens is the fact that the former All-Pro isn't even the best cornerback on the team. That title belongs to Chris McAlister. When factoring in the amazing range of safety Ed Reed, just image what Rolle will do with such a loose leash facing No. 2 receivers this year.

6. Edgerton Hartwell, LB, Atlanta Falcons

Former Team: Baltimore Ravens
Experience: 5th year (27 years old)
How acquired: Signed as free agent
Contract: Six years, $26.25 million ($8 million signing bonuses)
2004 Resume: 97 tkl., 1 FF

Most football fans do not know too much about Hartwell because he spent the first four years of his career making plays in Ray Lewis's shadow. However, now that he is stepping into the starting middle linebacker role in Atlanta (a team that will play three home games on Monday night this year), the world will finally get a chance to see an athletic 6'1", 250-pounder shine as a defensive standout. Hartwell's game is best summarized by the simple fact that he has an uncanny nose for getting to the football and making tackles.

7. Laveranues Coles, WR, New York Jets

Former Team: Washington Redskins
Experience: 6th year (27 years old)
How acquired: Traded for WR Santana Moss
Contract: Restructured deal; only details released are $5 million in bonuses
2004 Resume: 90 rec., 950 yds., 1 td.

Coles began his career as a Jet, before signing with the Redskins as a restricted free agent in 2003. He has spent two years away from the Meadowlands, but once training camp rolls around, it will seem like he never left. Coles offers the same type of quickness that Santana Moss gave the New York offense, with less breakaway speed but more strength and toughness to go over the middle. Most important will be his close relationship with quarterback Chad Pennington. Both men cried when Coles left New York in 2003. Now the rest of the AFC East can cry at his return.

8. Pat Williams, DT, Minnesota Vikings

Former Team: Buffalo Bills
Experience: 8th year (32 years old)
How acquired: Signed as free agent
Contract: Three years, $13 million ($6 million in bonuses)
2004 Resume: 53 tkl., 3 sacks, 1 int.

Pat Williams has been a stellar tackle in the NFL for most of his career, with the past three or four seasons being his best thus far. Graciously listed at 315 pounds, Williams is a vigorous blocker-eater in the middle of a young Viking defensive line. Williams can draw double teams by anchoring against the run, and every now and then he'll explode with a burst and make a play in the backfield. However, his most important contribution will be simply the attention he receives from offensive lines. His presence will allow Minnesota's young star defensive tackle Kevin Williams, among others, to prosper even more.

9. Kendrell Bell, LB, Kansas City Chiefs

Former Team: Pittsburgh Steelers
Experience: 5th year (27 years old)
How acquired: Signed as free agent
Contract: Seven years, $5 million+ per year, ($10 million guarantees)
2004 Resume: 8 tkl. (3 games)

Kansas City's signing of the oft-injured Kendrell Bell was one of the largest gambles in free agency this year. But considering the Chiefs' linebacking situation a season ago and looking at the return they can get if Bell stays healthy for them, this is a gamble that was definitely worth taking. Bell is a big-bodied superathlete who, thanks to his outstanding power, can take on blockers at the point of attack and disrupt an entire team's interior running scheme. He also has the ability to rush the passer up the middle, which was evident in 2001, when he recorded nine sacks and was named NFL Defensive Rookie of the Year.

10. Reggie Hayward, DE, Jacksonville Jaguars

Former Team: Denver Broncos
Experience: 5th year (26 years old)
How acquired: Signed as free agent
Contract: Five years, $25 million
2004 Resume: 10.5 sacks

The only element that was missing from Jacksonville's budding young defense in 2004 was a destructive pass-rusher up front. The Jags forcefully tried to create such a presence by converting linebackers—such as Greg Favors and Jason Gildon—to defensive end, but it was to no avail. Now Jacksonville can trust Hayward to be their prime pass-rusher in 2005. With a pair of giant tackles as effective as Marcus Stroud and John Henderson, Hayward should be able to use his outstanding burst and quickness against frequent single-man blocking. Hayward is not fully developed as a run defender, but at 270 pounds, he gives Jacksonville a much better option in this department, compared to what they had a year ago.

Biggest Winner

Minnesota Vikings—Bringing in Smoot and Sharper will boost the pass defense tremendously. Adding Williams, veteran middle linebacker Sam Cowart, and linebacker Napoleon Harris will do wonders for the run defense. Despite losing Moss on offense, they still added depth with quarterback Brad Johnson and receiver Travis Taylor, who can be a solid No. 4 option.

Biggest Loser

Washington Redskins—They lost their best receiving threat in Coles by trading him for Moss, a player who lacks the size, toughness, and consistency to fit in with Joe Gibbs's ball control philosophy. Worse yet, they got suckered into paying a large portion of Coles's contract, and early on, Moss wound up holding out and getting a new contract from Washington anyway. On defense, the Skins lost their leading tackler from last year, Antonio Pierce. Losing Pierce himself isn't as bad as it may seem, but the fact that he left for division rival New York because Washington couldn't afford him was embarrassing. Oh, by the way: That young cover corner the team had in Smoot? Gone.

Painting a New Picture

Rookies

Alex Smith, QB, San Francisco 49ers
Drafted: 1st overall out of Utah

In case anyone failed to notice, the San Francisco 49ers have had some pretty darn good quarterbacks over the past 25 years. The first was a man named Joe Montana, who became known for his habit of winning Super Bowls. Following Montana was a left-hander named Steve Young, who claimed a title himself during his Hall of Fame career. Even more recently was Jeff Garcia, who did well during his short tenure as San Francisco's starting signalcaller.

Now the Niners are putting their stock in Alex Smith. The No. 1 overall draft pick out of Utah does not have the supporting cast that the aforementioned quarterbacks did, but he has a lot of the ingredients needed to prepare a winning quarterback. San Francisco drafted Smith because they (and the rest of the league, for that matter) became enchanted with his intangibles: Great leadership, sound mechanics, strong work ethic, a perfect record as the Utes' starter last year, high character, and most of all, Einstein-level intelligence. The man earned his degree from Utah in *two years,* for crying out loud!

The difference between Smith and Montana (or even Young and Garcia) is that being a first-round draft pick, the immediate expectations on him are much greater. Montana was a third-round pick out of Notre Dame, Young came over from Tampa Bay and began his career in the USFL, and Garcia went undrafted out of San Jose State and didn't even reach the NFL until he was 29.

Smith, 21, has the potential to grow into a star, but it will likely take him some time. He does not have terrific arm strength to match his accuracy, he is coming from a quarterback-friendly system in Utah that allowed him to work primarily out of the shotgun, and he is working with as much proven talent as *American Idol* judge Simon Cowell on a first-day audition show. One thing helping Smith is his ability to move around the field; mobility is often the greatest bailout tool that flustered young quarterbacks have to rely on.

The Niners will certainly make the 21-year-old their starter on opening day. And if Smith's track record is any indication of what's to come, it's safe to say that San Francisco more than likely drafted something closer to the next Montana, as opposed to the next Ryan Leaf.

The Running Backs

For the first time in the history of the common draft, three running backs were selected in the top five picks. Auburn had their tandem of Ronnie Brown and Carnell "Cadillac" Williams go to the Miami Dolphins at No. 2 and Tampa Bay Buccaneers at No. 5, respectively. The Chicago Bears drafted Texas's Cedric Benson at No. 4.

To see three running backs go so early in the draft was not necessarily startling, but it was certainly peculiar, considering that last year, the first running back taken was St. Louis's Steven Jackson, who lasted until pick No. 24. The rumor circulating around the football world is that running backs are becoming interchangeable. This is actually *true* to an *extent*, but in the face of talents as impressive as Brown, Benson, and Williams, such a hypothesis must be temporarily tossed aside.

So how will each do at the pro level? For starters, none of these guys will be a bust, mainly because all three have proven to be players of high character—the importance of which in today's game Ricky Williams has helped make clear. Brown was "Cadillac" Williams's backup at Auburn, but he never once complained about his role off the bench. In much the same fashion, "Cadillac" never complained about sharing his workload with Brown. Benson is a passionate player who shed tears of joy on draft day, as well as tears of hurt because of the way he felt he had been treated during the scouting process. (Benson, being a power-runner from Texas, was inundated with Ricky Williams comparisons. He even cut his trademark dreadlocks to help distance himself from his troubled predecessor.)

On the field, each player offers his own unique array of skills. Brown is an all-around threat, showing a great burst and acceleration, displaying soft, receiver-quality hands, and possessing the blocking skills of a veteran. He can step in and gain 1,200 yards his rookie season. He is a surefire star who will enjoy great success for years to come.

Benson, as mentioned, is a power-runner who was a workhorse in college. He'll fit well in Chicago's new offense, which is returning to a slower, more grind-it-out style of play. He can carry the ball 25 times a game and wear teams down by the fourth quarter.

Williams is the fanciest, most elusive runner of the bunch. Of the three, he will likely have the most inconsistent rookie year, but that isn't to say he won't succeed. He is familiar with Jon Gruden (Gruden fell in love with Williams when he coached him at the Senior Bowl), and he has the diverse set of skills needed to thrive in Tampa Bay's detailed system.

Years from now, people will look back on the 2005 draft, examine these three running backs, and say, "Now those were some prospects who panned out."

Matt Jones, WR, Jacksonville Jaguars
Drafted: 21st overall out of Arkansas

Matt Jones is the most intriguing selection in this year's NFL draft. The reason is that many scouts see him as the best pure athlete ever to enter the NFL. Yes—*ever*. He is 6'6", 242 pounds, and he runs a 4.39 (as in under 4.4). He took over as the starting quarterback for the Razorbacks in 2002. He was also a key member of Arkansas' basketball team for three years. (Be reminded that Arkansas is not Treasure Valley Community College; it is a major sports powerhouse in the SEC.)

Jones enters the league as a wide receiver, but he was announced as a tight end on draft day. Some teams have said they would use him as a halfback or even a running back. There was also talk of him becoming a kick returner.

Jones is obviously a great athlete who can excel in the right situation. The question is: Is Jacksonville the right situation? Let's hope for James Harris, Jaguars vice president and head of player personnel, that the answer is *yes*, because many experts had Jones rated as a third-round, and no better than a second-round, prospect.

His ability to catch the ball will not be as big an issue as people think, but his desire to play the game might. Jones has the reputation for having a blasé attitude and a questionable approach toward practice. Typically, prospects like that are immediate red-flag guys, but then again, Jones is clearly not your typical prospect.

Mike Williams, WR, Detroit Lions
Drafted: 10th overall out of USC

A year ago Mike Williams was considered to be one of the five best players in a loaded draft class. This year he was the 10th-overall selection in a fairly weak draft class. Perhaps that is what spending a year away from the game will do to a player's status.

Last year Maurice Clarett, who had been dismissed from the Ohio State football team and was only two years removed from Warren Harding High School, had the fortitude to challenge the NFL's rule that says players cannot enter the draft unless they are three years removed from high school. He took the league to court, and an overly liberal activist U.S. district judge, Shira Scheindlin, ruled that Clarett had the right to enter the NFL draft, going against the NFL collective bargaining agreement. As it turned out, Judge Scheindlin's ruling was overturned by a 2nd U.S. Circuit Court of Appeals, and a Clarett appeal was shunned by the U.S. Supreme Court. However, during the time that it looked like Clarett would be successful in entering the NFL, Williams, then an All-American stud receiver at USC, declared for the draft after his sophomore season. But when the Clarett decision was reversed in mid-April, Williams was kept out of the draft and denied eligibility by the NCAA.

Williams spent the past year working out on his own in Southern California. He also received some firsthand help from former Minnesota Viking Cris Carter. A huge target with average speed but amazing strength and big, strong hands, Williams steps into Detroit as a can't-miss rookie. In fact, he is so can't-miss that the Lions used their first-round pick on him, despite already having a first-round receiving star from a year ago (Roy Williams) and a potential star—albeit injury-prone—No. 2 overall pick from two years ago (Charles Rogers).

Mike Williams gives the Lions three young top-10-drafted receivers to work with. Williams can dominate single coverage on the weakside of the field and serve as the tough possession-receiver who can move the chains on third down. He'll begin the season as the team's No. 3 receiver, working out of the slot.

Mid-round Gems

 Barrett Ruud, LB, Tampa Bay Buccaneers
Drafted: 2nd round (36th overall) out of Nebraska

A mediocre athlete who plays above his level. Ruud is a gutsy player who has great strength and feel for the game. He was productive in the Big 12 and could perhaps be an even larger version of Zach Thomas.

 Matt Roth, DE, Miami Dolphins
Drafted: 2nd round (46th overall) out of Iowa

An active defensive end who was projected to go late in the first round—but slipped, likely because of a lack of top-end speed and concerns about his ability to control his emotions. Not an ideal fit for Miami's new scheme, but too much of a steal for Nick Saban to pass up.

Justin Miller, CB, New York Jets
Drafted: 2nd round (57th overall) out of Clemson

A player who could have gone in the latter part of the first round, but a late-night arrest prior to the draft hurt him. A good athlete with the speed and playmaking abilities to start regularly, but not until he can hone his raw skills. He can also return kicks and convert interceptions into touchdowns.

 Adam Terry, OT, Baltimore Ravens
Drafted: 2nd round (64th overall) out of Syracuse

Terry, with his long-armed, 6'8" frame is a great find for the Ravens, because they need an upgrade at right tackle. He offers the athletic skills to start right away and get better over time.

Kevin Everett, TE, Buffalo Bills
Drafted: 3rd round (86th overall) out of Miami, Fla.

A Hurricane tight end following Bubba Franks, Jeremy Shockey, and Kellen Winslow. Somewhat raw, especially as a blocker, and still needs to fill out his good frame. Tore his ACL in spring, which will wipe out most of his rookie season, but once he returns, he will be the pass-catching option the Bills need at this position.

Chris Canty, DE, Dallas Cowboys
Drafted: 4th round (132nd overall) out of Virginia

Canty is a first-round talent who, because of injuries and some character concerns, slipped to the fourth round. He is a hybrid end who shouldn't have any problems with toughness and discipline, as long as Bill Parcells is around. Injuries (including one to his eye) may ultimately keep him from having a monstrous rookie season, though.

Biggest Winners

 Arizona Cardinals—They upgraded their secondary by drafting cornerback Antrel Rolle in the first round and Eric Green in the third; both will contribute right away. J.J. Arrington is not a big-time runner, but he can at least start as a rookie. Finally, the Cards added a pair of former Virginia Cavaliers: linebacker Darryl Blackstock and guard Elton Brown. Both will be key starters by next season.

Baltimore Ravens—They got the receiver they desperately needed (Mark Clayton), they found their future right tackle in Adam Terry, and they even snagged a prospected first-round defender (Dan Cody) with the 53rd-overall pick.

Dallas Cowboys—Their switch to a 3–4 became official when they managed to get an outstanding trio of linebackers with Demarcus Ware, Kevin Burnett, and Chris Canty. Furthermore, they targeted Marcus Spears at No. 11 and wound up getting him at No. 20.

Biggest Losers

 Denver Broncos—After trading their first-round pick, the only news this team could make was selecting malcontent running back Maurice Clarett. Keep in mind, the Broncos were already overcrowded at this position heading into the draft.

St. Louis Rams—They needed a right tackle and they wound up getting a left one in first round pick Alex Barron. Not a *big* problem, but considering that Orlando Pace was given a long-term deal to hold down the left side—and recalling just how devastating the poor blocking at right tackle has been to this team—it would have been nice to see them find a more reliable player to fill this position. In addition, St. Louis needed a safety who excels in pass coverage, which is not where Oshiomogho Atogwe's strengths lie.

NFL Economics

The NFL exhibits the greatest parity of any major sport. The league enjoys some of the world's most extraordinary venues. The Super Bowl has become an American holiday. Free agency has changed the game of football and the way teams approach the off-season.

What do all of these typical observations about the NFL have in common? They are all tied to the concept of money. *Money.* That's it, that's the name of the game.

While the league has managed to maintain its traditional image and quality product on the field, it has mastered the concept of adjusting to the new economic times off it. From the Andrew W. Mellon days of teams like the Canton Bulldogs or the Chicago Cardinals being valued in the $500 range to the more current John Snow times of clubs like the Washington Redskins or Dallas Cowboys being worth upward of $900 million, one thing has become certain: The NFL understands the basic concept of the dollar.

Spring, a season that was once a time of withdrawal and depression for NFL fans, has become a hotbed of excitement, thanks to the free-agency market and draft frenzy. Television used to be a simple factor of the game. Now, networks like CBS and FOX are buying six-year broadcasting rights for $3.7 and $4.3 billion, respectively.

The odd part about the economic side of football is that while it impacts the game greatly, nobody outside of the experts in the front offices seems to fully understand how it all works. Here is a breakdown of what exactly is going on.

Note: All information is based on the NFL's collective bargaining agreement, which expires in 2008. The owners and players union are expected to have an agreement that would extend the deal well before the start of the 2007 season, which is when the salary cap is scheduled to disappear.

Revenue Sharing

Everything in the league begins and ends with revenue sharing. First off, revenue sharing is basically a socialistic idea designed to maintain a system in which each team has an equal opportunity to be competitive. Former NFL commissioner Pete Rozelle summed it up best when, before retiring, he reminded his peers that the goal should be for a team in Green Bay, Wisconsin, to have the same chance of winning as a team from New York.

In 2004 the league raked in a record $5.2 billion in revenue. With revenue sharing, the money from national broadcasting contracts (the league's greatest source of income), national sponsorships, one-third of ticket earnings from all games played, and a 12 percent royalty rate on every piece of NFL merchandise is essentially placed into a hat and distributed equally among the 32 teams. All in all, each team is allotted approximately $100 million per year.

This isn't to say that teams cannot make money on their own. What separates franchises like the Redskins (valued at a league-

Since paying $800 million to buy the team in 1999, Redskins owner Daniel Snyder has helped escalate the value of his organization past the $1 billion mark.

high $1.1 billion, according to *Forbes*) from the Arizona Cardinals (a league-low $552 million) are elements like home market, stadium value, local sponsors, broadcasting deals, and luxury suites. Individual teams are still allowed to market their own product.

Salary Cap

Although teams do not gross equal income each year, they do play under the same spending rules when it comes to signing new players. The salary cap began in 1993, when the league adopted its current collective bargaining agreement in an effort to prevent player salaries from skyrocketing to an Alex Rodriguez level. It is the annual limit (as determined by the league's revenue from the previous year) that a team can spend on its player payroll. *Player* is the operative word there, because salaries for coaches, trainers, scouts, and so forth, do not count against a team's cap. This year, the salary cap for each team is approximately $85 million, which is an all-time high. The brilliance behind the salary cap is that, as it is commensurate with the *league's* revenue, everybody shares the same goals. The more money the teams make, the more money the league gets, the more money the owners have, and the more money the players receive.

Free Agency

The reason NFL players agreed to cut back on their growing salaries by introducing a salary cap was that, in exchange, they were given the new concept of free agency. Free agency allows players the freedom to market themselves to any team after a certain period of time. In the past, when a player was drafted by a certain organization, that player was stuck there for a majority of his career, unless he could somehow manage to be traded. Now, when a player has five or more accrued seasons with one team, he can become an unrestricted free agent. A player with either three or four accrued seasons can become a restricted free agent. An accrued season is simply when a player is active for at least six of his team's games in a given year.

Restricted vs. Unrestricted Free Agent

An unrestricted free agent is, for lack of a better term, an unemployed football player. He is allowed to sign with any team that he so desires, no strings attached.

A restricted free agent is able to sign with any team that he so desires, but his prior team has the right of first refusal. In other words, the prior team has seven days to match any offer made to that player by another franchise. If an offer is matched, the player and his prior team then enter into a binding contract on their own (i.e., the player is stuck with his old squad). If that player agrees to a deal with a new club, under certain financial circumstances, his old team can receive compensation from the player's new club, which comes primarily in the form of draft picks.

Franchise Players

In an effort to prevent superstars from drastically shuffling the competitive balance in the league too frequently, the NFL allows each team to declare one of their unrestricted free agents as their franchise player every season. When a franchise player is "tagged," as they say, that player is obligated to sign a one-year contract to remain with his team. The value of the contract is simply the average of the top five salaries of other players in the league who play that player's position. For example: The league's five highest-paid quarterbacks will make just over $40 million in combined salaries this season, so if a team were to declare their quarterback as their "franchise player," that player would get a one-year contract worth just over $8 million.

A franchise player can still choose to sign with a new team, though. In doing so, however, the new team must give the player's prior team two first-round draft picks in compensation, a hefty price that makes signing franchise players a rare occurrence.

How a Player Counts against His Team's Salary Cap

Many wonder how the Atlanta Falcons can pay Michael Vick $100 million over 10 years and not have it result in the immediate destruction of their salary cap. The reason for this is that the system is not so simplistic. A three-year, $15 million contract does not count $5 million against the cap each season.

Instead, what teams do is called "back loading" a contract. Instead of paying out the contract evenly over three years, a team might pay $1 million in the first year of the deal, $2 million in the second, and $12 million in the third and final year. The amount of money that a player's contract pays him in a given year is his "base salary." Of course, this is just an example. In reality, a player's contract is not allowed to increase by more than 30 percent of a previous season's income in the final year of a contract.

Releasing Players

Contracts in the NFL are not guaranteed. In order to avoid paying such outrageous sums in salaries to players, teams will take the Wal-Mart approach and release a player prior to the final big money years of his deal. Once a player is released, he automatically becomes an unrestricted free agent. This is why teams cut so many talented veteran players. If a team cuts a player, then they avoid having to pay that player's salary for the season, thus freeing up space under the team's salary cap.

Signing Bonuses

Before asking why in the world players would negotiate long-term back-loaded contracts that they know will be taken away from them before their money arrives, figure in the signing bonus aspect of a deal. As teams grow more familiar with the salary cap and with operating within its rules, they are referring to the use of signing bonuses more often.

A player's signing bonus is the only guaranteed part of his contract. The signing bonus is part of a player's salary. It is prorated over the length of the contract.

For example, let's go back to the imaginary player who signed a three-year, $15 million deal. Suppose that player received a $6 million signing bonus with his contract. Under these terms, that player immediately receives all $6 million of that money, but the franchise does not have to immediately spend $6 million against the team's cap. Instead, the player's signing bonus would count for $2 million against the team's salary cap each year for three years.

If the team chooses to release that player before his contract expires, then the value of what remains of the player's signing bonus would count against the cap immediately. If there are two years left in the player's deal, at $2 million a year in signing bonuses, then the team would end up paying $4 million against the cap, even though the player has been cut and is no longer on the team.

In addition, signing bonuses do allow players and teams the ability to renegotiate a new "cap-friendly" contract later in deals (when the big-money years of a back-loaded contract occur). This provides a nice reward for a player and a logical alternative for a team to avoid releasing a key member of the franchise. Of course, they're essentially taking out a loan, because they will have to continue to pay that player's signing bonus down the road. Not to mention that this is where teams like Washington begin to have an advantage over teams like Arizona, because the Redskins have more money to spend right away on players' signing bonuses (as previously alluded to).

The San Diego Chargers made quarterback Drew Brees their franchise player this year, signing him to a one-year, $8.078 million contract.

© Tom Dahlin/WireImage.com

NFC EAST

 1. **Philadelphia Eagles**

 2. **Dallas Cowboys**

 3. **New York Giants**

 4. **Washington Redskins**

Few can argue against the Eagles being the best team in this division. Andy Reid and his staff have done an incredible job of running this club. Philly is stacked on both sides of the ball, and they have star veteran players who are all very familiar with the system. The Cowboys should improve from last year, even though they're in a serious transition phase defensively. The Giants players are going to have trouble tolerating Tom Coughlin this season, while the Redskins simply have too many negative issues compounding in their program.

NFC NORTH

 1. **Minnesota Vikings**

 2. **Detroit Lions***

 3. **Green Bay Packers**

 4. **Chicago Bears**

Losing Randy Moss is not going to significantly hinder Minnesota's offense because they still have Daunte Culpepper and a large group of talented receivers to whom he can rifle the ball this year. However, Minnesota's vast improvements on *defense* will be the ultimate difference maker. It feels foolish to pick Joey Harrington's team ahead of Brett Favre's, but Detroit is only getting better at this point and the Packers did little over the offseason to improve their subpar defense. Don't sleep on Chicago, they have a good thing going, but at this point they're too inexperienced to play well for 17 whole weeks.

*Wild Card

NFC SOUTH

 1. **Carolina Panthers**

 2. **Atlanta Falcons***

 3. **New Orleans Saints**

 4. **Tampa Bay Buccaneers**

Carolina is finally healthy again. They were strong late in the season last year, despite having nothing to work with, which shows how adroit the coaching staff is. Consequently, the Panthers have also become deeper and more experienced by having to play so many young backups a year ago. Atlanta is still the most dangerous team in the NFC South—and it would not be a surprise to see them reclaim this division or even get hot late in the year and make a strong run through the playoffs. However, they have a dangerous amount riding on one player (Michael Vick). The Saints never live up to their potential; they lack leadership in every imaginable way—don't be seduced by their talent. The Bucs are in a rebuilding stage.

NFC WEST

 1. **St. Louis Rams**

 2. **Arizona Cardinals**

 3. **Seattle Seahawks**

 4. **San Francisco 49ers**

This is probably the weakest division in football. The Rams are not an upper-tier team, but they have the type of offense that can win games for them during the regular season. Projecting the Seahawks to finish third is a very risky move—touché—but the point needs to be made that they have underachieved in recent years and now appear to be worse off heading into this season. Arizona is one or two years away from exploding, and it's likely that they'll show faint signs of that throughout the season. The 49ers, as everyone knows, are nowhere near competitive right now.

AFC EAST

 1. **New England Patriots**

 2. **Buffalo Bills***

 3. **New York Jets**

 4. **Miami Dolphins**

Until someone can claim their crown, the Patriots are the default pick to win everything. Bill Belichick's team has proven to be worthy of such respect. Besides, even with losing Romeo Crennel and Charlie Weiss, New England may have still *improved* over the offseason, thanks to upgrades in the secondary. The Bills would be a shoo-in to make the playoffs, if not for the fact that they are relying on an unproven quarterback (J.P. Losman) to lead them in 2005. They'll still contend for a Wild Card spot, though. The Jets look like they're about as strong as they were a year ago, but in this day and age, a team must *get better* in order to have a chance. Nick Saban will help Miami, but right now he still has to repair a lot of the damage from 2004.

AFC NORTH

 1. **Baltimore Ravens**

 2. **Cincinnati Bengals**

 3. **Pittsburgh Steelers**

 4. **Cleveland Browns**

Baltimore's improvements on offense—plus the success that they'll have on defense now that they're running a 46 scheme—are too much to ignore. As long as Kyle Boller can prove to be adequate, this team is going to be very potent, week in and week out. Predicting the Steelers to finish third is a huge risk—agreed—but they have been known to follow strong seasons with disappointing ones. Plus, the maturing Bengals are bound to move up in the standings at some point. The only true guarantee in the entire AFC is that the Browns will finish last in the North.

*Wild Card

AFC SOUTH

 1. **Indianapolis Colts**

 2. **Jacksonville Jaguars**

 3. **Houston Texans**

 4. **Tennessee Titans**

Indy is unstoppable on offense, which means they'll win at least 12 regular season games. Of course, they'll still have trouble facing a team like New England or Baltimore in the playoffs. It is somewhat of a toss-up between Houston and Jacksonville. The Jaguars should come out ahead, because they are better up front on both sides of the ball. However, Houston *does* have more budding young playmakers. Tennessee is not a team to be scoffed at—they'll pull off a few upsets late in the season, but right now they're simply too young to thrive.

AFC WEST

 1. **Kansas City Chiefs**

 2. **San Diego Chargers***

 3. **Denver Broncos**

 4. **Oakland Raiders**

The Chiefs learned their lesson last season and now know that they must tend to defense, at least a little bit. They did so by adding five new major defensive contributors over the offseason. Offensively, Kansas City is slightly less prolific, but is still capable of lighting up the scoreboard each week. The Chargers overachieved last year, but they are still a good team that can vie for a playoff spot. It's too hard to erase the memories of Denver's past two playoff losses in Indy. The Raiders will be more fun to watch this season, but having Randy Moss does not mean winning more games. If it did, then Minnesota wouldn't be in the position they're in today.

AFC CHAMPIONSHIP	NFC CHAMPIONSHIP
New England Patriots over Indianapolis Colts	Philadelphia Eagles over Minnesota Vikings

 SUPER BOWL XL
Patriots 30, Eagles 21

Doesn't get much more boring than this, right? Patriots beating the same Eagles that they defeated last year in the Super Bowl? Sorry, but it's hard to be creative and pick some enticing dark-horse team when there are clearly two clubs that tower above the rest of the NFL. A fearless prediction is fun, but it would mean sacrificing the integrity of *Touchdown 2005*. It is no coincidence that the Eagles and the Patriots have been the most consistent, best-managed franchises in the league for the past four years. New England deserves to be the Super Bowl favorite until somebody dethrones them. The Eagles are simply the most complete team in the NFC—bar none.

AFC East

Buffalo
Bills

Miami
Dolphins

New England
Patriots

New York
Jets

Looking Forward

How They'll Finish
1. New England Patriots
2. Buffalo Bills
3. New York Jets
4. Miami Dolphins

Ready to Break Out

**Vince Wilfork,
New England Patriots**

Nose Tackle
6'2"—325 pounds
2nd year—23 years old
Drafted: 1st round out of Miami, Florida.

One of the main culprits of success for New England's 3–4 defense has been the talent that the team has had at the nose tackle position. In '03, it was Ted Washington. In '04, they had Keith Traylor. This year, the Patriots will feature another gifted force, only he will not be slipping on the downside of his career—in fact, he's still riding the chairlift up. The man is Vince Wilfork.

Wilfork saw decent playing time as a rookie last season, playing in all 16 games and starting 6 of them. Wilfork's 42 tackles and 2 sacks do not do justice in portraying his contributions, though.

Vince Wilfork

This year, Wilfork will take over the full-time duties up front in the middle and it would not be too great of shock to see his name on the AFC Pro Bowl roster when all is said and done. Wilfork does not simply have the outstanding size to attract double teams, he has the athleticism, too. He is very active in his area, he has an unbelievable burst, and he delivers a tremendous initial pop. Wilfork is dominant because of his sheer power, but also because he works to finish plays—something most young defensive linemen do not learn to do until later in their careers.

Hot Seat

**Chad Pennington,
New York Jets**

There is not a lot of pressure going around the AFC East (unless Ricky Williams returns to the Dolphins), but this is an opportunity to examine the heat that Jets quarterback Chad Pennington may begin to feel this year.

Pennington is 29 years old, which seems ancient when considering that he is often regarded as an "up-and-coming star." However, the "up-and-coming" part is over; *this* is it, he's *here*—now it's time to perform.

There has been some speculation that Pennington cannot win the big game—which he probably disproved last year. But come on, this is *New York*. Until Pennington can start sliding rings on his fingers, there will be skeptics. The media likely won't go easy on him, either—not after he told a roomful of reporters last season that getting to hang around world-class athletes was a privilege for them. Such comments really irk sportswriters, because often they are the ones who are bitter because they couldn't play the game themselves. . . . *What?* Don't look here, that doesn't apply to—well, whatever, right?

New York has a valiant rushing attack, they have a strong offensive line, and Pennington got his favorite receiver (Laveranues Coles) back this year. Now he has to deliver.

Best Offseason Move

New York Jets trading Santana Moss for the more productive Laveranues Coles—*and* saving money in the process.

Worst Offseason Move

Nick Saban bothering to even speak to Ricky Williams.

Best Under-the-Radar Offseason Move

The plethora of additions that New England has made to their cornerback position. They added veterans Chad Scott and Duane Starks, got Tyrone Poole back and healthy again, and drafted Ellis Hobbs in the third round.

Biggest Question

How in the world can any of the "other three teams" in the AFC East expect to catch the Patriots in '05?

Corey Dillon

QUICK HITS

TEAM BESTS		BEST PLAYERS	
Passing Game	Patriots	Pure Athlete	Jonathan Vilma, Jets
Running Game	Jets	Big Play Threat	Lee Evans, Bills
Offensive Line	Patriots	Best Use of Talent	Zach Thomas, Dolphins
Pass Rush	Jets	Worst Use of Talent	David Boston, Dolphins
Run Defense	Bills	On the Rise	Lee Evans, Bills
Pass Defense	Bills		Jonathan Vilma, Jets
Special Teams	Patriots		Terrence McGee, Bills
Coaching Staff	Patriots	On the Decline	Wayne Chrebet, Jets
Home Field	Patriots		Tim Bowens, Dolphins
			Donnie Abraham, Jets
		Best Leader	Tom Brady, Patriots
		Unsung Hero	Trey Teague, Bills
		Impact Rookie	Ronnie Brown, Dolphins

Looking Back

🏈 Buffalo Bills 2004

PASSING STATISTICS

PLAYER	CMP	ATT	YDS	CMP%	YDS/A	LNG	TD	TD%	INT	INT%	SACK	YDS	RAT
Drew Bledsoe	256	450	2932	56.9	6.52	69	20	4.4	16	3.6	37	215	76.6

RUSHING STATISTICS

PLAYER	ATT	YDS	AVG	LNG	TD	FUM	LST
Willis McGahee	284	1128	4.0	41	13	3	2
Travis Henry	94	326	3.5	19	0	0	0
Shaud Williams	42	167	4.0	27	2	0	0

RECEIVING STATISTICS

PLAYER	REC	YDS	AVG	LNG	TD	FUM	LST
Eric Moulds	88	1043	11.9	49	5	1	1
Lee Evans	48	843	17.6	69	9	1	1
Mark Campbell	17	203	11.9	27	5	1	0
Willis McGahee	22	169	7.7	16	0	1	0

RETURN STATISTICS

PLAYER	KICKOFFS ATT	YDS	FC	AVG	LNG	TD	PUNTS ATT	YDS	FC	AVG	LNG	TD
Terrence McGee	52	1370	0	26.3	104	3	0	0	0	0.0	0	0
London Fletcher	4	86	0	21.5	23	0	0	0	0	0.0	0	0

KICKING STATISTICS

PLAYER	1-20	20-29	30-39	40-49	50+	TOT	PCT	AVG	LNG	XPM/A	PTS
Rian Lindell	0/0	13/14	10/11	1/3	0/0	24/28	85.7	28.1	43	45/45	117

PUNTING STATISTICS

PLAYER	PUNTS	YDS	AVG	LNG	TB	TB%	IN20	IN20%	RET	YDS	AVG	NET
Brian Moorman	77	3325	43.2	80	9	11.7	17	22.1	37	315	8.5	39.1

DEFENSIVE STATISTICS

PLAYER	TACKLES TOT	SOLO	AST	SACK	TLOSS	MISC FF	BK	INT INT	YDS	AVG	LNG	TD	PD
London Fletcher	144	101	43	3.5	4.5	2	0	0	0	0.0	0	0	4
Takeo Spikes	99	71	28	3.0	6.5	4	0	5	122	24.4	62	2	17
Terrence McGee	87	81	6	2.0	1.5	0	0	3	21	7.0	21	0	15
Nate Clements	78	61	17	0.5	2.5	5	0	6	77	12.8	35	1	14
Aaron Schobel	73	47	26	8.0	8.5	5	0	0	0	0.0	0	0	4
Jeff Posey	66	44	22	1.0	2.5	0	0	1	3	3.0	3	0	2
Lawyer Milloy	62	44	18	4.0	0	0	0	2	20	10.0	11	0	5
Pat Williams	53	43	10	2.5	7	0	0	1	20	20.0	20	1	1
Sam Adams	40	28	12	5.0	7.5	0	0	1	0	0.0	0	0	3
Kevin Thomas	40	31	9	1.0	0	1	0	0	0	0.0	0	0	1

2004 Team Stats

OFFENSE

Scoring:	24.7 (7)
Yards per Game:	293.2 (25)
Pass Yards per Game:	176.1 (27)
Rush Yards per Game:	117.1 (13)
Sacks Allowed:	38 (18)
3rd Down Percentage:	35.8 (20)

DEFENSE

Scoring:	17.8 (8)
Yards per Game:	264.3 (2)
Pass Yards per Game:	164.0 (3)
Rush Yards per Game:	100.3 (7)
Sacks:	45 (t3)
3rd Down Percentage:	36.0 (t13)
Takeaways:	32 (t3)

🐬 Miami Dolphins 2004

PASSING STATISTICS

PLAYER	CMP	ATT	YDS	CMP%	YDS/A	LNG	TD	TD%	INT	INT%	SACK	YDS	RAT
A.J. Feeley	191	356	1893	53.7	5.32	38	11	3.1	15	4.2	23	136	61.7
Jay Fiedler	101	190	1186	53.2	6.24	71	7	3.7	8	4.2	25	165	67.1

RUSHING STATISTICS

PLAYER	ATT	YDS	AVG	LNG	TD	FUM	LST
Sammy Morris	132	523	4.0	35	6	1	0
Travis Minor	109	388	3.6	34	3	0	0
Leonard Henry	46	141	3.1	53	0	1	1

RECEIVING STATISTICS

PLAYER	REC	YDS	AVG	LNG	TD	FUM	LST
Chris Chambers	69	898	13.0	76	7	0	0
Randy McMichael	73	791	10.8	42	4	2	0
Marty Booker	50	638	12.8	45	1	0	0
Derrius Thompson	23	359	15.6	36	4	0	0

RETURN STATISTICS

PLAYER	KICKOFFS ATT	YDS	FC	AVG	LNG	TD	PUNTS ATT	YDS	FC	AVG	LNG	TD
Wesley Welker	57	1313	0	23.0	95	1	43	464	12	10.8	71	0
Bryan Gilmore	5	114	0	22.8	53	0	0	11	0	0.0	11	0

KICKING STATISTICS

PLAYER	1-20	20-29	30-39	40-49	50+	TOT	PCT	AVG	LNG	XPM/A	PTS
Bill Gramatica	0/0	2/2	1/1	0/0	0/0	3/3	100.0	29.0	30	0/1	9

PUNTING STATISTICS

PLAYER	PUNTS	YDS	AVG	LNG	TB	TB%	IN20	IN20%	RET	YDS	AVG	NET
Matt Turk	98	4088	41.7	67	10	10.2	29	29.6	44	241	5.5	39.3

DEFENSIVE STATISTICS

PLAYER	TACKLES TOT	SOLO	AST	SACK	TLOSS	MISC FF	BK	INT INT	YDS	AVG	LNG	TD	PD
Zach Thomas	145	118	27	2.0	7	0	0	0	0	0.0	0	0	4
Morlon Greenwood	101	75	26	0.0	3.5	0	0	0	0	0.0	0	0	3
Sammy Knight	96	65	31	0.0	2	2	0	4	32	8.0	32	0	4
Jason Taylor	68	49	19	9.5	4.5	2	0	1	-3	-3.0	-3	0	11
Jeff Zgonina	63	46	17	5.0	5	0	0	0	0	0.0	0	0	3
Patrick Surtain	58	44	14	1.0	3	0	0	4	2	0.5	2	0	11
Junior Seau	57	42	15	1.0	4	0	0	0	0	0.0	0	0	1
Sam Madison	47	40	7	0.0	1.5	3	0	0	0	0.0	0	0	7
Bryan Robinson	41	30	11	0.0	3	0	0	0	0	0.0	0	0	4
David Bowens	40	30	10	7.0	4	3	0	0	0	0.0	0	0	6

2004 Team Stats

OFFENSE

Scoring:	17.2 (t27)
Yards per Game:	275.3 (29)
Pass Yards per Game:	191.6 (21)
Rush Yards per Game:	83.7 (31)
Sacks Allowed:	52 (t29)
3rd Down Percentage:	34.5 (24)
Giveaways:	36 (32)

DEFENSE

Scoring:	22.1 (20)
Yards per Game:	305.9 (8)
Pass Yards per Game:	162.0 (2)
Rush Yards per Game:	143.9 (31)
Sacks:	36 (t21)
3rd Down Percentage:	32.3 (5)
Takeaways:	17 (t27)

New England 2004

PASSING STATISTICS

PLAYER	CMP	ATT	YDS	CMP%	YDS/A	LNG	TD	TD%	INT	INT%	SACK	YDS	RAT
Tom Brady	288	474	3692	60.8	7.79	50	28	5.9	14	3.0	26	162	92.6

RUSHING STATISTICS

PLAYER	ATT	YDS	AVG	LNG	TD	FUM	LST
Corey Dillon	345	1635	4.7	44	12	4	3
Kevin Faulk	54	255	4.7	20	2	0	0
Patrick Pass	39	141	3.6	19	0	0	0

RECEIVING STATISTICS

PLAYER	REC	YDS	AVG	LNG	TD	FUM	LST
David Givens	56	874	15.6	50	3	0	0
David Patten	44	800	18.2	48	7	0	0
Deion Branch	35	454	13.0	26	4	0	0
Daniel Graham	30	364	12.1	48	7	0	0

RETURN STATISTICS

PLAYER	KICKOFFS					PUNTS					
	ATT	YDS	FC	AVG	LNG	TD	ATT	YDS	FC	AVG	LNG	TD
Bethel Johnson	41	1016	0	24.8	93	1	4	8	1	2.0	6	0
Patrick Pass	6	115	0	19.2	24	0	0	0	0	0.0	0	0

KICKING STATISTICS

PLAYER	1-20	20-29	30-39	40-49	50+	TOT	PCT	AVG	LNG	XPM/A	PTS
Adam Vinatieri	0/0	13/13	7/7	11/12	0/1	31/33	93.9	34.0	48	48/48	141

PUNTING STATISTICS

PLAYER	PUNTS	YDS	AVG	LNG	TB	TB%	IN20	IN20%	RET	YDS	AVG	NET
Josh Miller	56	2350	42	69	5	8.9	19	33.9	31	365	11.8	35.4

DEFENSIVE STATISTICS

PLAYER	TACKLES					MISCELLANEOUS		INTERCEPTIONS					
	TOT	SOLO	AST	SACK	TLOSS	FF	BK	INT	YDS	AVG	LNG	TD	PD
Rodney Harrison	129	90	39	3.0	2.5	3	0	2	12	6.0	12	0	8
Tedy Bruschi	120	76	44	3.5	4	2	0	3	70	23.3	36	0	6
Ted Johnson	78	56	22	1.0	1.5	1	0	0	0	0.0	0	0	1
Mike Vrabel	67	52	15	5.5	3.5	0	0	0	0	0.0	0	0	3
Eugene Wilson	65	57	8	0.0	0	2	0	4	51	12.8	24	0	7
Willie McGinest	51	37	14	9.5	2.5	2	0	1	27	27.0	27	0	6
Ty Warren	49	39	10	3.5	5.5	2	0	0	0	0.0	0	0	1
Vince Wilfork	42	29	13	2.0	0.5	0	0	0	0	0.0	0	0	3
Roman Phifer	40	30	10	1.5	1	0	0	1	26	26.0	26	0	2
Richard Seymour	40	27	13	5.0	2	1	0	0	0	0.0	0	0	1

New York Jets 2004

PASSING STATISTICS

PLAYER	CMP	ATT	YDS	CMP%	YDS/A	LNG	TD	TD%	INT	INT%	SACK	YDS	RAT
Chad Pennington	242	370	2673	65.4	7.22	48	16	4.3	9	2.4	18	103	91.0

RUSHING STATISTICS

PLAYER	ATT	YDS	AVG	LNG	TD	FUM	LST
Curtis Martin	371	1697	4.6	25	12	2	0
LaMont Jordan	93	479	5.2	33	2	0	0
Chad Pennington	34	126	3.7	16	1	2	1

RECEIVING STATISTICS

PLAYER	REC	YDS	AVG	LNG	TD	FUM	LST
Santana Moss	45	838	18.6	69	5	0	0
Justin McCareins	56	770	13.8	43	4	1	0
Wayne Chrebet	31	397	12.8	35	1	0	0
Jerald Sowell	45	342	7.6	34	1	1	1

RETURN STATISTICS

PLAYER	KICKOFFS					PUNTS					
	ATT	YDS	FC	AVG	LNG	TD	ATT	YDS	FC	AVG	LNG	TD
Jonathan Carter	17	374	0	22.0	40	0	0	0	0	0.0	0	0
LaMont Jordan	14	284	0	20.3	40	0	0	0	0	0.0	0	0

KICKING STATISTICS

PLAYER	1-20	20-29	30-39	40-49	50+	TOT	PCT	AVG	LNG	XPM/A	PTS
Doug Brien	0/0	9/10	4/6	10/11	1/2	24/29	82.8	35.5	53	33/34	105

PUNTING STATISTICS

PLAYER	PUNTS	YDS	AVG	LNG	TB	TB%	IN20	IN20%	RET	YDS	AVG	NET
Toby Gowin	80	3057	38.2	58	8	10.0	22	27.5	34	221	6.5	35.5

DEFENSIVE STATISTICS

PLAYER	TACKLES					MISCELLANEOUS		INTERCEPTIONS					
	TOT	SOLO	AST	SACK	TLOSS	FF	BK	INT	YDS	AVG	LNG	TD	PD
Eric Barton	107	78	29	2.5	6.5	1	0	1	7	7.0	7	0	2
Jonathan Vilma	105	80	25	2.0	5.5	0	0	3	58	19.3	38	1	5
Erik Coleman	88	69	19	2.0	0.5	0	0	4	43	10.8	37	0	12
David Barrett	78	65	13	0.0	4	1	0	2	14	7.0	14	0	13
Reggie Tongue	72	56	16	0.0	2	1	0	1	23	23.0	23	0	5
Jason Ferguson	59	39	20	3.5	2.5	2	0	0	0	0.0	0	0	0
Shaun Ellis	57	38	19	11.0	4	2	0	0	0	0.0	0	0	4
Donnie Abraham	53	38	15	0.0	1.5	0	0	2	66	33.0	66	1	13
Dewayne Robertson	53	38	15	3.0	4.5	1	0	0	0	0.0	0	0	0
John Abraham	49	35	14	9.5	4	3	0	0	0	0.0	0	0	2

2004 Team Stats

OFFENSE

Scoring:	27.3 (4)
Yards per Game:	357.6 (7)
Pass Yards per Game:	224.3 (11)
Rush Yards per Game:	133.4 (7)
Sacks Allowed:	26 (5)
3rd Down Percentage:	45.1 (5)
Giveaways:	20 (8)

DEFENSE

Scoring:	16.2 (t2)
Yards per Game:	310.8 (9)
Pass Yards per Game:	212.5 (17)
Rush Yards per Game:	98.3 (6)
Sacks:	45 (t3)
3rd Down Percentage:	38.8 (21)
Takeaways:	30 (t5)

2004 Team Stats

OFFENSE

Scoring:	20.8 (17)
Yards per Game:	339.9 (12)
Pass Yards per Game:	190.6 (22)
Rush Yards per Game:	149.3 (3)
Sacks Allowed:	31 (17)
3rd Down Percentage:	42.5 (8)
Giveaways:	13 (1)

DEFENSE

Scoring:	16.3 (4)
Yards per Game:	304.9 (7)
Pass Yards per Game:	207.0 (14)
Rush Yards per Game:	97.9 (5)
Sacks:	37 (t17)
3rd Down Percentage:	38.0 (18)
Takeaways:	30 (t5)

Buffalo Bills

Predicted: 2nd ▪ 2004: 9-7 (3rd)

Draft

2	(55)	Roscoe Parrish	WR	Miami, Fla.
3	(86)	Kevin Everett	TE	Miami, Fla.
4	(122)	Raymond Preston	C	Illinois
5	(156)	Eric King	CB	Wake Forest
6	(197)	Justin Geisinger	OG	Vanderbilt
7	(236)	Lionel Gates	RB	Louisville

Not having a first-round pick was a bit of a problem, but the team is essentially including J.P. Losman as part of their draft class this year. Parrish is somewhat of a munchkin (5'10", 168 pounds), but he can be a playmaker in the slot. Everett is the tight end that this offense so desperately needed, but he'll miss the season with a torn ACL. Outside of the pair of Hurricanes, the Bills draft class seems destined for careers as backups.

Head Coach: Mike Mularkey (2nd year)
Offensive Coordinator: Tom Clements
Defensive Coordinator: Jerry Gray

Offense

QB:	J.P. Losman
RB:	Willis McGahee
FB:	Daimon Shelton
WR:	Eric Moulds
WR:	Lee Evans
TE:	Mark Campbell
LT:	Mike Gandy†
LG:	Bennie Anderson†
C:	Trey Teague
RG:	Chris Villarrial
RT:	Mike Williams
QB:	Kelly Holcomb†
RB:	Shaud Williams
WR:	Roscoe Parrish‡
TE:	Ryan Neufeld
OL:	Ross Tucker

Defense

LDE:	Chris Kelsay
DT:	Sam Adams*
DT:	Ron Edwards
RDE:	Aaron Schobel
SLB:	Jeff Posey
MLB:	London Fletcher
WLB:	Takeo Spikes*
CB:	Nate Clements*
SS:	Lawyer Milloy
FS:	Troy Vincent
CB:	Terrence McGee*
NB:	Kevin Thomas
DL:	Ryan Denney
LB:	Jabari Greer
K:	Rian Lindell
P:	Brian Moorman

* Pro Bowler '04
† veteran acquisition
‡ rookie

Report Card

Quarterback	C	Defensive Line	C+	Coaching	C+
Running Back	B	Linebacker	B–	Special Teams	A–
Receiver/Tight End	B+	Defensive Back	B+	Depth	C–
Offensive Line	B–			Intangibles	C

B eing a team that originated in the old AFL and plays their home games in Orchard Park, New York, in a down-to-earth stadium *not* named after a megacorporation but rather the team's longtime owner, Ralph Wilson, the Buffalo Bills almost seem like the AFC's version of the Green Bay Packers.

The city of Buffalo (population: 295,000, give or take) might be one of the most traditional towns in America. It rests on the shores of Lake Erie, in western New York, just 25 miles from Niagara Falls. The town was originally called Buffalo Creek, back when it was settled in 1780. Over time, Buffalo grew with the economic boom that resulted from the construction of the Erie Canal in the late 1790s.

With so much "water history" in the city of Buffalo, this year's hot question is fitting: Will the Bills sink or swim? Granted, by the time anyone knows for sure, the entire western side of New York will be buried in five feet of snow, but the point is that this team is looking to take that next step after winning 9 of their final 12 games last year.

Returning virtually the same core of starters from a defense that ranked second in yards allowed, Bills head coach Mike Mularkey recognizes that in order to have a chance in the competitive AFC East, his offense needs to put up more points in '05. Mularkey—a former tight end who was the offensive coordinator for the Steelers prior to coming to Buffalo—will do battle with a second-year quarterback (first year starting), a third-year running back (second year starting), a second-year receiver, and a new left side of the offensive line. However, aside from those linemen, virtually all of the other players on this team were in Mularkey's system a year ago, which means no time will be wasted on learning schemes and terminology. The Bills are ready to get right to work out there in western New York.

Willis McGahee

Offense

The second-year quarterback who is starting for the first time is **J.P. Losman**, a first-round draft choice who spent a majority of his rookie season healing a broken leg and learning from the sidelines. The Bills have a lot riding on the 24-year-old Losman; essentially his job is to take over an offense that could run the ball fairly well a year ago (117.1 yards per game—13th in the NFL) but could throw the ball about as well as Buffalo wings make a bison fly (176.1 yards per game, 27th in the NFL).

The Bills offense will have an entirely new look in '05 because Losman's game is predicated on his athleticism and mobility. The man he is replacing—Drew Bledsoe—played a style of football that was confined to the pocket, and absolutely nothing more (unless one counts Bledsoe walking off the field after an unsuccessful third down). **Mike Mularkey** and offensive coordinator **Tom Clements** have installed a wider variety of plays, including draws, bootlegs, and rollouts, that should take advantage of Losman's scrambling.

With a game plan that is tailored to Losman's style (although the Bills insist they are not basing their *entire* approach around him), it will be up to the 6'2", 217-pounder out of Tulane to lead this team. This is where the optimists and pessimists retreat into their respective corners. There are some who say that Losman won't lead well because he comes with the baggage of being a cocky jerk. Others say that he will be fantastic as a leader because he is such a confident young gun. One might think that the answer lies somewhere in between, but when examining this guy's demeanor and expressions, it's definitely a lot of *something*; only time will tell exactly what that something is. But know this about Losman: Had he been in this year's NFL draft, there are many who believe that he would have been selected No. 1 overall, ahead of Alex Smith. This gives some indication of how talented Losman is.

When the Buffalo coaching staff asserts that they are not crafting the playbook solely around Losman, they often claim that they are doing it for the good of the receivers as well. And considering the potential that resides in this position, one is inclined to believe them. The Bills feature a threesome of receivers that includes a productive 10th-year-veteran in **Eric Moulds**, a budding young superstar in second-year man **Lee Evans**, and a multitalented mega-athlete in rookie **Roscoe Parrish**.

Moulds is coming off one of his usual seasons: 88 catches for 1,043 yards. The 6'2", 210-pound Pro Bowl regular is 32 years old and has a slightly blemished track record when it comes to staying healthy, but he is still capable of putting up numbers as big in '05 as he did in '02. Moulds has always been a lead-by-example player who can thrive when surrounded by strong talent.

Strong talent does not begin to describe Evans. The first-round pick from a year ago lived up to his billing coming out of Wisconsin. Evans averaged 17.6 yards per catch, led the team with nine touchdown receptions, and showed an intriguing improvement as the season wore on. In fact, last year, Evans's production in September was minimal: three receptions for 77 yards and no scores. However, in the month of December, Evans had 21 catches for 336 yards and six touchdowns. Overall, he finished the year with 48 receptions for 843 yards and nine touchdowns.

Strengths

Cornerbacks

Both Nate Clements and Terrence McGee are fast, agile, and smart—a package of skills that spells major success, especially in today's game.

Wide Receivers

With the speed of Lee Evans and the athletic playmaking potential of rookie Roscoe Parrish, Eric Moulds can operate more effectively as a possession receiver in '05. Furthermore, having Josh Reed and Sam Aiken as the No. 4 and No. 5 targets isn't too shabby, either.

Weaknesses

Depth

The Bills are a talented team—on the first unit. After that, things seem to get a little hazy, particularly at the offensive tackle, tight end, and linebacker positions.

Offensive Experience

J.P. Losman will wind up being the most important passer, Lee Evans the most vital receiver, and Willis McGahee the most crucial runner for this team in '05, but these men have just 22 games of starting experience among them.

Evans has the type of speed rivaled only by the kind found in the inner breast pocket of a high-end "street pharmacist." However, most admirable about the 24-year-old is that he does not rely strictly on his pure talent. Despite being only 5'10", 197 pounds, Evans is capable of making plays in traffic and running the underneath routes against zone coverage. He spent the offseason improving his route running skills by working with wide receivers coach **Tyke Tolbert**.

The '05 season should be a great one for Evans, especially when considering that instead of lining up beside the questionable **Josh Reed**, he'll be next to the dangerous **Roscoe Parrish**. The Bills used their first draft choice on Parrish (55th overall) and have since been enchanted with the flashes of brilliance shown by the former Miami Hurricane during minicamps. Parrish has the type of abilities that are so natural and so "sick," they officially classify as "skillz."

Having three very talented receivers (and Reed, who is only in his third year and in a position to rebound from a poor sophomore season), Losman should have a fair shake in '05. However, Buffalo's offense would greatly benefit from having a multitalented tight end, which is something they don't have in **Mark Campbell**. The Bills thought they were getting this in rookie third-round pick **Kevin Everett** (another former Hurricane), but he tore his ACL in spring. However, Everett did not wind up having to undergo major reconstructive surgery on the knee, so there is an outside chance that he could return to play later in the season. Now they have Campbell—who is a limited receiver—and backup blocking specialist **Ryan Neufeld**. Don't be surprised if the team gives third-string player **Tim Euhus** a whirl; the second-year player has a nice frame (6'5", 249 pounds) and the receiving skills that Mularkey covets.

While he didn't quite go Kobe Bryant on everyone, running back **Willis McGahee** successfully ran his competitor, Travis Henry, out of town. As of late May, Henry was still on the roster, but he might as well be in Canada, going over Horseshoe Falls in a barrel (the American Falls and the Bridal Veil Falls on the American side of the Niagara River are said to have too many rocks for anyone to attempt the stunt).

McGahee's bumpy road to the NFL—which took a one-and-a-half-year detour to rehab a devastating knee injury—has been

> ## Write it Down:
>
> Wide receiver Lee Evans will be recognized as among the most lethal of weapons in the NFL by the time the season's over.

Progression:	**Offensive playmaking**—The Bills will have more big-play potential at the receiver position in '05, and the ability of J.P. Losman to scramble and turn "nothings" into "somethings" will be refreshing for this offense.
Regression:	**Left tackle**—Losing Jonas Jennings for Mike Gandy is a monumental step backward, especially if Gandy is unable to keep his job at this spot.

well publicized, but the 6'0", 228-pounder from (where else?) "The U," appears to have fully regained the shiftiness and balance that made him a blue-chip prospect. Last year McGahee started only 11 games for the Bills, but still amassed 1,128 yards and 13 touchdowns by season's end.

With Henry seemingly out of the picture, the backup running back in Buffalo will be **Shaud Williams**, a quick young slasher who could one day be a bang-up third-down back. The fullback for the Bills is **Daimon Shelton**, a soon-to-be 33-year-old who can still clear a path as a lead-blocker.

The success of the Bills offensive line may ultimately hinge on the play of newly acquired left tackle **Mike Gandy**. Not only will he be responsible for keeping pressure off the quarterback by protecting Losman's blind side (the Bills allowed 38 sacks last year, and Losman is said to have a tendency to hold on to the ball too long), but he is also the ticket to prosperity in the middle of the front five. The Bills are replacing Jonas Jennings at this spot, and while Gandy will definitely not do as much for this line as Jennings did, they still need him to at least prove capable of holding up. If he can't, then a domino effect takes place, with the minimum result being center **Trey Teague** moving to tackle and backup **Ross Tucker** getting inserted into the starting lineup.

Gandy has the necessary strength to do good things, but he'll need to show that he also has the quickness. The man next to Gandy, left guard **Bennie Anderson**, is new to the team as well. At 6'5", 345 pounds, Anderson does not have nimble feet, but fortunately the Bills signed the former Raven for his ability to maul in run-blocking.

The aforementioned Teague is very versatile and very critical to generating movement along the line on running plays. Teague, along with veteran right guard **Chris Villarreal**, is great at getting out in front and blocking in space. Right tackle **Mike Williams** is approaching a crossroads in his career. The 6'6", 360-pounder was the No. 4 overall pick out of Texas in '02, but has since only

The Bills' success this season will ultimately come down to how well second-year quarterback (and first-year starter) J.P. Losman can lead this offense.

moderately lived up to the hype. Williams gets a good knee bend and shows athleticism, but he looks uncomfortable with his footwork in pass protection. In all honesty, Williams will most likely never play at the premium left tackle slot, but with his power and leverage, he can still become a cogent right tackle. However, he must take that final step in elevating his entire game in '05.

Buffalo has good depth up front. Tucker is a utility lineman who has poor fundamentals but a knack for surviving when in the game. **Lawrence Smith** is an intriguing player; he started eight games in '04 and showed great potential. Before arriving in western New York, Smith spent the first two years of his career in Baltimore, where he was saddled with injuries and never once got on the field. Now healthy, Smith is a great talent because of his quickness and strong initial pop at the point of contact. However, he may still have trouble finding his way into the lineup this year.

Defense

The Bills have a defense that is highlighted by a stand-up secondary. This unit ranked third in passing yards given up last season, but even more impressive, they ranked first in allowing just 6.06 yards per pass *attempt*. They also tied for first in allowing just 53.7 percent of the throws against them to be completed, and they held opposing quarterbacks to a league-low 65.2 rating on average.

Such numbers are the result of a balanced defensive backfield that features a potent pair of young cornerbacks in **Nate Clements** and **Terrence McGee**, and a savvy pair of veteran safeties in **Lawyer Milloy** and **Troy Vincent**.

Entering his fifth season out of Ohio State, Clements is one of the most agile, coverage-capable corners in the NFL. His 6'0", 209-pound frame gives him size to go along with his outstanding speed and fluid hips. Clements has become the consummate playmaker at the cornerback position—last year he had six interceptions and forced five fumbles.

Clements also has good awareness and has matured enough that he is giving a solid effort on a regular basis. Despite this, the third-year player McGee (out of Northwestern *State*, of all places) might supplant his counterpart as the team's premier cornerback in '05. The reason for this is the 25-year-old's pure football intelligence. Don't think that McGee doesn't have tremendous God-given abilities as well; he has elite acceleration skills, speed, and an ability to elevate that could rival Tracy McGrady. However, his success this year will come from his development as a student of the game. Few players in the NFL understand and are as cognizant of the illegal contact rules as McGee is. Furthermore, much of his production comes from his familiarity with defending the deep pass (a difficult task) and his knowing how to time his breaks on the ball. The nickel back duties will go to **Kevin Thomas**, who has limited experience.

Strong safety **Lawyer Milloy** is the sagacious veteran leader in this secondary—well, one of them, anyway. In his 10th season in the NFL, Milloy is beginning to show signs of slowing down—which only means that he might be as bad as "average" in about three years. The Bills will use Milloy as their prime eighth man in the box and send him on frequent blitzes in '05. Last season, he had four sacks.

Vincent is a lot like former Buffalo mayor and U.S. president, Grover Cleveland. Cleveland is the only president in history who served two separate terms in office (1885–89 and 1893–97). Now, try to follow this connection: Vincent was a Pro Bowl–level player in Philadelphia, then moved to Buffalo last year. But he had his 1889–93 moment (see where this is going?) as the team's dime back, before moving to free safety this season. (Was that too much of a stretch?) It remains to be seen how well the 34-year-old will adjust to his new role. Vincent has the capacity to excel here, but second-year player **Rashad Baker** is a very talented young safety who has tremendous acceleration and range in pass coverage. He may push Vincent for playing time in '05.

The fact that Buffalo's defense tied for the third-highest total in sacks last season (45) had a lot to do with the success of the secondary. This year, despite losing defensive tackle Pat Williams, the Bills should continue their authority up front. The man replacing Williams may turn out to be a younger version of the former Buffalo notable. Fifth-year player **Ron Edwards** (6'3", 320 pounds) offers the same type of size that Williams did, and he has better quickness. Edwards could command a few double teams, although it's likely that a lot of the focus will be on his sidekick **Sam Adams**, a 335-pound veteran who has worked in the trenches and disrupted offenses for 12 years now.

The ends for the Bills are third-year player **Chris Kelsay** and the team's leading sacker over the past three years, **Aaron Schobel**, who has recorded 28 in that span. In addition to these starters, Buffalo will also throw fourth-year man **Ryan Denney** into the mix.

Kelsay has been slow to develop since being drafted in the second round out of Nebraska. This year should bring continued improvements for the all-around threat, but at the same time, he could *still* be developing late in the season. Kelsay is adept at beating blockers when he's playing at a good pace, and his overall presence is commendable—when he doesn't have to think too hard. However, too often he gets tied up in blocks or pushed out of position.

Schobel gets an outstanding jump off the snap (which explains his high sack totals), but what a lot of people do not recognize about the 262-pounder is his stellar impact in rush defense. Schobel is not a stout tackler when playing laterally near the line of scrimmage, but his motor and quickness allow him to get in position to disrupt plays. Denney knows all about having a motor. He plays with nice speed (especially in pursuit) and is very astute at getting around blocks.

In passing situations, the Bills usually leave Denney on the bench and send Kelsay over to join him. Then strongside linebacker **Jeff Posey** lines up at the end position on the front four and serves as a pass-rusher. This is all well and good, except that Posey didn't even produce enough sacks to carry home three quarts of milk from his local Orchard Park supermarket last season. The Bills are beginning to realize that the eighth-year

veteran is really only effective in a 3–4 scheme (in case it isn't apparent by now, Buffalo runs a 4–3!). Posey is like Samuel L. Jackson in *Changing Lanes*: He does not work well in traffic. This would not be a major problem for a *weakside* linebacker, but Posey's lining up on the side of the tight end where he'll have to square up and face opponents and play around piles. Yeah, that could be a problem.

The man who is the weakside linebacker for the Bills could play in traffic, he could play in a snowstorm, he could play in sand, indoors, outdoors, in Wyoming, in Japan, at midnight, in the morning, on New Year's—just about anywhere other than on the playoff stage. This man is **Takeo Spikes,** and he has never been to the postseason. (In fairness to Spikes, he spent five of his first seven NFL seasons in Cincinnati.)

Today, the 6'2", 242-pound Spikes is one of the top players in the AFC East. The best way to sum up this man is by simply relaying his stat line from '04, which reads something like a NASDAQ report: 99 tackles, 3 sacks, 4 forced fumbles, 5 interceptions, 122 return yards with 2 touchdowns on those picks, and 17 passes defensed! And *no*, do not go back and reread this—Spikes is indeed one man, even if his name *is* plural.

The middle linebacker for the Bills is **London Fletcher**. Fletcher has been the chief tackler for this team year in and year out (he had 144 takedowns last year, fifth-highest total in the NFL). Fletcher's numbers don't lie, but much like a *Newsweek* article, they do tend to mislead. He is an upper-tier player, but many of his contributions come a ways downfield. Fletcher's lack of size (5'10", 245 pounds) gives him some trouble at times, mainly when it comes to taking on blocks.

Special Teams

Kicker **Rian Lindell** was a stable 24/28 last year, although one must question his range when considering that the Bills had him kick only three field goals that were over 40 yards long (and zero from 50 yards and beyond). Punter **Brian Moorman** was seventh in the NFL at 43.2 yards per punt. The athletic cornerbacks handle the return duties, with McGee on kicks and Clements on punts. They are part of one of football's best special-teams units, under the direction of **Bobby April**.

The Bottom Line

The Bills are going to be an interesting team to watch in '05 because their entire season all but rests on first-time starter Losman. If he is able to generate some big plays for the passing attack, Buffalo has the offensive line and ground game to round out the offense—and there is no reason why the defense cannot repeat its hearty performance from '04. However, asking a young player to shoulder the load of this team is a necessary yet bold move, considering that the Patriots lurk around the corner, the Jets made the playoffs last year, and the Dolphins are more of a threat than they were in '04.

Miami Dolphins

Predicted: 4th ▪ 2004: 4-12 (4th)

Players Added

DL	Kevin Carter	(Ten)
OT	Damion Cook	(Cle)
CB	Mario Edwards	(TB)
FB	Heath Evans	(Sea)
QB	Gus Frerotte	(Min)
HE	Vonnie Holliday	(KC)
S	Tebucky Jones	(NO)
OT	Stockar McDougle	(Det)
LB	Donnie Spragan	(Den)
S	Travares Tillman	(Car)
NT	Keith Traylor	(NE)

Players Lost

OT	Tim Bowens	
QB	Jay Fiedler	(NYJ)
S	Arturo Freeman	(GB)
LB	Morlon Greenwood	(Hou)
S	Sammy Knight	(KC)
FB	Rob Konrad	(retired)
DT	Bryan Robinson	(Cin)
CB	Patrick Surtain	(KC)
DE	Jay Williams	(StL)

Draft

1	(2)	Ronnie Brown	RB	Auburn
2	(46)	Matt Roth	DE	Iowa
3	(70)	Channing Crowder	ILB	Florida
4	(104)	Travis Daniels	CB	LSU
5	(162)	Anthony Alabi	OT	Texas Christian
7	(216)	Kevin Vickerson	DT	Michigan St.

No doubt Nick Saban would have wanted to trade his No. 2 overall pick in return for more draft choices, but settling on Brown was definitely not a bad deal. Miami made the most out of their second- and third-round picks. Roth has first-round talent, but Saban will have to be a little creative in finding a way to use him. Crowder may have left school too early, but he'll be a good pro down the road, just as long as he can get bigger and stronger and avoid off-the-field trouble.

Head Coach: Nick Sabon (1st year)
Offensive Coordinator: Scott Linehan
Defensive Coordinator: Richard Smith

Offense

QB:	A.J. Feeley
RB:	Ronnie Brown‡
FB:	Heath Evans†
WR:	Chris Chambers
WR:	Marty Booker
TE:	Randy McMichael
LT:	Damion McIntosh
LG:	Jeno James
C:	Seth McKinney
RG:	Rex Hadnot
RT:	Stockar McDougle†
QB:	Gus Frerotte†
RB:	Lamar Gordon
WR:	David Boston
TE:	Donald Lee
OL:	Vernon Carey

Defense

LHE:	Vonnie Holliday†
DT:	Kevin Carter†
DT:	Keith Traylor†
RHE:	Jason Taylor*
SLB:	Donnie Spragan†
MLB:	Zach Thomas
WLB:	Junior Seau
CB:	Sam Madison
SS:	Tebucky Jones†
FS:	Travares Tillman†
CB:	Mario Edwards†
NB:	Reggie Howard
DL:	Jeff Zgonina
LB:	Channing Crowder‡
K:	Olindo Mare
P:	Matt Turk

* Pro Bowler '04
† veteran acquisition
‡ rookie

Report Card

Quarterback	C–	Defensive Line	C+	Coaching	C+
Running Back	B–	Linebacker	B	Special Teams	B+
Receiver/Tight End	B	Defensive Back	C	Depth	B–
Offensive Line	C–			Intangibles	C+

O kay, the party's over in South Beach. Turn off the hip-hop that's thumping from the stereo, say goodbye to the sexy bronze ladies, go park the mopeds by the sidewalk, pack up the cooler and lounge chairs, and somebody wake up Dave Chappelle. The fun is over for the Miami Dolphins. First-year head coach Nick Saban (*see* Painting a New Picture, page 5) has rolled into town and he's already angry about last year's dismal 4-12 record—even though he was at LSU during the time and had about as much to do with it as Castro has to do with capitalism.

Having epitomized a consistently good (but never great) NFL franchise for seven years (1997–2003), during which they posted win totals that never dipped below 9 but never exceeded 11, the Dolphins hit a bump in the road last season. Well, actually, they hit a crater. Everything that could have gone wrong went far worse than wrong. However, the hiring of Saban means the firing of last year. The '04 Dolphin season will be as forgotten in Miami as Dennis Haskins. (Who? Exactly.) And to begin with, Saban is implementing his famed hybrid 3–4 defense, a branch directly off the Belichick tree.

However, last year's problems were not on defense so much as they were on offense. This is where the eyebrows raise and the heads begin to look around. Saban certainly knows how to teach defense, but is he properly addressing the offense? Whether or not he is, only time will tell. But one thing's for sure: Saban's not going to waste time doing it.

Jason Taylor

Offense

The Dolphins know they are not going to have one of the upper-echelon offenses in the NFL this season—they haven't had that since the days of Dan Marino. All Miami wants to do is take a unit that ranked 27th in scoring (17.2 points per game) last year and make it good enough to rank somewhere in the top half of the league. If they can do that, they have a defense that they believe will keep up, thus allowing them to at least compete in each game.

So how does a team go from ranking near the bottom to somewhere in the respectable middle? For starters, they must eliminate the turnovers. The Dolphins gave away possession a league-high 36 times last year, many of which were attributed to quarterback **A.J. Feeley**. Feeley had 15 interceptions and fumbled 10 times, losing five of them. However, it could not have been entirely Feeley's fault—he was constantly under pressure and often in precarious third-down-and-long situations.

Recognizing this, Miami needs to find a way to avoid the vulnerable situations that allow teams to tee off on a blitz or crowd the passing lanes in zone coverage. There are several ways to do this: The Dolphins could add extra blockers up front, they could call more short-yardage passing plays and incorporate more three-step drops for the quarterback, they could run the ball more, they—WAIT!

There it is. *Run the ball.* Control the flow of the game, eat up the clock, sustain drives, and be in a position to convert a manageable third down. That's *it. Running!* That's the ticket to fewer turnovers, which is the ticket to more points, which is the ticket to more victories in '05. (And *no*, this point could not have been made with a simple introductory sentence or *two*—it had to be shown.) The Dolphins can improve on offense by running the football.

This is what **Nick Saban** and Miami offensive coordinator **Scott Linehan** are going to do this season. Before they can fix the various problems on offense, they must upgrade a rushing attack that averaged a pitiful 83.7 yards per game last year (31st in the league) and had a leading rusher, **Sammy Morris**, who gained a trivial 523 yards. Miami used the No. 2 overall pick in the draft to find the broom that should sweep up this mess: **Ronnie Brown** (*see* Painting a New Picture, page 8). Brown gives the Dolphins a versatile option in the backfield who can step in and immediately carry the load. He was not well known at Auburn because he split his carries with Cadillac Williams. Upon joining the Fins, it appeared that Brown would finally get his chance to be featured in an offense—until Saban opened up discussions with the most infamous pot puffer in the post–Bob Marley era: Ricky Williams.

The possibility of Saban welcoming even the *idea* of Williams rejoining the Dolphins organization is enough to cause a serious commotion. Bringing back Williams to form a dominant duo at the running back position could be the most foolish move in the NFL this year. Why bother? The team has already forgotten about Williams (and there is reason to believe that Williams has forgotten much of the team, too). The Fins drafted their star tailback No. 2 overall. Not to mention, because of his fondness for the type of grass that can't be found in the nearby Everglades, Williams would still be subject to a four-game suspension under the NFL's substance abuse policy. Plus, he is said to have lost considerable weight, which hurts his power-running style.

Write it Down:

Nick Saban comes across as desperate on offense for bringing back malcontent receiver David Boston and for even bothering to speak to Ricky Williams. Saban's arrival is great for this franchise, but would Bill Belichick handle things this way?

Strengths

Defensive Veterans

A major system overhaul is not as dramatic when there are leaders like Jason Taylor, Zach Thomas, Junior Seau, and Sam Madison around to help weather the "tropical" storm.

Receivers

Tight end Randy McMichael continues to improve as a big-play threat. Wideout Chris Chambers is *already* a big-play threat—now he's just trying to become more consistent. Marty Booker will be solid if he is used properly in this offense, and as long as David Boston is healthy, he is a great third receiver.

Weaknesses

Offensive Line

The fact that so much of the offense is dependent upon a front line that has underachieved from both an individual and a group standpoint is troubling. There are literally 10 players here who could end up starting at one spot or another this year. That speaks louder for the poor starting talent than it does for the depth.

Safety

Strong safety Tebucky Jones has been unable to live up to expectations for much of his career; now he finds himself playing out of position. For any of the 31 other teams in this league, free safety Travares Tillman is probably a backup.

It remains to be seen how Williams's return—if it does indeed pan out in the long haul (as in more than a few months)—affects this team. But overall, on the field—Williams or no Williams—Miami is going to be better at running the football in '05.

The focus now shifts back to Feeley. The fifth-year player out of Oregon should win the starting quarterback job, assuming he can fully comprehend Linehan's system by the time September rolls around. If Feeley is unable to pick up the new offense, Miami will have no choice but to go with veteran **Gus Frerotte**, a journeyman backup who played for Linehan in Minnesota and knows the scheme inside and out.

Either way the team goes, their boat is still going to be sinking off the Florida Keys this year. Frerotte won't work well, because if he could, he wouldn't be a 34-year-old who has started for five different teams in the past seven years. Feeley won't be great in this system because it requires everything that he lacks: Awareness in the pocket, patience to let slow-developing plays unfold, and the experience and confidence to make good reads. Feeley has admirable toughness and valor when it comes to giving his team everything he has, but if a person can only spare one quarter to give to a bum, no matter how kind the gesture may be, that bum's still not eating.

Miami will just have to make the most out of their quarterback situation in '05. The best they can do to help Feeley succeed is to give him the soundest protection possible. Going back to the importance of an improved rushing attack and factoring in the role that the run-blocking is going to play, it is evident that the offensive line may just be what makes or breaks (or in Miami's case, cracks or shatters) this offense in '05.

Unfortunately for the Dolphins, they have a front five that barely meets the common standards of mediocrity. The left side of the line features a pair of players who are so average they ought to have the names on the back of their jerseys replaced with the word *citizen*. This, of course, is referring to tackle **Damion McIntosh** and guard **Jeno James**. But let's keep in mind that being an average player in the NFL is not necessarily a bad thing. It's just . . . average.

This Season vs. Last Season

Progression: **Coaching**—With so many weak spots remaining from a year ago, a change in leadership is a great start in the rebuilding process.

Regression: **Secondary**—Losing a pair of Pro Bowl–caliber veterans like Patrick Surtain and Sammy Knight to the Chiefs will be detrimental, considering that there's nobody in Miami to replace them in '05.

McIntosh is a sixth-year pro who has suffered playing for one bad team after another. He began his career with the Chargers before leaving for South Beach last season. Given the chance, McIntosh could be a fine right tackle, but because of the dearth of talent that has surrounded him each year, he is always forced to work on the left side, where he doesn't have the quickness to thrive. This year will be no different.

James is also in his sixth season as a pro and his second with the Fins. The onetime Panther has Super Bowl experience to refer to, which helps explain why he is such a savvy blocker. James does not have any outstanding features, but as long as he's playing, Dolphins offensive line coach **Hudson Houck** (who is in his first year with Miami and is considered to be among the best assistant coaches in the game) knows he can trust what he has at the left guard slot.

The center is **Seth McKinney**, a blocker who is good in space but lacks the power to be very effective at the line of scrimmage. The right side up front for Miami is welcoming in new starters **Stockar McDougle** and **Rex Hadnot**, both of whom are shaky. McDougle starts only because he can throw his 335 pounds around. Hadnot's name is, unfortunately, symbolic of his game (pardon the rhyme). His lazy habits only intensify his many weaknesses. Don't be surprised if Miami's front line becomes a revolving door this year. All five reserves up front have started at some point in their careers and all in "last resort" circumstances. One player to keep a close eye on is **Vernon Carey**, who was a first-round pick last year. Carey is still trying to find his niche in the league; once he does, he should find a starting job as well.

When Feeley *does* have time to throw this year, he will have a very solid group of receivers to choose from. His favorite is going to be tight end **Randy McMichael**. McMichael is a fourth-year pro who led the team with 73 receptions in '04. While still a little green, the talented 6'3", 250-pound beast has great athleticism and the strong hands to haul in most balls thrown in his direction. The only glitch with McMichael is that his intense passion for winning sometimes allows his emotions to get the best of him.

Wide receiver **Chris Chambers** will be the best fit for Linehan's downfield system. In his fifth year out of Wisconsin, Chambers has the speed and playmaking mentality to be great— he just needs to become more consistent. **Marty Booker** epitomizes the possession receiver, showing the poise and strength to catch balls over the middle but lacking the speed and explosion to stretch the field. Miami will have to find special ways to get Booker involved in the offense this year—expect McMichael to run deeper routes, in order to allow Booker the room to work the underneath passing lanes.

The No. 3 receiver is the troubled **David Boston**, who has wasted a lot of his talent over his seven-year career. Steroid use has led to suspensions, which have been coupled with various injuries as well. Nevertheless, Saban appears willing to take Boston for his talent at this point, because it's a better option than relying on **Bryan Gilmore** or **Derrius Thompson**.

Defense

It may not make a whole lot of sense for Saban to come in and revamp a defense that gave up only 305.9 yards per game last season (eighth in the league), but team owner **Wayne Huizenga** gave Saban the keys to the car and told him to drive anywhere along the Gold Coast Megalopolis that he pleased. This means converting the most vanilla 4–3 defense in the game to a "31 flavors" hybrid 3–4. The Fins brought in six new players and inserted them into the starting lineup. Plus, they have changed the dynamics of the second and third strings.

Miami's new defense is based on its unpredictability and the difficulty that offenses have in reading it at the line of scrimmage. In other words, it's a carbon copy of the Patriots. The Dolphins will blitz from all angles, they'll play man-to-man coverage, zone coverage, etc. Saban's hybrid 3–4 (which incorporates 4–3 alignments) will not evolve into a *full-fledged* 3–4 this year— despite all the roster moves, Saban still does not have the necessary personnel to make a complete conversion. This is why Miami will continue to start four downlinemen in '05, with the ends, **Jason Taylor** and **Vonnie Holliday**, lining up in three- or four-point stances on first and second downs, and then likely standing up on passing downs.

Taylor—6'6", 255 pounds—is ideal for this role. The 31-year-old veteran is coming off his third Pro Bowl season, in which he led the team with 9½ sacks. Taylor is an all-around weapon who will continue to get to the quarterback in '05. He has some limited experience with linebacker responsibilities, which, along with his intelligence, effort, lanky frame, and outstanding athleticism, should allow him to soar in his hybrid role.

Starting Holliday is a bit of a surprise when considering that over the course of his eight-year career he hasn't come close to living up to expectations. At 290 pounds, Holliday does not have the versatility to thrive in a hybrid role. Second-round rookie **Matt Roth** *does*, and it is very likely that he will gradually eat away at Holliday's playing time this season.

The signing of former Rams and Titans defensive lineman **Kevin Carter** was huge for this team because the 290-pound veteran can play just about anywhere up front. He'll be a tackle on a four-man line and an end on a three-man line. Carter is very adept at playing the run, and he still has the ability to overpower

© Steven Murphy/WireImage.com

Despite playing a very physical and aggressive brand of football, Miami's soon-to-be 32-year-old linebacker Zach Thomas remains one of the most potent in the game today.

blocks and get to the quarterback (six sacks in '04). However, the one spot that Carter cannot play is nose tackle, which caused Miami to sign the aging yet still useful **Keith Traylor**.

In looking at the depth up front, the Dolphins are going to have to be creative in defining players' roles. **Larry Chester** is recovering from a back injury, and the odds of him making it through October are slim. **Jeff Zgonina** is a hard worker, but he doesn't really play a style of football that will command the necessary attention at nose tackle and he's not a natural defensive end. Seventh-year pro **David Bowens** is quick and effective against the run, but at 260 pounds, the team will be busy struggling to find ways to get him playing time at defensive end or outside linebacker. Finally, **Dario Romero** is a 307-pounder, but he still needs to hone his game, plus he holds his ground about as well as a strainer holds water.

The Dolphin linebackers feature two veterans who have already established a well-known reputation in the NFL: 32-year-old **Zach Thomas** and 36-year-old **Junior Seau**. Thomas was his typical self last year, ranking fourth in the league with 145 tackles. He will enjoy playing in the middle this season because Saban's scheme will make it far more difficult for blockers to locate him in '05. Seau decided to return for another year in Miami because he liked the prospect of playing the weakside/outside role in this system. Although he finished the season on injured reserve with a pectoral injury (bad boob) in '04, Seau should be just fine this year.

The newcomer to the squad is fourth-year man **Donnie Spragan**, who spent the first few years of his career in Denver. Spragan is capable of starting in this defense because he is surrounded by veterans like Thomas and Seau. He'll work on the strongside in 4–3 alignments and likely play in the middle in 3–4s. Spragan should be able to mask his mediocre explosiveness in this role, but if he doesn't become a more intrepid player, he could find himself on the bench.

The Dolphins will make good use of their depth at the linebacker position. Expect third-round rookie **Channing Crowder** to get some repetitions. Crowder left the northern part of the state in Gainesville (where he played his college ball) after his junior year, which many thought was too soon for him. However, the Miami coaching staff is impressed with the athletic ability of the 6'2", 247-pound Crowder, and they love the fact that he can play at any of the linebacker positions.

Third-year player **Eddie Moore** has been a project since joining the league; if he can stay healthy and make progress this year, he could challenge for some playing time as well. If the team is looking to amp up their energy, the best person to go with would be **Brendon Ayanbadejo**, who got limited experience filling in as a starter late last year. However, Ayanbadejo might be a little too suspicious for Miami's liking: He's only in his third season, but he'll turn 29 in September. Weird.

The Dolphins went from having a secondary that allowed just 6.49 yards per pass attempt last year (sixth best in the NFL) to having a group that features three new questionable players: A fill-in No. 2 corner, a disappointing strong safety who is playing out of position, and a free safety who is as established in the

league as Miami's flashy orange jerseys. However, the Dolphins *do* have one returning man, who just happens to be star cover corner **Sam Madison**. The ninth-year veteran is all that's left from a once-dangerous unit. Madison did not intercept a single pass last year because quarterbacks hardly threw his way. Of course, that was nothing—now being the only star in this unit, opponents will probably avoid Madison like poison. However, being matched up against opposing No. 1 wideouts and working in a scheme that will disguise his coverage so well, Madison may still have a few chances to jump routes and make big plays in '05. P.S.: Madison is allergic to tackling.

After the Fins traded Patrick Surtain, the No. 2 cornerback job was supposed to go to second-year man **Will Poole**, but he tore his ACL during the club's first minicamp. Oops. Now the job will be given to either **Mario Edwards** or **Reggie Howard**—it is impossible to say. The decision likely won't be made until late August, but whichever way the Dolphins lean (the guess here is Edwards, because of his size), they'll have a solid nickel back and a somewhat weak starter.

Strong safety **Tebucky Jones**, 31, has been a nice talent since coming into the league eight years ago. He has always had tremendous range in pass coverage, but he's never shown the mental capacity (from a football standpoint) to be a star. Moving from free safety to strong safety (albeit not as dramatic a switch in this scheme) will not be a good thing for him. However, the move must be made, because Jones has the size (6'2", 220 pounds) that free safety **Travares Tillman** (6'1", 190 pounds) doesn't. Tillman will be a liability here; the 27-year-old is on his third team in four years. Tillman has played in a total of just 13 games over the past two seasons and he has just 11 career starts on his resume.

Special Teams

For as many changes as have taken place in South Beach, there are still two important holdovers from last year's team: Kicker **Olindo Mare** and punter **Matt Turk**. Both players seem as if they have been around since Florida was ceded by Spain. However, both can still kick. Miami's '04 return duties were handled by **Wes Welker**, who is one of those underdogs that fans decide to fall in love with. Welker *earned* his popularity though; he averaged 23 yards on kicks (with one touchdown) and 10.8 yards on punts.

The Bottom Line

The Dolphins have undergone more changes than an eighth-grade gym class. The adjustments, of course, needed to be made. There is no way that this team is going to be able to pull enough together to challenge the three-time World Champions for this division—in fact, a run at the playoffs also seems fairly impossible for Miami at this point. This team can grow over the course of the season, but it's also conceivable that they'll become more fragmented.

New England Patriots

Predicted: 1st ▪ 2004: 14-2 (1st—Super Bowl Champions)

Players Added

LB	Monty Beisel	(KC)
LB	Chad Brown	(Sea)
WR/KR	Tim Dwight	(SD)
QB	Doug Flutie	(SD)
LB	Wes Mallard	(NYG)
CB	Chad Scott	(Pit)
CB	Duane Starks	(Ari)
WR	David Terrell	(Chi)

Players Lost

G	Joe Andruzzi	(Cle)
DB	Antuan Edwards	(StL)
TE	Zeron Flemister	
OT	Adrian Klemm	(GB)
CB	Ty Law	
QB	Jim Miller	
CB	Earthwind Moreland	
WR	David Patten	(Was)
LB	Roman Phifer	
NT	Keith Traylor	(Mia)

Draft

1	(32)	Logan Mankins	OG	Fresno St.
3	(84)	Ellis Hobbs	CB	Iowa St.
3	(100)	Nick Kaczur	OG	Toledo
4	(133)	James Sanders	S	Fresno St.
5	(170)	Ryan Claridge	OLB	Nevada–Las Vegas
7	(230)	Matt Cassel	QB	USC
7	(255)	Andy Stokes	TE	William Penn

It's hard to criticize anything the Patriots do in terms of drafting players, because if history repeats itself (like it has already), then half of these guys will be starting in Super Bowl XL. It's somewhat surprising that New England didn't make more of an attempt at snagging a cornerback in the first two rounds, but they needed a replacement for Joe Andruzzi, which is what Mankins can be. Hobbs is the right type of player for this team and could even pay off this year. Stokes was this year's Mr. Irrelevant.

Head Coach: Bill Belichick (6th year)

Offensive Coordinator: none

Defensive Coordinator: Eric Mangini

Offense

QB:	Tom Brady*
RB:	Corey Dillon*
FB:	Patrick Pass
WR:	Deion Branch
WR:	David Givens
TE:	Daniel Graham
LT:	Matt Light
LG:	Russ Hochstein
C:	Dan Koppen
RG:	Steve Neal
RT:	Brandon Gorin
QB:	Doug Flutie†
RB:	Kevin Faulk
WR:	David Terrell†
TE:	Christian Fauria
OL:	Tom Ashworth

Defense

LDE:	Ty Warren
NT:	Vince Wilfork
RDE:	Richard Seymour*
HE:	Willie McGinest
LILB:	Ted Johnson
RILB:	Chad Brown†
ROLB:	Mike Vrabel
CB:	Asante Samuel
SS:	Rodney Harrison
FS:	Eugene Wilson
CB:	Randall Gay
NB:	Tyrone Poole
DL:	Jarvis Green
LB:	Monty Beisel†
K:	Adam Vinatieri*
P:	Josh Miller

* Pro Bowler '04
† veteran acquisition
‡ rookie

Report Card

Quarterback	A+	Defensive Line	B+	Coaching	A+
Running Back	A–	Linebacker	B	Special Teams	B–
Receiver/Tight End	B+	Defensive Back	B	Depth	A+
Offensive Line	B			Intangibles	A+

It is almost surreal. This is an era of professional football that is marked by the almighty salary cap, a money-driven free agency market, an inordinately detailed rookie draft, scouting services that are elaborate enough to make the CIA jealous, and, of course, players of unprecedented athletic ability. All this prompts people to focus a great deal on the parity that is displayed in the NFL. Yet, in the midst of all this parity, this annual "shift in power," these "unforeseeable outcomes," a dynasty has emerged.

People began to see this forming back in 2003, when the New England Patriots (who had shocked the world by beating St. Louis in the Super Bowl just two years previously) began to march through the NFL with such ease that it started to look like a stroll down the Boston Freedom Trail. Counting the postseason, the Patriots in '03 won their final 15 games and claimed a second Lombardi Trophy in three years.

However, nobody was willing to step up and make a case for this team as a dynasty—and in looking at previous league powerhouses (such as the Cowboys from the '90s or the Steelers from the '70s), nobody should have; it would have been too soon. Instead, the countless sports critics throughout America simply shut up, the boisterous "experts" at home and in the sports bars piped down, and the other 31 teams throughout the league

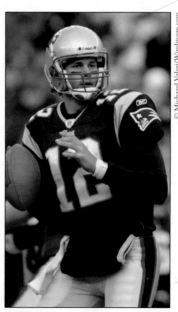

Tom Brady

accepted the role of chaser. Everybody stepped back and watched this franchise go to work, mesmerized by their NFL-record 19 consecutive wins, flabbergasted by the brilliance of the coaching staff, and awestruck by the selfless leadership and responsibility exhibited by each player on the roster, no matter how banged up, unknown, or low paid any of them were.

Where it stands now, the unassuming franchise from the serene New England colony of Massachusetts is above all of the speculation that highlights the game today. The Patriots are above criticism, they are above analysis, and they are above preseason rankings. Bill Belichick has done enough great things that losing his longtime offensive and defensive coordinators (Charlie Weiss and Romeo Crennel) should be regarded as a mere hiccup, because it was obvious that Belichick had already adjusted by July. The Patriots have proven themselves—they preach *team* and *actually* practice it. They are the predicted Super Bowl XL champions by default, because three rings in four years has earned them such respect. They know how it's done—the rest of the world can only watch and take notes.

Offense

No player better illustrates the Patriots than quarterback **Tom Brady**. Much like the team he plays for, Brady is underappreciated and overlooked in discussions about NFL superstars. It's almost as if he is too good to be true—as if people are afraid they might jinx him. With so much talk about players like Terrell Owens, Peyton Manning, Randy Moss, and Michael Vick—to name a few—the name Tom Brady somehow only gets touched upon. Sure, Brady does a few commercials (if he likes the product he's selling) and he participates in offseason events (such as hosting *Saturday Night Live*), but he is never thought of as some superstar tycoon. In reality, Brady should be in the same class as Michael Jordan, Tiger Woods, and Barry Bonds. If attention given to a player were commensurate with his performance on the field, Brady's name would *saturate* the airwaves. He is a 28-year-old wonder boy who has nothing but charisma and class off the field, and nothing but an ability to win on it. In reality, Americans don't know it, but they have accepted the fact that this man is No. 1; they are just blissfully discussing the candidates for "second best."

Brady's 28 touchdowns, 3,692 passing yards, and 92.6 quarterback rating from '04 are nothing more than sidebars to his three rings. Brady can win games in any fashion imaginable, from trying to move the chains in a low-scoring slugfest to going for the big numbers in a shoot-out. And wherever he goes, this offense will follow. The city of Boston has not seen a man who leads by example so well since the lanterns were hung on the Old North Church the night Paul Revere made his historic ride.

This past offseason, Brady and the Pats demonstrated in microcosm why this is the most well-managed and successful organization in football. Brady signed a long-term contract with the club, but—unlike past deals given to franchise quarterbacks such as Manning or Vick (and not to criticize them—they certainly deserve the money they earn)—Brady's contract did not break New England's bank. In fact, it was probably the best overall deal that any team and single player have agreed upon since the adoption of the salary cap in 1993. (Not coincidentally, the man negotiating for the Pats was general manager **Scott Pioli**, who himself rejected more money from other clubs over the offseason in order to stay in New England.)

Strengths

Chemistry

Frankly, everything on this team is a strength, both offensively and defensively. What makes so many weapons come together to form one arsenal is the leadership from the veteran players, the preparation of the coaching staff, and the harmony among all the people in this organization.

Depth

Injuries to starters have allowed many of the backups on this club to gain great experience. Furthermore, each week the game plan finds a way to fit virtually all players in uniform into the action on some level.

Weaknesses

Individual Pass-Blocking

It doesn't matter because this offensive line has been so solid as one unit anyway, but from a player-by-player standpoint, the Patriots are *somewhat* weak in pass-protection.

Special-Teams Coverage

Surprisingly, despite all the depth and veteran contributors, the Pats ranked 28th in both kickoff and punt coverage last year.

Of course, Brady doesn't carry his team by himself. Last season, the club traded for running back **Corey Dillon**, a bold move that worked out to the tune of utter domination on the ground. Dillon killed his evil reputation of being a locker-room cancer and finished third in the league in rushing, with 1,635 yards. Although he will turn 31 in October, there is nothing to indicate that Dillon will not continue to head a potent New England ground attack in '05. He has the vision, power, and balance to run between the tackles, but he also has the speed to turn the corner and get to the sideline. (Dillon averaged 5.6 yards per carry running outside last year.)

Perhaps most impressive about Dillon is that once he was able to operate behind a stable front five last year, he became the consistent player that he never was in Cincinnati. Dillon is the type of runner who can maintain long drives (like the ones that New England put together to doom Indy in the playoffs). He averaged five yards per carry on first down, and he also increased his yards per carry average by 0.7 in the second half of games.

Of course, there will be days when **Bill Belichick** (who will take over much of the offensive coaching responsibilities this year) will call on Brady to throw 40 or 45 times. When this happens, Dillon will take a backseat to **Kevin Faulk**, a seventh-year veteran who has established himself as the versatile third-down back on this team. In addition to the slashing Faulk, there is fullback **Patrick Pass**, who is essentially used as a halfback in this offense. Pass is a great short-yardage receiver—mainly in the flats, where he serves as Brady's dump-off option.

Pass's minimal contribution as a run-blocker is the result of two things: The first is that New England loves to use their bigger *defensive* linemen—such as **Richard Seymour** and **Dan Klecko**—as short-yardage lead-blockers; the second is that the Pats run a lot of single-back formations. From this, they show either a double tight end set or they line up three receivers.

The starting tight end this year will be fourth-year player **Daniel Graham**. Graham has come along gradually throughout his career, showing flashes of excellence as a downfield receiver and red zone option (seven touchdowns last season), but lacking the awareness and confidence to shoulder a big load. This year, he finally appears to be ready to step up. However, Graham's receiving skills did not earn him his starting job—his blocking

Write it Down:

Until another team in the league dethrones them, the New England Patriots deserve to be the *unquestioned* runaway favorite to win the Super Bowl.

This Season vs. Last Season

Progression: **Defensive backfield—**Thanks to their work over the offseason, the Patriots no longer lack depth in the secondary and now have more than 10 players who could all vie for playing time in '05.

Regression: **Left guard—**Last season's starter at this spot, Joe Andruzzi, is gone, leaving Russ Hochstein in his place. This marks a downgrade in both performance and leadership.

abilities did. Metaphorically, if there was a race to be the best blocking tight end in football, and the finish line was at the northern tip of the New England colonies, Graham would be approaching the Canadian border near Lancaster, New Hampshire, and whoever was in second place would still be as far south as New Haven, Connecticut.

The Patriots will use 11th-year veteran **Christian Fauria** and second-year player **Ben Watson** as the primary pass-catchers from the backup tight end spots this year. Fauria is nearing the conclusion of his career, but his long arms and soft hands still make him a viable receiving option. Watson is a gifted young player who was drafted No. 32 overall in '04, but he missed his rookie season with a knee injury. He has the potential to be a star later on down the road.

The Patriots have two of the league's brightest receivers, who are both still approaching the pinnacle of their careers. The first is MVP of Super Bowl XXXIX, **Deion Branch**, a 5'9", 193-pound stick of dynamite who can gouge defenses over the middle. The second is 25-year-old **David Givens**, who, like a true Patriot, settled for a one-year, $1.43 million contract over the offseason, knowing that he'll get his big-money deal in the near future. At 6'0", 215 pounds, Givens is thicker and stronger than Branch, and will be a more reliable possession receiver.

The depth at the receiver position is, as usual, splendid for New England. Although they lost David Patten, the team should still be adequate in the slot. They signed former first-round pick **David Terrell**, whose immaturity made him a letdown in Chicago. However, in the Patriot family, Terrell will have no choice but to grow up and play well, which means that his speed and desirable 6'3", 212-pound frame may actually translate into some meaningful production.

If Terrell doesn't work out, there's always **Bethel Johnson**, a third-year player who has even faster wheels and, occasionally, the presence of mind to make a big play. Finally, veteran **Troy Brown** (who last season epitomized New England's team concept in ignoring his chance to fulfill bonus clauses in his contract by switching to cornerback late in the year) is back, playing under a one-year deal.

With so many weapons on offense, it is no wonder the front line has been overlooked for so long. Nothing will change this year; aside from left tackle **Matt Light** (who is stellar in pass protection and outstanding in run-blocking), none of these players will likely make the Pro Bowl in '05. Instead, they'll just play to their strengths and thrive under the direction of offensive line coach **Dante Scarnecchia**.

The other no-names that make up this delicious New England clam chowder up front are guards **Russ Hochstein** and **Steve Neal**, center **Dan Koppen**, and right tackle **Brandon Gorin**—with maybe a flavored hint of utility lineman **Tom Ashworth** on the side. Every lineman for the Patriots is entering his third, fourth, or fifth year in the league. Each is smart, crafty, and mobile in run-blocking. And of course, they're good as one unit.

Defense

Despite ranking fourth in scoring offense (27.3 points per game) last year, the Patriots did absolutely nothing to dispel the old adage that says "Defense wins championships." New England held opponents to just 16.2 points per contest (which tied with the Eagles for second best in the league), and they tied for third with 30 takeaways. The Pats did not dazzle in any particular area (they ranked sixth against the run, 17th against the pass, and 21st on third down, while giving up loads of big passing plays), but they had the sheer moxie to stymie offenses. This speaks well for the coaching staff and, specifically, Romeo Crennel, who left New England over the offseason to become the head coach in Cleveland.

Before anyone interprets the loss of Crennel as an open invitation to end their respectful silence and start disparaging the Patriots, let's realize that the new defensive coordinator is **Eric Mangini**, who was the defensive backs coach here in '04, doing a job with a patchwork secondary that was nothing short of amazing. Mangini has a decade of NFL coaching experience, he joined the Pats when Belichick arrived in 2000, and he has earned his position just as much as Massachusetts legend Samuel Adams has earned the honor of having a beer named after him.

Nothing will be different with New England's defense this season. Well, actually, the *secondary* will be different; over the offseason, the Pats got *better* in the defensive backfield. New England said goodbye to the expensive Ty Law, which allowed them to have enough money to re-sign former Pittsburgh Panther and Steeler **Hank Poteat** and bring in veterans **Duane Starks** and **Chad Scott**. When factoring in the healthy return of 10th-year pro **Tyrone Poole** (who last season started five games before hurting his knee), the addition of third-round rookie **Ellis Hobbs**, and the development of young players **Asante Samuel** and **Randall Gay**, New England has gone from being Gillette razor–thin at the cornerback position to being Boston Harbor–deep.

With concerns about having to play receivers at nickel back and safeties at cornerback now a thing of the past, the Pats can go through training camp and the preseason with hearty competition for the starting cornerback jobs. Expect the

Veteran safety Rodney Harrison has helped hold down an unstable, yet still effective, secondary in New England for the past year.

emerging 24-year-old Samuel to earn one of the spots—his anticipation skills and range in zone coverage make him perfect in Belichick's crafty 3–4 scheme. The Patriots were listing Gay as the No. 2 corner throughout most of the offseason, but the second-year pro out of LSU is really more a fit for dime back duties. Gay is comfortable in this system, but he doesn't have the raw talent to excel.

Poole has proven before that he can be a surprise contributor in this defense, but at 33 he is slowing down. That leaves Starks—a former Super Bowl champion with the Ravens and, more recently, a solid contributor with the Cardinals—to win the No. 2 job. Starks should thrive in this role. He will have no trouble meeting the demands of physical play that this system calls for, and now that he'll operate out of more zone coverages, he should be even better at deflecting passes.

Strong safety **Rodney Harrison** is the do-all, say-all emotional leader for this secondary. He is very physical and most effective near the box. Free safety **Eugene Wilson** continues to get better each game. The third-year man out of Illinois was originally a cornerback, but his range and awareness in centerfield have made him a fixture at safety.

New England's 3–4 defense is built around the linebackers. Thanks to an assortment of alignments and blitz packages, the Patriots middle four can make a Boston Tea Party out of any offensive game plan, forcing teams to dump out certain plays, abandon the run, change blocking assignments, and so forth.

The starters for the Pats on the outside are the primary blitzers. They are veterans **Willie McGinest** and **Mike Vrabel**. After a season in which he recorded 9½ sacks and disrupted every short pass in sight, it is time to just accept the fact that the 33-year-old McGinest is like a fine wine: Better with age. Vrabel is a calm and collected ninth-year veteran who is still only 30. Although his sack total in '04 dropped to 5½, he will still be every bit as effective this season. More significant than his pass-rushing is that Vrabel is often the man responsible for setting the physical tone for which the Patriots pass defense has become so well known. He is fantastic at smacking receivers over the middle and disrupting a quarterback's timing.

The only truly negative element on this team heading into '05 is the questionable status of **Tedy Bruschi**. Bruschi, the heart and soul of this defense, suffered a mild stroke 10 days after the Super Bowl, jeopardizing his football future. Whether he joins the team in '05 or not, the Pats have the mind-set that he will not be available all year: They signed two free agent linebackers in **Chad Brown** and **Monty Beisel**.

Beisel joined New England because he was told he would have a chance to start. However, he may be mistaken. Assuming that the Pats elect to start the 6'4", 252-pound run-defending specialist **Ted Johnson** once again at one inside linebacker spot, Beisel would have to beat out Brown in training camp for the other—something that won't happen. Although Brown is 35, he still has outstanding speed and quickness and a mentality that is perfect for this system.

Beisel will likely have to come off the bench with pass-rushing specialist **Roosevelt Colvin** (who turns only 28 in September, is fully healthy, and is thus poised to step up this year) or play special teams with other linebackers like **Matt Chatham** and Pro Bowler **Larry Izzo**.

Pro Bowls appear to be in the cards for all three of the Patriots' young and talented defensive linemen. New England's two-gap defense will continue to make stars out of ends **Richard Seymour** and **Ty Warren** this year. It will also spark the coming-out party of second-year nose tackle **Vince Wilfork** (*see* Ready to Break Out, page 15).

In his fifth season out of Georgia, Seymour is already a three-time Pro Bowler in his own right. The 6'6", 310-pound force is a high-character player who is impossible to run against on the outside and difficult to block as a pass-rusher on the inside. Seymour is the only Patriots defensive lineman who plays all three downs.

It became known over the offseason that third-year pro Warren wants to join Seymour in being an every-down lineman up front. However, in yet another example of the near-perfect attitude throughout this Patriots team, Warren's ambitions did not become known as a result of him jabbering and complaining to the media, but rather by outsiders observing all of the extra work that he was putting in with defensive line coach **Pepper Johnson**. Expect Warren to get his wish soon (though maybe not until later in the year)—he is basically an improving B-version of Seymour, showing an impressive ability to keep separation as a forceful run-defender and displaying occasional pass-rushing skills.

New England's depth might keep Warren from becoming a three-down player, though. Fourth-year man **Jarvis Green** is a great interior pass-rusher off the bench, and last season's second-round pick (**Marquise Hill**) is expected to emerge into a greater role in '05.

Special Teams

Kicker **Adam Vinatieri** is almost as legendary around the Massachusetts area as Larry Bird or John Adams. New England was able to once again lock up Vinatieri for at least another year, thanks to the franchise tag—something that the 34-year-old, of course, didn't complain about. The punting situation in New England used to be something that could eagerly be cited as a weakness, but now, nope—the Patriots fixed that, too. **Josh Miller** averaged 42 yards per punt last season. The kick returner is the dangerous Bethel Johnson. On punts, New England is more concerned with playing it safe than they are with breaking a big one, which is why either the reliable Kevin Faulk or Troy Brown will likely do the job this year.

The Bottom Line

This team has to be everybody's favorite to win Super Bowl XL—there's just no way around it. It is wiser for a man to pick the Patriots and have them prove him wrong than it is for him to pick against them and end up looking foolish in the end. New England is the model for the perfect franchise in the NFL—in the front office, on the sideline, on the field, and in the locker room. In other words, they are the best *team* in football.

New York Jets

Predicted: 3rd ▪ 2004: 10-6 (2nd)

Players Added

RB	Derrick Blaylock (KC)	
OT	Ethan Brooks (Bal)	
WR	Laveranues Coles (Was)	
QB	Jay Fiedler (Mia)	
LB	Barry Gardner (Cle)	
TE	Doug Jolley (Oak)	
RB	Delvin Joyce (NYG)	
P	Micah Knorr (Den)	
DT	Lance Legree (NYG)	

Players Lost

TE	Anthony Becht (TB)	
K	Doug Brien (Chi)	
CB	Terrell Buckley	
QB	Quincy Carter	
LB	Sam Cowart (Min)	
DT	Josh Evans (retired)	
NT	Jason Ferguson (Dal)	
P	Toby Gowin (Atl)	
RB	LaMont Jordan (Oak)	
OT	Kareem McKenzie (NYG)	
WR	Santana Moss (Was)	

Draft

2	(47)	Mike Nugent	K	Ohio St.
2	(57)	Justin Miller	CB	Clemson
3	(88)	Sione Pouha	DT	Utah
4	(123)	Kerry Rhodes	S	Louisville
5	(161)	Andre Maddox	S	North Carolina St.
6	(182)	Cedric Houston	RB	Tennessee
6	(198)	Joel Dreessen	TE	Colorado St.
7	(240)	Harry Williams	WR	Tuskegee

Nugent was picked to make field goals and, thus, remove the bitter taste of last year's playoff meltdown caused partly by Doug Brien. Nugent is said to have 55-yard range. Miller is a great talent who showed character flaws after a late night of drinking led to his arrest, but New York has always been able to accept the gifted athletes in these sorts of situations. Pouha is a 26-year-old underachiever.

Head Coach: Herman Edwards (5th year)
Offensive Coordinator: Mike Heimerdinger
Defensive Coordinator: Donnie Henderson

Offense

QB:	Chad Pennington
RB:	Curtis Martin*
FB:	Jerald Sowell
WR:	Laveranues Coles
WR:	Justin McCareins
TE:	Doug Jolley†
LT:	Jason Fabini
LG:	Pete Kendall
C:	Kevin Mawae*
RG:	Brandon Moore
RT:	Adrian Jones
QB:	Jay Fiedler†
RB:	Derrick Blaylock†
WR:	Jerricho Cotchery
TE:	Chris Baker
OL:	Ethan Brooks†

Defense

LDE:	Shaun Ellis
DT:	Dewayne Robertson
NT:	James Reed
RDE:	John Abraham*
SLB:	Victor Hobson
MLB:	Jonathan Vilma
WLB:	Eric Barton
CB:	Donnie Abraham
SS:	Reggie Tongue
FS:	Erik Coleman
CB:	David Barrett
NB:	Ray Mickens
DL:	Bryan Thomas
LB:	Barry Gardner†
K:	Mike Nugent‡
P:	Micah Knorr†

* Pro Bowler '04
† veteran acquisition
‡ rookie

Report Card

Quarterback	B+	Defensive Line	A–	Coaching	B
Running Back	A–	Linebacker	C+	Special Teams	C
Receiver/Tight End	B	Defensive Back	C	Depth	C–
Offensive Line	B			Intangibles	B–

The New York Jets seem to have hopped on the subway at South Ferry in Manhattan, ridden all the way north past 103rd Street, clear up past Dykman Street, across the Hudson River, through the western side of the Bronx, and straight on out of the city. Their destination? Mediocrity.

Perhaps it is too harsh to introduce the Jets in such a manner, but the point is that New York was a solid playoff team a year ago (losing at Pittsburgh in the divisional round), but they have done little to improve in preparation for this season. Playing in the competitive AFC East and falling two steps back before taking a half-step forward translates into nothing more than a Wild Card—*if that*.

This year the Jets' head coach, Herman Edwards, is going to have to preach like he's never preached before. But it still won't be easy. One reason is that the New York coaching staff has rotated employees like a 7-Eleven. Edwards might be the most noble man in the NFL and he certainly deserves 100 percent respect from whoever has the honor of his presence, but there has been speculation that he may be difficult to work for as an assistant. The Jets have replaced countless assistants since Edwards's arrival in '01. This year, there is once again a handful of new coaches, including offensive coordinator Mike Heimerdinger and running back coach Dick Curl, who is

Curtis Martin

replacing Bishop Harris. Many remember Harris for his infamous sideline confrontation with Edwards during the team's Wild Card victory in San Diego last year.

Of course, coaches are great (turn back one page for proof), but the *players* are the ones who "play to win the game." With this in mind, the Jets will need a bunch of players to step up in '05.

Offense

New York running back **Curtis Martin** is a real headache to write about because he has a way of making certain "football authors" wonder why they even bother to offer analysis and make predictions. He simply defies all common sense. Take last season, for example: Martin, who was 31 at the time, was entering his 10th year in the league and appeared to be approaching his mortality. Although he had just rushed for 1,308 yards in '03, the consensus was that a decade of being a featured offensive weapon had finally taken its toll on the future Hall of Famer. Instead, Martin wound up claiming the NFL rushing title, gaining 1,697 yards, moving up to No. 4 on the all-time rushing list, and leaving many folks scratching their heads.

This year, writers—ahem—are in the same predicament; Martin is now a year older and, well, he's a year older, *okay?* How much longer can the quiet superstar continue on? Not wanting to underestimate him again, let's assume that Martin is capable of 1,400 yards in '05. That should be enough to produce another potent rushing attack for the Jets. (Last season, the team ranked third in the league at 149.3 rushing yards per game.)

What Martin brings to the offense is the type of consistency that only a clock can provide. He is not a home-run hitter and he is not a strikeout swinger; in fact, out of nearly 1,700 yards on the ground in '05, Martin's longest carry went for only 25. This speaks well to his ability to pick up four or five yards on a regular basis.

When Martin *does* get tired—something that is bound to happen once in a while this year—the Jets offense has a different look than the power-running that has been seen for the past couple of seasons with LaMont Jordan. Jordan is now in Oakland and fifth-year runner **Derrick Blaylock** (who was Priest Holmes's backup in Kansas City) is in place this season. Blaylock weighs a solid 210, but he is a quicker player who thrives on his shiftiness and ability to set up blocks.

New York ran the ball more often than all but two teams last season, which means that the 26-year-old Blaylock will likely see about eight carries a game in '05. Setting up his blocks on those eight carries shouldn't be hard, because All-World center **Kevin Mawae** will be clearing a path for him wherever he goes. Mawae is 34 and in his 12th year in the league, but he has yet to show any signs of slowing down. Simply put: Mawae is the best center in football. Everything that New York does on the ground is somehow related to Mawae. He anchors the line by pulling left or right and gets out in front as a lead-blocker.

Flanking Mawae on his sweeps and pulls will be left guard **Pete Kendall** and right guard **Brandon Moore**; both are set to be very good players in '05. Kendall is a 10th-year veteran who, after being cut by Dennis Green in Arizona last year, was thought to be washed up. However, he joined the Jets late in the summer and wound up having a season good enough to make his absence from Hawaii an official Pro Bowl snub. Kendall is an astute run-blocker who gets a good body on opponents and locks well. His technique and mobility on the ground make him the ideal fit for

this offense. Moore is nearly the antithesis of Kendall. The third-year pro out of Illinois started in all 13 games that he played last year, showing good potential but limited awareness. Moore's awareness issues are just a sign of his inexperience (heck, he actually began his career as a defensive lineman), something that goes away with—yes—more experience. Moore is going to work well in this offense because he is comfortable playing in space and has the technique to succeed as a run-blocker. In pass protection, he gets outdone at the point of contact, but he has the lower-body strength to recover and sustain his position.

On the right of Moore is where the problems will arise for New York in '05. They let their budding star, right tackle Kareem McKenzie, walk—literally *walk* (well, one would assume literally)—one locker room over in the Meadowlands to join the Giants. Unable to find a replacement, the Jets could go with second-year pro **Adrian Jones**, who has potential and has added bulk since joining the league (his weight is up from 286 to 296), but is still a project who would be a downgrade here in '05. A better option may be former Raven **Ethan Brooks**, who signed as a free agent late in the offseason. Brooks is not great in pass protection, but he has a 330-pound frame and solid dexterity when going forward in run-blocking.

It is darn near rude to mention left tackle **Jason Fabini** *last*, seeing as how the eighth-year pro is the nastiest, most aggressive player on this Jets offensive line. Fabini gets a great initial pop and is very tricky in how he baits defenders into getting too far upfield, allowing them to lay the bricks that form their own path out of a play.

The New York media that is touched upon with the Giants team report (pages 102–105) really pertains more to Jets quarterback **Chad Pennington**, who has gotten along with the big-city reporters about as well as prune juice gets along with the rectum. However, Pennington is by no means a prima donna— for crying out loud, the man joins Harlem's Bill Clinton (Harlem's Bill Clinton? Gosh, it still sounds odd) as New York's most famous Rhodes scholar *finalist*. Of course, Clinton *received* his Rhodes scholarship from Oxford in 1968. . . . Pennington played football at Marshall. (That might be the most unfair shot ever taken at a player.)

Write it Down:

If defensive tackle Dewayne Robertson and middle linebacker Jonathan Vilma continue to grow and emerge into what they are capable of becoming, the Jets will have the league's most dominant interior front seven for years to come.

This Season vs. Last Season

Progression: **Starting receiver—**The addition of Laveranues Coles is huge, because not only is he an upgrade over Santana Moss, but he is also a much better fit for this system.

Regression: **Tackle—**Both offensively and defensively. New York did not find an adequate offensive tackle on the right side to replace the departed Kareem McKenzie, and on defense they will pay all year for the losses of Josh Evans and Jason Ferguson.

Pennington may dream of one day owning a luxurious office in America's favorite ghetto-turned-folktown and have a wife in the Senate, but in the meantime he will aim his attention at rehabbing his surgically repaired right shoulder. Pennington is expected to be limited in training camp and throughout the preseason, but he should be fully prepared for action come September.

The Jets need Pennington like New Jersey needs the George Washington Bridge. **Herman Edwards**'s new offensive coordinator **Mike Heimerdinger** likely won't pass too much more than former coordinator Paul Hackett did, but when New York *does* toss the ball, they'll rely on the 29-year-old Pennington for his precision and accuracy. Pennington is a bright team leader who manages the game well and plays with poise. If he is unable to stay healthy for the duration of the season, newly acquired backup **Jay Fiedler** (a similar type of player, who comes with less accuracy but more mobility) would fill in.

Pennington should enjoy playing with former teammate (and now current teammate, once again) **Laveranues Coles** (*see* Painting a New Picture, page 7). Coles is in his sixth season in the league. He was traded back to the Jets (where he spent the first three years of his career) from the Redskins for Santana Moss.

Across from Coles—a player who, New York is very specific in noting, will line up two yards off the line of scrimmage as a flanker (those snooty Jets)—is "split end" **Justin McCareins**. McCareins is a lanky 6'2", 215-pound target in his fifth year in the league (his second in New York). He has what it takes to be a very viable third-down option; it seems as if every one of McCareins's 56 receptions last year was a crucial, tough catch.

The No. 3 receiver is going to be a problem for New York, unless second-year player **Jerricho Cotchery** can quickly emerge. Cotchery has the frame (6'0", 207 pounds) to be a decent possession receiver, but he caught only six balls last year. Letting

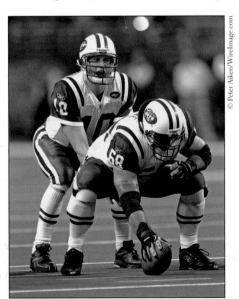

© Peter Aiken/WireImage.com

Jets quarterback Chad Pennington—like the rest of the offense—relies heavily on the services of the best center in the NFL: Kevin Mawae.

the concussion-prone **Wayne Chrebet** continue to play is almost as bad as granting a boxing license to 42-year-old Evander Holyfield. Chrebet has had a nice career, but it's time for him to purchase a nice home in the Hamptons.

Because New York focuses so much on maintaining drives and orchestrating a controlled passing attack, there is a premium placed on the pass-catching abilities of the tight end and fullback. This year, the Jets virtually traded away a 747 full of goods to get Oakland's **Doug Jolley**, and they are hoping that the fourth-year pro can use his unsuspecting quickness and soft hands to excel in this system. Jolley will start ahead of fourth-year man **Chris Baker**, who is a superb run-blocker.

Fullback **Jerald Sowell** isn't quite as smooth or cool as his last name implies, but he seems to have finally embraced his role as a receiver in the flats. The ninth-year veteran caught 45 passes last season.

Defense

Edwards hired the emotional and intense **Donnie Henderson** to spark some life into his young defense last year—something that Henderson did very well. New York ranked fourth in points allowed (16.3 per game) and seventh in yards given up (304.9 per game). They also came in fifth against the run (97.9 yards allowed per game) and generated an impressive 30 turnovers.

For the longest time, the Jets have been set on creating one of the most potent defensive lines in all of football. Now in '05, their young talents are basically all grown up and experiencing the prime years of their careers. In other words, it's payoff time for the Jets. New York has a pair of dynamic defensive ends in **Shaun Ellis** and **John Abraham**. However, this duo could become a . . . uh . . . well, whatever a single duo thing is called, if Abraham doesn't start enjoying being in New York. The 27-year-old was slapped with the franchise tag over the offseason, which prompted him to hold out of the team's minicamps in protest. Assuming Abraham signs his one-year tender sheet, the Jets can go back to game planning around the well-schooled abilities of the quick and athletic star. However, Abraham (who had 9½ sacks a season ago) may become a bit of a distraction if he does not have long-term financial security. Last year he created a controversy by refusing to play on a bad knee late in the season and during the playoffs because he knew it would jeopardize his negotiating leverage in pursuing a long-term contract. (In fairness to Abraham, he suffered an MCL injury and would have likely been rushing things had he played.)

Ellis, however, is getting paid, and as New York City's Cosmo Kramer would say, "He's out there and he's lovin' every minute of it!" The sixth-year pro broke into the league the same year that Abraham did, although it wasn't until around '03 that Ellis started producing like a star. Fortunately for the Jets, the 28-year-old produced again last season, recording a team-high 11 sacks. Ellis plays with good balance and a strong combination of speed and power.

Ellis is also very effective at dismantling one-on-one blocking, something that he will continue to see more and more of as 23-year-old tackle **Dewayne Robertson** improves. The Jets used a No. 4 overall draft choice on the Kentucky standout three years ago, and the gamble is starting to pay off. Robinson is incredibly quick and active in the trenches, showing an initial burst that would make a firecracker jealous. It is rare to see such a young player mature into a force that demands double teams; often, such respect is earned only with super production and veteran experience rather than just raw potential.

Despite his effectiveness, '05 is going to be a big year for the 317-pound Robertson. Regardless of how many double teams he sees, he must become more of a playmaker and improve his sack total and tackles in the backfield. Robinson's output this season may ultimately decide whether he is going to go on to become a superstar or just another good—but not great—Pro Bowler.

After putting forth so much effort to build an empire on the defensive line, the Jets have a gaping hole the size of Coney Island at the tackle position. The troubled and injured Josh Evans retired, and veteran Jason Ferguson was roped in by the Cowboys. This leaves **James Reed**—a one-gap player—to handle the nose tackle duties. That simply won't work for this team. New York could always go to free agent acquisition **Lance Legree**, a solid run-stopper, but they would be sacrificing too much quickness. Third-round rookie **Sione Pouha** may hear his name come up, but it is very unlikely that the 26-year-old could perform at a high enough level.

The Jets are sitting on an absolute gem in middle linebacker **Jonathan Vilma**. The '05 NFL Defensive Rookie of the Year appears to be one of those "once in a lifetime" talents. The agile 6'1", 230-pound Vilma is a superathlete out of—come on—the University of Miami, and his undersized frame is absolutely no hindrance to his game whatsoever. In fact, Vilma's best feature is his unmatched ability to avoid contact and shed blocks. Most impressive about the 23-year-old is that, even though he has natural skills that would allow him the ability to play brain-dead and still be good, Vilma is an intense student of the game. Last season, as a rookie who was not even expected to start, he not only took over the middle duties, but took responsibility for calling out the defensive signals as well.

Strongside linebacker **Victor Hobson** is only in his third year himself, and being 6'0" and 252 pounds, Hobson certainly has the size to play near the line of scrimmage and face blockers. However, the Jets love to match their defensive personnel with opposing offenses—meaning, when facing just about any alignment other than a traditional two-receiver, two-back, one–tight end formation, Hobson is expendable.

Weakside linebacker **Eric Barton** brings great energy and enthusiasm to this defense, but as he showed with his crucial personal foul penalty that allowed the playoff game last year against the Chargers to go into overtime, he must do a better job of playing under control. Then again, Barton is 27, so it's almost more likely that Mayor Bloomberg will call for a dramatic power-conservation effort in Times Square than that tackling machine Barton will actually slow down at this point.

New York's secondary was somehow able to survive last season, despite having a Knicks-like lineup. Perhaps Edwards's playing days as a cornerback had something to do with it. This year, the same cast of players returns, although they're still not worthy of much praise. Veteran cornerback **Donnie Abraham** had decided to call it quits before coming out for his 11th season,

but Edwards and the New York front office frantically talked the 31-year-old out of retirement, knowing that they would not be able to hold up in '05 without him. To convince Abraham to stay, the team agreed to give him Mondays off (in addition to the typical Tuesday break), in order to let him visit his family, who lives in his former home of Tampa, Florida.

The fact that a slowing-down player who had just two interceptions last season is this critical to the defensive backfield speaks volumes for how the Jets feel about their other cornerbacks. Positive things are often said about No. 2 starter **David Barrett**, a sixth-year pro out of Arkansas, because people see his solid statistics. However, Barrett is able to be around the ball and put up big numbers (78 tackles and 13 passes defensed in '05) because he gets challenged more than a Bush administration policy statement posted in Greenwich Village. Barrett gives up far too much separation and allows way too many receptions to get by, especially when teams throw at him deep downfield.

Barrett cannot become a nickel back—which is where he belongs—because the Jets don't have the depth to try anyone else out as a starter. **Derrick Strait** played well at times in '04, but the second-year man out of Oklahoma is thought to be nothing more than a No. 3 or No. 4. **Ray Mickens** is a veteran of 10 years, but he doesn't have enough size (5'8", 180 pounds) to match up with bigger receivers; plus, he missed all of last season with a knee injury. New York used a second-round pick on Clemson's **Justin Miller**, but he is still as green as the jersey he'll wear this year.

The safeties for the Jets are average. Strong safety **Reggie Tongue** can capitalize on opportunities presented to him, but he is not dynamic enough to create his own. Second-year free safety **Erik Coleman** will be very good one day, thanks to his ball skills and abilities in run support, but he will not fully blossom until he can improve his recognition skills.

Special Teams

After Doug Brien's playoff meltdown in Pittsburgh, the Jets were still steaming enough in April to use their first draft choice (which was a second-rounder) on Ohio State kicker **Mike Nugent**. Basically, Nugent will have to make about 29 of 30 field goals to fulfill expectations. Let's hope he has fun with that pressure in New York. The new punter is **Micah Knorr**. The Jets will have to find someone to replace Santana Moss on punt returns—expect it to be Justin McCareins. The speedy **Jonathan Carter** will likely have the full-time kick return duties in '05.

The Bottom Line

New York has pieced together a respectable club, and head coach Herm Edwards is a man who can *will* his players to victory. However, when a team wins 10 games and nearly reaches the AFC championship, the goal for the next season is to compete for a Super Bowl. The problem is, the Jets are not much different than a year ago—meaning they for darn sure do not have enough to compete with the Patriots. Jets fans will get their thrills late in December, when their team is in a playoff race, but expect nothing more after that.

AFC North

Baltimore
Ravens

Cincinnati
Bengals

Cleveland
Browns

Pittsburgh
Steelers

Looking Forward

How They'll Finish

1. Baltimore Ravens
2. Cincinatti Bengals
3. Pittsburgh Steelers
4. Cleveland Browns

Ready to Break Out

**Tommy Polley,
Baltimore Ravens**

Weakside Linebacker
6'3"—240 pounds
5th year—27 years old
Drafted: 2nd round in '01 out of Florida State

Polley is a very gifted linebacker who has not yet tapped into his potential. At 6'3", 240 pounds, he has a nice build, which he uses to show off his versatile athleticism.

Tommy Polley

Polley has always been regarded as something of an underachiever, and in reality, that is exactly what he has been. He began his career in St. Louis, a team that asked a lot of him but did not properly use his skills. They stuck Polley on the strongside, where he struggled to take on blocks and make powerful plays.

Now with the Ravens, Polley enters into a weakside role, in which he'll be far more successful. He'll be at ease, too, now that he has other veterans (hmmm . . . Ray Lewis?) around to assume the leadership duties. Lining up on the weakside will enable Polley to focus more on chasing the ball and playing on instincts, rather than having to read and react. Furthermore, Polley's low intensity will rise, now that he has a "dawg" like Lewis barking in his ear.

Hot Seat

**Kyle Boller,
Baltimore Ravens**

It is no secret what has been keeping Baltimore from prevailing deep in the playoffs in recent years. The Ravens have had an anemic passing attack, led by a struggling young quarterback, Kyle Boller.

However, the Baltimore front office and coaching staff are convinced that the former first-round draft pick is the man who can lead them in the future. Brian Billick has been very patient with Boller, but a football coach's patience can run only so deep.

Boller comes from the University of California, where he learned from one of the most respected quarterback teachers in the country, Jeff Tedford. However, there is speculation that Tedford produces great college players who fizzle as overhyped pro prospects. At Oregon, he had former Bengal (and current Frankfurt Galaxy) Akili Smith. Joey Harrington is another one of his ex-players who is on the hot seat in Detroit. Now Boller is finding himself trying to shake this image as well.

The Ravens paid a lot of money this past offseason to give their young quarterback an All-Pro receiver (Derrick Mason), plus the team invested a first-round draft choice in giving Boller wideout Mark Clayton. Consider that they have a Pro Bowl tight end in Todd Heap, stellar pass protection, and a very reliable rushing attack, and one quickly realizes that the Ravens are waiting on just one guy to step up this year. Pressure's on.

Best Offseason Move

Ravens signing a pair of former Titans in wide receiver Derrick Mason and cornerback Samari Rolle.

Worst Offseason Move

Browns tight end Kellen Winslow deciding to purchase a motorcycle *and then* attempting to pull wheelies on it.

Best Under-the-Radar Offseason Move

The Browns signing veteran guard Joe Andruzzi to help shore up the left side of their offensive line.

Biggest Question

Pittsburgh returns most of the personnel from last year's division championship team, but with the vast improvements in Baltimore and the inevitable progress being made in Cincinnati, can the Steelers prove they are still for real?

Jamal Lewis

QUICK HITS

TEAM BESTS		BEST PLAYERS	
Passing Game	Bengals	Pure Athlete	Ed Reed, Ravens
Running Game	Steelers	Big Play Threat	Ed Reed, Ravens
Offensive Line	Steelers	Best Use of Talent	Hines Ward, Steelers
Pass Rush	Steelers	Worst Use of Talent	William Green, Browns
Run Defense	Ravens	On the Rise	Troy Polamalu, Steelers
Pass Defense	Ravens		Levi Jones, Bengals
Special Teams	Steelers		Ben Roethlisberger, Steelers
Coaching Staff	Ravens	On the Decline	Orlando Brown, Ravens
Home Field	Steelers		Kimo von Oelhoffen, Steelers
			Peter Warrick, Bengals
		Best Leader	Ray Lewis, Ravens
		Unsung Hero	Dan Kreider, Steelers
		Impact Rookie	Mark Clayton, Ravens

Looking Back

Baltimore Ravens 2004

PASSING STATISTICS

PLAYER	CMP	ATT	YDS	CMP%	YDS/A	LNG	TD	TD%	INT	INT%	SACK	YDS	RAT
Kyle Boller	258	464	2559	55.6	5.52	57	13	2.8	11	2.4	35	247	70.9

RUSHING STATISTICS

PLAYER	ATT	YDS	AVG	LNG	TD	FUM	LST
Jamal Lewis	235	1006	4.3	75	7	2	0
Chester Taylor	160	714	4.5	47	2	1	1
Kyle Boller	53	189	3.6	19	1	4	2

RECEIVING STATISTICS

PLAYER	REC	YDS	AVG	LNG	TD	FUM	LST
Travis Taylor	34	421	12.4	47	0	1	1
Kevin Johnson	35	373	10.7	35	1	1	1
Randy Hymes	26	323	12.4	57	2	0	0
Todd Heap	27	303	11.2	37	3	0	0

RETURN STATISTICS

PLAYER	KICKOFFS ATT	YDS	FC	AVG	LNG	TD	PUNTS ATT	YDS	FC	AVG	LNG	TD
B.J. Sams	59	1251	0	21.2	64	0	55	575	12	10.5	78	2
Darnell Dinkins	1	7	0	7.0	7	0	0	0	0	0.0	0	0

KICKING STATISTICS

PLAYER	1-20	20-29	30-39	40-49	50+	TOT	PCT	AVG	LNG	XPM/A	PTS
Matt Stover	2/2	9/9	7/8	9/10	2/3	29/32	90.6	34.1	50	30/30	117

PUNTING STATISTICS

PLAYER	PUNTS	YDS	AVG	LNG	TB	TB%	IN20	IN20%	RET	YDS	AVG	NET
Dave Zastudil	73	2948	40.4	61	12	16.4	26	35.6	24	181	7.5	37.9

DEFENSIVE STATISTICS

PLAYER	TACKLES TOT	SOLO	AST	SACK	TLOSS	MISCELLANEOUS FF	BK	INTERCEPTIONS INT	YDS	AVG	LNG	TD	PD
Ray Lewis	147	106	41	1.0	6	1	0	0	0	0.0	0	0	6
Edgerton Hartwell	97	58	39	0.0	4.5	1	0	0	0	0.0	0	0	0
Gary Baxter	88	73	15	2.0	2.5	2	0	1	33	33.0	33	0	13
Will Demps	83	65	18	2.5	2.5	2	0	1	0	0.0	0	0	7
Ed Reed	78	67	11	2.0	4.5	3	0	9	358	39.8	106	1	17
Marques Douglas	72	51	21	5.5	6.5	1	0	0	0	0.0	0	0	2
Adalius Thomas	64	49	15	8.0	7	4	0	1	8	8.0	8	0	5
Kelly Gregg	61	45	16	1.5	3	1	0	0	0	0.0	0	0	1
Terrell Suggs	60	45	15	10.5	6.5	1	0	0	0	0.0	0	0	1
Chris McAlister	42	38	4	0.0	1	0	0	1	51	51.0	51	1	9

Cincinatti Bengals 2004

PASSING STATISTICS

PLAYER	CMP	ATT	YDS	CMP%	YDS/A	LNG	TD	TD%	INT	INT%	SACK	YDS	RAT
Carson Palmer	263	432	2897	60.9	6.71	76	18	4.2	18	4.2	25	178	77.3
Jon Kitna	61	104	623	58.7	5.99	30	5	4.8	4	3.8	6	41	75.9

RUSHING STATISTICS

PLAYER	ATT	YDS	AVG	LNG	TD	FUM	LST
Rudi Johnson	361	1454	4.0	52	12	4	4
Kenny Watson	26	161	6.2	25	0	2	1
T.J. Houshmandzadeh	6	51	8.5	16	0	0	0

RECEIVING STATISTICS

PLAYER	REC	YDS	AVG	LNG	TD	FUM	LST
Chad Johnson	95	1274	13.4	53	9	1	0
T.J. Houshmandzadeh	73	978	13.4	62	4	0	0
Kelley Washington	31	378	12.2	28	3	0	0
Matt Schobel	21	201	9.6	76	4	1	1

RETURN STATISTICS

PLAYER	KICKOFFS ATT	YDS	FC	AVG	LNG	TD	PUNTS ATT	YDS	FC	AVG	LNG	TD
Cliff Russell	39	872	0	22.4	40	0	0	0	0	0.0	0	0
Kenny Watson	13	240	0	18.5	32	0	0	0	0	0.0	0	0

KICKING STATISTICS

PLAYER	1-20	20-29	30-39	40-49	50+	TOT	PCT	AVG	LNG	XPM/A	PTS
Shayne Graham	0/0	7/7	10/12	7/8	3/4	27/31	87.1	36.3	53	41/41	122

PUNTING STATISTICS

PLAYER	PUNTS	YDS	AVG	LNG	TB	TB%	IN20	IN20%	RET	YDS	AVG	NET
Kyle Larson	83	3499	42.2	66	7	8.4	21	25.3	51	378	7.4	37.6

DEFENSIVE STATISTICS

PLAYER	TACKLES TOT	SOLO	AST	SACK	TLOSS	MISCELLANEOUS FF	BK	INTERCEPTIONS INT	YDS	AVG	LNG	TD	PD
Brian Simmons	107	84	23	1.0	1	3	0	2	61	30.5	50	1	4
Madieu Williams	91	79	12	2.0	0.5	0	0	3	51	17.0	51	1	11
Landon Johnson	84	64	20	2.0	4.5	2	0	0	0	0.0	0	0	2
Justin Smith	71	47	24	8.0	3.5	2	0	0	0	0.0	0	0	2
Kevin Hardy	69	49	20	4.0	2.5	0	0	0	0	0.0	0	0	4
Tory James	63	60	3	0.0	2	2	0	8	66	8.3	23	0	13
Kim Herring	62	50	12	0.0	5.5	1	0	1	0	0.0	0	0	6
Kevin Kaesviharn	58	48	10	0.0	2	0	0	0	0	0.0	0	0	8
John Thornton	57	44	13	3.0	4.5	0	0	0	0	0.0	0	0	4
Duane Clemons	50	37	13	6.5	5	2	0	0	0	0.0	0	0	1

2004 Team Stats

OFFENSE

Scoring:	19.8 (20)
Yards per Game:	273.4 (31)
Pass Yards per Game:	144.5 (31)
Rush Yards per Game:	128.9 (9)
Sacks Allowed:	35 (13)
3rd Down Percentage:	35.1 (22)
Giveaways:	22 (14)

DEFENSE

Scoring:	16.8 (6)
Yards per Game:	300.2 (6)
Pass Yards per Game:	195.1 (10)
Rush Yards per Game:	105.1 (t8)
Sacks:	39 (12)
3rd Down Percentage:	34.4 (8)
Takeaways:	29 (t8)

2004 Team Stats

OFFENSE

Scoring:	23.4 (10)
Yards per Game:	321.3 (18)
Pass Yards per Game:	206.3 (17)
Rush Yards per Game:	14.9 (17)
Sacks Allowed:	31 (t7)
3rd Down Percentage:	40.2 (11)
Giveaways:	30 (t26)

DEFENSE

Scoring:	23.2 (21)
Yards per Game:	335.3 (19)
Pass Yards per Game:	206.4 (13)
Rush Yards per Game:	128.9 (26)
Sacks:	37 (t17)
3rd Down Percentage:	36.7 (17)
Takeaways:	30 (t5)

Cleveland Browns 2004

PASSING STATISTICS

PLAYER	CMP	ATT	YDS	CMP%	YDS/A	LNG	TD	TD%	INT	INT%	SACK	YDS	RAT
Jeff Garcia	144	252	1731	57.1	6.87	99	10	4.0	9	3.6	24	99	76.7
Kelly Holcomb	59	87	737	67.8	8.47	55	7	8.0	5	5.7	5	31	96.8

RUSHING STATISTICS

PLAYER	ATT	YDS	AVG	LNG	TD	FUM	LST
Lee Suggs	199	744	3.7	39	2	6	3
William Green	163	585	3.6	46	2	3	2
Jeff Garcia	35	169	4.8	21	2	3	3

RECEIVING STATISTICS

PLAYER	REC	YDS	AVG	LNG	TD	FUM	LST
Dennis Northcutt	55	806	14.7	58	2	0	0
Antonio Bryant	42	546	13.0	55	4	0	0
Andre' Davis	16	416	26.0	99	2	0	0
Steve Heiden	28	287	10.3	30	5	1	1

RETURN STATISTICS

	KICKOFFS					PUNTS					
PLAYER	ATT	YDS	FC	AVG	LNG	TD	ATT	YDS	FC	AVG	LNG	TD
Richard Alston	46	1016	0	22.1	93	1	0	0	0	0.0	0	0
Dee Brown	13	243	0	18.7	30	0	0	0	0	0.0	0	0

KICKING STATISTICS

PLAYER	1-20	20-29	30-39	40-49	50+	TOT	PCT	AVG	LNG	XPM/A	PTS
Phil Dawson	0/0	11/11	6/8	6/9	1/1	24/29	82.8	33.5	50	28/28	100

PUNTING STATISTICS

PLAYER	PUNTS	YDS	AVG	LNG	TB	TB%	IN20	IN20%	RET	YDS	AVG	NET
Derrick Frost	85	3404	40	54	4	4.7	24	28.2	48	313	6.5	36.4

DEFENSIVE STATISTICS

	TACKLES				MISCELLANEOUS		INTERCEPTIONS				
PLAYER	TOT	SOLO	AST	SACK	TLOSS	FF	BK	INT	YDS	AVG	LNG	TD	PD
Robert Griffith	118	97	21	1.0	8	0	0	1	18	18.0	18	0	3
Warrick Holdman	76	54	22	0.5	2	0	0	0	0	0.0	0	0	2
Anthony Henry	76	67	9	0.0	0	0	0	4	83	20.8	51	0	12
Andra Davis	70	55	15	0.5	2	0	0	3	35	11.7	30	0	6
Kenard Lang	62	50	12	7.0	9.5	2	0	0	0	0.0	0	0	4
Chaun Thompson	58	38	20	2.5	0.5	0	0	0	0	0.0	0	0	3
Kevin Bentley	51	38	13	0.0	1.5	1	0	0	0	0.0	0	0	0
Daylon McCutcheon	50	45	5	0.0	0	0	0	2	0	0.0	2	0	9
Alvin McKinley	49	31	18	3.0	2.5	0	0	0	0	0.0	0	0	1

2004 Team Stats

OFFENSE

Scoring:	17.2 (t27)
Yards per Game:	280.1 (28)
Pass Yards per Game:	176.5 (25)
Rush Yards per Game:	103.6 (23)
Sacks Allowed:	41 (t21)
3rd Down Percentage:	29.1 (31)
Giveaways:	34 (t29)

DEFENSE

Scoring:	24.4 (24)
Yards per Game:	325.9 (15)
Pass Yards per Game:	181.3 (5)
Rush Yards per Game:	144.6 (32)
Sacks:	32 (t27)
3rd Down Percentage:	36.1 (15)
Takeaways:	25 (t17)

Pittsburgh Steelers 2004

PASSING STATISTICS

PLAYER	CMP	ATT	YDS	CMP%	YDS/A	LNG	TD	TD%	INT	INT%	SACK	YDS	RAT
Ben Roethlisberger	196	295	2621	66.4	8.89	58	17	5.8	11	3.7	30	213	98.1

RUSHING STATISTICS

PLAYER	ATT	YDS	AVG	LNG	TD	FUM	LST
Jerome Bettis	250	941	3.8	29	13	1	0
Duce Staley	192	830	4.3	38	1	3	2
Verron Haynes	55	272	4.9	18	0	0	0

RECEIVING STATISTICS

PLAYER	REC	YDS	AVG	LNG	TD	FUM	LST
Hines Ward	80	1004	12.6	58	4	1	0
Plaxico Burress	35	698	19.9	48	5	1	0
Antwaan Randle El	43	601	14.0	39	3	3	2
Verron Haynes	18	142	7.9	26	2	0	0

RETURN STATISTICS

	KICKOFFS					PUNTS					
PLAYER	ATT	YDS	FC	AVG	LNG	TD	ATT	YDS	FC	AVG	LNG	TD
Ricardo Colclough	26	566	0	21.8	48	0	1	13	0	13.0	13	0
Antwaan Randle El	21	527	0	25.1	41	0	42	347	13	8.3	60	0

KICKING STATISTICS

PLAYER	1-20	20-29	30-39	40-49	50+	TOT	PCT	AVG	LNG	XPM/A	PTS
Jeff Reed	1/1	8/9	12/13	5/8	2/2	28/33	84.8	33.1	51	40/40	124

PUNTING STATISTICS

PLAYER	PUNTS	YDS	AVG	LNG	TB	TB%	IN20	IN20%	RET	YDS	AVG	NET
Chris Gardocki	67	2879	43	61	6	9.0	24	35.8	34	252	7.4	39.2

DEFENSIVE STATISTICS

	TACKLES				MISCELLANEOUS		INTERCEPTIONS				
PLAYER	TOT	SOLO	AST	SACK	TLOSS	FF	BK	INT	YDS	AVG	LNG	TD	PD
James Farrior	95	73	22	3.0	7	3	0	4	113	28.3	41	1	12
Troy Polamalu	94	72	22	1.0	3	0	0	5	58	11.6	26	1	14
Chris Hope	90	63	27	0.0	0	1	0	1	41	41.0	41	0	5
Larry Foote	69	58	11	3.0	5.5	1	0	1	1	1.0	1	0	2
Deshea Townsend	56	51	5	4.0	0	1	0	4	54	13.5	39	1	11
Willie Williams	54	43	11	1.0	1.5	0	0	1	0	0.0	0	0	6
Joey Porter	54	42	12	7.0	7	3	0	1	3	3.0	3	0	12
Aaron Smith	44	35	9	8.0	6	3	0	0	0	0.0	0	0	1
Clark Haggans	38	30	8	6.0	3	2	0	0	0	0.0	0	0	1
Chad Scott	29	27	2	0.0	0	0	0	1	23	23.0	23	0	7

2004 Team Stats

OFFENSE

Scoring:	23.2 (t11)
Yards per Game:	324.0 (16)
Pass Yards per Game:	170 (28)
Rush Yards per Game:	154 (2)
Sacks Allowed:	36 (14)
3rd Down Percentage:	42.9 (6)
Giveaways:	16 (t5)

DEFENSE

Scoring:	15.7 (1)
Yards per Game:	258.4 (1)
Pass Yards per Game:	177.2 (4)
Rush Yards per Game:	81.2 (1)
Sacks:	41 (t7)
3rd Down Percentage:	32.6 (6)
Takeaways:	28 (t10)

Baltimore Ravens

Predicted: 1st ■ 2004: 9-7 (2nd)

Players Added

WR	Derrick Mason	(Ten)
LB	Jim Nelson	(Ind)
LB	Tommy Polley	(StL)
CB	Samari Rolle	(Ten)
G	Keydrick Vincent	(Pit)

Players Lost

G	Bennie Anderson	(Min)
CB	Gary Baxter	(Cle)
LB	Peter Boulware	
OT	Ethan Brooks	(NYJ)
LB	Cornell Brown	
DE	Marques Douglas	(SF)
DB	Corey Fuller	
LB	Ed Hartwell	(Atl)
WR	Kevin Johnson	(Det)
FB	Harold Marrow	(Ari)
C	Casey Rabach	(Was)
WR	Travis Taylor	(Min)
RB	Jamel White	(Det)

Draft

1	(22)	Mark Clayton	WR	Oklahoma
2	(53)	Dan Cody	DE	Oklahoma
2	(64)	Adam Terry	OT	Syracuse
4	(124)	Jason Brown	C	North Carolina
5	(158)	Justin Green	FB	Montana
6	(213)	Derek Anderson	QB	Oregon St.
7	(234)	Mike Smith	LB	Texas Tech

The Ravens may have had the best draft in the entire AFC. They snagged Clayton, a player whom many absolutely love. He is somewhat small, but very shifty and dangerous after the catch. He'll start opposite Derrick Mason this year. Cody is a passionate player who, as long as he can keep his emotions under control, can start regularly someday. He was supposed to go in the middle of the first round. Terry will likely start at right tackle before the year's over, and Anderson could be a stellar backup in this league.

The great American writer Edgar Allan Poe—who was born in Baltimore, Maryland, in 1809—did not realize the full significance of his words when he wrote his epic poem *The Raven*, which was published a year after his death. Although his eerie midnight tale in which the Raven quoth "Nevermore" is great, the real significance of Poe's piece was that it may have (to use a proper literary term) foreshadowed the '05 Baltimore Ravens football team.

Not even Poe himself could have put into words the fear that this Ravens defense will strike in opponents this year. Led by All-World superstar Ray Lewis and NFL '04 Defensive Player of the Year Ed Reed, the Ravens once again have a unit that is good enough to carry them through the playoffs and into Super Bowl contention. Granted, the defense is making a switch to a 46 defense, they are not as smart as that veteran group from 2000, and—like the offense—they are adjusting to a new coordinator (Rex Ryan). However, what makes Baltimore's defense unique is that they are not simply a solid bunch who will force a lot of punts—they are a playmaking bunch who will force a lot of turnovers and score a lot of immediate points off of those turnovers.

Head Coach: Brian Billick (6th year)
Offensive Coordinator: Jim Fassel
Defensive Coordinator: Rex Ryan

Offense

QB:	Kyle Boller
RB:	Jamal Lewis
FB:	Alan Ricard
WR:	Derrick Mason†
WR:	Mark Clayton‡
TE:	Todd Heap
LT:	Jonathan Ogden*
LG:	Edwin Mulitalo
C:	Mike Flynn
RG:	Keydrick Vincent†
RT:	Orlando Brown
QB:	Anthony Wright
RB:	Chester Taylor
WR:	Clarence Moore
TE:	Terry Jones
OL:	Adam Terry‡

Defense

LDE:	Anthony Weaver
DT:	Kelly Gregg
DT:	Dwan Edwards
RDE:	Terrell Suggs*
SLB:	Adalius Thomas
MLB:	Ray Lewis*
WLB:	Tommy Polley†
CB:	Chris McAlister*
SS:	Ed Reed*
FS:	Will Demps
CB:	Samari Rolle†
NB:	Deion Sanders
DL:	Jarret Johnson
LB:	Dan Cody‡
K:	Matt Stover
P:	Dave Zastudil

* Pro Bowler '04
† veteran acquisition
‡ rookie

Report Card

Quarterback	C	Defensive Line	B–	Coaching	A–
Running Back	A–	Linebacker	A–	Special Teams	B+
Receiver/Tight End	B–	Defensive Back	A+	Depth	C
Offensive Line	B–			Intangibles	B–

Ray Lewis

Of course, if Poe were to write a truly frightening poem, he could focus on the drudgery that is the Baltimore offense, which, over the years, has been horrific, to say the least. Improving on this side of the ball is where the first stanza of the Ravens season begins in '05.

Offense

Since the '02 NFL season, the Ravens offense has ranked 26th, 21st, and most recently, 31st in yards per game. Granted, this ranking is often overanalyzed and misleading, but *come on!* After a while, the writing on the wall becomes clear: Something needs to be fixed. Upon closer examination, it's not hard to figure out what that something is. In '02, the Ravens ranked 27th in passing offense, which, had they known at the time would have been so much better than their dead-last ranking in '03 (and their second-to-dead-last ranking in '04), would have been a cause for celebration down at Mo's Fisherman Wharf.

This past offseason, Baltimore went into action. However, they did not dump their third-year quarterback **Kyle Boller** (as so many impatient morons have insisted they should). Instead, the team signed former Titan wideout **Derrick Mason** (*see* Painting a New Picture, page 6). In addition to signing Mason, Baltimore used their first-round draft pick on Oklahoma receiver **Mark Clayton**. Couple this with the re-signing of **Randy Hymes** and toss in a rising star at tight end (**Todd Heap**), and one might just be tempted to say that the Ravens are establishing something that resembles an actual passing attack.

In other words, Baltimore has essentially pushed all of their chips over in Boller's corner. Choosing to surround Boller with so many receiving weapons is the third enormous wave of commitment Ravens general manager **Ozzie Newsome** and company have shown the former Cal Bear. The first was when they drafted Boller with the 19th-overall pick in '03, and the second was when they made him the starter that same year. Now they've arrived at this season, in which they've chosen to build around his skills.

But after a season in which Boller recorded a quarterback rating of 70.9 (82.5 in wins and 59.3 in losses, by the way), while averaging a comical 5.5 yards per attempt, many are arguing that he does not have enough skills to justify their faith. However, what many don't realize is that at the tender age of 24, Boller is still a work in progress. He was the youngest starting quarterback in the league last season, yet his team still finished above .500. The 6'3", 220-pounder has all of the tools needed to thrive in the NFL, whether it's arm strength, intelligence, accuracy, or unexpected mobility. Furthermore, Boller plays for head coach **Brian Billick**, one of the best offensive minds in the league. Boller's offensive coordinator is **Jim Fassel**. The two developed a nice rapport last season when Fassel was the team's quarterbacks coach. Finally, the *new* quarterbacks coach in Baltimore is (has everybody placed their bets?) **Rick Neuheisel**, who was great at instructing passers when he was the head coach at the University of Washington. The bottom line is that Boller simply has too much going for him to fail. Will he become Peyton Manning this season? No. Will he be what leads this team to a Super Bowl in '05? Certainly not. But will Boller continue to struggle like he has thus far in his career? Absolutely, positively, yes—wait, *no*, the answer is *no*. Sorry.

In examining the men who are expected to help Boller and the Ravens average more than just 144.5 passing yards per game this season, the assumption that can be made is that Baltimore is placing a premium on receivers running for yards after the catch. Mason has had a nice "RAC rep" for years. Clayton is said to be one of the most polished route runners to enter the league in quite some time; he is great at beating defenders with double moves and he knows how to work against zone coverage. The fifth-year tight end Heap should finally come fully into his own in '05. Heap missed a large chunk of last season with an ankle injury, but the 6'5", 252-pounder is healthy now. Heap has a great feel for making tough catches, he stretches the field as well as any tight end in the game, and he is improving his football IQ and blocking with every passing day. Because the Ravens place such a heavy emphasis on establishing the run (over 30 attempts per game last season), expect them to go with a few double tight end sets in '05. Backup tight end **Terry Jones** has solid experience as a fourth-year player, but he may see some of his playing time this season go to **Daniel Wilcox** or **Darnell Dinkins**.

Although last year's receiving corps was not quite good enough to be pathetic (say, Travis Taylor as the leader in yards with 421—no, no typo here, 4-2-1), Baltimore did discover two young talents almost by accident: **Clarence Moore** and **Randy Hymes**. This year, the two will likely compete for the No. 3 job (there is an outside chance that the No. 2 spot will be open, but that would require Clayton falling off the roof of one of the city's lovely brick homes or drowning in the Chesapeake Bay). Expect Moore to win the job with ease. At 6'6", he has an outstanding frame that could give the Ravens a superb target in the red zone. Furthermore, Hymes played well at times last year, but he lacks the speed to be anything more than a No. 4. Don't sleep on **Devard Darling**, either—he was a third-round pick last year who missed most of the season with a heel injury.

Regardless of how many nifty adjustments are made in the passing game, the surf and turf of this Baltimore offense is still going to be **Jamal Lewis** and the rushing attack. However, the 26-year-old Lewis enters the '05 season on much different terms than he has in any of his previous five years: Lewis is getting out of prison. He spent four months of his offseason locked up as a

Write it Down:

Football fans need to quit riding Kyle Boller and just realize that he is only going to continue to get better, especially in '05.

This Season vs. Last Season

Progression: **Wide receiver—**Replacing the disappointing Travis Taylor and difficult-to-live-with Kevin Johnson with Pro Bowler Derrick Mason and first-round rookie Mark Clayton needs no explanation.

Regression: **Pass protection—**Kyle Boller may have some initial trouble this year, because the right side of the offensive line features Keydrick Vincent and Orlando Brown, two shaky pass-blockers.

Defense

Anytime there is a discussion about the Ravens defense, the focus is automatically going to shift to **Ray Lewis**. Excuse the cliché, but he is the heart and soul of this team. No football player better depicts defense than Baltimore's middle linebacker. He is an intrinsic leader and an intrepid destroyer. In fact, Lewis may just be the best player in the NFL.

result of pleading guilty to facilitating a cocaine deal back in 2000. (He also spent two months in a halfway house after his release.) However, much like when Ray Lewis had his legal troubles, the Ravens have stood behind their star runner, never once entertaining the idea of trading the 245-pound sledgehammer. (Good thing, too: Baltimore likely would have wanted too many cigarettes for Lewis anyway.)

When on the field and healthy, Lewis is perhaps the most punishing between-the-tackles power-runner in the game. But after not working out during the offseason (Lewis spent his time with Bubba rehabbing his surgically repaired ankle) and going through the life-changing experience of being incarcerated, how ready can Lewis be, come September? The Ravens think he'll be great. Billick pointed out that Lewis, for the first time in nearly two years, now has the weight of his legal troubles completely off his back. Furthermore, reading between the lines, Baltimore enjoyed the luxury of knowing that their star runner was focusing on football this past spring and summer, and not gaining weight or having too much fun.

The Ravens rushing attack is aided by solid sidebar players such as fullback **Alan Ricard** and the shifty **Chester Taylor**—who is capable of being a spot-starter, but most of all, the ground game reaps the benefits of outstanding run-blocking from the offensive line.

The Ravens boast one of the best left tackle-guard tandems in all of football. The tackle is the 6'9", 345-pound perennial Pro Bowler **Jonathan Ogden**. That would make the guard seventh-year veteran **Edwin Mulitalo**.

Ogden did not have his best season last year, as he uncharacteristically struggled at times in pass protection. However, the 31-year-old has set the bar so high that if an opposing defender simply *breathes* on his quarterback, it equals a bad play. Ogden will be his usual dominant self in '05. At 345 pounds, Mulitalo is one of the most potent run-blockers in all of football. However, he does not thrive strictly on power; Mulitalo is also smart and superb at angling his blocks and sealing off defenders.

The Ravens downgraded at center by moving **Mike Flynn** over to replace the departed **Casey Rabach**. Flynn spent some time at guard last season, but he will now play solely in the middle. The eighth-year pro is not a weak player (he locks into opponents and can do a decent job of driving in run-blocking), but he is not as athletic as Rabach was.

A step back at the center position is nullified by a step forward at the right guard spot. Former Steeler **Keydrick Vincent** is in his fifth year and tipping the scales at a healthy 325 pounds. For years, the Ravens have had to overextend their efforts to run to the left side, but with the strength and nastiness of Vincent now residing on the right, Baltimore should be able to add more balance to their rushing attack in '05.

Vincent offers extreme limitations as a pass-blocker, though, which is not at all good when considering that right tackle **Orlando Brown** is 34 and slowing down. Vincent lacks lateral speed, and Brown has poor footwork. The Ravens will probably end up starting second-round rookie **Adam Terry** at right tackle before too long. Terry is tall (6'8"), has long arms, and plays with better balance.

That said, the Ravens produced last year's NFL Defensive Player of the Year, but it was not Lewis. Although Lewis finished third in the NFL with 147 tackles, the man receiving the hardware was strong safety **Ed Reed**, who became arguably the best playmaker since William Shakespeare, leading the league with nine interceptions. Reed is the best ballhawk in the league today. He has the kind of range that only the state of Montana can compete with, and thanks to his studious dedication to watching film (especially with Lewis), he has developed great awareness to accompany his anticipation skills. The fun is not over once Reed makes a pick; in fact, an even better thrill kicks in: Reed averaged 39.8 yards per runback off his interceptions last season, including a 106-yard touchdown return to seal a win against the Browns in week 9.

This year, expect Reed to be even better in *all* phases of the game, but specifically in run support, thanks to the duo of potential shutdown corners on the field. These corners are 28-year-old **Chris McAlister** and 29-year-old **Samari Rolle** (*see* Painting a New Picture, page 6). With McAlister and Rolle locking in on opposing receivers week in and week out, Baltimore will have what is far and away the most dynamic cornerback tandem in the AFC. McAlister is already of shutdown status, having the athletic abilities to match any opponent he faces. He has also matured in recent years and improved his discipline, which has proven to be a crucial step forward in his career.

Having two first-class corners is not going to be what causes the Ravens to drastically improve upon their 17 picks from last season, because great corners do not necessarily leave their mark by intercepting passes (although it certainly doesn't hurt). Where

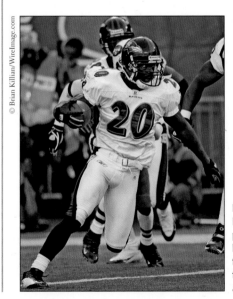

Reigning NFL Defensive Player of the Year Ed Reed is poised to have an even bigger season this year, thanks to the improvements that the Ravens have made at the cornerback position.

Rolle's addition to this secondary will be most noticeable is in the amount of passing yards given up by the club (last year Baltimore allowed a 10th-ranked 195.1 yards per game—a number that should drop in '05). Rolle's presence will also benefit free safety **Will Demps**. It has already been established that Reed is going to be much better with a solid tandem of cornerbacks beside him, but fourth-year pro Demps should progress even more.

Demps is an instinctive player who has improved his awareness and tackling with each game. This season, making the proper reads and getting in position should be close to second nature for him, as he will have more freedom to let loose his playmaking mentality.

The only potential concern about this secondary was the nickel back situation, which was designated to **Dale Carter**, a once-troubled veteran who missed all of last season with a blood clot in his lungs. However, Carter will probably find himself working in dime packages this year because **Deion Sanders** has strutted back into town and signed for the No. 3 job. How good a secondary can this be when the free safety is up-and-coming, the strong safety is the reigning defensive MVP, the cornerbacks are two of the league's few shutdown-capable talents, and the first man off the *bench* is *Prime Time*? P.S.: Backup safety **Chad Williams** is a talented player as well. Williams is a strong tackler who is productive when on the field.

The defensive backfield in Baltimore is amazing, but the front seven is under a bit of construction. New defensive coordinator **Rex Ryan** (who is replacing Mike Nolan, the new head coach in San Francisco) is canceling the 3–4 experiment and installing a variation of the 4–3 defense, known as the 46 defense. Fortunately, the move shouldn't be too tough, because Ryan will have Lewis holding things down in the middle.

The switch to the 46 will benefit Number 52 the most, because with a pair of meaty tackles like **Kelly Gregg** and **Dwan Edwards** occupying blockers up front, Lewis should have an easier time getting to the ball carrier in '05. The change also allows newly acquired linebacker **Tommy Polley** (*see* Ready to Break Out, page 35), a fifth-year pro who had been with St. Louis prior to heading east for Maryland, to man the weakside.

The strongside linebacker is **Adalius Thomas**, a sixth-year player who registered a career-high 8½ sacks in '04. However, those sacks came in a 3–4, where Thomas had fewer responsibilities. This year, the Ravens might use the 6'2", 270-pounder in pass coverage, an area where he can thrive on being physical. Thomas is a naturally gifted athlete, but if he wants to keep his starting position, he will have to break his lazy habit of giving a half effort. Otherwise, the team will find a way to bring second-round rookie **Dan Cody** into the mix. Cody was drafted as a defensive end out of Oklahoma, but Baltimore is moving the 270-pounder to a two-point stance, likely to better utilize his speed.

This move is interesting because the Ravens tried a similar approach with **Terrell Suggs** a few years ago, only to learn that even in a 3–4, the pass-rushing ace was simply not sound enough with pass coverage or making reads from the linebacker spot. If it

isn't obvious by now, Suggs has returned to the defensive end position. The 22-year-old has recorded 22½ sacks over his first two seasons in the NFL, so getting to the quarterback in '05 shouldn't be a problem. However, as a downlineman, Suggs must expand his pass-rushing repertoire and learn to better use his speed and quickness in run defense. Initially, Suggs might be slow to grasp these new obligations, but the man is simply too talented to fail.

On the left side of the front four will be end **Anthony Weaver**, a player who is just about as poor a fit for playing in a 4–3 scheme as one can be. Weaver has decent size (6'3", 290 pounds), which should help him against the run, but his limitations in agility—as well as his inconsistency—spell trouble as an every-down end. This is why it would not be at all shocking to see third-year player **Jarret Johnson** take over for Weaver before the season is over. Johnson plays with great energy, showing a nice step off the line of scrimmage and strong skills in pursuit.

Much the way the battle at Maryland's Fort McHenry during the War of 1812 helped inspire American Francis Scott Key to write "The Star-Spangled Banner," a switch to a 46 might finally inspire more Pro Bowl voters to pencil in Gregg at one of the tackle positions in '05. The 29-year-old Gregg is one of the most potent interior defensive linemen in the game. He has a great first step, outstanding power, and the lateral mobility to be active against the run. Gregg may have to carry the inexperienced Edwards along this year, but now that he's finally starting on a four-man front, he should be able to do an even better job of tying up blockers and getting in opponents' backfields this season.

Special Teams

The Ravens have a very stellar duo in kicker **Matt Stover** and punter **Dave Zastudil**. Stover is 37—gosh, just yesterday he seemed 36. He made 29/32 attempts last year, so he's still plenty valuable. Zastudil has an especially important job because anytime a team has a defense as fervid as Baltimore's is, it is important to have the means of capitalizing on field position. Hence, the punter can be crucial. Little-known **B.J. Sams** came out of nowhere to average 21.2 yards per kick return and 10.5 yards per punt return last season, all while displaying big-play potential. In fact, Sams ran two punts back for touchdowns.

The Bottom Line

The Ravens are the clear-cut favorite to win the AFC North, if for no other reason than their defense is explosive enough to outscore most offenses in this league. Boller will make his greatest leap as a pro, and as long as Jamal Lewis is healthy and a free man, he is good for an easy 1,000 yards. Finally, not enough credit is given to Billick, but he does a fantastic job of tying so many tough characteristics together and forming a football team.

Cincinnati Bengals

Predicted: 2ⁿᵈ ▪ 2004: 8-8 (3ʳᵈ)

Players Added

DE	Elton Patterson (Jax)
DT	Bryan Robinson (Mia)

Players Lost

S	Rogers Beckett
LB	Frank Chamberlin (Hou)
LB	Kevin Hardy
P	Kyle Richardson (Cle)
DT	Tony Williams (Jax)

Draft

1	(17)	David Pollack	DE	Georgia
2	(48)	Odell Thurman	ILB	Georgia
3	(83)	Chris Henry	WR	West Virginia
4	(119)	Eric Ghiaciuc	C	Central Michigan
5	(153)	Adam Kieft	OT	Central Michigan
6	(190)	Tab Perry	WR	UCLA
7	(233)	Jonathan Fanene	DE	Utah

The Bengals selected a pair of Georgia linebackers with their first two picks. Pollack would probably fit better in a 3–4, but then again, last year in college he showed the moxie of a player who can work anywhere if given the opportunity. Thurman will be a middle linebacker his entire career, as he lacks the speed and quickness to play outside but is more than solid between the hashes. Henry is a major talent who must disprove doubts about his character.

Head Coach: Marvin Lewis (3rd year)
Offensive Coordinator: Bob Bratkowski
Defensive Coordinator: Chuck Bresnahan

Offense

QB:	Carson Palmer
RB:	Rudi Johnson*
FB:	Jeremi Johnson
WR:	Chad Johnson*
WR:	T.J. Houshmandzadeh
TE:	Reggie Kelly
LT:	Levi Jones
LG:	Eric Steinbach
C:	Rich Braham
RG:	Bobbie Williams
RT:	Willie Anderson*
QB:	Jon Kitna
RB:	Chris Perry
WR:	Chris Henry‡
TE:	Tony Stewart
OL:	Larry Moore

Defense

LDE:	Duane Clemons
DT:	Bryan Robinson†
DT:	John Thornton
RDE:	Justin Smith
SLB:	David Pollack‡
MLB:	Odell Thurman‡
WLB:	Brian Simmons
CB:	Deltha O'Neal
SS:	Kim Herring
FS:	Madieu Williams
CB:	Tory James
NB:	Keiwan Ratliff
DL:	Langston Moore
LB:	Landon Johnson
K:	Shayne Graham
P:	Kyle Larson

* Pro Bowler '04
† veteran acquisition
‡ rookie

Report Card

Quarterback	B–	Defensive Line	C+	Coaching	B–
Running Back	B	Linebacker	C+	Special Teams	C+
Receiver/Tight End	B	Defensive Back	B	Depth	C
Offensive Line	B			Intangibles	C–

What is about to be said may sound funny, but it needs to be stated: The glass slipper could be sitting on the steps somewhere in Cincinnati. Wait! Wait! Don't laugh, just listen. The NFL is known for its Cinderella stories ('04 Chargers, '03 Panthers—anyone read those tales?). True, the people in the southern Ohio/northern Kentucky region have not had a happy ending since the Boomer Esiason days, but hey, there was once a class of people in an even worse situation: They were known as Red Sox fans.

The Bengals have the perfect formula to compute a surprisingly successful season in '05. They have a strapping young quarterback in Carson Palmer (whom Esiason has dubbed the best signalcaller in the AFC North), they have a strong core of talented receivers for Palmer to throw to, they can run the ball, and their offensive line will be the best it's been in years.

Cincinnati's problems have been most evident on the defensive side of the ball, but in recent years the team has drafted some players, signed some players, and moved some players. It looks like things could finally be working. And let's not forget, not only do the Bengals have a great defensive mind coaching them in Marvin Lewis, they also have one of the league's brightest and most passionate head coaches fresh on the scene. Looking at Lewis and seeing how he structures his football team, one just gets the feeling that the Bengals are not going to be bad forever.

However, this team will still be playing with the stripes of shame on their helmets, they'll still be mocked by ignorant fans who don't know what they're talking about but who nevertheless help form public opinion, and they'll still be expected by their town to fall short. After all, when *Monday Night Football* rolled

tions of people .

Chad Johnson

© Dan Bieneke/WireImage.com

 42   Cincinnati Bengals

back into Cincy for the first time in 15 years last season, the headline on one *Cincinnati Enquirer* column read: "Please, Bengals, Don't Embarrass Us." Ouch.

Offense

A s alluded to earlier, Cincinnati quarterback **Carson Palmer** is in a position to step up and lead his team to a playoff run in '05. Is the time right for Palmer? Is this the year that he must elevate his play? Well, *no*—Palmer is still only 25 and in his third season. Considering that he didn't take a single snap in his first year (when current backup **Jon Kitna** ran the show), the former No. 1 overall pick still looks like a developing prospect from here.

However, Palmer was adequate last season—after all, he led his squad to a respectable 8-8 record. While he certainly deserves at least one more year of hands-on-experience before being subjected to lofty expectations, his stellar play thus far may rob him of the benefits of being regarded as a young, on-the-job learner. Palmer is an athletic 6'5", 230-pound stud with a rocket arm. He can move well in the pocket or buy himself some time by scrambling outside. He has proven to be dependable under pressure (although his quarterback rating in the fourth quarter last year *was* a shabby 65.6). However, what should be focused on with Palmer is how he radically improved as he gained experience last season. Palmer's quarterback rating in September was 60.9. In October, he posted a 64.2. By November, Palmer was performing well enough to have a rating of 84.9. Finally, in the winter month of December, either the Christmas season or some other factor inspired him to play well enough to post a rating of 121.1.

If he continues at this pace, Palmer's rating by the year 2009 will read like a Social Security number. (Of course, the rating system maxes out at 158.2, but *that's* not the point.) With the talented receivers that the Bengals have put around Palmer, such outlandish improvements go from seeming "impossible" to just "unlikely." Star receiver **Chad Johnson**, for example, is one more great season away from becoming *superstar* receiver Chad Johnson. The fifth-year player had a career season in '04, catching 95 passes for 1,274 yards and nine touchdowns.

Johnson's 6'1", 192-pound frame, coupled with his speed, makes him a darting finesse-style receiver. He runs good routes, he is explosive, and he's a very diligent worker who shows a passion for the game. However, at times, Johnson is more like a supermodel than a superstar: Fun to look at, but too high maintenance to be around. His desire to be the best comes dangerously close to compromising his desire to help his team. Johnson is not a bad guy. In fact, he's like a normal version of Dennis Rodman: People tend to overlook some of the things he does because they want so badly to have a reason to like him. But the bottom line is that when the Bengals are in the heat of battle and trying to win a football game, head coach **Marvin Lewis**, offensive coordinator **Bob Bratkowski**, and Palmer do not have time to listen to one player whining. Some might say that Johnson is just young and emotional. *Nonsense.* He's a 27-year-old adult—he can behave like one just like the rest of society is forced to do every day. He's far too gifted a player and far too intelligent an individual to shortchange himself with a negative attitude.

Outside of Johnson, the Bengals have starter **T.J. Houshmandzadeh**, who, minus the personality, is eerily similar to his counterpart. Both are 6'1", both weigh in the 190s, and both are in their fifth year out of Oregon State. Houshmandzadeh

(73 receptions for 978 yards) did not have as productive a year in '04 as Johnson, but considering that he played in only two games the previous season and had a career total of just 62 catches coming into the '04 season, Houshmandzadeh sure amassed some nice accomplishments.

This year should be even better for Houshmandzadeh. He gives the Bengals the tough, physical, over-the-middle possession-receiver mentality that they don't have in Johnson. He is also adept at running after the catch. Overall, Houshmandzadeh is in the game to make tough grabs in short-yardage situations and move the chains on third down. Sixth-year pro **Peter Warrick** has the ideal skills to be a slot receiver, but his delayed recovery from his mild fibula fracture (nothing mild about it), which kept him out for most of last season, has left his future with the team in doubt. Third-year player **Kelley Washington** was also expected to at one time fill the No. 3 receiver role, but his offseason shoulder surgery has caused the Bengals to lose some interest. Washington could even find himself *fifth* or *sixth* on the depth chart—if at all—in '05.

Enter **Chris Henry**, a third-round draft pick out of West Virginia. At 6'4", 197 pounds, the receiver has the kind of lanky size that scouts drool over. However, Cincinnati's drafting Henry is the type of gamble that only hometown boy Pete Rose could understand. While very talented (especially in the red zone), Henry comes with character concerns and perhaps skills that are too raw to even bother cooking.

The tight ends for the Bengals are **Reggie Kelly** (the "starter"), **Tony Stewart** (the "backup"), and **Matt Schobel** (the "third-stringer"). As the quotes might indicate, the Bengals really have no idea what they're doing here. Kelly should be a No. 2, because his primary function is to block. Stewart is *listed* as the current No. 2, but in no way is he a better pass-catching option than Schobel. Finally, the man who should be the *real* No. 1 isn't even on the roster. In fact, nobody really knows who that man is; all that is known is that it's definitely *not* one of *these* guys.

After Corey Dillon packed up and left "the Queen City," running back **Rudi Johnson** was able to step into the starting role

Write It Down

Chad Johnson can be a great receiver because he is gifted and passionate about becoming the best in the game, but it is time for him to grow up and be more of a leader on this team.

This Season vs. Last Season

Progression: **Passing attack—**Carson Palmer will be better in '05, his starting wideouts will be more comfortable in this offense, and the receiver talent on the bench will be improved as well (assuming that rookie Chris Henry pans out and returning players Peter Warrick and Kelley Washington are healthy).

Regression: **Tight end—**It's hard to "regress" when the Bengals have not changed their personnel at this position in three years, but that's *exactly* the problem. The NFL is becoming more tight end oriented each day, and Cincy does not have the talent to take advantage.

and gain 1,454 yards, along with 12 touchdowns. This year, Cincinnati made the fifth-year pro their franchise player, meaning Johnson will once again be playing for a contract. Don't expect this to be a problem, though—after all, the man has been trying to prove people wrong since he came into the league in '01. Johnson is used to being doubted—the man's name is *Rudi* for crying out loud! It is more than okay to doubt Rudi on third down. He catches the ball about as well as Sean Penn catches a joke. This means that second-year player **Chris Perry** (a first-round draft choice from a year ago) will likely get his chance to compete in '05. Perry must outperform **Kenny Watson** in training camp, though.

Although Johnson is a stout 5'10", 220 pounds, he is not the inside runner that he appears to be. In fact, he averaged just 2.3 yards per carry up the middle last year. This season, the Bengals will focus on sending Johnson to the outside more often. Fullback **Jeremi Johnson** does not have the agility to be great as a lead-blocker going east and west, but the offensive tackles for the Bengals are good enough to pick up the slack.

Those tackles would be **Levi Jones** on the left and Pro Bowler **Willie Anderson** on the right. Jones is entering his fourth season in the league and is quietly becoming one of the game's rising linemen. While he has not performed at a high enough level to get any postseason accolades, he has played well enough to show fans that he was indeed worthy of being the 10th-overall pick in '02. Jones has tremendous strength, which allows him to drive defenders in run-blocking. His most impressive element is his ability to comprehend assignments and improve. Jones has developed a great grasp on the fundamentals, his awareness has risen over the years, and he now plays with a nice mean streak. (Ooh, ooh—oxymoron alert!) Because of these traits, Jones is able to disguise his mediocre foot speed and average agility in pass protection.

Anderson is a well-versed 10th-year veteran who is still only 30 years old and in the prime of his career. The 340-pound right tackle has the size to dominate in run-blocking, but he may actually be a better pass-blocker.

Former Heisman Trophy winner and first-overall pick Carson Palmer is in his third season in the NFL and second as a starter. He has all the tools needed to lead his club on a playoff push in 2005.

Between the tackles are guards **Eric Steinbach** and **Bobbie Williams** and center **Rich Braham**. Steinbach is a third-year player who might just be the most crucial piece to the puzzle up front. His mobility is the hinge on which many of Cincy's running plays swing. But he must improve his strength (at 6'6", he weighs only 297 pounds)—especially in the lower body—so that he can become more stable in pass protection.

Williams creates holes in the ground game by locking onto opponents and using his 330-pound body to drive them. He is somewhat inconsistent, but still definitely worthy of his starting role. The 34-year-old Braham was re-signed out of necessity this year. He'll have to play well if he wants to keep the impressive fourth-round rookie **Eric Ghiaciuc** from taking his job in '05.

Defense

The Bengals know exactly what they need to do to improve on defense in '05: Stop the run. Cincy ranked 26th in rush defense last year, giving up 128.9 yards per game.

Improving the run defense will open a lot of doors for this team. Not only will they likely allow fewer than their 23.2 points per game in '04 (ranked 21st), but they'll put themselves in more opportunities to rush the passer, *and* they'll have more chances to force turnovers—something they did very well last year (30 takeaways, tied for third highest in the league).

Saying they'll stop the run is one thing; doing it is another. The Bengals have decided that the best way to improve in this area is by enhancing the linebacker position. Thus, they drafted a pair of Georgia linebackers with their first two picks this year: Strongside man **David Pollack** in the first round and middle man **Odell Thurman** in the second. Pollack was given a starting job right away and, likely, a manual for being the headliner on an NFL front seven. Pollack is said to epitomize a playmaker. In his senior year with the Bulldogs, he had 17 tackles for a loss and 12½ sacks. At 6'2", 265 pounds, Pollack is really more fit to play an outside role in a 3–4, rather than a strongside role in Cincy's 4–3. However, regardless of where he lines up, the Bengals will frequently blitz their star. As far as improving the run, though, it will mainly be up to how well Pollack can understand the nuances of the pro game (he'll be just fine—he's a smart, high-character man). Pollack does not have the exceptional speed to fall back on, however, which means that he will have to be accountable for finding alternative ways to outplay opponents.

The Bengals are indicating that Thurman may crack the starting lineup in '05. Although he is athletic and particularly effective at stopping the run on the inside, Thurman has a few character concerns from his days at Georgia, plus many in the football industry question his mental capacity. (Thurman had academic trouble at Georgia and is said to have scored very low on the Wonderlic Test at the combine.) It is not fair to question Thurman's intelligence from this standpoint, but it must be said about all players that someone can be fast and explosive, but if he's not very bright he has no chance of succeeding at the pro level. However, because of injury concerns with veteran **Nate Webster** and second-year player **Landon Johnson**, he will likely snag the starting duties in '05.

Webster is returning from surgery on his kneecap, which kept him out of all but three games a year ago. If Johnson can ever learn to shed blocks, the middle linebacker job will be his. He is a good tackler (84 as a rookie last year) who quickly closes with a strong impact at the point of attack, but right now he may be too much of a liability to start. Johnson tends to get driven out of plays because of his inability to handle blocks. When this happens to a middle linebacker, running lanes for opposing offenses quickly open up. The word *liability* has as much to do with weakside linebacker **Brian Simmons** as the word *normal* has to do with Michael Jackson. Simmons, an eighth-year pro out of North Carolina, led the team with 107 tackles a year ago. He is one of those players who always appear on the television screen, no matter what. New defensive coordinator **Chuck Bresnahan** would be wise to take advantage of Simmons's speed and change-of-direction skills on the weakside, by placing a load of the underneath coverage responsibilities on him, much like the Bills currently do with former Bengal Takeo Spikes.

Simmons is an unknown star who is definitely not the culprit for the poor run defense. To be blunt (and probably, a little too harsh), the main cause of Cincy's poor run defense is tackle **John Thornton**. Thornton has solid size (6'3", 297 pounds) and he moves well—showing good quickness and lateral mobility—but in this scheme, the Bengals need him to move north and south and work to clog running lanes. Thornton simply doesn't do that. Instead, he attempts to *guess* which direction plays are going, moving around so much that on any particular down, Thornton looks like he is leaving to take a day trip to Indiana, maybe returning to Ohio for a few hours, then possibly heading south on Interstate 71 to Louisville or driving east toward West Virginia—anyway, that's the idea. He basically has ADD in run defense. If Thornton can't hold still, the Bengals should consider bringing in second-year player **Langston Moore**. Moore is a 303-pound brute who plays much larger than his size. He features great quickness in getting off blocks, and if properly directed by defensive line coach **Jay Hayes**, he could learn to play with the necessary leverage to stop the run.

Fortunately for the Bengals, they were able to sign former Dolphin **Bryan Robinson**. Robinson is exactly the player they need to fill the clogger role. He'll offer nothing as a pass-rusher (zero sacks in Miami last year), but the Cats have ends **Duane Clemons** and **Justin Smith** to pressure the quarterback.

Clemons probably deserves as much scathing criticism for his run defense as Thornton. He pays attention to the run like Howard Stern pays attention to censors. However, the 10th-year veteran *does* display a ferocious effort—he just applies it to pass-rushing. Smith has not lived up to his fourth-overall draft status from five years ago, but the 26-year-old is still a solid all-around player. He is quick, effective with his first move, and good in pursuit. Last season, Smith led the team with eight sacks.

Cincy has very good depth up front. In addition to the aforementioned Moore, veteran **Carl Powell** has had his moments as a starter, but his lack of ideal strength makes him more of a situational player. Second-year pro **Robert Geathers** is a third-down pass-rusher who will surely improve upon his 3½ sacks this year. In fact, it may not be long before Geathers replaces Clemons in the starting lineup. The two are very similar, although Geathers plays with better control and thus is more likely to stop the run.

The front seven will undoubtedly have to have a good month in August in order to be prepared for the show in September. Fortunately for the Bengals, the defensive backfield will be stable.

The Bengals have a pair of cornerbacks who are a constant threat to intercept a pass. The first is **Tory James**, who has put together tremendous back-to-back seasons—especially last year, when he picked off eight balls and earned his first trip to the Pro Bowl. The 32-year-old James is an efficient player who tackles well, operates with good awareness and anticipation, and has a knack for making the plays that his teammates normally wouldn't.

The second cornerback for the Bengals is **Deltha O'Neal**, a talented player who has squandered his once boundless potential with bouts of immaturity. O'Neal seemed to come around last season, though. If he continues to behave properly and not let his cocky ego get in the way of his outstanding athletic talent, Cincy will subtly have one of the top cornerback tandems in the NFL.

Nickel back **Keiwan Ratliff** began to show his potential late in the schedule of his '04 rookie season. Ratliff does not yet have the awareness to be a starter, but he is certainly capable of covering the slot receiver this year. He has the ability to quickly react to the reads he makes, and his closing speed in man coverage is excellent.

With Rogers Beckett gone, veteran **Kim Herring** is moving into Beckett's strong safety spot, which allows second-year player **Madieu Williams** to slide into the starting free safety role in '05. Herring should be fine playing near the box this year—the move is actually great for him because it will better highlight his power, hiding his second-rate speed. The real thrill is going to be watching what *Williams* can do in '05. The second-round pick from a year ago has an incredible feel for the game. Williams shows an uncanny ability to read a quarterback at the line of scrimmage and disguise his intentions. Once the ball is snapped, Williams's football IQ translates into good pass coverage. He also has the physicality to play the run. Williams is not especially explosive or particularly fast, and he doesn't have breathtaking strength, either. However, he simply knows how to play football, which is the best foundation on which to build a strong career.

Special Teams

Kicker **Shayne Graham** showed great long-distance accuracy last season, making seven of eight field goals in the 40-yard range and three of four in the 50-yard variety. A kicker with monstrous power is a huge plus for a football team. Punter **Kyle Larson** did nothing as a rookie to deserve to be made fun of this year (averaging 42.2 yards per boot), but he's a punter, so ha-ha. The Bengals used Houshmandzadeh on punt returns last season—a role in which he was downright average. Some guy named **Cliff Russell** ran back kicks, averaging 22.4 yards per return but failing to make a return that was longer than 40 yards.

The Bottom Line

Cincinnati is said to be the "northernmost southern city and southernmost northern city" in the United States. This principal has applied to Marvin Lewis's team the past two years, as they've posted their "somewhere in the middle" record of 8-8 in each of his two seasons. However, this year, one has to believe that Cincy is at least a game or two better than they were in '04, lending some credibility to the idea that they might just contend for a playoff spot. Or possibly the division title?

Cleveland Browns

Predicted: 4th ▪ 2004: 4-12 (4th)

Players Added

G	Joe Andruzzi (NE)
CB	Gary Baxter (Bal)
G	Cosey Coleman (TB)
QB	Trent Dilfer (Sea)
RB	Reuben Droughns (Den)
NT	Jason Fisk (SD)
P	Kyle Richardson (Cin)
FS	Brian Russell (Min)
OT	L.J. Shelton (Ari)
OL	Marcus Spears (Hou)
LB	Matt Stewart (Atl)

Players Lost

LB	Kevin Bentley (Sea)
DE	Courtney Brown (Den)
G	Damion Cook (Mia)
DE	Ebenezer Ekuban (Den)
QB	Jeff Garcia (Det)
LB	Barry Gardner (NYJ)
G	Kelvin Garmon
OL	Joaquin Gonzalez (Ind)
S	Robert Griffith (Ari)
CB	Anthony Henry (Dal)
QB	Kelly Holcomb (Buf)
LB	Warrick Holdman (Was)
S	Earl Little (GB)
Q	Luke McCown (TB)
DT	Michael Myers (Den)
CB	Lewis Sanders (Hou)
OT	Ross Verba
DT	Gerard Warren (Den)

Draft

1	(3)	Braylon Edwards	WR	Michigan
2	(34)	Brodney Pool	S	Oklahoma
3	(67)	Charlie Frye	QB	Akron
4	(103)	Antonio Perkins	CB	Oklahoma
5	(139)	David McMillan	DE	Kansas
6	(176)	Nick Speegle	OLB	New Mexico
6	(203)	Andrew Hoffman	DT	Virginia
7	(217)	Jon Dunn	OT	Virginia Tech

Edwards is considered by many to be the best player in this draft because of his combination of size, strength, jumping ability, and speed. He does tend to drop passes, though. Nevertheless, Cleveland should have a Pro Bowl receiver in him. Pool is a true free safety who can go get the football as a center fielder. Frye is an interesting pick: Is he here to be a long-term backup or is Cleveland looking to one day start him?

Head Coach: Romeo Crennel (1st year)
Offensive Coordinator: Maurice Carthon
Defensive Coordinator: Todd Grantham

Offense

QB:	Trent Dilfer†
RB:	Lee Suggs
FB:	Terrelle Smith
WR:	Braylon Edwards‡
WR:	Antonio Bryant
TE:	Steve Heiden
LT:	L.J. Shelton†
LG:	Joe Andruzzi†
C:	Jeff Faine
RG:	Cosey Coleman†
RT:	Ryan Tucker
QB:	Charlie Frye‡
RB:	Reuben Droughns†
WR:	Dennis Northcutt
TE:	Aaron Shea
OL:	Enoch DeMar

Defense

LDE:	Orpheus Roye
NT:	Jason Fisk†
RDE:	Alvin McKinley
LOLB:	Kenard Lang
LILB:	Andra Davis
RILB:	Ben Taylor
LOLB:	Chaun Thompson
CB:	Daylon McCutcheon
SS:	Sean Jones
FS:	Brian Russell†
CB:	Gary Baxter†
NB:	Antonio Perkins‡
DL:	Andrew Hoffman‡
LB:	Matt Stewart†
K:	Phil Dawson
P:	Kyle Richardson

* Pro Bowler '04
† veteran acquisition
‡rookie

Report Card

Quarterback	C	Defensive Line	D+	Coaching	C
Running Back	C−	Linebacker	C	Special Teams	C+
Receiver/Tight End	C+	Defensive Back	C	Depth	C−
Offensive Line	B−			Intangibles	C−

Dennis Northcutt

The city of Cleveland, which is located where the Cuyahoga River meets Lake Erie, has not seen so much renovation since the mid-80s, when the town was known by the deplorable title of "The Mistake by the Lake." At that time, the city regrouped after years of economic struggle by refurbishing the Lake Erie shoreline, building the Rock and Roll Hall of Fame, fixing the public schools, and getting the Cleveland Grand Prix—just to name a few things. Today, the Ohio town is being referred to as the "New American City."

With this in mind, it seems the Cleveland Browns are attempting to become the "New American Football Team." Since their reinstatement into the NFL in '99, the Browns have posted the worst record in football over that span (30-66) and have made just one cameo appearance in the playoffs ('02). It is no wonder there have been so many tweaks and adjustments made in the Dawg Pound this year. The most significant adjustment was the hiring of former Patriots defensive coordinator Romeo Crennel (*see* Painting a New Picture, page 5).

Crennel's arrival gives the Browns an entirely new coaching staff in '05. It also means substantial personnel moves made on a roster that features no star and little hope. On offense, a new starting quarterback will lead at least three other first-year Browns in the lineup. Defensively, Cleveland has axed the 4–3 in favor of Crennel's notable 3–4. The change has given the Browns three new starters and reshuffled several of the returning players, as many are undergoing position changes. And the players who are not switching positions will still be handling very different responsibilities this year.

All in all, Crennel has replaced 17 major contributors from last year's club, welcomed in a rookie class that will get right to work, and readmitted several key figures who missed significant time due to injury in '04. That said, this team is still miles away from living up to Ohio native Drew Carey's famous phrase "Cleveland Rocks!"

Offense

Let's just throw one thing out there right now and clear the air of any confusion: The Browns offense is going to be bad this year. Oh sure, the receiving corps is looking much better, especially now that the team drafted **Braylon Edwards** with the third-overall pick, and, yes, the front five is stronger, too. But these are the exact types of elements that can fog a person's perception. This is why the air is being cleared—to prevent people from falling victim to the poison of disappointment that floats in the water of a half-full glass.

Cleveland ranked 27th in scoring last season (17.2 points per game) and 28th in yards (280.1 per game). This year, behind new veteran quarterback **Trent Dilfer** and a less-fractured set of skill-position players, the Browns *might* be able to eke into the top 25 of both categories. Dilfer's arrival means absolutely nothing except for stability at the quarterback position. Of course, as Cleveland learned last season with Jeff Garcia, Kelly Holcomb, and Luke McCown (all of whom are now gone), stability under center is not something that should be taken for granted. The Browns did draft quarterback **Charlie Frye** (a local boy who played college ball at nearby Akron) in the third round, but it is extremely unlikely that Crennel will put the ball in Frye's inexperienced hands anytime soon. Frye could be groomed for Cleveland's future starting quarterback position, but as for '05, he'll likely be a nonfactor.

Essentially, the Browns are doing something that no NFL team has ever seemed truly willing to do: They're investing all of their stock in Dilfer. The 33-year-old has been one of the greatest backup quarterbacks/fill-in starters since "accidentally" winning a Super Bowl with the Ravens in 2000. Off the field, Dilfer has become one of the team leaders for this club, but on the field, the Browns will have to rely on his supporting cast to carry them in '05.

That supporting cast was supposed to feature the young and talented tight end **Kellen Winslow**, but the former Miami Hurricane suffered a torn ACL, among other things, in a serious motorcycle accident in May. Considering that Winslow missed virtually his entire rookie season with a broken leg, one can only hope that at this point in his career, he doesn't become one of the tragic stories of a world-class athlete never getting to display his skills at the highest level. As it stands now, Winslow's career is dangerously close to slipping away (an ACL tear is much more than a serious knee injury when a player goes without playing for

virtually two years). Not to mention, Winslow has lost a lot of dough for violating the terms in his contract (*see* Startling Statistics, page 49).

Winslow's absence means that once again, seventh-year veteran **Steve Heiden** will be the starter on opening day and backup **Aaron Shea** will be the second receiving option. Neither is a bad player, but neither is close to capable of fulfilling the huge plans that Cleveland's new offensive coordinator, **Maurice Carthon**, had brewed up for Winslow.

Any improvements to the Browns' struggling passing game will have to come from the receiver position. The man who will attract the attention in this department is Edwards. The 6'3", 211-pound rookie out of Michigan is the most highly touted receiver entering the NFL in '05. With great speed, masterful levitation, and an apparent playmaker flair, Edwards is expected to immediately produce on the big stage. (He has even drawn comparisons to Terrell Owens.) Over his final three years with the Wolverines, Edwards hauled in 249 receptions, amassed 3,503 receiving yards, and celebrated 39 touchdowns.

However, there is one red flag with Edwards (which, in the pros, will either become crimson or pink, depending on how he responds), and that is his attitude. Early in college, Edwards was immature. Being a high draft pick in the NFL can greatly impact a person. Not since William Jennings Bryan has the state of Ohio seen someone work as hard to further his own celebrity status and wealth as Edwards already has. He has purchased cars, jewelry, and a few friends to join his posse. However, let's not paint Edwards in an unfair manner, either. He has a very close relationship with his father, he matured during his collegiate career (even opting to return for a senior season in Ann Arbor), and he has yet to prove that he is indeed the next Michael Westbrook.

The No. 2 receiver across from Edwards will likely be former Pitt Panther **Antonio Bryant**, an emotional basket case who joined the Browns in October last season after getting himself kicked out of Dallas midway through the year. A focused Bryant can be an upper-tier wideout in the NFL; he has good athleticism, runs nice routes over the middle, and shows a knack for making tough catches in traffic. However, a pouting and complaining Bryant is a hindrance to a football team and at best, a so-so receiver.

The man who might be able to compete with Bryant for the No. 2 job is **Andre Davis**. However, Davis—in his fourth year out of Virginia Tech—missed nine games last season because of a toe

Write It Down

The Cleveland Browns are as big a lock to finish last in their division as any team in the AFC.

This Season vs. Last Season

Progression: **Stability—**Considering that Butch Davis and his coaching staff were lame ducks last year and the quarterback position was a revolving door, the Browns can feel good about having a firm leader in Romeo Crennel and a trusted veteran signal caller in Trent Dilfer. Slowly but surely, this team is finding an identity.

Regression: **Defensive depth—**Last season, the Browns had a variety of players whom they could rotate on defense. Granted, none of them were any good, but the options came in handy as injuries continued to strike the team. This year, Cleveland is very thin in all areas defensively.

has drawn attention for his vast display of tattoos and his habit of showering right before kickoff. In the very near future, Faine will be getting attention for his near-perfect technique in pass protection. However, he must develop more as a run-blocker before he can be considered an upper-echelon center.

injury. He has never in his career totaled more than 576 receiving yards in a given year and he has proven inconsistent when asked to serve as more than a complementary option. Davis is not a weak enough player to be a No. 4 receiver, but that is likely where he'll end up on the depth chart if he doesn't start. The No. 3 wideout will probably be the 27-year-old veteran **Dennis Northcutt**, because he is extremely shifty and quick and has proven to be a good receiver in the slot.

Ever since the Browns drafted **William Green** in the first round in '02, their running back situation has been a mess. Green has been a major nuisance to this team, as his host of off-the-field problems has significantly compromised his production on the field. Green will enter the season as the team's No. 3 running back, behind returning starter **Lee Suggs** and former Bronco **Reuben Droughns**, for whom the Browns traded a pair of defensive linemen.

However, Green is fresh from his best offseason as a pro, leaving **Romeo Crennel** and the rest of the Browns organization impressed with his dedication to working out with his teammates every day. It appears that Green is trying to do the right thing. Now all that remains to be seen is which, if either, will come first: Green's last-chance mistake or his second-chance opportunity.

Trading for Droughns was more of an avenue to dump defensive lineman Ebenezer Ekuban—Cleveland is just hoping that they get lucky with the sixth-year runner. What they'll likely discover about Droughns is that although he gained 1,240 yards as a product of Denver's system last year, he does not have the speed or quickness to be a major threat week in and week out in the NFL.

This leaves Suggs to fill the starting role. One hundred of his 199 carries a year ago came as a starter, but his 3.7-yards-per-carry average does little to show that he can be a feared back at the pro level. At 210 pounds, the 25-year-old is a downhill runner who has the power to fit well with the team's fullback **Terrelle Smith**—a thick lead-blocker who can crush defenders. But at some point, Suggs will have to rely on the change-of-direction skills that he has not yet proved to possess. Furthermore, Suggs must learn to run to the left as effectively as he runs to the right. Last year, he averaged just 3.2 yards per carry going left, with six fumbles (as opposed to 3.8 yards per carry to the right, and no fumbles).

Suggs won't be able to point the finger at the offensive linemen on the left side this year. Newly acquired tackle **L.J. Shelton** is a solid player who, after being let go in Arizona, will be playing with a chip on his shoulder. Former Patriot **Joe Andruzzi** (*see* Benoit Citizen Hall of Fame, page 184) is one of the premier run-blockers in the NFL, thanks to his outstanding technique.

The right side of the front line features tackle **Ryan Tucker** and guard **Cosey Coleman**. Tucker is a 320-pound veteran who has been known to be a force in run-blocking, but he is coming off a quadriceps injury that caused him to miss nine games in '04. Coleman left the Buccaneers over the offseason. He's an average lineman, but he plays with good energy.

The center for the Browns is third-year man **Jeff Faine**, who

Defense

Upon inheriting this defense, Crennel probably feels as if he's been tasked with of those enormous 1,000-piece puzzles that must be put together before September. He is undoubtedly forcing some sharper-edged pieces into rounder spots, knowing that if he pounds them together with his fist, he may just get them to fit.

However, forced pieces often result in an ungraceful picture of slop and chaos. This is what is poised to happen with the Browns defense in '05. Crennel and defensive coordinator **Todd Grantham** are stuck trying to run a 3–4 with a subpar defensive line, a group of underdeveloped linebackers, and a secondary that does not enjoy the kind of safeties that Crennel got used to having in New England.

Crennel will have to shift the focus of his 3–4 toward improving Cleveland's awful run defense, which allowed 144.6 yards per game last season (worst in the NFL). Teams simply could not wait to line up and ram the ball down the Brownies' throats. In this scheme, the impact that the three defensive linemen have in stopping the run is often overlooked. Ultimately, the nose tackle is the key, which means that first-year Brown **Jason Fisk** (who was the backup nose tackle in San Diego) will have to play beyond himself this year. At 295 pounds, Fisk may lack the bulk needed to command double teams in the middle. He can get a decent push, but he isn't destructive enough to be a potent starter in '05. Furthermore, he will turn 33 early in the season, which suggests that his inevitable decline is looming.

The Browns seem to be relying on Fisk almost as much as the Cavaliers are relying on LeBron James. If Fisk is ineffective, the team will likely have to go with sixth-round rookie **Andrew Hoffman**. Such limited depth is the result of starting former tackles **Orpheus Roye** and **Alvin McKinley** at defensive end this year. Roye's quick first step and ability to split double teams (as well as his 320-pound frame) would make him a much better option at the nose tackle spot, but Crennel likely doesn't trust Roye's inconsistency or the lack of leverage with which he plays. McKinley has made a minimal impact over his six-year career. A move to the outside is the best thing that could have happened to him—because his active nature is more likely to pay off there. But this doesn't change the fact that McKinley is a backup-level player who just happens to be on a team that is bad enough to be using him as a starter.

Crennel is going to have to work like an Amishman to make this linebacking unit function right this season. His first mission should be to make sure that fourth-year player **Andra Davis** is comfortable and ready to go, because Davis is the closest thing that he'll have to a playmaker up front. The 6'1", 255-pound Davis will start alongside **Ben Taylor** on the inside. From here, Davis will be responsible to stuff the run, but also, because of his three interceptions and six passes defensed last year, the team will likely have him do some work in coverage.

Taylor missed virtually all of the '04 season with a back injury. He has the football IQ to understand his role on the inside, and

Veteran Kenard Lang will be making the switch from defensive end to outside linebacker, where he'll play the role of Willie McGinest in Romeo Crennel's 3–4.

Startling Statistics

150 Amount in dollars that Kellen Winslow was fined for his misdemeanor charge of "disregarding safety" in his motorcycle accident.

5,000,000 Roughly the amount in dollars that Kellen Winslow was forced to repay the Cleveland Browns as a result of violating the terms of his contract, which forbid him to engage in risky acts such as riding a motorcycle.

he might be versatile enough to move outside at times, but from a raw skills standpoint, Taylor lacks the power to dominate against the run. Furthermore, the team may have to go with the inexperienced **Mason Unck** in place of Taylor on third downs.

The outside linebackers will be **Kenard Lang**—who has played defensive end in every one of his nine seasons until now—and **Chaun Thompson**. Lang is perhaps the biggest question mark on this defense. Despite weighing 280 pounds, the 30-year-old moves with a relatively good rhythm and flow, and he even has limited experience in pass coverage from his work in zone blitzes. But in his outside linebacker role, Lang will blitz on a majority of plays, meaning he should increase his sack total of seven from a year ago. However, Lang has always been a bit of an underachiever, and making such a dramatic position change at this stage of his career a somewhat risky move.

Thompson is a younger and more athletic version of Crennel's former linebacker Roman Phifer. In his third year out of West Texas A & M, Thompson has a nice 6'2", 250-pound build, something that is required to play in this scheme. Thompson is well equipped to handle pass-coverage duties, and as long as he can learn to use his size to be more physical (which he almost certainly will), he can slide right into this puzzle as a smooth, well-fitting corner piece.

Former Falcon **Matt Stewart** is on the roster and may prove to be too safe an option to leave on the bench. The Browns are rolling the dice with Lang and Taylor, plus they are counting on an increased level of play from Davis and Thompson. With so many quiet uncertainties, Crennel may want to use Stewart's stellar speed and comfortable presence near the line of scrimmage in some fashion this year. Stewart is very reliable in this sense.

A lot of people will look at Cleveland's 181.3 passing yards per game allowed last year (fifth fewest in the league) and think that the Browns have a potent secondary, but if the Society Center in downtown Cleveland is Ohio's tallest building at 948 feet, does that mean Columbus is *not* the state's largest city? Looks can be deceiving.

For starters, the Browns ranked so well in pass defense in '04 only because nobody threw against them. Offenses were so successful running on the orange and brown that there was no reason to attempt any passes. Second, whatever success this team had in pass defense last year is irrelevant, because Cleveland has

three new starters and a first-year nickel back heading into week 1 of this season.

The new starters are cornerback **Gary Baxter**, strong safety **Sean Jones**, and free safety **Brian Russell**. The nickel back is rookie **Antonio Perkins**. With so many new faces under those solid orange helmets in '05, the only man whom the fans in the Dawg Pound will recognize in September is **Daylon McCutcheon**. McCutcheon is a seventh-year cornerback who lines up against the opposing team's No. 2 receiver. He is a quick player with solid talent, but he would make a much better nickel back.

Baxter will help alleviate some of the pain at the cornerback position. The former Raven is in his fifth year in the league and is, for the first time, playing as a big-money man under lofty expectations. Baxter improved annually during his time in Baltimore, but making the quantum leap to a leading role will be a huge adjustment for him. He is adept in man coverage and can stay with receivers downfield, but Baxter must become more consistent if he is to thrive as a No. 1 corner.

Jones was a second-round pick last year but—seemingly like everybody on this team—he missed the entire season with a torn ACL. Jones has very limited experience, which will show in '05, but his talent is superior enough to that of backup **Michael Jameson** that the Browns will have to suffer through the bumps in the road.

Ex-Viking Russell has been overrated since picking off nine passes in '03. Last year, he had just one interception, because of fewer tipped balls falling in his lap. The former undrafted rookie out of San Diego State is a nice success story, but as far as this season goes, the Browns will soon realize Russell's lack of authority and host of limitations. It will be a test of patience to see how long Crennel can go before giving in to the idea of starting the second-round rookie, **Brodney Pool**, at free safety in '05.

Special Teams

Kicker **Phil Dawson** was a mediocre 24/29 last season. But the 30-year-old has had seasons in which he was among the most accurate kickers in the league, so the Browns have nothing to be concerned about. Cleveland has brought in punter **Kyle Richardson**—who has not played in over a year—to compete with **Derek Frost**. Expect Richardson to easily win the job. Northcutt is the punt returner for this team; he is dangerously electrifying in this role. However, the team has considered relieving Northcutt of all return duties so that he can focus more on becoming a better receiver. If this is the case, Cleveland will go with the rookie Perkins as their return artist. Perkins was great in this role at Oklahoma.

The Bottom Line

Do not expect the Browns to compete in the AFC North anytime soon. Crennel may be a good head coach in his first year, but unless he can transform himself into Gepetto and handcraft better players, he's not going to win this season. Cleveland simply does not have any stars. Name one player whom the Browns can turn to when in trouble. The only possible option is Braylon Edwards, an unproven rookie. This spells significant trouble for the team in '05.

Pittsburgh Steelers

Predicted: 3rd ▪ 2004: 15-1 (1st)

Players Added
WR Cedrick Wilson (SF)

Players Lost
LB	Kendrell Bell (KC)
WR	Plaxico Burress (NYG)
DT	Kendrick Clancy (NYG)
TE	Jay Riemersma
OT	Oliver Ross (Ari)
CB	Chad Scott (NE)
OG	Keydrick Vincent (Bal)

Draft
1	(30)	Heath Miller	TE	Virginia
2	(62)	Bryant McFadden	CB	Florida St.
3	(93)	Trai Essex	OT	Northwestern
4	(131)	Fred Gibson	WR	Georgia
5	(166)	Rian Wallace	ILB	Temple
6	(204)	Chris Kemoeatu	OG	Utah
7	(228)	Shaun Nua	DE	BYU
7	(244)	Noah Herron	RB	Northwestern

Heath Miller is one of the best picks any team made in this draft. He is a Jason Witten–type receiver who understands the game in a variety of ways. Furthermore, a good tight end is a perfect fit for Ben Roethlisberger and the Pittsburgh offense. Both McFadden and Essex are mediocre prospects, but each could provide some depth. Gibson is a well-spoken man with the height and receiving skills to offer unique contributions on offense.

Head Coach: Bill Cowher (14th year)
Offensive Coordinator: Ken Whisenhunt
Defensive Coordinator: Dick LeBeau

Offense
QB:	Ben Roethlisberger
RB:	Duce Staley
FB:	Dan Kreider
WR:	Hines Ward*
WR:	Cedrick Wilson†
TE:	Heath Miller‡
LT:	Marvel Smith*
LG:	Alan Faneca*
C:	Jeff Hartings*
RG:	Kendall Simmons
RT:	Max Starks
QB:	Tommy Maddox
RB:	Jerome Bettis*
WR:	Antwaan Randle El
TE:	Jerame Tuman
OL:	Trai Essex†

Defense
LDE:	Aaron Smith*
NT:	Casey Hampton
RDE:	Kimo von Oelhoffen
LOLB:	Clark Haggans
LILB:	James Farrior*
RILB:	Larry Foote
ROLB:	Joey Porter*
CB:	Ricardo Colclough
SS:	Troy Polamalu*
FS:	Chris Hope
CB:	Deshea Townsend
NB:	Willie Williams
DL:	Travis Kirschke
LB:	James Harrison
K:	Jeff Reed
P:	Chris Gardocki

* Pro Bowler '04
† veteran acquisition
‡ rookie

Report Card
Quarterback	A–	Defensive Line	B	Coaching	B+
Running Back	B+	Linebacker	B+	Special Teams	B
Receiver/Tight End	B–	Defensive Back	C+	Depth	C
Offensive Line	B+			Intangibles	A–

These next four pages will be an utter delight for all of the traditional, old-fashioned purists out there. It is time to take a look at the Pittsburgh Steelers, arguably the best example of what a professional football team is supposed to be. The Steelers come from a blue-collar town that established itself as a true American city during the days of Andrew Carnegie and his steel mills. They are owned by Dan Rooney, who did not purchase the team with $800 million made off his booming Internet company, but inherited it from his father, Art, who was one of the league's true pioneers.

The Rooney family simply knows how to do business. They are honest, passionate, and, most of all, loyal to their program. Amazingly, in this day and age, when everybody in the football world is looking for a quick fix, the Rooneys have modeled their team on stability. This is best seen in head coach Bill Cowher, who has now been with the franchise for 14 years! Since when in the NFL does *that* happen? How, in 14 years, has some bigger-than-life superstar not come along and run the coach right out of Three Rivers—er . . . ugh—*Heinz* Field. Okay, Heinz Field, like the ketchup—so the Steelers are not old-fashioned in *every single* dimension. Cut em' *some* slack.)

The bottom line is that this is a classic NFL organization. They're just a true, down-to-earth, levelheaded, blood-and-guts football team. Who in their right mind can't appreciate that?

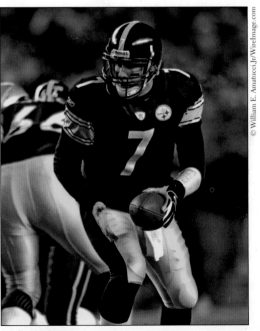

Ben Roethlisberger

Offense

In no fashion are the Steelers more traditional than in their offensive approach. Vince Lombardi, Chuck Knoll, Jim Brown, John Madden, Dick Butkus—every one of them, every football purist to ever grace the earth— would tip their cap to the way **Bill Cowher's** team plays offense. The Steelers run the ball—they're a grind-it-out offense. They don't care that it is darn near against the rules to keep the ball on the ground in the NFL today. Offensive coordinator **Ken Whisenhunt** is going to scoff at passing innovations and force opponents to show their heart and display their toughness up front in the trenches. If they are not man enough, the power-running of **Jerome Bettis** and **Duce Staley** is going to devour them. Why, the Steelers could even have one of the best young quarterbacks to ever enter the league (like that **Ben Roethlisberger** guy, for example), and they would *still* be a running team.

Pittsburgh ran the ball a league-high 618 times last season. They threw the ball a league-low 358 times. The 618 rushing attempts generated an average of 154 yards per game, which was good for second in the NFL. However, it isn't just the Steelers' rushing yardage that kills opponents, it's the rhythm with which they play. Because they can run the ball so effectively, Pittsburgh is able to dictate the pace of the game.

This year, helping to dictate that pace will be Staley, who enters the season completely healthy. Staley is a 30-year-old veteran who has 242 pounds of sheer muscle strapped to his frame. He is a hard-nosed runner who loves to lower his shoulder, initiate contact, and deliver a pop while grinding north and south.

Staley spent the first seven years of his career in Philadelphia, where he split carries with many other tailbacks. Prior to the 2004 season, Staley wanted a featured role, so he hit the Pennsylvania Turnpike and drove west to the steelmaking town that was established by the British and named after late-18th-century prime minister William Pitt. There, Staley hoped to finally have an opportunity to be an every-down-back in the NFL, but darned if he didn't hurt a hamstring and open the garage door for "The Bus" to drive through. Nobody could have foreseen the 33-year-old Bettis rushing for 941 yards and 13 touchdowns last season—with the amount of pounding that Bettis has taken since joining the league 13 years ago, not only should he have long since been retired, he probably should be outright dead by now. Instead, "The Bus" just keeps driving along, not stopping to pick anyone up and accelerating to run over defenders every Sunday.

Staley and Bettis will once again split carries in '05, a role with which both classy men are fine, just as long as the Steelers keep winning. No matter who is in the game, the man who will be providing the lead-blocking is **Dan Kreider**. The sixth-year veteran is simply one of the best classic fullbacks in all of football. In passing situations, the Steelers could go with Staley (he is a decent receiver out of the backfield and he is a very good blocker as well), but they'll probably elect to use backup fullback **Verron Haynes**, because of his quickness.

Perhaps now is a good time to dwell more on that quarterback who was mentioned earlier. For anyone who doesn't know, Roethlisberger became the Steelers starting quarterback early in the season last year (after veteran **Tommy Maddox** went down in week 2) and took the league by storm. The 6'5", 241-pounder from Miami, Ohio (a Mid-American Conference school),

produced a rating of 98.1, completed 66.4 percent of his passes, and averaged 8.9 yards per attempt. Oh yeah, he also posted a record of 13-0 as a starter during the regular season.

Unfortunately for the Steelers, Roethlisberger got banged up and, consequently, unraveled during the postseason, looking like the 23-year-old rookie that he was supposed to be all along. But as Kurt Vonnegut would say, "So it goes." Roethlisberger's playoff woes should take nothing away from the brilliance that he showed last season.

The '05 season promises greater expectations as well as greater potential for success for the 24-year-old Roethlisberger. Many cynics believe that because the Steelers predicate their offense so much on running the ball, Roethlisberger's success comes largely from the fact that he is merely the beneficiary of being surrounded by good talent. The players around the quarterback certainly help shorten his learning curve (yes, of course that's true); however, Roethlisberger's ability to orchestrate Pittsburgh's ball-control offense is equally as impressive as the system itself. His role requires leadership, poise on third down (where Roethlisberger posted a rating of 101.1 last year), patience, and playmaking skills that can be employed when things break down.

Roethlisberger has outstanding mobility (particularly behind the line of scrimmage), he sees the field relatively well, he has a strong arm, and, most important, he oozes the "It" that is so often talked about.

This season, Roethlisberger might be even more dangerous, now that he has a tight end who can be a major receiving threat in rookie **Heath Miller**. The Steelers used their first-round draft choice on the former Virginia Cavalier. Miller gives Pittsburgh the second short-yardage target that was missing from the offense a year ago. Furthermore, the team does not sacrifice a lot of blocking by adding him, because they still have veteran **Jerame Tuman** to come off the bench when need be.

The prime short-yardage receiver is **Hines Ward**, a 29-year-old warrior who has made four consecutive Pro Bowls. Ward is the heart and soul of the offense, he is the source of toughness, and, this year, with the handful of new downfield plays created by Whisenhunt, he'll likely be the best big-play threat as well.

Of course, the Steelers would prefer that that title be awarded to fourth-year player **Antwaan Randle El**, an electrifying and

---

Write it Down:

Ben Roethlisberger is already one of the top 10 quarterbacks in the NFL, but that will not be enough for this team to match their success from a year ago.

Strengths

Identity

The Steelers know exactly what they are going to do week in and week out: Run the ball on offense and blitz on defense. They care little for what their opponents are doing—Pittsburgh wants to make teams play to *their* game.

Offensive Line

Most of the dynamite is focused on the left, where Pro Bowlers Marvel Smith and Alan Faneca reside, but don't forget about Pro Bowler Jeff Hartings and the potential of the younger right linemen, guard Kendall Simmons and tackle Max Starks.

Weaknesses

Deep Threat

The Steelers are going to have trouble stretching the field in '05. Hines Ward is a possession receiver in every sense of the term, Cedrick Wilson is a poor man's Ward (Charlie Bucket–poor), and Antwaan Randle El lacks the size to overmatch defenders on jump balls.

Offensive Line Depth

Every time Pittsburgh crumbles, it seems as if a lack of depth on the front line is to blame. If injuries occur, this year will be no different, as the Steelers have very inexperienced players on their bench.

Progression: **Tight end**—No offense could have benefited from getting a viable receiving tight end more than Pittsburgh's. They found exactly what they needed in rookie Heath Miller.

Regression: **Right offensive line**—Although both Kendall Simmons and Max Starks are capable of having good seasons, the initial outlook has to be that they are inferior to Keydrick Vincent and Oliver Ross.

multitalented slot receiver. Randle El is a threat to run (eight attempts on end-arounds and reverses last year), he can throw (record-setting quarterback for the Indiana Hoosiers from 1998–2001), and, of course, he can catch (43 receptions in '04). He is also a dangerous punt returner. Amazingly, Randle El was also drafted by the Chicago Cubs back in 1997, and he played on the Hoosiers basketball team for "The General," Bobby Knight! In other words, he has some nice athletic genes.

While Randle El may be the team's second-best wide receiver, newly acquired **Cedrick Wilson** will likely capture the No. 2 job. Wilson symbolizes a major drop-off from the downfield skills of Plaxico Burress (who is now with the Giants), but he was the best that Pittsburgh could do. The problem is that whichever way the Steelers choose to lean this year (Randle El or Wilson), they are still going to have an inconsistent player with questionable experience and awareness.

Anyone who started on the Steelers offensive line last season and failed to make the Pro Bowl probably feels like a loser. After all, three of Pittsburgh's five starters up front got invited to Hawaii, and (oh, this is ironic) the two who didn't have been replaced this season.

The men who kicked back on the beach and basked in the glory of being fat, rich, and loved were left tackle **Marvel Smith**, left guard **Alan Faneca**, and center **Jeff Hartings**. This year, all three are back and ready to go, although Faneca is the only virtual guarantee to return to Hawaii this season. In his eighth year out of LSU, Faneca is the anchoring force that leads this run-blocking unit. He has the athletic capacity to make any block—whether it's near the line or in the open field—and he plays with good power and toughness. Smith is a sixth-year pro who possesses good agility. When he faces inferior competition, he serves well as a run-blocker by taking good angles and highlighting his balance and mobility. However, for a 321-pound beast, he lacks a great initial pop.

Hartings will be 33 in September, but as long as his mind has yet to deteriorate, his game will remain strong as well. The best

Two of the cogs in Steelers football are running back Jerome Bettis and head coach Bill Cowher. Cowher has been the head man in Pittsburgh for 14 years now, which is the longest tenure among all head coaches in the NFL.

way to describe Hartings is to explain that he is the type of solid presence in the middle who will help make a bad play average, an average play good, and a good play great.

The soft spot up front is undoubtedly the right side of the line. Right guard **Kendall Simmons** is a powerful player who can engulf defenders, but he is rebounding from a torn ACL suffered last August. Next to him is tackle **Max Starks**, a second-year player who made a few cameo appearances in 10 games last season. Starks is a gifted young talent, but some have questioned his passion for the game.

Defense

Much the way the Steelers have stayed true to running the football—recently, that is—they have been loyal to playing an aggressive 3–4 defense that strives to attack opponents and dictate the tempo of the game. In '04, the Steelers clearly had the best defense in all of football. They ranked first in points allowed (15.7 per game), first in yards allowed (258.4), first against the run (81.2 yards per game), and an atrocious fourth—*fourth!*—against the pass (177.2 yards allowed per game).

It is good news for Pittsburgh that they are essentially returning the same cast of players in '05. One reason the Steelers have such a potent 3–4 (a 3–4 that does little to be cute and disguise intentions, as is seen in New England) is that, while most teams settle for mediocrity out of their three-man defensive line, the Steelers present impact players.

Left defensive end **Aaron Smith** made the Pro Bowl in '04, thanks to his team-leading eight sacks. Smith is an eighth-year player who has really come into his own over the past few seasons. As implied, he is adept at pressuring the quarterback, but he is even more committed to playing the run. Smith has the 6'5", 298-pound size to handle blockers and he has gotten stronger in recent years, something that has allowed him to push the pile and further disrupt blocking schemes.

The other defensive end is 34-year-old **Kimo von Oelhoffen**, a 12th-year veteran out of Boise State. Von Oelhoffen has begun his natural decline (his sack total dropped from eight in '03 to just one last year), but he is still a stellar run-defender, thanks to his strong lower body and inclination to always keep his legs pumping. However, this year, expect von Oelhoffen to begin sharing more time with 30-year-old **Travis Kirschke**. Kirschke is a versatile backup who can hold up against the run on the outside or play tackle when the Steelers go into their four-lineman set on passing downs.

Analogous to the way Pittsburgh was settled in the 1750s because it was a strategic location at which to build a fort where the Allegheny and Monongahela rivers converge, the Steelers nose tackle position has become the perfect location for the front line to converge. The man being converged upon is **Casey Hampton**, a fifth-year pro out of Texas who has a load of power in his 325-pound body. However, Hampton will be unable to collapse defensive lines this season if he doesn't stay healthy (he missed most of last season with a right knee injury). If Hampton were unavailable, the Steelers would once again rely on the undersized yet overachieving **Chris Hoke** to fill in the middle.

The Pittsburgh defense did not earn the nickname "Blitzburgh" for no reason—with an active linebacking unit, the Steelers essentially have four players whom they feel comfortable sending after the quarterback. The name that everyone loves to throw

© William E. Amatucci, Sr/WireImage.com

around is **Joey Porter**, who has been to the Pro Bowl a time or two and is one of the best blitzing linebackers in the NFL.

However, after '04, the name that everyone *should* be throwing around is **James Farrior**. The ninth-year pro out of Virginia is coming off a career-season. In fact, playing the inside, Farrior was probably the best all-around linebacker in football for 17 weeks last year. He recorded the kind of balanced numbers that only Alan Greenspan could appreciate: 95 tackles, three sacks, three forced fumbles, four interceptions, one touchdown, and 12 passes defensed. It is hard to say exactly what got into Farrior last year—he has never been more than a middle-tier player throughout his career. Whatever it was, defensive coordinator **Dick LeBeau** has to be praying that it returns in '05, because Farrior's speed and instincts help make LeBeau's job much easier.

As for Porter, he is a prolific star (seven sacks in '04) who has great athleticism on the outside. However, someone should label the 28-year-old for what he truly is: A dirty player. Porter is productive, but his immaturity, disrespect for opponents, and occasional cowardly approach to the game leave him just shy of being a bona fide thug on the field.

Between the inside linebacker Farrior and the outside linebacker Porter sits inside man **Larry Foote**, an improving fourth-year player who is one of this team's integral forces against the run. Although Foote weighs just 239, he shows good strength in how he faces up to contact and accepts a man-to-man challenge. He does not play the game at a very fast rate, but what Foote lacks in "foot" speed (ha!), he makes up for in his clever angle to the football.

The final starting linebacker is **Clark Haggans**, a fifth-year player who is used primarily as an extra pass-rusher. On third downs, the Steelers will line up Haggans and Porter as downlinemen. However, Haggans is only average in such a role—frankly, his game is too vanilla to be dominant. Opponents can quickly figure out exactly what he is trying to do, which is beat offensive linemen around the corner with his speed-rush. The best way for LeBeau to utilize Haggans is to scratch the idea of him playing end and just allow him to operate off the line of scrimmage. From there, Haggans could stay active, use his pursuit skills, and read offenses. He is not *completely* foreign to pass coverage, so he wouldn't be too much of a liability in this role.

The most surprising element in Pittsburgh's unexpected fortune in '04 was the play of the secondary. In fact, it was downright startling that the Steelers defensive backs were as good as they were. But with this in mind, it is hard to say with a lot of conviction that they can match their output again this year. One man who is certainly going to be great again is strong safety **Troy Polamalu**, a third-year player out of USC. Polamalu absolutely exploded last season, totaling 94 tackles, 14 passes defensed, and five interceptions—strong enough numbers to send him to Hawaii. If he isn't already a superstar, Polamalu will surely become one this year. He's only 5'10", 212 pounds, but that's 5'10", 212 pounds of sheer athleticism. Best of all, Polamalu's greatest attributes are not his Tarzan-like strength and range, but rather his intelligence. The 24-year-old sees plays unfold

extremely well (especially those going underneath the coverage), which helps him manufacture turnovers for this defense.

Next to Polamalu is where the problems could begin. Free safety **Chris Hope** is a respectable player who certainly has a cheery name that could brighten up even the city of Pittsburgh (which was once known around America as "Smoke City"). However, his range in pass coverage is not convincing enough to prove that he is guaranteed to have another starter-level season. Then again, Hope *is* playing for a new contract this year.

Pittsburgh had a commendable starting cornerback in **Willie Williams**, a player who rose from the dead at the age of 34 to make a great late-season run as a starter in '04. However, Williams will be 35 in December, and Pittsburgh may not be committed to relying on him much longer—no matter how clever and crafty he can be. Williams will likely lose his job to second-year player **Ricardo Colclough**, an astoundingly quick player who has big-play potential.

The No. 1 corner appears to be **Deshea Townsend**, another player who is in the final year of his contract. Townsend is adequate in man coverage, but opposing offenses still have a tendency to pick on him. That said, he is a solid tackler who will not allow too many big plays. He is also a capable blitzer, as his sack total matched his interception total of four.

Third-year man **Ike Taylor** is too good to leave off the field. He shows flashes of excellence from time to time and is a very confident individual. However, the Steelers drafted cornerback **Bryant McFadden** in the second round this year, and it is unlikely that they want him to sit on the bench for too long. Consequently, someone from this Steeler secondary is bound to have their playing time diminish in '05.

Special Teams

Steelers kicker **Jeff Reed** has had some tough times at Heinz Field, but he was able to pull things together last year and make an admirable 28/33 field goals. Reed has decent range, but he is still a solid season away from proving that he is consistent year in and year out. Punter **Chris Gardocki** averaged 43 yards per punt last season, leaving 24 inside opponents' 20 yard line and giving up only six touchbacks. Randle El is the punt return artist for this squad. He is not real reliable in getting a solid runback each time, but who the heck cares? Just as long as he has a few major returns, all will be well. Colclough handles most of the kick return duties.

The Bottom Line

The Steelers were 15-1 last season and are returning nearly the same group this year. But historically, Pittsburgh has not been able to post strong campaigns in succession. Roethlisberger is more experienced, but at the same time more vulnerable to teams being better prepared for him. The running backs are old and have also had trouble being great in consecutive years, and the passing attack really lacks downfield options now that Burress is gone. Defensively, Pittsburgh is the same unit they were a year ago, but the secondary is still not immune to giving up some big passes.

AFC South

Houston
Texans

Indianapolis
Colts

Jacksonville
Jaguars

Tennessee
Titans

Looking Forward

How They'll Finish
1. Indianapolis Colts
2. Jacksonville Jaguars
3. Houston Texans
4. Tennesse Titans

Ready to Break Out

**Rashean Mathis,
Jacksonville Jaguars**

Cornerback
6'1"—200 pounds
3rd year—25 years old
Drafted: 2nd round in '03 out of Bethune Cook

It is a good thing that the Jaguars unstable secondary will be able to rely on the rising young star Rashean Mathis this year. Mathis is a unique story. He came into the league out of Bethune Cook, a small college from the Mid-East Atlantic Conference. In addition to lacking the first-rate experience at the collegiate level, Mathis also lacked experience at his pro position of cornerback, because in college he was an extraordinary safety.

When he arrived in the NFL, the Jaguars coaching staff had Mathis try his hand at playing cornerback. Jacksonville absolutely loved what they saw; as a rookie, Mathis even turned off a few teammates by infringing upon the veterans' playing time.

However, those teammates obviously came around. Now they have a bright talent who will help them dramatically in '05. Mathis will excel for a variety of reasons. At 6'1", he has rare height for a cornerback (most defensive backs are under 6'0" because high school and

Rashean Mathis

college coaches cannot resist the temptation of training the tall players to be wide receivers). In addition to size, Mathis has tremendous recovery speed, a great feel for locating the ball in man coverage, and a keen sense for recognizing what a receiver is trying to do and preventing him from succeeding.

Hot Seat

**Ron Meeks,
Indianapolis Colts**

For anyone who is a little embarrassed/curious/perplexed that they don't know who Ron Meeks is, he is the name behind the label "Colts defensive coordinator."

Meeks is on the hot seat because it is his unit that is perceived to be the reason Indy can never win an AFC Championship. A lot of people will fail to realize that this past season Peyton Manning and his men scored only three points in the playoff loss to New England; all they'll complain about is that blasted Colts defense that can't match the offense. Nobody ever said that hot seats have to be fair—they just have to be hot.

Meeks will have trouble getting his group to succeed in '05. The Colts will be dynamic at rushing the quarterback, but they lack the size needed to play the run. Furthermore, Meeks will be working with a somewhat young pack of players. Best of luck.

Best Offseason Move

The Colts managing to maintain their offensive trio of stars by locking up Marvin Harrison in a long-term deal and placing the franchise tag on Edgerrin James.

Worst Offseason Move

The Texans failing to draft or sign a premier left tackle.

Best Under-the-Radar Offseason Move

The Jaguars adding a capable pass-rusher in Reggie Hayward.

Biggest Question

Do the Colts finally have enough toughness and defense to win the AFC title this season?

Marvin Harrison

QUICK HITS

TEAM BESTS		BEST PLAYERS	
Passing Game	Colts	Pure Athlete	Dwight Freeney, Colts
Running Game	Colts	Big Play Threat	Andre Johnson, Texans
Offensive Line	Colts	Best Use of Talent	Brad Meester, Jaguars
Pass Rush	Colts	Worst Use of Talent	Robaire Smith, Texans
Run Defense	Jaguars	On the Rise	Andre Johnson, Texans
Pass Defense	Texans		Dunta Robinson, Texans
Special Teams	Texans		Jacob Bell, Titans
Coaching Staff	Colts	On the Decline	Kyle Brady, Jaguars
Home Field	Colts		Marcus Coleman, Texans
			Brad Hopkins, Titans
		Best Leader	Peyton Manning, Colts
		Unsung Hero	Jeff Saturday, Colts
		Impact Rookie	Adam "Pac Man" Jones, Titans

Looking Back

Houston Texans 2004

PASSING STATISTICS

PLAYER	CMP	ATT	YDS	CMP%	YDS/A	LNG	TD	TD%	INT	INT%	SACK	YDS	RAT
David Carr	285	466	3531	61.2	7.58	69	16	3.4	14	3.0	49	301	83.5

RUSHING STATISTICS

PLAYER	ATT	YDS	AVG	LNG	TD	FUM	LST
Domanick Davis	302	1188	3.9	44	13	2	2
David Carr	73	299	4.1	24	0	5	0
Jonathan Wells	82	299	3.6	14	3	1	1

RECEIVING STATISTICS

PLAYER	REC	YDS	AVG	LNG	TD	FUM	LST
Andre Johnson	79	1142	14.5	54	6	1	1
Jabar Gaffney	41	632	15.4	69	2	0	0
Domanick Davis	68	588	8.6	38	1	2	2
Derick Armstrong	29	415	14.3	44	1	0	0

RETURN STATISTICS

PLAYER	KICKOFFS						PUNTS					
	ATT	YDS	FC	AVG	LNG	TD	ATT	YDS	FC	AVG	LNG	TD
J.J. Moses	59	1303	0	22.1	49	0	36	309	13	8.6	27	0
Todd Washington	2	27	0	13.5	16	0	0	0	0	0.0	0	0

KICKING STATISTICS

PLAYER	1-20	20-29	30-39	40-49	50+	TOT	PCT	AVG	LNG	XPM/A	PTS
Kris Brown	0/0	7/7	3/5	6/9	1/3	17/24	70.8	34.9	50	34/34	85

PUNTING STATISTICS

PLAYER	PUNTS	YDS	AVG	LNG	TB	TB%	IN20	IN20%	RET	YDS	AVG	NET
Chad Stanley	73	3009	41.2	57	7	9.6	19	26.0	30	265	8.8	37.6

DEFENSIVE STATISTICS

PLAYER	TACKLES					MISCELLANEOUS			INTERCEPTIONS					
	TOT	SOLO	AST	SACK	TLOSS	FF	BK		INT	YDS	AVG	LNG	TD	PD
Jamie Sharper	139	103	36	2.0	7.5	3	0		0	0	0.0	0	0	9
Dunta Robinson	88	76	12	3.0	0	3	0		6	146	24.3	61	0	19
Jay Foreman	79	57	22	0.0	1.5	0	0		0	0	0.0	0	0	1
Kailee Wong	71	56	15	5.5	4	1	0		3	0	0.0	0	0	14
Aaron Glenn	63	57	6	0.0	0	0	0		5	40	8.0	23	0	14
Jason Babin	63	54	9	4.0	4.5	0	0		0	0	0.0	0	0	5
Marcus Coleman	56	46	10	0.0	0	0	0		2	116	58.0	102	1	9
Robaire Smith	52	33	19	2.0	3.5	0	0		0	0	0.0	0	0	9
Seth Payne	51	37	14	2.0	3.5	0	0		0	0	0.0	0	0	0
Glenn Earl	44	36	8	0.0	2	0	0		0	0	0.0	0	0	0

2004 Team Stats

OFFENSE

Scoring:	19.3 (21)
Yards per Game:	320.5 (19)
Pass Yards per Game:	202.9 (18)
Rush Yards per Game:	117.6 (12)
Sacks Allowed:	49 (26)
3rd Down Percentage:	38.4 (12)
Giveaways:	22 (t14)

DEFENSE

Scoring:	21.2 (t15)
Yards per Game:	341.1 (23)
Pass Yards per Game:	225.9 (24)
Rush Yards per Game:	115.2 (13)
Sacks:	24 (32)
3rd Down Percentage:	43.4 (29)
Takeaways:	25 (t17)

Indianapolis Colts 2004

PASSING STATISTICS

PLAYER	CMP	ATT	YDS	CMP%	YDS/A	LNG	TD	TD%	INT	INT%	SACK	YDS	RAT
Peyton Manning	336	497	4557	67.6	9.17	80	49	9.9	10	2.0	13	101	121.1

RUSHING STATISTICS

PLAYER	ATT	YDS	AVG	LNG	TD	FUM	LST
Edgerrin James	334	1548	4.6	40	9	6	2
Dominic Rhodes	53	254	4.8	55	1	1	1
Peyton Manning	25	38	1.5	19	0	1	1

RECEIVING STATISTICS

PLAYER	REC	YDS	AVG	LNG	TD	FUM	LST
Reggie Wayne	77	1210	15.7	71	12	0	0
Marvin Harrison	86	1113	12.9	59	15	1	1
Brandon Stokley	68	1077	15.8	69	10	1	1
Edgerrin James	51	483	9.5	56	0	0	0

RETURN STATISTICS

PLAYER	KICKOFFS						PUNTS					
	ATT	YDS	FC	AVG	LNG	TD	ATT	YDS	FC	AVG	LNG	TD
Dominic Rhodes	48	1188	0	24.8	88	1	0	0	0	0.0	0	0
Brad Pyatt	10	230	0	23.0	32	0	8	47	5	5.9	13	0

KICKING STATISTICS

PLAYER	1-20	20-29	30-39	40-49	50+	TOT	PCT	AVG	LNG	XPM/A	PTS
Mike Vanderjagt	0/0	6/6	9/11	5/7	0/1	20/25	80.0	33.3	47	59/60	119

PUNTING STATISTICS

PLAYER	PUNTS	YDS	AVG	LNG	TB	TB%	IN20	IN20%	RET	YDS	AVG	NET
Hunter Smith	54	2443	45.2	62	3	5.6	21	38.9	29	395	13.6	37.9

DEFENSIVE STATISTICS

PLAYER	TACKLES					MISCELLANEOUS			INTERCEPTIONS					
	TOT	SOLO	AST	SACK	TLOSS	FF	BK		INT	YDS	AVG	LNG	TD	PD
Cato June	104	80	24	0.0	5	0	0		2	71	35.5	71	0	9
David Thornton	85	66	19	0.0	3	2	0		1	5	5.0	5	0	1
Nick Harper	77	59	18	0.0	0.5	0	0		3	12	4.0	12	0	8
Rob Morris	76	56	20	3.0	4.5	1	0		1	17	17.0	17	0	2
Idrees Bashir	58	41	17	0.0	0	1	0		0	0	0.0	0	0	1
Jim Nelson	52	40	12	0.0	0	0	0		1	0	0.0	0	0	5
Jason David	51	47	4	0.0	2	1	0		4	36	9.0	34	1	15
Mike Doss	48	41	7	1.0	2	3	0		2	32	16.0	32	0	2
Raheem Brock	47	36	11	6.5	6.5	1	0		0	0	0.0	0	0	4
Montae Reagor	43	36	7	5.0	6	1	1		0	0	0.0	0	0	2

2004 Team Stats

OFFENSE

Scoring:	32.6 (1)
Yards per Game:	404.7 (2)
Pass Yards per Game:	288.9 (1)
Rush Yards per Game:	115.8 (15)
Sacks Allowed:	14 (t1)
3rd Down Percentage:	42.7 (7)
Giveaways:	15 (t3)

DEFENSE

Scoring:	21.9 (t18)
Yards per Game:	370.6 (29)
Pass Yards per Game:	243.3 (29)
Rush Yards per Game:	127.3 (24)
Sacks:	45 (t3)
3rd Down Percentage:	41.9 (26)
Takeaways	35 (t1)

🏈 Jacksonville Jaguars 2004

PASSING STATISTICS

PLAYER	CMP	ATT	YDS	CMP%	YDS/A	LNG	TD	TD%	INT	INT%	SACK	YDS	RAT
Byron Leftwich	267	441	2941	60.5	6.67	65	15	3.4	10	2.3	25	114	82.2

RUSHING STATISTICS

PLAYER	ATT	YDS	AVG	LNG	TD	FUM	LST
Fred Taylor	260	1224	4.7	46	2	3	2
LaBrandon Toefield	51	169	3.3	16	0	0	0
Greg Jones	62	162	2.6	12	3	1	0

RECEIVING STATISTICS

PLAYER	REC	YDS	AVG	LNG	TD	FUM	LST
Jimmy Smith	74	1172	15.8	65	6	2	1
Troy Edwards	50	533	10.7	36	1	2	2
Fred Taylor	36	345	9.6	64	1	0	0
Ernest Wilford	19	271	14.3	46	2	0	0

RETURN STATISTICS

PLAYER	KICKOFFS ATT	YDS	FC	AVG	LNG	TD	PUNTS ATT	YDS	FC	AVG	LNG	TD
Jermaine Lewis	21	386	0	18.4	26	0	23	227	7	9.9	50	0
Troy Edwards	15	335	0	22.3	45	0	3	26	1	8.7	14	0

KICKING STATISTICS

PLAYER	1-20	20-29	30-39	40-49	50+	TOT	PCT	AVG	LNG	XPM/A	PTS
Josh Scobee	0/0	10/10	8/11	5/7	1/3	24/31	77.4	32.9	53	21/21	93

PUNTING STATISTICS

PLAYER	PUNTS	YDS	AVG	LNG	TB	TB%	IN20	IN20%	RET	YDS	AVG	NET
Chris Hanson	84	3592	42.8	69	9	10.7	28	33.3	38	429	11.3	37.7

DEFENSIVE STATISTICS

PLAYER	TACKLES TOT	SOLO	AST	SACK	TLOSS	MISCELLANEOUS FF	BK	INTERCEPTIONS INT	YDS	AVG	LNG	TD	PD
Mike Peterson	126	99	27	5.0	6.5	1	0	0	0	0.0	0	0	1
Akin Ayodele	93	80	13	2.0	1	2	1	0	0	0.0	0	0	3
Donovin Darius	89	69	20	0.0	1	2	0	5	80	16.0	37	0	7
Dewayne Washington	77	72	5	0.0	2	1	0	2	0	0.0	0	0	9
John Henderson	76	67	9	6.5	3	0	0	0	0	0.0	0	0	4
Deon Grant	65	53	12	1.0	0	0	0	2	4	2.0	4	0	8
Rashean Mathis	62	55	7	0.0	0.5	1	0	5	42	8.4	21	0	21
Marcus Stroud	54	42	12	4.5	2.5	2	0	0	0	0.0	0	0	3
Daryl Smith	48	43	5	2.0	2.5	0	0	1	0	0.0	0	0	4
Greg Favors	35	24	11	4.5	0.5	0	0	0	0	0.0	0	0	4

2004 Team Stats

OFFENSE

Scoring:	16.3 (29)
Yards per Game:	313.1 (21)
Pass Yards per Game:	197.4 (19)
Rush Yards per Game:	15.6 (16)
Sacks Allowed:	32 (t9)
3rd Down Percentage:	36.9 (t14)
Giveaways:	17 (t7)

DEFENSE

Scoring:	17.5 (7)
Yards per Game:	320.9 (11)
Pass Yards per Game:	109.8 (16)
Rush Yards per GameL	111.1 (11)
Sacks:	37 (t17)
3rd Down Percentage:	41.0 (24)
Takeaways:	22 (t23)

🏈 Tennessee Titans 2004

PASSING STATISTICS

PLAYER	CMP	ATT	YDS	CMP%	YDS/A	LNG	TD	TD%	INT	INT%	SACK	YDS	RAT
Billy Volek	218	357	2486	61.1	6.96	48	18	5.0	10	2.8	30	216	87.1
Steve McNair	129	215	1343	60.0	6.25	37	8	3.7	9	4.2	13	95	73.1

RUSHING STATISTICS

PLAYER	ATT	YDS	AVG	LNG	TD	FUM	LST
Chris Brown	220	1067	4.9	52	6	6	4
Antowain Smith	137	509	3.7	43	4	2	1
Steve McNair	23	128	5.6	23	1	2	1

RECEIVING STATISTICS

PLAYER	REC	YDS	AVG	LNG	TD	FUM	LST
Drew Bennett	80	1247	15.6	48	11	2	0
Derrick Mason	96	1168	12.2	37	7	0	0
Ben Troupe	33	329	10.0	33	1	2	0
Eddie Berlin	20	278	13.9	31	1	0	0

RETURN STATISTICS

PLAYER	KICKOFFS ATT	YDS	FC	AVG	LNG	TD	PUNTS ATT	YDS	FC	AVG	LNG	TD
Jason McAddley	38	849	0	22.3	45	0	0	0	0	0.0	0	0
Troy Fleming	18	316	0	17.6	30	0	0	0	0	0.0	0	0

KICKING STATISTICS

PLAYER	1-20	20-29	30-39	40-49	50+	TOT	PCT	AVG	LNG	XPM/A	PTS
Gary Anderson	0/0	4/5	4/4	9/12	0/1	17/22	77.3	36.7	45	37/37	88

PUNTING STATISTICS

PLAYER	PUNTS	YDS	AVG	LNG	TB	TB%	IN20	IN20%	RET	YDS	AVG	NET
Craig Hentrich	73	3117	42.7	64	8	11.0	20	27.4	29	184	6.3	40.2

DEFENSIVE STATISTICS

PLAYER	TACKLES TOT	SOLO	AST	SACK	TLOSS	MISCELLANEOUS FF	BK	INTERCEPTIONS INT	YDS	AVG	LNG	TD	PD
Keith Bulluck	152	104	48	5.0	7.5	1	0	2	25	12.5	25	0	13
Brad Kassell	102	77	25	0.0	3	1	0	0	0	0.0	0	0	1
Lamont Thompson	65	57	8	0.0	0	1	0	4	77	19.3	37	1	6
Tank Williams	52	43	9	1.0	2	1	0	1	13	13.0	13	0	1
Kevin Carter	49	26	23	6.0	4	1	0	0	0	0.0	0	0	1
Andre Dyson	41	36	5	0.0	0	0	0	6	135	22.5	44	0	15
Carlos Hall	41	27	14	2.5	4.5	0	0	0	0	0.0	0	0	1
Andre Woolfolk	41	37	4	0.0	0.5	0	0	1	25	25.0	25	0	6
Albert Haynesworth	37	27	10	1.0	6.5	2	0	0	0	0.0	0	0	3
Donnie Nickey	32	29	3	0.0	0.5	0	0	0	0	0.0	0	0	1

2004 Team Stats

OFFENSE

Scoring:	21.5 (15)
Yards per Game:	342.9 (1)
Pass Yards per Game:	226.0 (10)
Rush Yards per Game:	116.9 (14)
Sacks Allowed:	44 (t23)
3rd Down Percentage:	34.1 (25)
Giveaways:	29 (24)

DEFENSE

Scoring:	27.4 (30)
Yards per Game:	357.8 (27)
Pass Yards per Game:	237.9 (26)
Rush Yards per Game:	119.8 (18)
Sacks:	32 (t27)
3rd Down Percentage:	33.3 (7)
Takeaways:	26 (t14)

Houston Texans

Predicted: 3rd ▪ 2004: 7-9 (3rd)

Players Added

CB	Phillip Buchanon (Oak)
LB	Frank Chamberlin (Cin)
LB	Morlon Greenwood (Mia)
LB	Zeke Moreno (SD)
OT	Victor Riley (NO)
TE	Marcellus Rivers (NYG)
CB	Lewis Sanders (Cle)
DL	Daleroy Stewart (SF)
KR	Reggie Swinton (Det)

Players Lost

S	Eric Brown
LB	Jay Foreman (Oak)
CB	Aaron Glenn (Dal)
S	Marlon McCree (Car)
KR	J.J. Moses
LB	Jamie Sharper (Sea)
OL	Marcus Spears (Cle)
CB	Kenny Wright (Jax)

Draft

Round	(Pick)	Player	Pos	College
1	(16)	Travis Johnson	DT	Florida St.
3	(73)	Vernand Morency	RB	Oklahoma St.
4	(114)	Jerome Mathis	WR	Hampton
5	(151)	Drew Hodgdon	C	Arizona St.
6	(188)	Ceandris Brown	S	Louisiana–Lafayette
7	(227)	Kenneth Pettway	OLB	Grambling

In selecting Johnson, the Texans could be contemplating a future shift to a 4–3 defense, but more likely they'll transform the 290-pounder into a defensive end. Morency is said to have starter capabilities down the road, but his questionable mental capacity (11 on the Wonderlic test) and current skill level make him a mild option in the immediate future. Mathis will have to prove he can keep up, considering the major jump that comes from leaving Hampton for the NFL.

Head Coach: Dom Capers (4th year)

Offensive Coordinator: Chris Palmer

Defensive Coordinator: Vic Fangio

Offense

QB:	David Carr
RB:	Domanick Davis
FB:	Moran Norris
WR:	Andre Davis*
WR:	Jabar Gaffney
TE:	Mark Bruener
LT:	Seth Wand
LG:	Chester Pitts
C:	Steve McKinney
RG:	Zach Wiegert
RT:	Todd Wade
QB:	Tony Banks
RB:	Jonathan Wells
WR:	Corey Bradford
TE:	Billy Miller
OL:	Victor Riley

Defense

LDE:	Gary Walker
NT:	Seth Payne
RDE:	Robaire Smith
LOLB:	Jason Babin
LILB:	Morlon Greenwood
RILB:	Kailee Wong
ROLB:	Antwan Peek
CB:	Dunta Robinson
SS:	Glenn Earl
FS:	Marcus Coleman
CB:	Phillip Buchanon
NB:	DeMarcus Faggins
DL:	Travis Johnson‡
LB:	Zeke Moreno†
K:	Kris Brown
P:	Chad Stanley

* Pro Bowler '04
† veteran acquisition
‡ rookie

Report Card

Quarterback	B–	Defensive Line	B–	Coaching	B–
Running Back	B–	Linebacker	C	Special Teams	B–
Receiver/Tight End	B–	Defensive Back	B–	Depth	C+
Offensive Line	C+			Intangibles	C–

Andre Johnson

Before beginning and getting too in-depth on anything, a promise needs to be made: Throughout these next four pages covering the Houston Texans, there will not be a single joke that refers to the phrase "Houston, we have a problem." It is time to stop this nonsense. It is time to let the movie *Apollo 13* go. Too many people believe they are being clever, unique, or intellectual when they humorously reference the five words that made Tom Hanks's career. (And no, those words are not "My name's Forest. Forest Gump.") Forget Houston's problem—just let it go. It's not funny anymore, okay?

Now that that's out of the way, how about those Texans? What needs to be said to introduce them is pretty simple: They've grown up. The Texans do not have an illustrious history, but they are hoping that 2005 can be the year that one begins to form.

During the offseason, there was pandemonium around Reliant Stadium in downtown Houston. The Texans locker room was overflowing with hysteria, as the team's veteran players could not believe that four defensive starters had been replaced and that only three of the team's original 19 players selected from the expansion draft during the club's inaugural '02 season were still with the franchise.

However, such reactions were not received even mildly throughout the NFL. In fact, the Texan players' reactions were regarded a lot like those of a small child who is on an airplane for the first time, in awe of everything, making loud noises, and pointing out the obvious. The other passengers on the plane either ignore the kid or smirk at the innocence of youth. Nobody reacts along with the youngster because there's nothing to react to—it's just the way planes are. This is just the way the NFL is.

The Texans hit the runway and went into takeoff this past offseason, gasping and pointing out the window, asking "What's dat?" and making a big deal about normal roster moves (such as four veteran defensive players being shown the exit). But Houston's plane has now arrived at its destination (reality), and the Texans are currently walking up the jet ramp and into the '05 season. The luxury of being a developing expansion club is over. If the Texans do not respond well to this, someone might soon be saying, "Houston, we have a—" Oops. Sorry. Gosh, that's sure a hard one to avoid.

Offense

Don't look now, but Texans quarterback **David Carr** has grown up. He's no longer the fresh-faced, young, No. 1 overall draft pick who is scheduled to become the team's franchise quarterback. No, Carr's now approaching his fourth season in the league; he's 26 years old. He *is* the franchise quarterback.

So, Carr has been starting in the NFL for the past three years now? What's the verdict—boom or bust? The evidence is minimally helpful in giving an answer—although it is apparent that he's not a *bust*—but how much of a success is he? Carr has helped lead the Texans to more wins with each year that he's been the starting quarterback. Houston was 4-12 in Carr's rookie season ('02), 5-11 in his sophomore season ('03), and a more respectable 7-9 last season. Furthermore, Carr's quarterback rating has risen from 62.8 as a rookie, to 69.5, to 83.5 in '04.

Obviously, Carr has improved with each step of his career, but at this stage in his professional life, annual improvements take on less meaning, as immediate results become the a priori issue. About one-third of the starting quarterbacks in the league have less experience than he does. With his pacifier in the trash can, Carr will be expected to lead this team to the playoffs in '05. He certainly has the skill to do so. Carr has outstanding leadership traits (which come in handy, considering that he is actually one of the elder statesmen on this offense); he is tough, plays with poise, and has solid playmaking ability. Carr's arm strength is not a question, and his accuracy has greatly improved (61.2 completion percentage in '04 versus low- to mid-50s over his first two years).

However, if the Texans are going to improve their 21st-ranked scoring attack from a year ago (19.3 points per game), they will have to give Carr better protection up front. The ground game will be stable under the services of third-year player **Domanick Davis**, and Carr has a young superstar receiver to throw to in **Andre Johnson**. However, as Houston has learned in recent years, talented skill players mean very little if the front five cannot keep defenders out of the backfield.

Houston's problems up front center around poor pass protection, which was highlighted by the 49 sacks the team gave up last year (26th in the NFL, and Carr's underrated mobility prevented that number from climbing even higher). The main problem has been the left tackle position, where third-year player **Seth Wand** resides. Wand started all 16 games for Houston last season, but toward the end of the year the team was having to substitute him on passing downs because of his dreadful inability to fight off a pass-rush. Wand has good size (6'7", 330 pounds) and is capable of occasionally clearing a path in run-blocking, but the man is simply not a left tackle; he has inconsistent footwork and poor quickness. Perhaps it's the fact that Houston is

the largest city in America without zoning laws, because Wand sure as heck does not belong where he is.

Texans head coach **Dom Capers** and his coaching staff know this. They spent the offseason experimenting with ways to fix the problem. They have tried moving Wand inside to play guard and shifting last season's starting left guard, **Chester Pitts**, to the left tackle spot (where the 26-year-old Pitts played during his first two years in the league). Pitts does not have elite quickness, but he is a very mobile run-blocker, which implies that he would be serviceable on the outside in pass protection.

However, if Pitts were suited to play left tackle, Houston would not have moved him to guard in the first place. With this in mind, the Texans heavily pursued a possible trade for St. Louis's Orlando Pace prior to the draft, but they ultimately had to settle for signing eighth-year veteran **Victor Riley**, a player who fell out of favor in New Orleans. Riley is a powerful 340-pound beast, but he is also a very similar version of Wand. He does not have the quickest feet, he has been a right tackle throughout his career, and there's not even a guarantee that his move to "H-Town" will alter the off-the-field lifestyle that has caused problems for him in the past.

The Texans would prefer to sign a veteran free agent to come in and fill the left tackle role, but there are not any viable options to choose from. Thus, Riley will probably win the job in training camp. Wand is destined to end up on the bench this year (beside other trial starters such as **Milford Brown**, **Todd Washington**, and **Fred Weary**), and Pitts will remain at left guard.

The right side of the front five is much more stable for the Texans. Tackle **Todd Wade** is a solid sixth-year player out of Mississippi, who spent the first stages of his career in Miami before joining Houston last year. At 6'8", Wade has great height, which he is able to take advantage of by playing with a strong base and sound balance. He's not the type of player to be destructive or particularly zealous, but he's smart, athletic, and reliable.

The right guard is **Zach Wiegert**, a 32-year-old veteran who still gets the job done with his strength and energy. Wiegert is very explosive coming out of his stance, he is able to dictate to opponents, and he is capable of powering his way to the second level. Center **Steve McKinney** benefits greatly from playing next to Wiegert. The better-than-average but worse-than-proficient McKinney is almost a poor man's Casey Wiegmann. McKinney

Write It Down

If the Texans can make enough things click on offense this season, third-year player Andre Johnson will emerge as the best wide receiver in the NFL.

This Season vs. Last Season

Progression: **Offensive skill position**—With a young group of offensive weapons (quarterback David Carr, running back Domanick Davis, receivers Andre Johnson and Jabar Gaffney) now a year older and approaching their third season together, Houston's offense will be more mature in '05.

Regression: **Inside linebacker**—Losing two veteran cogs in Jamie Sharper and Jay Foreman, who were the top two leading tacklers on the team a year ago, is going to hurt.

won't dominate in any fashion, but he has a great feel for the game, he can help generate movement in run-blocking (if paired with the right teammates), and he is comfortable playing in space.

If the Texans can patch together a serviceable offensive line, this offense can become a dangerous force to be reckoned with. Houston ranked 12th in rushing last season (117.6 yards per game), thanks mainly to Davis. The NFL Offensive Rookie of the Year from '03 appears to be the real deal, meaning the Texans have found their first franchise running back in team history. Davis does not have dazzling raw talent, he's not a huge threat to break off a 65-yard scamper, and he isn't going to embarrass many defenders on *SportsCenter*. However, the 5'9", 221-pounder runs with a strong presence, he has good vision, he sets up his blocks well, and he can break tackles. Davis is also very versatile; last year he caught 68 passes (the second most for a running back in the NFL, behind only Philly's Brian Westbrook) for 588 yards.

Although Davis had just 309 rushing attempts last season (on which he totaled 1,188 yards), Houston is going to make an effort to decrease his workload in '05. The team drafted running back **Vernand Morency** in the third round this year, plus they re-signed fourth-year veteran **Jonathan Wells**. Morency can be a quicker change-of-pace back for the Texans. He is a 24-year-old rookie, but he spent three years of his life playing minor league baseball, so his experience in shoulder pads is still limited. Wells is a vanilla runner who brings little to the table. Perhaps he can use his 252-pound size to help in pass protection on third down (an area where Davis struggles), but all in all, Wells is about as effective as jaywalking laws. Houston starts **Moran Norris** at fullback, although backup **Jarrod Baxter** should see a few snaps as well. The 254-pound Norris is a pure lead-blocker who can operate north and south but doesn't have the balance or footwork to do much else. He delivers a good pop and shows decent power, but he lacks the premium lower-body strength needed to drive opponents.

Perhaps the best lower body in Houston—in fact, the best *entire body* for that matter—belongs to Andre Johnson. (Well, actually, the best body in Houston belongs to Beyoncé Knowles, the lead singer of Destiny's Child. However, Jay-Z has already staked his claim there.) The 6'3", 219-pound Johnson just *looks like* a superstar. Entering only his third year in the league, the former Miami Hurricane is already coming off his first Pro Bowl season. Johnson (a former No. 3 overall pick) has 2,118 receiving yards over his first two seasons—which marks the best output among all of the top-five draft picks during the past 20 years. It is not the least bit unreasonable to think that Johnson could emerge as the best receiver in the NFL this season. He has amazing strength, incredible speed, and magnetic hands. He can make tough short-yardage catches over the middle, he can explode for deep routes downfield, he can win a jump ball near the sideline, and he is more lethal than Danny Glover when it comes to running after the catch.

Johnson's progress as a superstar may ultimately hinge on whether the Texans can produce a No. 2 receiver who is good enough to ease some of the attention that will be paid to him. Entering training camp, the men competing for the other starting job were fourth-year player **Jabar Gaffney** and eighth-year veteran **Corey Bradford**. The reality is that each player is a prime slot

receiver, but neither is a starter. Gaffney is a reliable target who can make tough catches (especially when a play breaks down), but he is too constricted to running shorter routes. Bradford is just the opposite; he loves to stretch the field, but he's proven to be inconsistent in all other areas. Expect Gaffney to win the job this year, for the reason that he has a much better rapport with Carr.

The starting tight end is **Mark Bruener**, although judging from his four receptions a year ago, something says that he might be a better blocking tight end off the bench. The receiving tight end is **Billy Miller**, a seventh-year veteran who is more like a wide receiver. Miller runs good routes, he has the long arms needed to haul in tough catches, and, well, he at least *makes an effort* to block, God bless him. The Texans are below standard at the tight end spot, but don't blame them—they're trying. Houston spent a second-round draft pick on Michigan's **Bennie Joppru** back in '03, but sadly, Joppru has yet to play in the NFL. He missed the first two seasons of his career with a groin injury, and this past spring, he tore the ACL in his right knee during a noncontact drill.

Defense

Much in the same way that military leader and Texas Revolution legend Sam Houston is firmly entrenched in the glory of the Lone Star State, Dom Capers's 3–4 defense (which is coordinated by **Vic Fangio**) is firmly entrenched in the Texans game plan. Capers doesn't care that his 3–4 has been a dud for the duration of the team's existence—the 3–4 is what he knows, and it's what he's going to run.

There is nothing wrong with Capers's decision—well, nothing wrong now that the Texans have replaced four of the starters from last year (remember those kids on the airplane?), becoming younger and faster on this side of the ball. Vast changes were definitely needed—Houston's pass-rush was as successful last season as the city's oil industry in the mid-1980s. The Texans produced a measly 24 sacks in '04, a number that was eight lower than the team's pass-rush ranking in the NFL. (Think about it . . . come on . . . do the math . . . eighth lower—*Yes!* They ranked 32nd. Dead *last*.)

The problem heading into this season is that, despite the youth movement, it's questionable how much this team has improved at the linebacker position. The showcase player will be second-year pro **Jason Babin**, who recorded four sacks as a rookie last season. Babin, the left outside linebacker, is a 6'2", 259-pound athletic

In just his second season as a pro, Texans cornerback Dunta Robinson is already among the elite defensive players in the game.

mogul who has great pass-rushing experience from his college days at Western Michigan, where he played defensive end. The '05 season brings a great deal of promise for the 25-year-old Babin. He has tremendous speed, change-of-direction skills, and all-around mobility. He has proven to be a player who can one day dominate, but his mental skills are yet to catch up with his physical prowess. With time and experience, Babin will become smarter and more instinctive. Expect him to make positive strides in '05, but not approach his summit until '06.

The other outside linebacker is **Antwan Peek**. He will have to improve his awareness and show that he's able to hold up in run support, but this is the team's best option for success. Peek already has outstanding athletic skills (mainly as a pass-rusher), but if he can develop more fundamentals in other areas, the Texans can make things work.

Peek's insertion into the lineup moves veteran **Kailee Wong** to inside linebacker. The speedy seventh-year player out of Stanford won't be quite as effective there, but he has experience playing in the middle. Wong (5½ sacks a year ago) has the athleticism to be effective in virtually all instances, but he struggles ever so slightly with getting off blocks. He is a playmaker, but he doesn't have enough speed and pizzazz to be this defense's ultimate difference maker—he must have adequate players working around him.

The team signed former Dolphin **Morlon Greenwood** over the offseason, stabilizing the other inside linebacker spot. Greenwood's arrival seemed even more critical after Houston lost veterans Jamie Sharper and Jay Foreman (the team's most consistent tacklers over the past couple of years). The fifth-year pro who grew up in Kingston, Jamaica, but played his college ball in Syracuse, is coming off the best season of his career, in which he recorded 101 tackles. However, Greenwood, who has always had good speed and athleticism, has been slow to develop adequate awareness in his career. After finally stepping up his game in Miami's 4–3 defense last season, getting acquainted with a new home and learning an entirely new role in a 3–4 scheme may not be the best thing for Greenwood right now.

Houston has a solid front line. The club believes that nose tackle **Seth Payne** is slowing down (the Texans made this clear when they used the 16th-overall draft choice this year to select Florida State defensive tackle **Travis Johnson**), but Payne is still only 30 years old. He plays with a nice burst and occupies blockers by weighing 315 pounds and staying active against the run.

Johnson will likely become a defensive end in this scheme and eventually replace veteran **Gary Walker**. Walker, 32, is a 324-pound giant who can bull against the run (part of the reason Houston ranked 13th in rush defense a season ago), but recently he's begun to move about as well as an armadillo in quicksand. However, that may be all Walker needs to do in order to contribute as a backup end/nose tackle in '05.

Robaire Smith is the end on the right side. Smith is a talented player who was signed to a big contract as a free agent last year. On certain plays, he's worth every penny of what he earns; on other plays, he's worthless. Smith has the talent to pressure the quarterback and anchor the run defense, but he has yet to play with a consistent effort in his career.

The Texans ranked 24th in pass defense last season, allowing opposing quarterbacks to complete 64.9 percent of their throws

against them (second-worst in the league). But don't blame cornerback **Dunta Robinson**. In only his second year out of South Carolina, the 5'10", 174-pound Robinson easily rates among the 10 best players at his position. Robinson lived up to his first-round billing in '04, intercepting six balls, defensing 19 passes, forcing three fumbles, connecting on 88 tackles, and notching three sacks. His speed is superb, but even better is the fact that he might be the quickest player in the game today. Plus, he has great change-of-direction skills and his timing in jumping routes is stupendous. Finally, believe it or not, Robinson's a budding young superstar cornerback who is not averse to playing the run.

To help increase their speed and playmaking skills in the defensive backfield, Houston traded for Raiders cornerback **Phillip Buchanon**, a talented fourth-year player out of the University of Miami. Buchanon has the skills to be a Pro Bowler, but he must become more consistent and improve his presence in solo coverage. Buchanon has fluid hips and terrific closing speed, but unless he can become more comfortable covering the deep ball, he's destined to struggle.

Downfield passing did not kill this team last season, which is amazing considering how sorry the safeties were. This year, the Texans return essentially the same pair of players who finished '04, with **Glenn Earl** at the strong safety spot and veteran **Marcus Coleman** at free safety. Earl is a stout hitter who is physical near the line of scrimmage, but he is a liability in pass defense. He's not as bad in zone coverage, but the Chiefs have shown the world the damage that an overdose of zone coverage can cause to a football team. The 10th-year veteran Coleman may need a little zone coverage himself in '05. The longtime cornerback was converted to safety a year ago, to help mask his declining speed. However, it's questionable how much range Coleman has.

The nickel back duties will be given to **DeMarcus Faggins**, who is not prolific but is better than the newly acquired **Lewis Sanders**.

Special Teams

Although he missed 7 out of 24 field goals in '04, the Texans still decided to re-sign kicker **Kris Brown** this past offseason. Last year, Brown was bothered by a pelvic injury (boy, of all the problems for a kicker to have), but he's healthy now and ready to go. **Chad Stanley** surpassed the 3,000-yard mark in punting yards last season (not sure how good that is or what it means, but there it is). J.J. Moses was the return specialist a year ago, but he's now gone, leaving a hole in kickoff return duties. Robinson would probably be pretty good in this role, but expect one of the backup running backs or receivers to handle the job. Buchanon will return punts, an area where he can be a deadly weapon in the right circumstance.

The Bottom Line

The Texans grew up this past offseason, but it's still hard to be convinced that this team is ready to emerge in '05. It is common sense that they won't catch the Colts for the division title, which means they must be evaluated as a wildcard contender. But Houston's uncertainty with the front five may ultimately be too much for the offense to overcome. Defensively, the team may have too many soft spots mixed in with new faces. Then again, the Texans are the only team in the NFL right now who have improved their win total in each year of their existence, so who knows.

Indianapolis Colts

Predicted: 1st ▪ 2004: 12-4 (1st)

Players Added
OL	Joaquin Gonzalez (Cle)
OG	Marico Portis (Ten)

Players Lost
FS	Idrees Bashir (Car)
OG	Rick DeMulling (Det)
LB	Rob Morris
LB	Jim Nelson (Bal)
G	Tupe Peko (Car)
TE	Marcus Pollard (Det)
DE	Brad Scioli

Draft
1	(29)	Marlin Jackson	CB	Michigan
2	(60)	Kelvin Hayden	CB	Illinois
3	(92)	Vincent Burns	DE	Kentucky
4	(129)	Dylan Gandy	OG	Texas Tech
4	(135)	Matt Giordano	S	California
5	(148)	Jonathan Welsh	DE	Wisconsin
5	(165)	Rob Hunt	C	North Dakota St.
5	(173)	Tyjuan Hagler	OLB	Cincinnati
6	(202)	Dave Rayner	K	Michigan St.
7	(243)	Anthony Davis	RB	Wisconsin

The Colts predictably got defensive with their draft, taking two cornerbacks and an end with their first three selections. The addition of Jackson will either pan out really well–if he can translate his physical style to the pro game–or really awful–if he can't avoid getting in trouble off the field. Hayden has just one year of experience playing cornerback, so his transition into the NFL will be a long one. Burns is basically the same type of player that they already have too many of on the roster: a speedy and undersized defensive end.

Head Coach: Tony Dungy (4th year)
Offensive Coordinator: Tom Moore
Defensive Coordinator: Ron Meeks

Offense
QB:	Peyton Manning*
RB:	Edgerrin James*
HB:	Dallas Clark
WR:	Marvin Harrison*
WR:	Reggie Wayne
WR:	Brandon Stokley
LT:	Tarik Glenn*
LG:	Jake Scott
C:	Jeff Saturday
RG:	Dylan Gandy‡
RT:	Ryan Diem
QB:	Jim Sorgi
RB:	Dominic Rhodes
WR:	Aaron Moorehead
TE:	Ben Hartsock
OL:	Joaquin Gonzalez

Defense
LDE:	Raheem Brock
DT:	Montae Reagor
DT:	Josh Williams
RDE:	Dwight Freeney*
LOLB:	David Thornton
MLB:	Gary Brackett
ROLB:	Cato June
CB:	Nick Harper
SS:	Bob Sanders
FS:	Mike Doss
CB:	Donald Strickland
NB:	Marlin Jackson‡
DL:	Robert Mathis
LB:	Rob Morris
K:	Mike Vanderjagt
P:	Hunter Smith

* Pro Bowler '04
† veteran acquisition
‡ rookie

Report Card
Quarterback	A+	Defensive Line	B	Coaching	B+
Running Back	A–	Linebacker	C	Special Teams	C+
Receiver/Tight End	A+	Defensive Back	C+	Depth	C
Offensive Line	B–			Intangibles	B+

There is no hope for any individual who needs to read these next four pages to know what the Indianapolis Colts are all about. Last season, Indy ranked second in yards gained offensively and 29th in yards allowed defensively. In a way, the Colts resemble the transportation system in their hometown. The city of Indianapolis is known not only as the state capital of Indiana but also as the Crossroads of America, because more interstate freeways and federal highways cross the town than any other city in the United States. With Edgerrin James hauling down the road and Peyton Manning tossing touchdowns to his trio of speedy receivers buzzing around the field, Indy's high-powered offense is like the town's active highway system. However, Indianapolis is also the largest city in the country that does not have a natural body of navigable water. This tidbit symbolizes the Colts defense. They have a lot of nice individual boats and ships, but no waters to sail them toward success.

For years the Colts have produced sports-car athletes to accelerate their offense, but at the same time, defensively, they've had *Titanic*-like shipwrecks. This season, it is obvious that the Colts will once again drive on offense, but the question remains whether they'll avoid sinking on defense. If the answer is "No, they won't avoid it," then they'll drown, leaving the answer to the annual Super Bowl question the same old "No—not this time."

Peyton Manning

Offense

Critiquing offensive coordinator **Tom Moore**'s unit is like critiquing da Vinci's *Mona Lisa*: There's not a complaint to be made, a function to improve, or a weakness to expose. Last season, Indy's offense seemed to do more impressive things with numbers than Pythagoras, Euclid, and Newton *combined*. The Colts led the league in scoring (31.6 points per game) and passing (288.9 yards per game), they tied for first for the fewest sacks allowed (14), and they turned the ball over only 15 times.

Since there's now a laundry list of numbers going, it seems like an optimum time to get the **Peyton Manning** introduction out of the way. Manning, who claimed the NFL MVP award in '04, is coming off arguably the greatest regular season for a quarterback in NFL history—if not in history, then easily the best since Dan Marino's magical 1984 season. Last year, Manning broke Marino's single-season touchdown record by tossing 49. Manning also threw for 4,557 yards, completed 67.6 percent of his passes, and registered a rating that could be mistaken for a credit card number.

However, in the end, Indy rested in the same position as usual: Under the cold, sharp cleats of the New England Patriots. For the 29-year-old Manning, the reputation of being the best player in the NFL who "can't win the big one" is already active. The label will stick like Hawthorne's scarlet A—from now until the day Manning actually does get his Colts to the Super Bowl.

But how in the world can it be Manning who is culpable for this team's inability to reach the promised land? If his numbers grew any bigger, they'd have to start listing them in scientific notation. Despite the fact that blaming Number 18 for the Colts' shortcomings is ridiculous to the extent of being *laughable*, the 6'5", 230-pound gunslinger has, like a true leader, embraced the burden. After all, no one can argue with the fact that Manning *does* still have to prove that he can beat New England.

Bill Belichick and those pesky Patriots are more than a thorn in Manning's side—they're a six-foot-long medieval dagger with perforated edges, twisting and turning through Manning's rib cage. They're the only obstacle between him and his coveted ring. Since becoming the head coach in New England, Belichick is 4-0 against Manning's Colts, including the past two postseasons, in which Manning took his crew outside of the comforts of the RCA Dome and into the Dante's Inferno that is Gillette Stadium, only to get beaten down in a windy blizzard of snow and linebackers.

This year, Manning will try, try again. Although he's the best pocket passer in the NFL today, he isn't satisfied with his quarterbacking performance. He can revolutionize play-action passing, have the greatest understanding of his offensive scheme, and hold the highest football IQ in the game, but it's not going to scratch his itch. Sure, Manning's career is still Canton-bound if he doesn't win a title. (Just look at how people revere the career of his fellow Indiana icon, the recently retired Pacers shooting guard Reggie Miller.) Still, Manning's looking to get better. Over this past offseason, he, Moore, and quarterbacks coach **Jim Caldwell** sat down and reviewed the tape of the '04 season (head coach **Tony Dungy** was likely off at some elementary school desperately scouting a young athletic gem who could help shore up his defense in '05). The three offensive brains counted 17 drives from last year that ended without a touchdown because of a Manning mistake. Manning is confident he'll correct those errors, which can only mean one thing for the rest of the league: Watch out!

The battalion of players surrounding "General Manning" includes the best receiving threesome in the NFL today: All-World star **Marvin Harrison**, up-and-coming deep-threat **Reggie**

Write It Down
Peyton Manning will throw for precisely 45 touchdowns this season.

Strengths

Passing attack

Does this really have to be explained? Fine. Peyton Manning, Marvin Harrison, Reggie Wayne, Brandon Stokley. There.

Pass rush

A lot of people don't realize that Dwight Freeney is not the only force up front (although if he were, this would still be one of the team's strengths). Thanks to the speed of ends Raheem Brock and, especially, Robert Mathis—as well as the quickness at the tackle position—the Colts were able to total 45 sacks last season, which tied for the third most in the NFL.

Weaknesses

Defensive Size

Everything about this defense is small. The ends are too light to play the run, the tackles are quick but not at all wide, the linebackers all weigh under 235, and the secondary features a few players who are short enough that, if painted with the proper shade of orange, could pass as Oompa Loompas.

Strength

Indy is not a soft team, per say, but nothing about this club spells *strong*. The front line is undersized and finesse-oriented, the receivers prance around the field (*true*, they kill opponents doing it), and the defense is full of players who prefer to go after the ball rather than an opposing player.

Wayne, and slot-receiving ace **Brandon Stokley**. Last year, these three did the unthinkable: Each had over 1,000 yards and 10 touchdowns.

The 33-year-old Harrison has at least another five good years left in him. This is quite remarkable considering he has been performing at the highest of levels for virtually all of his previous nine seasons. However, Colts president **Bill Polian** demonstrated his belief in Harrison's future when he signed the wideout to a seven-year, $67 million deal, with $23 million guaranteed. (And to think that Harrison's *receiving* numbers were once considered huge.) Although Wayne led the team in yards and touchdowns last year, Harrison is undoubtedly the No. 1 wideout in this lineup. His quickness and precision in route running, as well as his sure hands and well-developed cognition with Manning and the offensive scheme, allow him to attract the double coverage that is crucial for the success of his teammates.

The 26-year-old Wayne is in his fifth season out of the University of Miami and is finally proving to be worthy of the first-round draft pick that the team spent on him five years ago. At 6'0", 198 pounds, Wayne has the athletic frame needed to be a versatile threat, but his main focus is using his speed to help stretch the field. In '05, Wayne can continue to grow and be productive, just as long as he continues to mature and develop patience.

Stokley is by no means a star player—at 5'11", 197 pounds, he does not have the raging raw skills to be an uncontrollable force. However, the seventh-year veteran is humble, smart, and perfect operating out of the slot in this offense. Stokley runs slants and crossing routes over the middle as well as anyone in the NFL and is a very reliable target on third down.

Was it mentioned that the Colts are pretty darn good at running, as well? Never mind their mediocre 115.8 rushing yards per game last year (15th in the NFL)—after all, it's hard to accumulate yards on the ground when the ball is always flying through the air and into the end zone. Just know that seventh-year player **Edgerrin James** is indeed one of the premier running backs in the NFL. James is coming off a 1,548-yard season (fifth best in the league). There *is* one *minor* problem with the former Miami Hurricane: He isn't quite thrilled to be a member of the Colts organization. After Indy slapped James with the franchise tag, the running back and his agent (Drew Rosenhaus, of

This Season vs. Last Season

Progression: **Defensive cohesion—**The Colts defense has a plethora of young players who have learned the same system together for four years now. That can only help their cause in '05.

Regression: **Guard—**Although the system should hide this weakness fairly well, over the offseason the Colts lost the fairly skilled Tupe Peko and the very effective Rick DeMulling. They replaced them with a pair of second-year players Jake Scott and rookie Dylan Gandy, neither of whom have gone through an entire 16-game season as starters before.

course—perhaps it's time to start putting his name in boldface type) worked like crazy to orchestrate a trade that could send James to a team that was willing to give him a long-term deal. However, with the rookie class being so running-back-heavy, and James being a 28-year-old workhorse who has had his share of major knee operations, no team took the bait.

This means that James might opt to hold out for a good portion of the team's training camp. However, he has already hinted that while he's not pleased with a one-year contract, he'll live with it and be ready to go once training camp opens.

It should also be mentioned that James knows the Colts have a very capable backup in **Dominic Rhodes**, who has shown his best speed and burst since he suffered his own major knee injury in '02.

The Colts operate out of a three-receiver, one-back set, but one would never be able to tell by looking at the alignments they create by motioning halfback **Dallas Clark**. The third-year player out of Iowa is a crucial component of this offense. Clark (along with James, who is a very good pass-catcher) is a solid receiving threat. He has soft hands and hidden athleticism in his 6'3", 252-pound frame. Clark isn't the most nimble of players, but when teams work so hard to contain all of the other weapons on this Colts offense, only to see this guy make a play, it's absolutely deflating. This year, Indy will also utilize the blocking skills of second-year player **Ben Hartsock**. His contributions will be most critical in the red zone.

By the way, the Colts *do* have an offensive line. While this year's group will certainly be a step or two below those of past seasons (due to the youth at the guard position), there is nothing to indicate that this team will struggle up front. The guards being alluded to are second-year players **Jake Scott** and fourth-round rookie **Dylan Gandy**. Scott was drafted to play tackle last year, but after injuries forced him into the interior line, the Colts discovered that his lack of size (280 pounds) and power could be masked at the guard position. Scott is an alert player who works well within this scheme.

Center **Jeff Saturday** will have quite a task in anchoring this line in '05. However, Saturday will come through on Sundays—he always does. The seventh-year player has been one of the most consistent contributors on this team for years. He is a savvy run-blocker who forms holes by having the awareness to be creative in his angles and the mobility to get out in front.

Indy's left tackle is **Tarik Glenn**, a 29-year-old Pro Bowler who has great size (6'5", 332 pounds) and quickness getting out of his stance. Glenn is outstanding in pass protection. Right tackle **Ryan Diem** also boasts outstanding size (6'5", 331 pounds) and presents more power than anyone on the front five. Diem's mobility is almost comical (think circus elephant, small bike), but he has such a firm grasp on fundamentals that he's able to survive.

Defense

The Colts have a charming offense, but if they are to become a complete football team bidding for the Lombardi Trophy, they're going to have to get significantly better on defense. The Colts ranked 18th in allowing 21.9 points

per game last year, but as previously stated, they were 29th in yards given up, with 370.6 per game. Simply put, teams are able to move the ball on this unit far too easily.

Dungy and defensive coordinator **Ron Meeks** have tried to duplicate the dynamic defense that the head coach had while in Tampa Bay. The Colts run a Cover 2 scheme that encourages big plays. Believe it or not, last year Indy led the NFL with 35 takeaways, a fact that could actually be bad, considering that they accomplished their main mission of forcing turnovers, yet still came up short in the end.

It should be noted that Indianapolis will never be among the elite defensive units in the NFL, simply because human nature will always rule: When an offense is capable of putting up 35 points in any given week, it is only natural for the defense to play too loose with a lead or for opponents to play with too great a sense of urgency to contain. However, the Colts must find some way to abate such developments and keep them at a more reasonable level in '05. And the best place to begin is up front, with a talented defensive line.

Indianapolis's defense is headed by end **Dwight Freeney**, a fourth-year player out of Syracuse. The 6'1", 268-pound Freeney is a superfast and superexplosive demon who impacts a football game more than any other defensive player in the NFL today. After posting a league-high 16 sacks (as well as four forced fumbles) in '04, the 25-year-old Freeney enters this season as the most feared defensive lineman in all of football. Nobody in the game attracts more double teams than Freeney—there's simply no alternative option to blocking him. Freeney is so strong, so quick, and so potent that unless he has to fight through two linemen, he is going to pressure the quarterback 9 times out of 10. If he continues on with the standard he's set, Freeney is poised to become one of the greatest defensive ends to ever play the game.

Freeney isn't the only Colt lineman who can play at an Indy-500 pace. Backup end **Robert Mathis** also reached double digits in sacks last season ($10\frac{1}{2}$), to go along with six forced fumbles. The reason Mathis comes off the bench is that weighing just 235 pounds, he does not have the girth or strength to play the run. In fact, there was once again the annual talk about moving him to outside linebacker, but even there, he *still* might not

Defensive end Dwight Freeney is far and away the most dominant defenisve lineman in the NFL today. No player on this side of the ball demands more respect and attention than Freeney does.

have the ideal size to be destructive. Mathis is strictly a speed-rusher on third downs.

The man starting ahead of Mathis is fourth-year player **Raheem Brock**. Brock (6'4", 274 pounds) is a favorite of defensive line coach **John Teerlinck**. The Colts love to use him in a variety of ways, including at defensive tackle on third downs. While Brock is a fine player (6½ sacks a year ago), he, too, is somewhat of a liability in rush defense.

The problem with the run defense for the Colts up front is that with this threesome of speed-rushing ends, there is not enough size to win battles at the line of scrimmage. Freeney isn't so much a problem because of his monstrous athleticism, but since he's only able to occupy the right side of the line, Indy is substantially weak against the run on the left. What the Colts really need are two enormous nose tackles who can occupy blockers and get a consistent push up front. Instead, what they have is a pair of 285-pound finesse-oriented players in **Montae Reagor** and **Josh Williams**.

A person could watch tape on Reagor for five minutes and learn his game: The spin move. That's it—that's Reagor. He defers to the spin move on virtually every play, and when that's not working, he spins some more. Reagor gets more spin than a presidential debate. His spin move shouldn't be made fun of, though (it's no twirl); Reagor actually wins most first-step battles at the line of scrimmage, which is how he gets penetration. However, Indy needs a clogger in the middle, which is something he's simply not.

Williams also plays with a good burst, plus he has better strength than his counterpart. Williams plays in traffic as is needed, but his productivity is much lower than Reagor's, not to mention that he struggles to hold his ground.

The Colts are fairly deep at tackle, although they do not have any 300-pounders. **Larry Tripplett** plays with the energy of a man who knows his playing time is decreasing by the day, showing a frantic effort that is a nice change of pace off the bench. Indy also drafted end **Vincent Burns** in the third round this year. They were listing Burns as a defensive tackle throughout the offseason, but at 265 pounds, he doesn't have the necessary size to compete there.

A pair of voracious man-eating tackles would go a long way toward helping a linebacking unit that, frankly, is going to *need* a lot of help in '05. The linebacking unit faces the same dilemma as the front four: Very fast and athletic, but undersized. The new middle linebacker is **Gary Brackett** (5'11", 235 pounds), a career-long backup who is starting in place of **Rob Morris**. Brackett is really more fit for pass coverage duties in nickel packages.

Indy does not give preference to a weakside and a strongside linebacker, instead opting to feature two outside linebackers who can play accordingly. This is good in the sense that neither of the tiny outside linebackers—**David Thornton** (6'2", 230 pounds) or **Cato June** (6'0", 227 pounds)—has the burden of being labeled a "strong" linebacker. Thornton pretty much got stuck with the strong duties last year and basically vanished because of it.

June has somewhat of a sissy name (perfect for a man who plays in a city that is located on the Tipton Till Plain—wheeee!), but if speed means anything in this world, then this man is as rugged as *X-Men*'s Wolverine. June is a third-year player out of Michigan.

(The Wolverine reference was unintentional—honestly, a strange coincidence.) While he is a fast tackler who closes well and defends the pass even better, he has the kind of fragile strength that allows him to get knocked down if breathed on wrong.

In a perfect world, June would be a big, thick safety (like Brian Dawkins or Roy Williams), but instead, the Colts have the 5'8" **Bob Sanders**. (First it was lightweight players; now they're *short*? Jeez—pretty soon the Lollipop Guild will form in the RCA Dome and start welcoming opponents to Munchkin Land.) The strong safety is the 5'10" **Mike Doss**.

Sanders will man the free safety spot. He has great quickness and closing speed, but he's still a developing player. Doss had a bad offseason in which he drew the fury of his coach by getting arrested on gun charges. Doss reportedly fired gunshots into the air of an Akron, Ohio, nightclub, scaring gobs of people and critically wounding two ceiling tiles. Here's hoping he's that decisive and aggressive on the *field* this year. However, he'll have to wait to get on the field, because the NFL suspended him for the first two games of this season. Former cornerback **Joseph Jefferson** was converted to safety this year, in order to add depth and fill in during Doss's absence.

The cornerbacks for the Colts will be **Donald Strickland**, who's back at his natural position but was probably better at safety, and **Nick Harper**. Harper, who has excellent timing when it comes to playing the ball, was re-signed over the offseason. However, he was also temporarily jailed for spousal abuse. He too could be facing suspension.

The Colts starting cornerbacks know they must perform better this year; the team has **Jason David**, a fourth-round pick last season who started 11 games, and they also drafted Michigan's **Marlin Jackson** in the first round and Illinois' **Kevin Hayden** in the second. Neither player was drafted early so they could come in and sit on the bench.

Special Teams

Everybody knows and loves—err, *hates*, sorry—everybody knows and *hates* kicker **Mike Vanderjagt**. Nobody has an opinion on punter **Hunter Smith** because, with this prolific offense, nobody ever sees him. The backup running back, Rhodes, handles most kickoff returns. Punt return assignments are practically awarded to whoever has the stickiest receiver gloves at the time. The Colts care very little about punt returns. **Brad Pyatt** may get the job this year, or **Troy Walters**—neither is very good.

The Bottom Line

This is the same old regular season powerhouse that puts up huge numbers on offense and allows huge numbers on defense. As usual, at some point in the playoffs, the numbers allowed on defense will become much larger than the numbers allowed on offense. It's tough to see Manning struggle to move along in the postseason because he truly is an amazing player, but with such a lack of size and first-rate experience on defense this year, Indy is going to struggle to change their image in '05.

Jacksonville Jaguars

Predicted: 2ⁿᵈ ▪ 2004: 9-7 (2ⁿᵈ)

Players Added

DT	Martin Chase (NYG)
CB	Terry Cousin (NYG)
DE	Reggie Hayward (Den)
OG	Brent Smith (NYJ)
LB	Nate Wayne (Phi)
DE	Marcellus Wiley (Dal)
DT	Tony Williams (Cin)
CB	Kenny Wright (Hou)

Players Lost

DL	Lionel Barnes
CB	Juran Bolden (TB)
FB	Marc Edwards
LB	Tommy Hendricks
KR	Jermaine Lewis
DE	Elton Patterson (Cin)
CB	Dewayne Washington
OT	Bob Whitfield (NYG)

Draft

1	(21)	Matt Jones	WR	Arkansas
2	(52)	Khalif Barnes	OT	Washington
3	(87)	Scott Starks	CB	Wisconsin
4	(127)	Alvin Pearman	RB	Virginia
5	(157)	Gerald Sensabaugh	S	North Carolina
6	(185)	Chad Owens	WR	Hawaii
6	(194)	Pat Thomas	ILB	North Carolina St.
7	(237)	Chris Roberson	CB	Eastern Michigan

Taking Jones in the first round was as big as a draft day gamble can get. Finding Barnes in the second round was outstanding. He is a solid right tackle who will be expected to replace Mike Pearson, should Pearson not recover from a knee injury suffered last year. As long as he can stay inspired to play, Barnes has the natural ability needed to thrive in the league. Starks is small, which hurts his upside, but he plays hard and has enough athletic gifts to make it work.

Head Coach: Jack Del Rio (3rd year)
Offensive Coordinator: Carl Smith
Defensive Coordinator: Mike Smith

Offense

QB:	Byron Leftwich
RB:	Fred Taylor
FB:	Greg Jones
WR:	Jimmy Smith
WR:	Reggie Williams
TE:	Kyle Brady
LT:	Mike Pearson
LG:	Vince Manuwai
C:	Brad Meester
RG:	Chris Naeole
RT:	Maurice Williams
QB:	David Garrard
RB:	LaBrandon Toefield
WR:	Matt Jones‡
TE:	George Wrighster
OL:	Ephraim Salaam

Defense

LDE:	Marcellus Wiley
DT:	Marcus Stroud*
DT:	John Henderson*
RDE:	Reggie Hayward†
SLB:	Daryl Smith
MLB:	Mike Peterson
WLB:	Akin Ayodele
CB:	Rashean Mathis
SS:	Donovin Darius
FS:	Deon Grant
CB:	Kenny Wright†
NB:	Terry Cousin†
DL:	Paul Spicer
LB:	Nate Wayne†
K:	Josh Scobee
P:	Chris Hanson

* Pro Bowler '04
† veteran acquisition
‡ rookie

Report Card

Quarterback	B–	Defensive Line	B+	Coaching	B
Running Back	C+	Linebacker	B–	Special Teams	C
Receiver/Tight End	C	Defensive Back	C+	Depth	B
Offensive Line	B–			Intangibles	C–

Marcus Stroud

After the Jacksonville Jaguars proved to be a surprisingly dangerous fourth-quarter team last season, they became known around the NFL as the "Cardiac Cats." The clever name derived specifically from the early parts of September, when the Jags won all of their first three games in the final seconds, beating the Bills by three, the Broncos by one, and the Titans by three.

The quick start helped push this team to a 9-7 record, which still was not enough to propel them into the playoffs. This year, virtually the same pack of cats is back and sharpening their claws for a breakout run to the playoffs. Head coach Jack Del Rio has a fairly young team to work with, particularly on offense, where the Jags struggled in '04.

The city of Jacksonville (which is located in northeast Florida) has been somewhat obscure on the national front, considering the attention paid to Miami because of its party image (thank you, South Beach), Orlando because of its family image (thank you, Disney World), or Fort Lauderdale because of its spring break image (thank you, MTV?). However, this Duval County city, which is named after former Florida governor and U.S. president Andrew Jackson, is actually—by far—the state's most heavily populated city. That population also just got a taste of how great the vibe of a Super Bowl can be (with ALLTELL Stadium hosting Super Bowl XXXIX).

What this means is that these cardiac cats will not be embraced as cute kittens for long—they're under pressure to start scratching their way to the top of the league this season. But playing in the ultracompetitive AFC and falling in the same division as the Colts, how reasonable is it to expect this team to emerge from the pack in '05?

Offense

Jack Del Rio is a smart man—he knows exactly what needs to be fixed in order for his squad to contend for a playoff spot in '05: The offense. Jacksonville's offense was close to dormant last season. The Jaguars averaged 313.1 yards per game (21st in the NFL—not *horrendous*, but not good), but they had more trouble scoring than a *Star Wars* junky at a teen pregnancy prevention conference (16.3 points per game).

Jacksonville's main problem was that they never established an identity. They started a young quarterback in **Byron Leftwich**, who, coming out of Marshall as the seventh-overall pick in '03, has always been associated with the term *gunslinger*. However, they also recognized that veteran running back **Fred Taylor** was the bread and butter of their offense. Former offensive coordinator Bill Musgrave didn't want to be the one to have to sort out whether this unit should become an aerial force or a ground powerhouse, so he left in January to become the Redskins' quarterbacks coach. The Jaguars decided to hire **Carl Smith**—who had been working as the quarterbacks coach for the USC Trojans—to take over as the new offensive coordinator. Smith has previous NFL experience in New Orleans, were he worked long enough to establish a play-calling reputation that made him out to be as conservative as Michael Savage. However, Smith has said he intends to shake off his undesirable image by implementing more three and four receiver sets in '05. Of course, just as every new defensive coordinator says upon joining a new team that he is going to blitz and play more aggressively, every new offensive coordinator claims that he is going to open up the playbook, be loose, throw downfield—blah blah blah. It's just the popular thing to say; it has nothing to do with what will actually happen.

However, considering the status of Jacksonville's star running back, Taylor, Smith may actually be forced to put his "big-play, downfield passing" money where his mouth is. Taylor's status, exactly, is—well, um, see, honestly—nobody quite knows his status. Taylor sprained the MCL in his left knee in late December of last year. He went in for an arthroscopic procedure shortly after that and never returned to the field. He spent the entire offseason on the sideline—he never even ran.

The Jaguars have been mum on Taylor's condition, saying the 29-year-old will be ready come August. However, regardless of whether Taylor is running in August, his situation only raises more concerns that the days of "Fragile Freddie" are returning. The talented Taylor has been one of the fastest and most agile players in the NFL throughout his seven years as a pro. But early in his career, he also was one of the most injury prone. The fact that Taylor's standard—and mild—surgical procedure has left such a negative and dramatic impact should cause every alarm in northern Florida, from the Atlantic Ocean to the Gulf of Mexico, to sound and flash red. Something isn't right.

Jacksonville will likely end up having someone else spearhead their rushing attack in '05. The Jags will explore all veteran

Write It Down

Because of Fred Taylor's mysterious knee injury, the featured back in Jacksonville this season is going to wind up being LaBrandon Toefield. Keep in mind that even if Taylor is able to play this year, he'll still have missed virtually all of his offseason training.

Strengths	Weaknesses
Defensive Line Despite the presence of Marcellus Wiley, Jacksonville will have a potent front four, now that pass-rushing dynamo Reggie Hayward has joined Pro Bowl tackles Marcus Stroud and John Henderson.	**Uncertainty** On offense, nobody quite knows for sure what to expect out of Fred Taylor and the running game. The receiving corps is very hit or miss, with unproven raw talents like Reggie Williams and Matt Jones being relied upon heavily. Defensively, the linebackers are yet to establish defined roles and the personnel in the secondary is yet to be determined.
Depth Competition in practice is always a good thing. With so many backups who are vying for meaningful roles this season, the Jaguars are sure to develop some quality depth along the way.	**Pass Defense** Whoever starts at the No. 2 cornerback spot this season is going to be a huge target for quarterbacks to pick on. This never bodes well for any defense.

options on the market, but unless they can land a trade for Buffalo's Travis Henry, it is going to be difficult to find a player who can match Taylor's 1,200-plus rushing yards. Expect the team to attempt to go with third-year player **LaBrandon Toefield**. Smith is very familiar with Toefield (mainly from watching him play at LSU), and he is giddy about the combination of quickness and power shown by the 5'11", 232-pound back. However, Toefield has never been a major contributor at the pro level.

Whoever lines up in the backfield this season (whether it's Taylor or Toefield) will be back there with second-year player **Greg Jones**. The Jaguars are attempting to transform their power-runners (this includes the 250-pound Jones and 252-pound veteran **Chris Fuamatu-Ma'afala**) into fullbacks. Both players will still be used as ball carriers near the goal line, but having them serve primarily as lead-blockers may prove to be too ambitious an objective for the Jaguars coaching staff.

It is clear that the Jags will enter this season with a great deal of uncertainty about their rushing attack. With this in mind, Leftwich and his receivers will have to elevate their play and improve upon last year's 25th-ranked 6.46 average yards gained per pass attempt. At 6'5", 245 pounds, Leftwich has a demonstrative presence in the pocket. He has a powerful arm that is capable of producing an accurate spiral, but he will need to grow this season from a mental standpoint. He plays the game methodically, showing virtually no speed, and having a timely windup and release on his throws. This is fine, as long as Leftwich can learn the offensive system well enough to make his torpid nature a tool that can be used to control the rhythm of a game.

The most important man in Jacksonville could very well be **Steve Walters**, the wide receivers coach. Walters is charged with helping second-year player (and last year's first-round pick) **Reggie Williams** shake off a horrendous rookie season. At the same time, he is also responsible for teaching first-round pick **Matt Jones** (*see* Painting a New Picture, page 8), a former quarterback at Arkansas, how to play the receiver position. The progress that Walters is able to make during training camp with these two very young and very untested players may ultimately determine the fate of Jacksonville's offense in '05.

Progression: **Pass-rush—**The addition of Reggie Hayward is going to be huge for this defense, because not only will it generate more sacks, but it will also allow other players to operate more comfortably in their natural roles.

Regression: **Running back—**It is likely that Fred Taylor will be limited this year, plus Jacksonville is going through the transition of replacing a veteran fullback with the younger and more versatile Greg Jones and Chris Fuamatu-Ma'afala—a unique experiment that will take some time to get rolling.

Williams is a 6'4", 223-pound athlete who has the speed to be a playmaker downfield and the strength to move the chains in short-yardage passing. Last year, he was drafted No. 9 overall out of Washington, a program that passed a great deal. He started 15 games as a rookie, but despite these favorable factors, he never became comfortable. Williams finished the season with only 27 catches.

With Williams being a question mark and Jones an even *bigger* question mark, the Jags are fortunate to have a veteran presence in 36-year-old **Jimmy Smith** at the No.1 wideout spot. Smith is certainly nearing the end of his career, but he still has solid quickness, a keen sense for reading and attacking a defense, and very reliable hands. Last year, Smith caught 74 passes for 1,172 yards and six touchdowns.

The Jaguars also have backups **Troy Edwards**, who is inconsistent but capable of darting through a secondary from time to time, and the 6'4" second-year-player **Ernest Wilford**, who is outstanding in the red zone. Tight end **Kyle Brady** will see his role diminish as the season goes along. Brady is 33 and has forgotten how to catch. His 278-pound frame will be great for blocking, but the Jags will look to backups **George Wrighster** and **Todd Yoder** more often this year.

As long as everyone is able to stay healthy this season, Jacksonville is going to have a reliable front five. The health concerns are directed mainly at fourth-year tackle **Mike Pearson**, an athletic finesse blocker, who missed all but four games last season with torn ligaments in his left knee. Pearson's status for '05 is very much up in the air, which is one of the reasons the Jaguars drafted Washington's **Khalif Barnes**. The second-round pick does not have tremendous size (6'6", 305 pounds), but he's extremely fast for a lineman and capable of adding the necessary strength to one day start in the NFL. However, that day might not be coming this season, which is why the team may look to use backup **Ephraim Salaam**, if need be. Salaam is a solid veteran who has started virtually his entire eight-year career.

Young flame-thrower Byron Leftwich is charged with re-boosting an offense that last year was inconsistent and, at times, lethargic.

The right tackle is **Maurice Williams**, who doesn't dominate but defines *sturdy* better than Paris Hilton defines *dirty*. Williams plays with great fundamentals and control. Next to him is guard **Chris Naeole**, a ninth-year veteran who is not spectacular but is trustworthy in a group. Naeole's best feature is his mobility, from lateral movement to run-blocking to operating around the line of scrimmage in pass protection. He doesn't have great power, though.

Left guard **Vince Manuwai** is a third-year player who shows good strength in delivering an initial pop. The challenge with him is finding ways to maximize his potential. It's helpful that next to Manuwai is center **Brad Meester**, an intelligent and vocal leader of this offense. Meester is not a gifted player, but he works hard and is able to find ways to get the job done.

Defense

The Jaguars defense is very reminiscent of the Panthers from '03. The similarities run deeper than the fact that both teams have mascots from the cat family and both joined the NFL in 1995. For starters, prior to '03, when he became the second head coach in Jacksonville's franchise history, Del Rio spent a year as the defensive coordinator in Carolina, laying the groundwork for the output that carried the Panthers to the Super Bowl the following season.

Although **Mike Smith** is the defensive coordinator for this team, the man actually directing the Jaguars is Del Rio. (Come on, with a name like Mike Smith, you didn't actually think he would be more than a henchman anyway, right?) Del Rio predicates his defense on having a dominant front four, as he believes that the unit that controls the line of scrimmage will likely control the game. (Huh, makes sense.) This season, Del Rio may finally have the lineup he wants up front. He has a pair of young Pro Bowl tackles in **Marcus Stroud** and **John Henderson**, and his club signed two free agents to come in and be his starting ends: **Reggie Hayward** (*see* Painting a New Picture, page 7) from Denver and **Marcellus Wiley** from Dallas.

The tackles are the key to Jacksonville's success on this side of the ball. At the age of 27, Stroud is one of the premier defensive linemen in the game. He has amazing quickness for a man who is 6'6", 312 pounds, and of course, he has outstanding power as well. This past offseason, the Jaguars rewarded Stroud with a long-term contract that included $13.28 million in guaranteed money. The Jaguars are placing a lot of trust in their fifth-year star; Stroud's greatest assets are his energy and tenacity, two elements that can disappear once a player gets a large amounts of dead presidents in his pocket. However, Stroud has pledged to play hard and continue to improve this season.

Although Henderson made it to Hawaii last year, Jacksonville would be better off if the fourth-year pro took the same oath that Stroud has taken. Henderson is not exactly this team's version of Vince Carter, but the former first-round draft pick could stand to get more production out of his powerful 6'7", 328-pound frame.

The best way to exemplify what Henderson must do to improve is to look at his pregame routine. Prior to kickoff, Henderson goes into the training room and has trainer **Joe Sheehan** slap him across the face as hard as possible. (Sheehan knows he's done the job right if he can draw a little blood. Seriously.) Henderson then proceeds out the door and down the tunnel, walking like a beast freed from his chain and cursing like a drunken Redd Fox. What

Henderson needs to do is find some way to consistently reenact such enthusiasm once he's on the field.

Henderson does one of two things each down: Either he feasts off the attention that Stroud attracts (which is mainly where Henderson's 6½ sacks and 76 tackles a year ago came from) or he attracts his own double team. It is here that Henderson must learn to be more productive. When opponents work hard to get extra bodies on him, he tends to give up and allow himself to be ineffective.

The Jags are right to think Hayward will help boost their mediocre pass-rush from a year ago (37 sacks, tied for 17th in the NFL). However, they are sorely mistaken if they think Wiley is worth the jersey he wears. Last season, he was the third most unproductive thing in Texas Stadium—right behind the worn-out tackling dummies in the equipment room and the leaky Gatorade cooler on the opponent's sideline. (One would think that the Jaguars had learned their lesson when they gave a big contract to defensive end Hugh Douglas a few years ago. Douglas also became ineffective and was soon released.)

Jacksonville has decent depth up front. Veteran **Paul Spicer** is back healthy (he'll likely start once the team realizes just how bland Wiley is), **Rob Meier** is a feisty backup who, when healthy, can be effective, and second-year player **Bobby McCray** started late in the season last year, at times showing intriguing speed around the corner. The team also has second-year player **Anthony Maddox** (who can develop into a very good pro one day) and former Bengal **Tony Williams** to back up the Pro Bowlers at defensive tackle.

The cats from the town known as "The Winter City in the Summer Land" have a linebacking unit that can be as pleasant as 80 degrees and sunny, or as disappointing as 45 degrees with high winds and showers. It all depends on how the two young players grasp their roles. These players are **Akin Ayodele** and **Daryl Smith**. Linebackers coach **Brian VanGorder** must decide exactly how he wants to use the fourth-year player Ayodele and the second-year pro Smith. During the offseason, it appeared that Smith was working on the strongside, which would leave Ayodele on the weakside (the middle duties are firmly held down by the team's leading tackler from last season, **Mike Peterson**). Smith is adept at taking on blocks and tackling with good form, but at 6'2", 234 pounds, he does not possess the size needed to hold up at the strongside position. Ayodele *does* have the size; he's 6'2", 251 pounds. Furthermore, Ayodele is a little better than Smith at playing in traffic. At the same time, Smith is more athletic in space.

Logic would say that Smith should play the weakside and Ayodele the strong. However, all this could change if the Jaguars decide that they want to get free agent acquisition **Nate Wayne** in the starting lineup to use his speed and veteran experience. But replacing either of these young potential stars with a middle-tier veteran like Wayne would be foolish. Wayne is versatile, but he's a much better fit to be an effective utility linebacker off the bench. On the bench, he could bond with veteran **Greg Favors**, who has returned to his normal linebacker position after he concluded his one-year experiment at defensive end last season.

How's this for a career headed downhill: **Dave Campo** was the head coach of the Cowboys from 2000 through '02, the defensive coordinator for the Browns from '03 through '04, and now the secondary coach for the Jaguars in '05. At this rate,

Campo will be the No. 2 ticket taker for the Mustangs of Mandarin High School by the year 2009.

Campo *does*, however, have a somewhat critical job this season. He has the talented young **Rashean Mathis** (*see* Ready to Break Out, page 55) starting at one of the cornerback positions, but he must decide on who to start at the No. 2 spot. The list of candidates resembles a Duval County phone book: Veteran **Kiwaukee Thomas** (likely not worth investing in), ninth-year pro **Terry Cousin** (a career nickel back who will probably be asked to serve in this role again in '05), **Kenny Wright** (a veteran who is very useful in practice but not necessarily on Sundays), rookie **Scott Starks** (tough and speedy, but undersized at 5'8", 175 pounds), second-year player **Chris Thompson** (who played sparingly as a fifth-round draft choice last season), and an undrafted free agent in his second year named **David Richardson** (a dark-horse candidate who is actually one of the front runners). Wow. Don't go thinking the answer to who will get the nod is coming from here.(Thompson. Shhhhh.)

Strong safety **Donovin Darius** was very public about his unhappiness with being given the franchise tag by the Jags for a third consecutive year. What's funny is that the hard-hitting, freelancing star has actually been among the highest-paid defensive backs in the game over the past three seasons because of all the high-priced one-year contracts that he gets stuck with. Over the offseason, Darius pleaded for a trade (citing Miami or Minnesota as his preferential suitors), but to no avail. Now he'll show up this year and be ready to perform at a high level in the black and teal/sea green/aqua/dark cyan/turquoise/dark aquamarine uniform once again.

The free safety is **Deon Grant**, but the 26-year-old is shaky as an open-field tackler and slightly more likely to give up a big play than manufacture his own. Not saying it will happen, but don't be stunned if backup **Deke Cooper** captures the starting free safety job at some point this season.

Special Teams

Since virtually every other member of the Jacksonville coaching staff has somehow had his name printed in these past four pages, we might as well throw in special-teams coach **Pete Rodriguez**, one of the most respected assistants in the game. Rodriguez will have a second-year kicker in **Josh Scobee** and a veteran punter in **Chris Hanson**. (Who still hasn't lived down his epic ax injury from October of '03.) Hanson returned last season, averaging 42.8 yards per punt. The Jaguars are going to have to search hard during the preseason for a quality return artist to replace the departed Jermaine Lewis.

The Bottom Line

The Jaguars began their climb last season, finishing 9-7. This year, the tendency is to think that they are poised to take that final step forward. However, a lot of components of this team seem fragmented. There are a lot of players on this roster who are injury prone (most notably, running back Fred Taylor), and it seems as if the team is having to force some of their young players into gelling. Maybe all this is overanalyzing, but Jacksonville is going to have to push hard to make things work in '05.

Tennessee Titans

Predicted: 4th ▪ 2004: 5-11 (4th)

Players Added
DE	Kyle Vanden Bosch (Ari)	

Players Lost
WR	Eddie Berlin (Chi)	
DL	Kevin Carter (Mia)	
CB	Andre Dyson (Sea)	
DE	Carlos Hall (KC)	
RB	Robert Holcombe (KC)	
WR	Derrick Mason (Bal)	
OL	Jason Mathews (retired)	
WR	Jason McAddley (SF)	
TE	Shad Meier (NO)	
OT	Fred Miller (Chi)	
K	Joe Nedney (SF)	
OG	Marico Portis (Ind)	
CB	Samari Rolle (Bal)	
S	Lance Schulters	
RB	Antowain Smith (NO)	

Draft
1	(6)	Adam Jones	CB	West Virginia
2	(41)	Michael Roos	OT	Eastern Washington
3	(68)	Courtney Roby	WR	Indiana
3	(96)	Brandon Jones	WR	Oklahoma
4	(108)	Vincent Fuller	CB	Virginia Tech
4	(113)	David Stewart	OT	Mississippi St.
4	(136)	Roydell Williams	WR	Tulane
5	(142)	Damien Nash	RB	Missouri
5	(150)	Daniel Loper	OT	Texas Tech
6	(179)	Bo Scaife	TE	Texas
7	(218)	Reynaldo Hill	CB	Florida

Jones is a quick, ball-hawking playmaker who is already being asked to carry the load in a somewhat depleted secondary. Roos comes from a small Big Sky school and he hasn't fully developed his power. He does, however, have good agility. He would replace Fred Miller at right tackle, but Roos clearly has left tackle skills. Jones is more of a physical receiver than Roby and can be more aggressive over the middle. Then again, Roby has more shiftiness and quickness.

Head Coach: Jeff Fisher (12th year)
Offensive Coordinator: Norm Chow
Defensive Coordinator: Jim Schwartz

Offense
QB:	Steve McNair
RB:	Chris Brown
FB:	Troy Fleming
WR:	Drew Bennett
WR:	Tyrone Calico
TE:	Erron Kinney
LT:	Brad Hopkins
LG:	Zach Piller
C:	Justin Hartwig
RG:	Benji Olson
RT:	Michael Roos‡
QB:	Billy Volek
RB:	Damien Nash‡
WR:	Brandon Jones‡
TE:	Ben Troupe
OL:	Jacob Bell

Defense
LDE:	Bo Schobel
DT:	Rien Long
DT:	Albert Haynesworth
RDE:	Travis LaBoy
LOLB:	Peter Sirmon
MLB:	Brad Kassell
ROLB:	Keith Bulluck
CB:	Adam Jones‡
SS:	Tank Williams
FS:	Lamont Thompson
CB:	Andre Woolfolk
NB:	Michael Waddell
DL:	Antwan Odom
LB:	Rocky Calmus
K:	Ola Kimrin
P:	Craig Hentrich

* Pro Bowler '04
† veteran acquisition
‡ rookie

Report Card
Quarterback	B	Defensive Line	C	Coaching	A–
Running Back	C+	Linebacker	B	Special Teams	C
Receiver/Tight End	C+	Defensive Back	C+	Depth	C
Offensive Line	C			Intangibles	B–

Keith Bulluck

Heading into last season, the Tennessee Titans knew they were approaching the reform years, but they were hoping that they could muster up enough firepower to make one final playoff run. (They had lost to New England in the divisional round of the playoffs the previous year.) However, as things turned out, one final "Music City Miracle" (*whew*, got that reference out of the way early) was simply not in the cards. The first indication came when the team had to release running back Eddie George, a revered icon of Titan football who had been with the Baby Blue and White long enough to remember what life was like as an Oiler. The second indication came when veteran player on top of veteran player (including quarterback Steve McNair) went down with injury. The third indicator came in January, when the misery was finally over and this team was left looking down on the carnage of an 11-loss season.

Now it's undeniable: The Titans are in a rebuilding stage. Head coach Jeff Fisher has nothing to be ashamed about in his club having to regroup. Sure, owner Bud Adams will try to play George Steinbrenner a time or two this year, and the team's home games in the beautiful Coliseum (located in downtown Nashville, along the banks of the Cumberland River) will not have the same energy and flair come late October. But *darn it*, this team has been a pretty well-run franchise for the better part of the past decade. They'll make the best of their situation this year. Heck, between their first- and second-string lineups, Tennessee will play at least 25 players who, heading into this season, have two years or less of experience. That spells significant trouble in the short run, but just think how solid this team's nucleus will be in a year or two, when those 25 players are in their prime.

Offense

Just because the Titans finished the season as the "top-ranked offense" in '04 (leading the league with 342.9 yards per game) doesn't mean that they will prosper on this side of the ball in '05. The only reason the Titans were able to move the ball on offense last year was because they were constantly playing from behind, which enabled them to play against soft, prevent zone defense and fewer blitzes. Tennessee still ranked a mediocre 15th in scoring last season (21.5 points per game).

This year, the Titans are making an adjustment that could be prodigious: They hired the well-known **Norm Chow**, who was the mastermind behind the offensive success that led to back-to-back national championships at USC over the past two years. Chow—who many believe should have been given an NFL job far earlier in his career—intends to improve this Tennessee offense by correcting the protection scheme up front and complicating the playbook to include more pre-snap motion and shifts, all in an effort to confuse defenses. Chow has also said that he wants the team to spend less time in the huddle this year.

Essentially, this all pertains to one position on the field: Quarterback. Considering the dramatic changes in philosophy (not to mention losing so many veteran players), one can't help but wonder why **Steve McNair** decided to delay his looming retirement and return for an 11th season. Yes, McNair is only 32, but over his career, the man has been banged up more than a bass drum in the Vanderbilt marching band. (*see* Startling Statistics, page 73.) McNair had a miserable season last year, missing half of his team's games with a bruised sternum.

It is unlikely that McNair will be able to stay healthy for the duration of the season in '05. Chow could attempt to strengthen the pass protection by running a nine-man line that features an extra tight end, three hippos, *and* Kirstie Alley—and McNair would *still* be roughed up each week. Tennessee has a great backup in **Billy Volek**—a player who, quite frankly, may have made a poor decision in choosing to continue to be a part of this franchise. Volek is a fairly accurate passer, he knows how to get the ball downfield, and he has proven capable of throwing 40-plus times a game. Last year, when Volek was filling in for an injured McNair, he posted a solid rating of 87.1. However, the sixth-year pro out of Fresno State is now 29 years old, meaning that he's likely to have a legacy as a backup. It would not be surprising—or unreasonable—for Jeff Fisher and the Titans to ultimately make Volek the starting quarterback at some point this season.

But if enough things go right, McNair will play well enough that the Titans won't have to make that decision. However, a

tweak in the blocking assignments can only do so much; Tennessee is still going to have to get something out of their linemen. This is where the problems might occur.

First off, the most important position on the offensive line (left tackle) is occupied by a slowing-down, 13th-year veteran (**Brad Hopkins**) who will turn 35 in September. Hopkins has been on the decline for the past few years, but has always been able to survive with the fundamentals and technique that come from having a great depth of experience. However, this past offseason, he humiliated the Titans organization when he was arrested for domestic assault on his wife, Ellen. (He pleaded guilty to the assault.) It is very likely that Tennessee will gradually phase Hopkins out of the picture during the rebuilding process this year.

Expect rookie **Michael Roos** to take over the left tackle duties at some point this season. Roos (who is currently slated to start at right tackle) is a second-round pick out of Eastern Washington. The Titans love the 6'5", 320-pounder's upside; he did not even begin playing football until his senior year in high school *and* he has been working as an offensive lineman for only three years. And yet, Titans offensive line coach **Mike Munchak** likes how poised, polished, and NFL-ready Roos is.

Moving Roos to left tackle (likely sometime around November) would also allow Tennessee to get second-year player **Jacob Bell** on the field. Bell, a fifth-round draft choice last season, has the tools to be a Pro Bowler. He has a good burst, with the power and intensity to drive in run-blocking. Bell started 14 games last season and showed veteran traits in areas such as angling his blocks, playing with good technique, and improvising on busted plays.

As previously stated, Bell may see action at tackle this year, though he operated primarily at left guard in '04. However, this was because veteran **Zach Piller** tore a biceps muscle in September, causing him to miss the entire season. Piller is back this year and safe in his starting role. His fellow starting guard, **Benji Olson**, is an eighth-year veteran with a pair of Pro Bowls to his name. Olson is a powerful 320-pound force who plays with a mean streak and can create running lanes by bulldozing up front. Between the guards is center **Justin Hartwig**, a fairly skilled fourth-year player who is very effective blocking north and south. Hartwig isn't a dynamic force, but he is a solid presence who can work well with veterans around him.

Write it Down:

By the time the season begins to wind down, the Titans will have discovered two outstanding young bookend tackles in Jacob Bell and Michael Roos.

Progression: **Downfield passing**—Tennessee was more of a controlled, intermediate passing team with Derrick Mason, but in an effort to try something new, the club will feature the lanky Drew Bennett and the athletic Tyrone Calico, both of whom have the speed to stretch the field. New offensive coordinator Norm Chow is also a man who is more inclined to go deep.

Regression: **Experience**—Losing as many veterans as this team did (especially when considering how much Pro Bowl and playoff experience a lot of those players had) was probably necessary for the long run, but it will be painful in the short run.

The Titans running game (which ranked 14th a season ago) is headed by third-year player **Chris Brown**, who gained 1,067 yards on just 220 carries in '04. However, like the banjos and guitars that fill the streets of Nashville's famous recording industry center, Music Row, Brown comes with a few strings attached. He weighs 219 pounds, but he is also 6'3", which gives him a somewhat thin and fragile frame. Even worse is that, like former Titan Eddie George, Brown runs very upright. But the difference between George and Brown is that when the moment was right, George knew how to lower his shoulder, deliver a blow, and withstand the impact. Brown doesn't. Injuries left Brown either sidelined or severely hampered late in the season last year; he carried the ball only 54 times during the months of November and December. Furthermore, he had six fumbles in just 11 games played.

The Titans would have used their first-round pick to draft running back Cedric Benson, but he was off the board when their turn arrived at No. 6. Tennessee also gave heavy consideration to trading for Buffalo's Travis Henry (something they may still opt to do). However, as it stands now, the only man competing with Brown for playing time this year is fifth-round rookie **Damien Nash**.

A player to learn is **Ben Troupe**, a second-year pro out of Florida. The 6'4", 262-pound Troupe is the NFL's next major pass-catching star at the tight end position. Troupe is very fast for his size, he has great athleticism, and he is versatile enough to even split out as a wide receiver. However, he'll likely have a quiet first half of the season and begin the year second on the depth chart, behind **Erron Kinney**. Troupe missed a lot of the offseason activities, recovering from surgery that he underwent to repair a broken fifth metatarsal in his left foot. Eventually, the 275-pound Kinney will assume his more natural, blocking-oriented, No. 2 job, leaving room for Troupe to step in and start.

The Titans have a great deal of untapped potential at the receiver position. The new No. 1 target this season is **Drew Bennett**, a fifth-year pro who played quarterback at UCLA. Bennett is coming off the most explosive second half of a season for a receiver in recent memory. In the first eight games of last year, Bennett caught 33 passes for 388 yards (11.8 average) and one touchdown. Over the last eight games, he totaled 47 receptions for 859 yards (18.3 average) and 10 touchdowns. Not a bad turnaround.

The fluid and lanky 6'5" Bennett should be able to maintain his '04 second-half standard (well, actually, that's *quite* a standard, but the *point* is he'll play well) now that he has more confidence and job security. The No. 2 receiver is the supertalented **Tyrone Calico**, a third-year player with incredible speed and raw talent. Calico, however, missed virtually all of last season with knee problems, which stemmed from when Dallas's Roy Williams brought him down with a horse-collar tackle in a preseason game (horse-collar tackling was outlawed by the NFL this past offseason). The Titans foolishly tried to bring Calico back too soon last year, but this season, the time is finally right for him to be back on the field. Good thing, too.

The No. 3 job will likely go to third-round rookie **Courtney Roby**, because he offers the short-yardage receiving element that this offense is lacking. However, another third-round rookie, **Brandon Jones**, presents similar features, plus he can be electrifying at times.

Defense

Like all bad teams, the Titans experienced significant problems on defense in '04. The main issue was that they just plain couldn't *stop* anybody. Tennessee surrendered 27.4 points per game (30th in the NFL), and they allowed 357.8 yards of offense per contest (26th in the league).

Defensive coordinator **Jim Schwartz**'s group gave up a barrel full of big plays through the air last season. The Titans allowed 13 pass plays of 40 yards or more and 53 pass plays of 20 yards or more. Part of the trouble was that the secondary was littered with injuries to key starters, including cornerback Samari Rolle, free safety Lance Schulters, and strong safety **Tank Williams**. However, this season the Titans will be without two of those players (Rolle and Schulters) and they also lost their young, up-and-coming cornerback Andre Dyson in free agency. In other words, they need to find a way to adjust—fast.

This year, replacing Rolle and Dyson will be rookie sixth-overall pick **Adam "Pac Man" Jones** and former first-round pick **Andre Woolfolk**, who is in the third season of what has been an injury-riddled career. Replacing Rolle and Dyson with Jones and Woolfolk is essentially like going from Alan Jackson and Garth Brooks, two surefire country music stars, to Craig Morgan and Josh Turner, two *potentially* great but still unproven talents.

Tennessee had a chance to use their first-round draft choice on another cornerback named Rolle (Antrel Rolle, from Miami), but they decided to gamble a bit and take the 5'11", 187-pound Jones instead. Jones is not as strong or reliable as Rolle, but his speed and pizzazz make him a far more lethal big-play threat. He is also a likely candidate to run back punts. Woolfolk is a tall (6'2") defender who features similar attributes. Prior to entering the league out of Oklahoma, Woolfolk had played cornerback for only one season, spending his other years at wide receiver and

Running back Chris Brown is coming off a 1,000-yard season, but Tennessee has major concerns about his durability.

safety. Considering his lack of solid in-game experience, the athletic and potential paragon still might be a bit too green to thrive in '05. (Please excuse the rhyme.)

With Tennessee attempting to improve a pass defense that allowed opposing quarterbacks to complete 63.3 percent of their attempts (30th in the NFL) and throw for an average of 237.9 yards per game (26th in the NFL) by starting a pair of young players who have a combined total of two starts between them, the Titans are fortunate to at least have decent depth at the cornerback position. The nickel back is expected to be **Michael Waddell**, a second-year player who has not yet fully developed his confidence but shows a nice feel for playing the ball. The other reserve cornerback *has* fully developed his confidence; in fact, there is nothing reserved about him at all. This would be **Tony Beckham**, who claims that he'll be a starter this season—actually, he claims that "Tony Beckham" will be a starter. Beckham's mouth may run like an all-night printing press, but he is the longest-tenured veteran and outgoing leader for this secondary.

Strong safety Tank Williams has a very fitting name for a player at his position. The 6'3", 223-pounder can be a punishing tackler near the line of scrimmage, but he tends to play a little out of control at times. Williams is not inept in pass coverage, although the Titans don't often use him there. Part of the reason they rarely play two-deep with their safeties in coverage is because they feel that it is appropriate for them to ask their free safety to take on a great amount of responsibility in stopping the pass. The man being asked to do this in '05 will be **Lamont Thompson**, a fourth-year player who certainly has the range to live up to his task. However, Thompson must improve in one area that will actually be a concern for *all* Titan defensive backs this season: Staring at the quarterback less often.

The Titans hope to improve their pass defense by getting better pressure on the quarterback in '05. Defensive line coach **Jim Washburn** is not happy about the fact that Tennessee's defensive ends generated only 10½ sacks as a group last season. (The Titans, as a team, ranked 27th in the league with 32 sacks.) Washburn knows he has several talented early-round picks to play up front. He is expecting his plethora of young players to flourish in a way that the Volunteer State has not seen since the revolutionary 1930s days of cheap electricity from the Tennessee Valley Authority. At the ends, the Titans are starting a pair of second-year players with **Travis LaBoy** on the right side and **Bo Schobel** on the left.

LaBoy is undersized (253 pounds) but plays with good leverage and arm extension, getting solid initial contact and showing solid strength. However, he desperately needs to learn how to get off blocks more efficiently in '05. Schobel (who is the cousin of Buffalo's Aaron Schobel and also Cincinnati's Matt Schobel) played in only five games as a rookie last year. At 6'5", 264 pounds, he looks as if he should be playing for Jerry West and Mike Fratello on the Memphis Grizzlies. Schobel has decent quickness, but overall he does not seem to offer the necessary skills to start in the NFL.

It is a little curious that Tennessee doesn't start **Antwan Odom** ahead of Schobel. After all, Odom was drafted in the second round last season (two rounds ahead of Schobel), offers the same type of quickness as Schobel, and has a stronger build (6'4", 277 pounds). Odom has struggled to pick up the nuances

of the pro game, though, and will still be adjusting to a higher level of play in '05.

Between the ends are tackles **Rien Long** and **Albert Haynesworth** (with second-year player **Randy Starks** expected to see significant playing time off the bench). Long thrives on getting penetration, while Haynesworth (at 6'6", 320 pounds) thrives on his incredible, Hulk-like strength. Starks is a developing player who moves well in his defensive tackle realm, but he is also still getting acclimated to the NFL. (Last season, Starks was the youngest player in the NFL; he didn't turn 21 until December.)

It is an absolute travesty that sixth-year linebacker **Keith Bulluck** is not recognized as one of the top-echelon linebackers in the league. The superfast, highly energized 235-pounder is in the same class as Ray Lewis and Derrick Brooks. Bulluck—who mans one of the outside slots for Tennessee—recorded a league-high 152 tackles last season, with five sacks, two interceptions, and 13 passes defensed.

The other outside linebacker for the Titans is **Peter Sirmon**, a sixth-year pro. Sirmon preaches the concept of playing well within the system. He is, in a way, similar to middle linebacker **Brad Kassell**. Both players lack raging physical skills (emphasis on *raging*—each is adequate athletically, unless compared to Bulluck, of course), but they know exactly how to operate in the Titans scheme. They are both effective at the point of attack—although Kassell has been known to take some time with getting off blocks—and they're both sound tacklers.

Tennessee has solid depth at the linebacker position, which is a good thing considering the number of injuries that seem to have stricken this unit over the years. Perhaps most exciting about the key contributors off the bench is that each is named Rocky—how often does *that* happen? **Rocky Boiman** and **Rocky Calmus** are both fourth-year players who are capable of doing spot-duty in the middle. Of course, when either of them is on the field, it is a "Rocky" situation for the Titans. (Is that too desperate a pun? Does that go too far?)

Special Teams

There is no need for anyone to pretend they know who in the world kicker **Ola Kimrin** is. Apparently he is a second-year player who played in five games for the Redskins last season. The punter is **Craig Hentrich**, who, thanks to Fisher's fondness for trickery, has become one of the most exciting players in the game today—sorta. Tennessee loves fake punts and onside kicks; last year Hentrich threw the ball four times and also ran once for eight yards. (Gripping.) The Titans are hoping that "Pac Man" Jones can ignite their lethargic return game by evading the solid-colored ghosts of the other team and gobbling them up when they are flashing blue.

The Bottom Line

There is no doubt that the Titans are in a serious rebuilding stage. A person could find more fresh-faced youth running around the Coliseum in downtown Nashville than they could at Neverland Ranch. However, Tennessee is going about this the right way. They're developing young talent for the future, they are attempting to at least field a competitive squad this year, and they are finally regaining a handle on their salary cap. Still, they'll likely finish last in the AFC South this season.

AFC West

Denver
Broncos

Kansas City
Chiefs

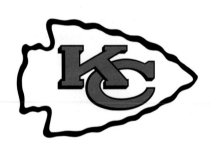

Oakland
Raiders

San Diego
Chargers

Looking Forward

How They'll Finish
1. Kansas City Chiefs
2. San Diego Chargers
3. Denver Broncos
4. Oakland Raiders

Ready to Break Out

**Toniu Fonoti,
San Diego Chargers**

Left Guard
6'4"—350
4th year—23
Drafted: 2nd round in '02 out of Nebraska

Fonoti has been a starter on the Chargers front five every year of his young career, although a foot injury wiped out his entire season in 2003. However, Fonoti returned to have a strong outing last year, starting all 16 regular season games, plus the wild card game.

Now entering his fourth season in the league—yet still not turning 24 until November—Fonoti is poised to supplant Dallas's Larry Allen as the most dominating guard in the game. No player in the NFL right now exhibits more sheer power and ferocity as a run-blocker than Fonoti. He has tremendous mobility as a run-blocker, with the ability to open up holes for runners by lead-blocking to the second level or to create space on the outside by pulling to the open field.

Fonoti is a beast, but there are areas where he could get better, namely, in pass protection. If he can improve his footwork and learn to keep his balance in pass-blocking, all while gaining awareness, he can become a rare All-World player.

Toniu Fonoti

Hot Seat

**Mike Shanahan,
Denver Broncos**

Since taking over the Broncos in 1995, Shanahan has been considered one of the best offensive-minded head coaches in the industry. However, it has not slipped anybody's mind that his teams have gone 0-3 in the postseason since John Elway retired in 1999. With Elway, Shanahan went 7-0 and won two Super Bowls.

The absence from the postseason had not been viewed with the greatest of concern for the few years following Number 7's retirement, because Denver was still competing admirably during the regular season and the offense was putting up good numbers. However, after back-to-back thrashings by the Indianapolis Colts in 2003 and 2004, people are beginning to look around uneasily and questions are starting to be asked.

If Shanahan cannot get his squad to reach the postseason and, more important, perform well there, this could be his last year coaching at a one-mile altitude.

Best Offseason Move

Raiders jump-starting their offense by trading for Randy Moss.

Worst Offseason Move

Broncos crowding their backfield even more by signing Ron Dayne and wasting a third-round pick on Maurice Clarett.

Best Under-the-Radar Offseason Move

The Chiefs convincing guard Will Shields to put off retirement for another year.

Biggest Question

With the Chiefs better on defense and the Raiders better on offense, can the Chargers prove they weren't a fluke in 2004?

QUICK HITS

TEAM BESTS	
Passing Game	Raiders
Running Game	Broncos
Offensive Line	Chiefs
Pass Rush	Chargers
Run Defense	Chargers
Pass Defense	Broncos
Special Teams	Chargers
Coaching Staff	Chargers
Home Field	Chiefs

BEST PLAYERS	
Pure Athlete	Ronald Curry, Raider
Big Play Threat	Randy Moss, Raiders
Best Use of Talent	Rod Smith, Broncos
Worst Use of Talent	G. Warren, Bronco
On the Rise	Ashlet Lelie, Broncos
	D.J. Williams, Broncos
	Antonio Gates, Chargers
On the Decline	Warren Sapp, Raiders
	Trevor Pryce, Broncos
	Johnnie Morton, Chiefs
Best Leader	Donnie Edwards, Chargers
Unsung Hero	Tony Richardson, Chiefss

Priest Holmes

Looking Back

Denver Broncos 2004

PASSING STATISTICS

PLAYER	CMP	ATT	YDS	CMP%	YDS/A	LNG	TD	TD%	INT	INT%	SACK	YDS	RAT
Jake Plummer	303	521	4089	58.2	7.85	85	27	5.2	20	3.8	15	90	84.5

RUSHING STATISTICS

PLAYER	ATT	YDS	AVG	LNG	TD	FUM	LST
Reuben Droughns	275	1240	4.5	51	6	5	3
Tatum Bell	75	396	5.3	29	3	0	0
Quentin Griffin	85	311	3.7	47	2	2	2

RECEIVING STATISTICS

PLAYER	REC	YDS	AVG	LNG	TD	FUM	LST
Rod Smith	79	1144	14.5	85	7	1	0
Ashley Lelie	54	1084	20.1	58	7	0	0
Jeb Putzier	36	572	15.9	39	2	0	0
Darius Watts	31	385	12.4	28	1	1	0

RETURN STATISTICS

PLAYER	KICKOFFS					PUNTS					
	ATT	YDS	FC	AVG	LNG	TD	ATT	YDS	FC	AVG	LNG	TD
Roc Alexander	19	386	0	20.3	32	0	0	0	0	0.0	0	0
Triandos Luke	15	306	0	20.4	32	0	19	135	8	7.1	21	0

KICKING STATISTICS

PLAYER	1-20	20-29	30-39	40-49	50+	TOT	PCT	AVG	LNG	XPM/A	PTS
Jason Elam	0/0	10/10	7/8	9/12	3/4	29/34	85.3	34.7	52	42/42	129

PUNTING STATISTICS

PLAYER	PUNTS	YDS	AVG	LNG	TB	TB%	IN20	IN20%	RET	YDS	AVG	NET
Micah Knorr	54	2243	41.5	66	6	11.1	12	22.2	26	240	9.2	37.1

DEFENSIVE STATISTICS

PLAYER	TACKLES					MISCELLANEOUS			INTERCEPTIONS				
	TOT	SOLO	AST	SACK	TLOSS	FF	BK	INT	YDS	AVG	LNG	TD	PD
D.J. Williams	106	81	25	2.0	10	1	0	1	10	10.0	10	0	7
Al Wilson	105	78	27	2.5	7	2	0	2	17	8.5	10	1	5
Kenoy Kennedy	82	68	14	2.0	2	2	0	1	21	21.0	21	0	9
Champ Bailey	81	72	9	0.0	4	0	0	3	0	0.0	0	0	12
Kelly Herndon	69	60	9	1.0	4.5	3	0	2	17	8.5	15	0	23
Donnie Spragan	66	46	20	1.0	3	1	0	0	0	0.0	0	0	6
John Lynch	65	50	15	2.0	3	3	0	1	2	2.0	2	0	10
Reggie Hayward	43	33	10	10.5	4	1	0	1	76	76.0	76	0	3
Marco Coleman	28	23	5	2.5	0	1	0	0	0	0.0	0	0	0
Monsanto Pope	24	19	5	1.0	1.5	0	1	0	0	0.0	0	0	2

Kansas City Chiefs 2004

PASSING STATISTICS

PLAYER	CMP	ATT	YDS	CMP%	YDS/A	LNG	TD	TD%	INT	INT%	SACK	YDS	RAT
Trent Green	369	556	4591	66.4	8.26	70	27	4.9	17	3.1	32	227	95.2

RUSHING STATISTICS

PLAYER	ATT	YDS	AVG	LNG	TD	FUM	LST
Priest Holmes	196	892	4.6	33	14	4	2
Larry Johnson	120	581	4.8	46	9	0	0
Derrick Blaylock	118	539	4.6	24	8	0	0

RECEIVING STATISTICS

PLAYER	REC	YDS	AVG	LNG	TD	FUM	LST
Tony Gonzalez	102	1258	12.3	32	7	0	0
Eddie Kennison	62	1086	17.5	70	8	1	1
Johnnie Morton	55	795	14.5	52	3	1	1
Larry Johnson	22	278	12.6	40	2	0	0

RETURN STATISTICS

PLAYER	KICKOFFS					PUNTS					
	ATT	YDS	FC	AVG	LNG	TD	ATT	YDS	FC	AVG	LNG	TD
Dante Hall	68	1718	0	25.3	97	2	23	232	17	10.1	46	0

KICKING STATISTICS

PLAYER	1-20	20-29	30-39	40-49	50+	TOT	PCT	AVG	LNG	XPM/A	PTS
Lawrence Tynes	0/0	5/5	7/8	3/6	2/4	17/23	73.9	35.2	50	58/60	109

PUNTING STATISTICS

PLAYER	PUNTS	YDS	AVG	LNG	TB	TB%	IN20	IN20%	RET	YDS	AVG	NET
Steve Cheek	42	1643	39.1	55	6	14.3	8	19.0	18	197	10.9	34.4

DEFENSIVE STATISTICS

PLAYER	TACKLES					MISCELLANEOUS			INTERCEPTIONS				
	TOT	SOLO	AST	SACK	TLOSS	FF	BK	INT	YDS	AVG	LNG	TD	PD
Scott Fujita	90	68	22	4.5	5.5	0	0	0	0	0.0	0	0	4
Kawika Mitchell	71	57	14	1.0	5.5	1	0	0	0	0.0	0	0	3
Greg Wesley	67	61	6	0.0	0	4	0	4	92	23.0	65	0	7
Eric Warfield	58	50	8	0.0	2	1	0	4	49	12.3	43	1	12
Monty Beisel	51	42	9	2.5	1	1	0	1	-1	-1.0	-1	0	1
Shaunard Harts	44	37	7	0.0	1	1	0	0	0	0.0	0	0	1
Jerome Woods	42	36	6	1.0	0.5	1	0	0	0	0.0	0	0	1
John Browning	39	32	7	4.5	3	1	0	0	0	0.0	0	0	1
William Bartee	38	34	4	1.5	0	0	0	0	0	0.0	0	0	7
Dexter McCleon	36	31	5	0.0	1	0	0	2	23	11.5	23	0	9
Eric Hicks	33	26	7	5.0	2.5	0	0	0	0	0.0	0	0	1
Jared Allen	31	29	2	9.0	4	0	0	0	0	0.0	0	0	0

Denver Broncos — 2004 Team Stats

OFFENSE

Scoring:	23.8 (9)
Yards per Game:	395.8 (5)
Pass Yards per Game:	249.9 (6)
Rush Yards per Game:	145.8 (4)
Sacks Allowed:	15 (3)
3rd Down Percentage:	37.9 (13)
Giveaways:	27 (21)

DEFENSE

Scoring:	19.0 (9)
Yards per Game:	278.7 (4)
Pass Yards per Game:	184.2 (6)
Rush Yards per Game:	94.5 (4)
Sacks:	38 (t14)
3rd Down Percentage:	31.1 (3)
Takeaways:	17 (t27)

Kansas City Chiefs — 2004 Team Stats

OFFENSE

Scoring:	30.2 2
Yards per Game:	418.4 1
Pass Yards per Game:	275.4 (4)
Rush Yards per Game:	143.1 (5)
Sacks Allowed:	32 (t9)
3rd Down Percentage:	47.2 (3)
Giveaways:	21 (t10)

DEFENSE

Scoring:	27.2 (29)
Yards per Game:	377.9 (31)
Pass Yards per Game:	263.3 (32)
Rush Yards per Game:	114.6 (12)
Sacks:	40 (t9)
3rd Down Percentage:	38.4 (20)
Takeaways:	18 (t25)

Oakland Raiders 2004

PASSING STATISTICS

PLAYER	CMP	ATT	YDS	CMP%	YDS/A	LNG	TD	TD%	INT	INT%	SACK	YDS	RAT
Kerry Collins	289	513	3495	56.3	6.81	63	21	4.1	20	3.9	25	144	74.8

RUSHING STATISTICS

PLAYER	ATT	YDS	AVG	LNG	TD	FUM	LST
Amos Zereoue	112	425	3.8	55	3	1	1
Tyrone Wheatley	85	327	3.8	60	4	0	0
Zack Crockett	49	232	4.7	47	2	0	0

RECEIVING STATISTICS

PLAYER	REC	YDS	AVG	LNG	TD	FUM	LST
Jerry Porter	64	998	15.6	52	9	2	2
Ronald Curry	50	679	13.6	63	6	1	0
Doug Gabriel	33	551	16.7	58	2	0	0
Doug Jolley	27	313	11.6	34	2	0	0

RETURN STATISTICS

PLAYER		KICKOFFS						PUNTS				
	ATT	YDS	FC	AVG	LNG	TD	ATT	YDS	FC	AVG	LNG	TD
Doug Gabriel	53	1140	0	21.5	64	0	2	7	2	3.5	7	0
Phillip Buchanon	0	0	0	0.0	0	0	21	121	7	5.8	18	0

KICKING STATISTICS

PLAYER	1-20	20-29	30-39	40-49	50+	TOT	PCT	AVG	LNG	XPM/A	PTS
Sebastian Janikowski	1/1	7/7	7/8	8/10	2/2	25/28	89.3	35.5	52	31/32	106

PUNTING STATISTICS

PLAYER	PUNTS	YDS	AVG	LNG	TB	TB%	IN20	IN20%	RET	YDS	AVG	NET
Shane Lechler	73	3409	46.7	67	14	19.2	22	30.1	35	413	11.8	41

DEFENSIVE STATISTICS

PLAYER	TACKLES					MISCELLANEOUS		INTERCEPTIONS					
	TOT	SOLO	AST	SACK	TLOSS	FF	BK	INT	YDS	AVG	LNG	TD	PD
Danny Clark	130	99	31	2.0	6.5	1	0	0	0	0.0	0	0	5
Ray Buchanan	87	65	22	0.0	0.5	1	0	1	27	27.0	27	0	6
Charles Woodson	74	60	14	2.5	0.5	2	0	1	25	25.0	25	0	9
Marques Anderson	72	55	17	0.0	2	1	0	1	23	23.0	23	0	2
Napoleon Harris	60	47	13	0.0	4	0	0	0	0	0.0	0	0	1
Phillip Buchanon	59	51	8	0.0	1.5	0	0	3	69	23.0	37	1	9
Bobby Hamilton	57	36	21	1.0	3.5	0	0	0	0	0.0	0	0	3
Tyler Brayton	45	36	9	2.5	0.5	0	0	1	24	24.0	24	0	7
Denard Walker	44	42	2	0.0	1	0	0	1	45	45.0	45	0	5
Warren Sapp	42	32	10	2.5	3.5	0	0	0	0	0.0	0	0	0

2004 Team Stats

OFFENSE

Scoring:	20.0 (18)
Yards per Game:	322.1 (17)
Pass Yards per Game:	241.1 (8)
Rush Yards per Game:	80.9 (32)
Sacks Allowed:	30 (6)
3rd Down Percentage:	35.3 (21)
Giveaways:	30 (t26)

DEFENSE

Scoring:	27.6 (31)
Yards per Game:	371.0 (30)
Pass Yards per Game:	245.3 (30)
Rush Yards per Game:	125.8 (22)
Sacks:	25 (31)
3rd Down Percentage:	47.4 (32)
Takeaways:	14 (t30)

San Diego Chargers 2004

PASSING STATISTICS

PLAYER	CMP	ATT	YDS	CMP%	YDS/A	LNG	TD	TD%	INT	INT%	SACK	YDS	RAT
Drew Brees	262	400	3159	65.5	7.90	79	27	6.8	7	1.8	18	131	104.8

RUSHING STATISTICS

PLAYER	ATT	YDS	AVG	LNG	TD	FUM	LST
LaDainian Tomlinson	339	1335	3.9	42	17	5	2
Jesse Chatman	65	392	6.0	52	3	1	0
Michael Turner	20	104	5.2	30	0	0	0

RECEIVING STATISTICS

PLAYER	REC	YDS	AVG	LNG	TD	FUM	LST
Antonio Gates	81	964	11.9	72	13	0	0
Eric Parker	47	690	14.7	79	4	1	1
LaDainian Tomlinson	53	441	8.3	74	1	1	0
Keenan McCardell	31	393	12.7	31	1	0	0

RETURN STATISTICS

PLAYER		KICKOFFS						PUNTS				
	ATT	YDS	FC	AVG	LNG	TD	ATT	YDS	FC	AVG	LNG	TD
Eric Parker	0	0	0	0.0	0	0	27	237	10	8.8	32	0
Drayton Florence	0	0	0	0.0	0	0	1	0	0	0.0	0	0

KICKING STATISTICS

PLAYER	1-20	20-29	30-39	40-49	50+	TOT	PCT	AVG	LNG	XPM/A	PTS
Nate Kaeding	1/1	9/11	2/2	5/6	3/5	20/25	80.0	34.0	53	54/55	114

PUNTING STATISTICS

PLAYER	PUNTS	YDS	AVG	LNG	TB	TB%	IN20	IN20%	RET	YDS	AVG	NET
Mike Scifres	69	2974	43.1	60	8	11.6	29	42.0	23	164	7.1	40.7

DEFENSIVE STATISTICS

PLAYER	TACKLES					MISCELLANEOUS		INTERCEPTIONS					
	TOT	SOLO	AST	SACK	TLOSS	FF	BK	INT	YDS	AVG	LNG	TD	PD
Donnie Edwards	151	106	45	1.0	2.5	2	0	5	49	9.8	30	1	14
Terrence Kiel	96	71	25	1.0	2	0	0	2	31	15.5	31	0	10
Randall Godfrey	87	70	17	2.0	6	3	0	0	0	0.0	0	0	3
Jerry Wilson	75	53	22	0.0	0	1	0	3	12	4.0	12	0	4
Steve Foley	65	48	17	10.0	3.5	5	0	2	4	2.0	4	0	12
Quentin Jammer	62	54	8	0.0	1	0	0	1	12	12.0	12	0	10
Ben Leber	58	47	11	2.0	2.5	0	0	0	0	0.0	0	0	1
Igor Olshansky	39	28	11	1.0	3	0	0	0	0	0.0	0	0	2
Sammy Davis	38	33	5	0.0	0	0	0	1	4	4.0	4	0	10
Stephen Cooper	33	25	8	0.0	2	0	0	0	0	0.0	0	0	2

2004 Team Stats

OFFENSE

Scoring:	27.9 (3)
Yards per Game:	347.0 (10)
Pass Yards per Game:	210.4 (16)
Rush Yards per Game:	136.6 (6)
Sacks Allowed:	20 (4)
3rd Down Percentage:	46.6 (4)
Giveaways:	15 (t3)

DEFENSE

Scoring:	19.6 (11)
Yards per Game:	335.0 (18)
Pass Yards per Game:	253.3 (31)
Rush Yards per Game:	81.7 (3)
Sacks:	???
3rd Down Percentage:	35.2 (10)
Takeaways:	28 (t10)

Denver Broncos

Predicted: 3rd ▪ 2004: 10-6 (2nd)

Players Added

DTE	Stephen Alexander	(Det)
DE	Courtney Brown	(Cle)
LB	Keith Burns	(TB)
OT	Anthony Clement	(Ari)
RB	Ron Dayne	(NYG)
DE	Ebenezer Ekuban	(Cle)
LB	Ian Gold	(LB)
DT	Michael Myers	(Cle)
WR	Jerry Rice	(Sea)
P	Todd Sauerbrun	(Car)
OL	Cameron Spikes	(Ari)
DT	Gerard Warren	(Cle)

Players Lost

p	John Baker	(Car)
RB	Reuben Droughns	(Cle)
DE	Reggie Hayward	(Jax)
RB	Garrison Hearst	
CB	Kelly Herndon	(Sea)
S	Kenoy Kennedy	(Det)
OG	Dan Neil	
LB	Donnie Spragan	(Mia)

Draft

2	(56)	Darrent Williams	CB	Oklahoma St.
3	(76)	Karl Paymah	CB	Washington St.
3	(97)	Domonique Foxworth	CB	Maryland
3	(101)	Maurice Clarett	RB	Ohio St.
6	(200)	Chris Myers	OG	Miami, Fla.
7	(239)	Paul Ernster	K	Northern Arizona

A subpar draft was low-lighted by the foolish selection of Clarett on the first day. Any running back can succeed in Denver's system, so the onus is on the former Buckeye. One can't help but wonder if his selection was more of an effort to disrupt the Raiders. Williams is the most gifted of the three corners, but he has character concerns. Paymah and Foxworth can both become nickel backs one day, but likely nothing more.

Head Coach: Mike Shanahan (11th year)
Offensive Coordinator: Gary Kubiak
Defensive Coordinator: Larry Coyer

Offense

QB:	Jake Plummer
RB:	Tatum Bell
FB:	Kyle Johnson
WR:	Rod Smith
WR:	Ashley Lelie
TE:	Jeb Putzier
LT:	Matt Lepsis
LG:	Ben Hamilton
C:	Tom Nalen*
RG:	Tyson Clabo
RT:	George Foster
QB:	Danny Kanell
RB:	Quentin Griffin
WR:	Darius Watts
TE:	Patrick Hape
OL:	Cooper Carlisle

Defense

LDE:	Trevor Pryce
NT:	Gerard Warren†
RDE:	Raylee Johnson
OLB:	DJ Williams
ILB:	Al Wilson*
ILB:	Terry Pierce
OLB:	Ian Gold†
CB:	Champ Bailey*
SS:	Nick Ferguson
FS:	John Lynch*
CB:	Lenny Walls
NB:	Darrent Williams‡
DL:	Raylee Johnson
LB:	Jason Sykes
K:	Jason Elam
P:	Todd Sauerbrun†

* Pro Bowler '04
† veteran acquisition
‡ rookie

Report Card

Quarterback	B–	Defensive Line	C	Coaching	B
Running Back	C+	Linebacker	A–	Special Teams	C–
Receiver/Tight End	B	Defensive Back	B–	Depth	B
Offensive Line	B+			Intangibles	C+

As the snow that caps the Rocky Mountains begins to melt down into the South Platte River, which runs through the city of Denver, Colorado, and just a short distance from Invesco Field, the annual hopes of taking that next step and maximizing potential begin to ooze into the Denver Broncos complex. Free agency is completed, the draft is over, and the season is fast approaching. With it comes new life for the blue and orange.

The Rocky Mountains are home to more than just piles of snow, volcanic remnants, and Coors beer; they are also home to the Broncos and all of their optimism. Each year the season begins with expectations a "mile high" for Mike Shanahan's team. But how can Shanahan keep convincing his troops that this is the year they will finally get over the wildcard hump? If the Broncos are Coors, then the Indianapolis Colts must surely be Budweiser, because they have completely annihilated their wild-horse counterparts in the playoffs two years in a row.

Denver begins the year with the same Elway-less offense that has been regularly productive for the past decade, but—perhaps showing the club's impatience—there is talk of installing more 3–4 schemes on defense for 2005. New defensive packages can be a good thing, but has this team done enough to make the world believe they are not just destined for another whipping in the first round of the playoffs?

Champ Bailey

Offense

No player knows more about the expectations in Denver than Broncos quarterback **Jake Plummer**. Plummer is approaching his third year with the franchise, and much to the dismay of Bronco fans, it is beginning to look more and more unlikely that he will magically transform himself into John Elway. However, in Shanahan's offense—which is coordinated by former quarterback **Gary Kubiak**—everything remains constant: Denver will always run the ball well, they will always have an effective front line, and they will always pass for large amounts of yardage. What many don't seem to understand is that the quarterback stays constant, as well. In other words, Plummer *isn't* changing. As much as everybody would love to believe that Plummer is still a young, raw kid who will learn from his mistakes when he throws interceptions (20 last year), that's just not the case. Plummer will turn 31 before the end of the season. He is what he is; there's no developing from here. *This is* Jake Plummer. The sooner fans can realize that, the better off everyone will be.

For Plummer to succeed, the Broncos need to find ways to put him in position to exploit his strengths. He has many strong qualities to offer an offense. After all, the Broncos were sixth in passing a year ago (249.9 yards per game), and Plummer threw for over 4,000 yards. With Plummer, Denver will try to move the pocket and allow him to use his mobility to make passes from outside the tackle box. He is at his best when he is able to move around. Of course, some of Plummer's improvising is what has led to the costly interceptions that have followed him throughout his entire career.

It is unreasonable to think that Plummer will not throw a horrendous pick from time to time (say, another left-handed special?), but it is not unreasonable to expect gifted receiving target **Ashley Lelie** to continue to elevate his game in 2005. Criticized throughout his young career for his inconsistency and tendency to drop the ball, the lanky 6'3" fourth-year target out of Hawaii finally started coming into his own last year. Relied on for his ability to stretch the field, Lelie caught 54 balls for 1,084 yards and seven scores. His 20.1 yards per catch was an astounding figure. This year, Denver will continue to use Lelie as their deep threat, but they wouldn't mind seeing his yards-per-catch numbers drop just a bit, if that would mean an increase in his total receptions. Fellow veteran receiver **Rod Smith**—who had another outstanding season last year, catching a team-high 79 passes for 1,144 yards—is now 35 years old. Although it is hard to argue that he is slowing down, science tells us that this is the year he becomes a No. 2 target. With this in mind, Lelie's improvements on shorter routes that require more physical toughness are vital to the ingress of the offense; last year Lelie caught just one pass in the red zone, an area where Denver, as a team, struggled.

The Broncos will not have to completely alter Lelie's style of play in 2005 because they were able to re-sign tight end **Jeb Putzier**. Putzier, who played wide receiver at Boise State, is entering his fourth season in the league, but his first as a starter. He made a strong showing in 2004, with 36 receptions.

Putzier will serve as the receiving force in the middle for the Broncos offense. Not since the days of Shannon Sharpe (pre-Ravens Shannon Sharpe, that is) have the Broncos had such a potentially dynamic pass-catching threat from the tight end position. While his footwork is still developing (he is often too slow in making his cuts and moving laterally), his knack for making the play is not. He averaged 15.9 yards per catch last season.

A weak aspect of Putzier's game has been his slow development as a blocker. Denver loves to set up their run-blocking by using their tight ends in a variety of ways—mainly lining them up in the backfield and going in motion. They have eighth-year veteran **Patrick Hape** for this, and they signed former Detroit Lion **Stephen Alexander** over the offseason. Alexander will be a nice addition to this offense, thanks to his passion for the game, his willingness to do whatever it takes to help his team win, and (listen up, Putzier) his effectiveness as a blocker. Another player who will get some time on the field is 290-pound **Dwayne Carswell**, who, as one might imagine, is primarily an extra blocking tight end.

Rounding out the passing game is **Darius Watts**, the No. 3 receiver. His is a name to remember; Watts is an electrifying player who possesses mind-boggling raw abilities. If he can become more consistent in getting open and catching the football in 2005, watch out.

Perhaps now the time is right to mention that living legend **Jerry Rice** signed a one-year deal late in the offseason to join the Broncos. Rice is now 43, but he is still more than capable of producing at the highest level. **Mike Shanahan** has stated that Rice will have to make the 53-man roster just like any other player, but that is nonsense. Shanahan (Rice's former offensive coordinator in San Francisco) did not sign the great Jerry Rice only to become the coach who cuts him in his farewell year. Rice will play as the No. 4, he'll get more snaps late in the year, and—Denver hopes—he'll teach the younger players a thing or two.

No matter who is catching passes or throwing them, the bread and butter of the Broncos offense is going to be the running game. The Broncos are coming off a typical season in which they started a fifth-string tailback for most of the year (Reuben Droughns) and still finished fourth in the league in rushing, at 145.8 yards per game. It's time to finally admit once and for all that any person capable of walking, even at a 10-year-old-Forrest-Gump level, can thrive in this Broncos offense.

The success on the ground is a result of the brilliant zone-blocking scheme implemented by offensive line coach Alex Gibbs in the mid-1990s. Gibbs is now working his magic in Atlanta, but Denver has **Rick Dennison**, who has been with the club since 1995 and is in his fourth year as the offensive line coach. Dennison has a nice core of players to work with, starting

Write it Down:

D.J. Williams's pure athleticism will be what keeps Denver's defense alive this year.

This Season vs. Last Season

Progression: **Passing attack**—Both Lelie and Putzier can rack up yards, and both should be more consistent in 2005.

Regression: **Front line pass-rush**—Bertrand Berry and his 11½ sacks left last season, and now Reggie Hayward and his 10½ sacks have also departed. Up front, Denver is either slow, injured, or old—or all three.

Anderson, **Ron Dayne**, and **Maurice Clarett**. For argument's sake, let's assume Dayne and Clarett will be too fat to contribute on a regular basis this year. Let's just focus on the other three.

Bell will be the starter on opening day. Unless he gets injured, it's very unlikely he'll have the job taken from him. Bell is a great fit for this scheme and was able to average 5.3 yards per carry in a substitute role late in the season last year. Griffin is a poor man's Barry Sanders, and can juke and jive his way past just about anybody. He must regain the favor of the Bronco coaches, though, by improving his hands in order to catch more passes and fumble fewer carries. Anderson is a team-first guy who can do duty at fullback and in short-yardage situations. He will likely back up starter **Kyle Johnson** at halfback and do spot work in games throughout the year.

with a pair of veterans in the middle: Center **Tom Nalen** and guard **Dan Neil**. Both players were around for the Super Bowl years in the late 1990s, and both know how to play the game. Nalen, who is 34, has not shown many signs of slowing down. He controls opponents with his crafty technique. Although Neil was cut for cap reasons early in the offseason, Neil will likely end up back with the team in '05, providing the same run-blocking dominance the team is accustomed to. Neil moves well and uses his hands extremely well; both he and Nalen get away with holding on every play. If for some reason Neil is not around, the Broncos will likely start 23-year-old **Tyson Clabo**. Clabo has great size (6'6", 314 pounds), but he must learn how to use it.

Next to Nalen on the right side of the front five is tackle **George Foster**, who is beginning his third year in the league and his second as a starter. Foster had a decent campaign last season, but he must improve his footwork in order to become more consistent in '05. He has massive strength and is the only Bronco lineman on the roster that the team drafted higher than the third round. Foster was selected twentieth overall in '03.

On the left side of the line is guard **Ben Hamilton**, who, at 283 pounds, lacks the strength to do more than merely survive in pass-blocking, but has the quickness to be a standout run-blocker. A lot of the agility that is required to effectively operate the zone-blocking scheme comes from the flexibility that Hamilton's quickness and particular technique in run-blocking supply. He opens holes and gets to the second level masterfully.

The best lineman up front is left tackle **Matt Lepsis**. Lepsis has the skills to play well anywhere on the offensive line. He has mediocre size (6'4", 290 pounds), but solid strength and a good strong base. Like his sidekick Hamilton, Lepsis offers a lot of flexibility in the run game. The Broncos also added a pair of former Cardinals to give them some depth. **Anthony Clement** will play second-string tackle and **Cameron Spikes** will work mainly as a backup guard.

The men who benefit the most from this front five are the runners. Droughns was traded to Cleveland (probably for a defensive lineman), but all in all, the Broncos have five names that people have heard of: **Tatum Bell**, **Quentin Griffin**, Mike

Defense

The Broncos had a fairly successful defense in 2004, at least on paper. They allowed only 19 points per game—ninth best in the NFL—and they were fourth in total yards given up, at 278.7 per contest. However, only a few numbers really tell the story from last year: 49—the number of points given up in the wildcard loss at Indy; 377—the number of passing yards in that game allowed to Peyton Manning . . . in the first half; 0—the number of championship rings this team will win if they continue in this fashion.

The Broncos decided in the offseason *not* to continue in this fashion. Responding to an inability to generate turnovers and big plays (only 17 takeaways a year ago), Denver is switching to more 3–4 schemes, which emphasize athleticism and allow for more variations.

In examining the Broncos depth and skill at the linebacker position, many wonder why they did not make such a move a year ago. They are two deep at every linebacker position. Nevertheless, one has to admire the change in philosophy this year, and when considering that **D.J. Williams** is entering his second season in the league, a person understands why it's smart to begin grooming the role for his career as soon as possible.

For the longest time, **Al Wilson** has been the leader of this defense. Let's not misconstrue anything here; Wilson still *is* the leader of this defense. But his reign as the brightest star in blue on this side of the ball will soon be over because it's only a matter of time before Williams becomes a fixture in the Pro Bowl. Williams, a second-year player out of the University of Miami, is as gifted as athletes come. Like Wilson—who is entering his seventh year in the league—Williams has tremendous speed. He has not quite developed the uncanny nose for the ball that Wilson possesses, and his intensity is only that of which a second-year player is capable, but the fact that a 23-year-old is even being compared to a veteran as good as Wilson says a lot.

This season, Wilson will man one of the inside linebacker positions, and Williams will play the outside (he was a weakside linebacker in Denver's 4–3 a year ago). Placed at the other outside linebacker slot will be **Ian Gold**. Gold began his NFL career as a Bronco, after being drafted by the team in the second round out of Michigan six years ago. But like so many in America today, he packed up his bags and moved to the sunny, carefree world of St. Petersburg, Florida. He did not retire to some Buena Vista complex, but rather resumed his playing career with the Buccaneers. The sunshine must be overrated because this past

Mike Shanahan hopes a new emphasis on a 3–4 defensive philosophy can finally help propel his team past the Wild Card round of the playoffs.

offseason Gold swallowed his pride and returned to a team that he likely thought he would never play for again. Now back with the Broncos, he provides the speed, and thus the playmaking capabilities, that every 3–4 defense needs somewhere in the box. At just 223 pounds, Gold does not have tremendous strength, but he is able to effectively take on blocks at the point of attack.

If Gold is going to become a leading playmaker in the Bronco's defense, he will have to improve his pass coverage. As it currently stands, Denver has a very good pass defender on the outside in Williams, but Gold is often nothing more than pyrite against the pass. What will likely happen is that Denver will substitute Gold in passing situations and bring in backup **Patrick Chukwurah**, or whoever else can rush the passer.

With **Donnie Spragan** now in Miami, the Broncos must find a second inside linebacker who can adequately line up with Wilson and stop the run. **Jashon Sykes** is a fourth-year player out of Colorado who has some experience, or there is also veteran backup **Keith Burns**. An intriguing player who had a productive season filling in for an injured John Mobley (who has since retired) in 2003 is **Terry Pierce**, but the fourth-year player missed most of last season with an MCL injury.

Perhaps the best part about the Broncos playing in more 3–4 defensive alignments this year is the fact that they will be putting one less defensive lineman on the field. The Broncos have added four new players up front: **Courtney Brown**, **Michael Myers**, **Gerard Warren**, and **Ebenezer Ekuban**. The funny side to this is that there was once a team that, as recently as a year ago, tried to win with this very same crop of players. They were called the Cleveland Browns, and they were terrible.

The Broncos did not mean to bring in four of Cleveland's defensive linemen—heck, nobody would ever do such a thing on *purpose*—but it's something that happened.

The key piece of this shoddy puzzle will be Warren, who at 325 pounds is being counted on as the new nose tackle. However, the only thing about him worth counting is the number of reasons why he can't be counted on. Warren is a great talent, who was the third-overall selection out of Florida in 2001. However, since entering the league, he has partied, gained weight, and avoided any activity that might accidentally improve his game. Every six or seven plays, he will use a great swim move or a powerful club to get in the backfield, but all in all, Warren is a lazy player who can pathetically be blocked one-on-one.

Denver didn't do much better with the other three Cleveland acquisitions. Brown has been an injury magnet since being the first-overall draft pick in 2000. Ekuban has improved his work ethic and gotten better as an all-around player, but he weighs just 275 pounds and has shown that he lacks the strength needed to anchor against the run, which is not good when playing up front on the outside in a 3–4. He could fill in as a backup pass-rushing end, but such a role is a small one in this defensive scheme. As for Myers . . . he's likely a nice guy, but watching him move is like watching frozen sap drip off an old pine tree. He can maybe help out as a backup defensive tackle.

The Broncos still have a slew of players they can refer to up front, but all of them come with an asterisk. **Trevor Pryce** believes his back has fully healed and thinks he is headed for a return to the Pro Bowl. Unfortunately, these thoughts resemble the lyrics to Mariah Carey's 1994 hit song "Fantasy," but if Pryce

can stay healthy, he does have good power to offer as an end. **Mario Fatafehi** is an active defensive tackle who is disruptive at times. He probably won't play nose tackle, but he *is* a possibility at end. One-time Lion **Luther Ellis** has good strength and is very adept in run support, but it is unlikely he can stay healthy for a full 16-game schedule. As alarming as it sounds, the Broncos may actually consider using a pair of 35-year-olds—**Marco Coleman** and **Raylee Johnson**, both of whom are under 275 pounds.

Fortunately for the Broncos, they have perhaps the best all-around cornerback in the league today: **Champ Bailey**. Bailey enjoyed a stellar first year with the team in 2004, picking off 3 passes, defensing 12, and recording 81 tackles. Being considered the best at his position does not take a whole lot of explanation; Bailey has great hips, agility, speed, and anticipation, plus he tackles well. He *can* be beaten deep if teams elect to go at him enough, but those teams also run the risk of turning the ball over because of it.

Many thought safety **John Lynch**—a former Buccaneer who is entering his 13th year in the league—was finished when he arrived in Denver. The rumors worsened when it became known that he would be playing the free safety position, a spot that requires more range and mobility in pass coverage. However, Lynch proved his doubters wrong, serving as a calm defender against the pass and an effective one-on-one tackler who gives great help in run support. One must expect similar results this year.

Denver all but needs Lynch to perform well in 2005 because penciled in as the starter at strong safety is the inexperienced **Nick Ferguson**. Fourth-year player **Sam Brandon** may push Ferguson. The Broncos lost cornerback Kelly Herndon to Seattle over the offseason. His subtraction doesn't hurt the starting lineup so much, because fourth-year player **Lenny Walls** has the long arms to go with his 6'4" frame and should be able to hold his own in man coverage. However, Walls's starting leaves a spot open at nickel back. It's safe to assume that Denver would rather see either of their three fast rookies (**Darrent Williams**, **Karl Paymah**, or **Domonique Foxworth**) start ahead of **Roc Alexander**, who was absolutely painted by Reggie Wayne in the play-offs last year.

Special Teams

3 5-year-old **Jason Elam** is one of the best kickers of his generation, but he has lost an awful lot of range. He now must sit out kickoffs and watch either backup kicker **Tyler Fredrickson** or the punter do duty. That punter happens to be **Todd Sauerbrun**, a former Panther who believes, as do many others, that he is the best in the game. The Broncos have lacked a decent return artist since the days of Glyn Milburn. They will pay again this year for their lack of explosion on runbacks.

The Bottom Line

It is not unreasonable to assume that the offense for the Broncos will be pretty good in 2005. The question, though, is this: With a defense that is transitioning to a 3–4 and that has some personnel issues rockier than the mountains surrounding the Mile High City, can Plummer and his group score enough points to win games on a consistent basis? Looking at the talent they have this year, compared to last year, the answer is no.

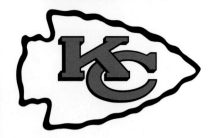

Kansas City Chiefs

Predicted: 1st ▪ 2004: 7-9 (3rd)

Players Added
LB	Kendrell Bell (Pit)
DE	Carlos Hall (Ten)
RB	Robert Holcombe (Ten)
S	Sammy Knight (Mia)
CB	Patrick Surtain (Mia)

Players Lost
LB	Monty Beisel (NE)
RB	Derrick Blaylock (NYJ)
HE	Vonnie Holiday (Mia)

Draft
1	(15)	Derrick Johnson	OLB	Texas
3	(99)	Dustin Colquitt	P	Tennessee
4	(116)	Craphonso Thorpe	WR	Florida St.
5	(138)	James Grigsby	ILB	Illinois St.
5	(147)	Alphonso Hodge	CB	Miami, Ohio
6	(187)	Will Svitek	OT	Stanford
6	(199)	Khari Long	DE	Baylor
7	(229)	James Kilian	QB	Tulsa
7	(238)	Jeremy Parquet	OT	Southern Mississippi

Johnson was a steal at No. 15; he has the natural ability to be an impact player immediately and a superstar down the road. However, he needs to increase his strength and learn to take on blocks. Thorpe can add some depth at the WR position, but his ability as a deep threat declined after he suffered a broken leg during his junior year. Colquitt went early, but generally punters and kickers taken early in the draft struggle to live up to expectations.

Head Coach: Dick Vermeil (5th year)
Offensive Coordinator: Al Saunders
Defensive Coordinator: Gunther Cunningham

Offense
QB:	Trent Green
RB:	Priest Holmes
FB:	Tony Richardson*
WR:	Eddie Kennison
WR:	Johnnie Morton
TE:	Tony Gonzalez*
LT:	Willie Roaf*
LG:	Brian Waters*
C:	Casey Wiegmann
RG:	Will Shields*
RT:	Jordan Black
QB:	Todd Collins
RB:	Larry Johnson
WR:	Dante Hall
TE:	Jason Dunn
OL:	John Welbourn

Defense
LDE:	Eric Hicks
DT:	Ryan Sims
DT:	Lionel Dalton
RDE:	Jared Allen
LOLB:	Scott Fujita
MLB:	Kendrell Bell[†]
ROLB:	Shawn Barber
CB:	Patrick Surtain[†]
SS:	Sammy Knight[†]
FS:	Jerome Woods
RCB:	Dexter McCleon
NB:	Eric Warfield
DL:	Carlos Hall[†]
LB:	Derrick Johnson[‡]
K:	Lawrence Tynes
P:	Dustin Colquitt[‡]

* Pro Bowler '04
[†] veteran acquisition
[‡] rookie

Report Card
Quarterback	B+	Defensive Line	B-	Coaching	B+
Running Back	A	Linebacker	B-	Special Teams	A
Receiver/Tight End	C+	Defensive Back	B-	Depth	A-
Offensive Line	A+			Intangibles	B

Perhaps the defense did not need just a simple schematic adjustment. After all, here we are in '05 with a Kansas City Chiefs team that is hoping to bounce back from a disappointing—and surprising—7–9 season. Heading into 2004, many believed Dick Vermeil and his explosive offense were just one good defensive coordinator away from the Super Bowl. As a result, the club brought back its onetime head coach Gunther Cunningham to manage the defense. When all was said and done, the offense had still done its part, ranking first in total yardage and second in scoring. But once again, the defense had entered the season as an unblemished cow and came out as a well-done Angus steak, ranking 31st in yards allowed and 29th in points given up.

This cause for concern became a cause for action this past offseason. The Chiefs took all of the railroads and freeways that lead into this town that borders Kansas where the Missouri River and Kaw River meet, and put them to good use. They loaded up a handful of new defensive players and shipped them in for the '05 season. In all, the Chiefs added five players who can contribute in meaningful roles right away. Perhaps that was it all along; perhaps the Chiefs just needed different players. At least it wasn't anything major, right?

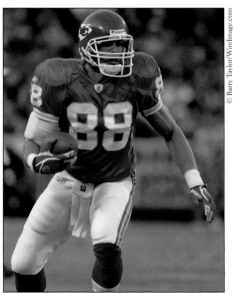

Tony Gonzalez

Offense

Many praise the offense that **Dick Vermeil** assembled in St. Louis (particularly the 1999 season) when his Rams team spread the field on their way to a Super Bowl title. However, what Vermeil's wide-open passing attack is doing these days in Kansas City might be even more impressive. The Chiefs were the oldest offense in the league last season, averaging around 30 years of age in their starting lineup. However, showing Strom Thurmond–like durability, they still ranked in the top five in passing, rushing, total first downs, and third-down success. This year, every starter is back and, according to God's laws, likely a year older, too.

Despite the grandfather factor creeping in, the Chiefs can still be expected to put up great numbers in '05, because **Al Saunders**'s offense will operate well as long as Kansas City's powerful front line is intact. The Chiefs return all of their starters up front, headed by three Pro Bowlers in left tackle **Willie Roaf**, left guard **Brian Waters**, and right guard **Will Shields**.

Despite turning 35 in April, the 6'5", 320-pound Roaf is still one of the premiere left tackles in the NFL. His ability to generate natural power from his notable bulk has made him an absolute bulldozer on run plays. Although he is not as agile as he once was, Roaf's familiarity with the game—combined with his solid lower-body foundation and long strides that allow him to cover a lot of ground with each step—make him almost as effective as he was during his days in New Orleans. It doesn't hurt that next to Roaf is the sixth-year veteran Waters, who is now being recognized as one of the best all-around interior linemen in the NFL. Waters has the upper-body strength to dismantle opponents in the ground game and easily handle his duties in pass-blocking. He has tremendous dexterity in open-field lead-blocking, as well.

Before training camp, there was speculation from the local Missouri media that Shields might retire, but such discussion is irrelevant at this point. Shields—who will be 34 in September—has started a club record 191 consecutive games and does not want to have his streak end now. Besides, why end when he is still getting great drive in run-blocking and playing at a Pro Bowl level?

Shields's greatest asset may be his character and awareness on the field, both of which will come in handy as the Chiefs try to integrate a young **Jordan Black** into the starting lineup as a right tackle in '05. Black is taking over at a position filled by **Chris Bober** and **John Welbourn** last year, both of whom are back for this season but playing second string at their more natural guard spots. Black, a fifth-round draft pick in 2003, has decent strength and shows respectable knowledge in using his hands and keeping defenders in front of him, but his inexperience will still make him the weak link up front.

The man who makes the entire front five operate so well is center **Casey Wiegmann**. The Chiefs rely heavily on the mobility of their offensive linemen to move the line and block downfield. Wiegmann sets the tone and leads these efforts from the center position.

The one person who has had his hands under Wiegmann's rear end more than anyone else in this world is quarterback **Trent Green**. Green is coming off a season in which he had a quarterback rating of 95.2 and ranked fourth in the league at 8.3 yards per pass attempt. As long as Green is protected in the pocket, he can read a defense and pick teams apart. However, Green's 35 years of age may begin to show this season; last year,

Write it Down:

Running back Larry Johnson will replace Priest Holmes by the start of next season, if not sooner.

Strengths

Offensive Line

The success on offense has been largely because of the stability and dominance of the front five.

Return Game

As long as Dante Hall is around, this will be a huge advantage for the Chiefs. They can either threaten a touchdown on every punt and kick return, or they can assure themselves of good field position.

Weaknesses

Defensive Blend

Kansas City must adjust to having five new contributors on defense and, most challenging of all, making the players from last year believe that the offseason changes are the ticket to a turnaround.

Health

On offense there are concerns about Priest Holmes's durability, and there are a slew of receivers returning from major surgery. Defensively, both middle linebackers (Kendrell Bell and Mike Maslowski) have attracted the injury bug in recent years, plus linebacker Shawn Barber is still not healthy after an ACL tear in 2004.

his inability late in games to rely on his natural skills really hurt the team.

A person could make the argument that tight end **Tony Gonzalez** is the No. 1 reason Kansas City's offense has generated so much production over the past four years. In fact, that person would probably win the argument. The athletic 6'5" Gonzalez remains the best tight end in the game today. He is even coming off a career year in which he became the first tight end since Shannon Sharpe in '93 to lead the league in receptions, with 102. Gonzalez has outstanding range and a great presence for playing in the middle of the field. His ability to play between the hash marks is what opens things up for the team's mediocre receivers.

Perhaps the word *mediocre* is unjust in describing **Eddie Kennison**. After all, the man is coming off of his first career 1,000-yard season, in which he led the team with eight touchdown receptions. However, in terms of being a No. 1 option, Kennison is only mediocre. He has great speed and can stretch the field by getting behind a defense, but his skills are somewhat limited beyond that, making him a better fit as a second option on the outside.

The other starter for the Chiefs is **Johnnie Morton**. Since his early days with Detroit, Morton has been a stellar target in the NFL, but lately he has been making far too many mistakes at inopportune moments. When this happens, Morton's "patience" starts getting called "slowness." His tendency to drop balls in traffic transforms his "courage to at least go over the middle" to a "lack of focus," and he gets remembered not so much as the guy who once jokingly told Jay Leno to "kiss his ass," but as the guy who got accused of cheating the game in the BALCO steroids scandal.

The Chiefs would love to find a third receiver who could make defenses pay for collapsing on Gonzalez, but such a threat from the slot has been hard to come by. **Dante Hall** does not have the hands to be much more than a return man, **Chris Horn** plays hard but lacks the raw skill needed to thrive, and both **Marc Boerigter** and **Sammie Parker** are coming back from devastating knee injuries suffered a year ago.

Speaking of injury, the focus must shift to Chiefs running back **Priest Holmes**. Holmes has been a touchdown machine for the past three years (69 total), but the machine is beginning to malfunction ever so slightly. A hip injury prematurely ended his

Progression: **Firepower**—Although the Chiefs will once again be good on offense, they will also be a year older and a year slower.

Regression: **Secondary**—Adding Patrick Surtain and Sammy Knight will help shore up last season's elementary unit.

season in '02, and just last year Holmes missed half of his team's games because of a knee problem. When healthy, the shifty and versatile Holmes can be the most statistically productive back in the game, but one must wonder if he *can* stay healthy for a full year. The chances of him playing 16 games *are* better than one might think; Holmes will be 32 in October (an age that most running backs never last long enough to see), but he spent a majority of his college career backing up Ricky Williams at the University of Texas. Once he got to the professional ranks, Holmes spent two of his first three seasons playing behind Jamal Lewis in Baltimore. In other words, Holmes has not taken as many hits as, say, a 33-year-old Jerome Bettis.

Look for the Chiefs to tone down the workload on Holmes this year, if not to protect his health then to get third-year runner **Larry Johnson** on the field more often. Johnson has had his spats with Vermeil, but last year he proved he deserves more opportunities after gaining 452 yards and scoring seven touchdowns as the starter during the month of December. In fact, don't be surprised if talks of Johnson replacing Holmes start surfacing this season.

Two men who are unheralded figures in Kansas City's offense are fullback **Tony Richardson** and backup tight end **Jason Dunn**. Richardson is a Pro Bowler who does an outstanding job providing the lead-blocking services for this team. Dunn is used primarily as a blocking tight end—especially as an extra pass-blocker, a job he excels at—and his role on the team really helps the offense establish its vast array of dimensions.

Defense

As for that Chiefs defense, well, the key in '05 will be successfully integrating the new faces added during the offseason. The city that calls itself "the Heartland of America" (because of its ideal location in the central states) has a flourishing agricultural economy because a wide variety of products are shipped to and from the area. The Chiefs are merely taking the concept that their town has created and applying it to their defense. They chose to ship in new products. Up front, they attempted to improve a run-defense that was decent, but certainly not great, a year ago. They traded a fifth-round pick to Tennessee for lineman **Carlos Hall**, they signed former Steelers linebacker **Kendrell Bell** (*see* Painting a New Picture, page 7) and they used the No. 15 overall draft pick to select Texas linebacker **Derrick Johnson**.

That said, the additions of a pair of Dolphins in the secondary will be the most crucial to Kansas City's improvement in '05. The Chiefs ranked dead last against the pass last year, giving up a pitiful 263.3 yards per game and an even more shameful 8.53 yards per attempt. To improve these numbers, Kansas City signed veteran strong safety **Sammy Knight** and traded a pair of draft picks for cornerback **Patrick Surtain** (*see* Painting a New Picture, page 6). The addition of Surtain will be huge for them, because his potential to occasionally provide shutdown skills will only broaden the scope of what other defensive backs on the team are able to do. However, it might be the addition of Knight that makes the greatest difference.

Knight brings something that nobody else in the Kansas City defensive backfield offers: A willingness to reach for a big play. Knight is a cruel hitter who goes for the kill and throws his body into players. Plus, he will always look for ways to strip a player of the ball. Once more, Knight is also great at playing the deep pass—which is something that Kansas City's other safeties (**Jerome Woods**, **Shaunard Harts**, and **Greg Wesley**) have seriously struggled to do over the past two seasons. Knight's skills have led to 35 interceptions over his previous eight years in the league.

Woods will be the one who joins Knight in the backfield this year, although he has not done much to prove that he deserves this job. Woods's backup, Wesley, has the pass coverage skills to play free safety, but his sloppy habits make him far too prone to penalties. Harts, a fourth-year pro out of Boise State, was re-signed to a new contract over the offseason and appears ready to start in the very near future. The only problem is that his biggest asset is his hitting. His style of play really makes him an extra linebacker; as he becomes more effective the closer he is to the line of scrimmage. But playing in the box is Knight's role, meaning Harts will once again have to come off the bench to contribute. He lacks the pass coverage skills to play free safety in the NFL.

Backup cornerback **William Bartee** is also moving to safety this year, a position that he played in college. The Chiefs are hoping that Bartee can increase his number of big plays in this role—the team is looking to improve upon their shabby interception total (11) from a year ago. It should be noted that Warfield may be facing a suspension from the league, due to pleading no contest to his third DUI this past January. He was on house arrest throughout most of May.

Defensive coordinator **Gunther Cunningham** would like his cornerbacks to be physical enough to handle man coverage. However, outside of Surtain, no Chiefs corner has proven capable of such duties. The starter opposite Surtain is **Dexter McCleon**, who is more fit for the nickel role and will likely struggle now that he will see more passes thrown his way in 2005. McCleon is at his best when he's physical, but he doesn't have the strength to be consistent with this style of play.

Many believe that **Eric Warfield**—who is listed as the nickel back—is the best returning corner from a year ago. However,

© Wesley Hitt/WireImage.com

Veteran guard Will Shields is one of the cogs on the best offensive line in football.

such notions are simply false; Warfield is like an 18th-century Quaker in his refusal to get physical, and he attracts as many flags as a United Nations meeting. Plus, he gets burned deep a lot. However, with Bartee returning to safety, the nickel back duties will fall into Warfield's lap.

One way to cause more turnovers is to boost the pass rush up front. This year, Kansas City will start **Jared Allen**, who, as a fourth-round rookie out of Idaho State last year, led the team with nine sacks. Allen will make the transition from a situational pass-rusher to starter just fine. He is still learning how to read offenses, but he knows how to beat one-on-one blocking, he finishes plays well, and, best of all, he just has a *feel* for playing football and getting in an opponent's backfield.

Eric Hicks will start on the left side at defensive end. Hicks is a discerning team leader in the locker room. On the field, he can play both the run and the pass. He won't bring a lot of energy to the table (Hicks plays a somewhat reticent style of football), but he gets off the snap well and knows how to be productive. The Chiefs probably wouldn't mind seeing him increase his total of five sacks from a year ago, something he is capable of.

One of the more interesting figures to watch this season will be defensive tackle **Ryan Sims**. Since being drafted sixth overall out of North Carolina in '02, Sims has been nothing short of a disappointment. However, unlike other letdown tackles (hmmm . . . Gerard Warren, anyone?), Sims's struggles have not been related to a lack of effort or focus. He still has an explosive first step, he operates low to the ground, and he sees plays unfold. Sims plays with the effort and change-of-direction skills to stop the run, but he has a surprising shortage of power in his 315-pound frame.

Next to Sims will be **Lionel Dalton**, a player one scout has said "leads the league in second chances." Dalton's second chance with the Chiefs is now heading into its second year. He is never going to be anything more than average, and one of the main reasons why is his tendency to do what is asked of him and *only* what is asked of him.

Kansas City enjoys solid depth in their front four. They have Hall, who is agile enough to reach the quarterback or make plays against the run from the end position. They also have another end in **Jimmy Wilkerson**, who has potential as a pass rusher, but must learn to play with better discipline. In the middle is **John Browning**, a man searching for an identity after being bounced around the defensive line, from the inside to the outside, the past couple of years. Nobody knows where to play him; the truth is nobody will *ever* know where to play him. There is also **Junior Siavii**, who was a second-round pick in '04, but missed most of the season with an ankle injury.

Kansas City has not been terrible against the run over the past few seasons, but that could be in large part because teams are so anxious to pass against them. Nevertheless, bringing in Bell to add strength and force up the middle was a smart move. Not to mention that it gave the Chiefs a reason to put oft-injured **Mike Maslowski** on the bench, along with his lazy companion **Kawika Mitchell**. Maslowski, in fact, could be forced to end his playing days and might end up on the Kansas City coaching staff in the very near future.

Flanking Bell on his left side will be **Scott Fujita**, a player who should excel now that he has more talent around him. Fujita is one of those guys who always appear on the television screen and around the action. He is good at spotting the ball and recognizing what direction a play is going and his 4½ sacks last season are a testament to his sturdy pass-rushing skills.

Shawn Barber is scheduled to start at the right outside linebacker slot, but he has been slow to recover from a knee injury that ended his season last year and left him on the shelf for most of this year's training camp. Don't be surprised to see the rookie Johnson snag this job before the season becomes too old. Johnson has unbelievable raw talent, mainly in the name of speed. He has the potential to be a superstar in the NFL, and playing beside the girth of Bell, he should be able to operate in more space and avoid having to take on blockers.

If Johnson isn't ready to go, Bell spent a lot of time working at this spot during minicamps, so he may be the choice to play here.

Special Teams

Dante Hall is still the most dangerous return artist in the league today. Teams are afraid to kick to him (the Chiefs returned a league-low 34 punts last year), which gives the offense great field position. Kicker **Lawrence Tynes** has terrific range but was able to make only 17/23 kicks last season. The Chiefs drafted punter **Dustin Colquitt** in the third round this year. It's his job to lose from here on out.

The Bottom Line

It is not unrealistic in the least bit to think the Chiefs can bounce back and win the AFC West in 2005. They have an offense that has been so efficient over the years, even a step or two back would still leave them in pretty good shape. Be that as it may, the key to this team's success is still going to be the defense. They have added better starters, gotten healthy, and improved their depth. With this in mind, the noise that will flow out of Arrowhead stadium, across Interstate 70, and throughout the rest of the league should consist of less booing and more cheering.

Oakland Raiders

Predicted: 4th ▪ 2004: 5-11 (4th)

Draft

1	(23)	Fabian Washington	CB	Nebraska
2	(38)	Stanford Routt	CB	Houston
3	(69)	Andrew Walter	QB	Arizona St.
3	(78)	Kirk Morrison	ILB	San Diego St.
6	(175)	Anttaj Hawthorne	DT	Wisconsin
6	(212)	Ryan Riddle	DE	California
6	(214)	Pete McMahon	OT	Iowa

The Raiders are really pressing the cornerback issue: Two years ago they drafted Nnamdi Asomugha in the first round; this year they traded up to get Washington, who has the speed to quickly adjust to the NFL and maybe even start right away. They traded away Phillip Buchanon for the picks that became Routt and Morrison; neither will contribute right away. Walter will be the No. 3 quarterback this year. Hawthorne was a first-round prospect who fell hard because of inconsistent effort and a positive drug test for marijuana.

There are certain things that just let everyone know that the world is okay, that the good old times are still alive—like when Russia and the United States are competing, when the New York Yankees are winning, or when Walter Matthau and Jack Lemmon were making movies together. Another of these is when the Oakland Raiders are considered to be the "bad boys" of the NFL.

Such a day has returned to the Black Hole. The Raiders sailed the high seas of the NFL this past offseason, plundering and pillaging teams for free agents, draft prospects, and probably even a few cheerleaders on the side. By the time all the ships had stopped burning or sinking, the Raiders stood with a collection of booty worthy of a hip-hop music video.

Oakland traded for Minnesota's controversial receiver Randy Moss, signed hard-nosed runner LaMont Jordan, and drafted defensive tackle Anttaj Hawthorne, who tested positive for marijuana at the combine. Add these to players who were already present, such as Warren Sapp and second-year safety Stuart Schweigert (who found trouble a time or two while at Purdue), and not to forget Charles Woodson and Marques Anderson, both of whom embarrassed the team with their arrests for public drunkenness last December. Of course, a question—and it is an important topic of concern—must be posed: Does Al Davis know what he is doing in mixing the questionable characters on this team, or are these pirates of the AFC going too far? At what point

Head Coach: Norv Turner (2nd season)
Offensive Coordinator: Jimmy Raye
Defensive Coordinator: Rob Ryan

Offense

QB:	Kerry Collins
RB:	LaMont Jordan†
FB:	Zack Crockett
WR:	Randy Moss†
WR:	Jerry Porter
TE:	Teyo Johnson
LT:	Barry Sims
LG:	Langston Walker
C:	Jake Grove
RG:	Brad Badger
RT:	Robert Gallery
QB:	Marques Tuiasosopo
RB:	Justin Fargas
WR:	Ronald Curry
TE:	Courtney Alexander
OL:	Ron Stone

Defense

LDE:	Derrick Burgess†
DT:	Warren Sapp
NT:	Ted Washington
HE:	Tyler Brayton
SLB:	Sam Williams
MLB:	Danny Clark
WLB:	Travian Smith
CB:	Charles Woodson
SS:	Derrick Gibson
FS:	Stuart Schweigert
CB:	Nnamdi Asomugha
NB:	Fabian Washington‡
DL:	Bobby Hamilton
LB:	DeLawrence Grant
K:	Sebastian Janikowski
P:	Shane Lechler

* Pro Bowler '04
† veteran acquisition
‡ rookie

Report Card

Quarterback	C+	Defensive Line	C+	Coaching	C–
Running Back	C+	Linebacker	C–	Special Teams	B
Receiver/Tight End	A	Defensive Back	C+	Depth	C+
Offensive Line	B			Intangibles	D–

Charles Woodson

does a "bad boy" become a "bad guy"? Will the revamped Raiders be a more energized team in 2005, or are they just destined to watch their ship sink deeper?

Offense

If it wasn't already clear, the Raiders will have a much different look on offense in '05. Basically, what will be seen are 10 players doing their thing near the line of scrimmage and one player repeatedly running fly patterns 40 yards downfield. That one player will be newly acquired receiver **Randy Moss** (*see* Painting a New Picture, page 6), who was the biggest name to change uniforms this past offseason.

It is obvious what Moss brings to Oakland and their offense; he can stretch the field better than anyone in the NFL and he commands attention from defenses in a way that perhaps only Atlanta's Michael Vick can match. But with Moss, it's more fun to carp about who he is as a person rather than what he is as a football player. Oakland is the perfect fit for Moss—not because the organization understands him and can "relate" to persons of his ilk, but because he can do whatever the hell he wants and get away with it. It will be a lot like a Donald Trump marriage: There's lots of money and high publicity, but inevitable turmoil behind the scenes. And it will end like a Trump marriage: It will take some time, but ultimately go nowhere.

For anyone who likes to believe that human beings are capable of growing and prospering if given a chance, first take in a production of *Waiting for Godot*, then watch the Raiders this year. Moss isn't going to "grow"; he isn't going to "mature." This is his eighth year in the league and people are still talking about his behavior. He will attract attention and get his team nationally televised games in prime time, but the Raiders are not going to win with this guy. Nobody will. His selfishness and lack of heart are too much to overcome. After all, for the past several years, Moss was surrounded by more talent in Minnesota than he is now in Oakland, and where did the Vikings wind up in the end?

Of course, Moss is still a good player who will provide great statistical production. The beneficiaries of this will be quarterback **Kerry Collins** and the supporting cast of receivers in silver and black.

Although the team drafted Arizona State's **Andrew Walter** in the third round this year and is still carrying 26-year-old backup **Marques Tuiasosopo** on the roster (veteran **Rich Gannon** is expected to retire), Collins appears to be **Norv Turner**'s man for the short-term future. Collins is not among the better half of quarterbacks in the NFL and isn't likely to single-handedly win any games, but he does have the right skills to succeed in this offense. Coordinator **Jimmy Raye** is going to spread the field, allow Moss to attract defenders, and let Collins use his strong arm to attack defenses. Last year Collins attempted 84 passes that were 21 yards or more downfield (17 of them were 41 yards or more); this year the Raiders may double those figures.

While Collins is executing three- and five-step drops in the pocket, other receivers such as **Jerry Porter** and **Ronald Curry** will be working against one-on-one coverage, trying to get open. Expect both to succeed at this. Porter is like the Danny DeVito of the NFL: He's very talented and does a lot of good things, but he will never be known as a leading man. Early in his career, he came off the bench behind a pair of legends in Tim Brown and Jerry Rice. Last year, he fell just two yards shy of 1,000 on the season, but Oakland's pitiful record kept him out of the spotlight. Now he starts the season as a No. 2 target, thanks to the arrival of

Moss. Don't expect the athletic speedster to complain much; in this offense Porter can still have 80 catches for 1,200 yards. Curry—entering his third season in the league—is perhaps the best pure athlete in the NFL. He was a starting small forward on the North Carolina basketball team in college and he was also the Tarheels quarterback. As a slot receiver, Curry has the opportunity to create mismatches against lesser athletic competition, and he can beat teams in a variety of ways. However, he is still learning the position, and while catching 50 passes for six scores in 2004, Curry appeared poised for a breakout season in 2005—until he tore his Achilles tendon in December. The injury can be devastating to a player, so Curry may begin the season behind the eight ball.

Another player who has the skills to break out is tight end **Teyo Johnson**, who managed to crawl out from under the gobs of tight ends that continually kept him buried in the depth chart for the first two years of his career. Now that he's emerged to see the light of day as a starter, Johnson can show off his 6'6", 260-pound frame, solid footwork, and general receiving abilities. There are concerns about his attitude, but, hey, Randy Moss is around, so no worries.

For everything that Moss will bring to the passing game, it might be easy to overlook the contribution that newly acquired running back **LaMont Jordan** will make to the ground game. Oakland ranked dead last in running the football in 2004, gaining just 80.9 yards per outing. With players like Tyrone Wheatley and Amos Zereoue in the backfield, Turner lost confidence in the run (a very un-Turner-like reaction), and the Raiders rushed the ball a league-low 328 times.

Both Wheatley and Zereoue are gone now. Jordan gives the Raiders a go-to guy on the ground in 2005. As Curtis Martin's backup in New York for four years, he showed tremendous strength and power at the point of attack, making him a potential 25-carries-a-game guy. Of course, Jordan likely won't get more than 18 or 19 attempts a game, but if he can handle the workload for a full season and make good use of his burst in timing his runs, he can be a 1,000-yard back. The Raiders will continue to defer to **Zack Crockett** for their fullback duties.

J.R. Redmond will replace the 230-pound Jordan in passing situations. The regular backup is the speedy **Justin Fargas**, who still must improve his awareness and receiving skills to thrive in this role. As it stands right now, Fargas is best known for being the son of Antonio Fargas, who played Huggy Bear on the 1970s television series *Starsky & Hutch*.

Write it Down:

Randy Moss is a great talent, but a poor football player. He is far from a winner, which the Raiders will find out before all is said and done.

This Season vs. Last Season

Progression: **Offense**—The entire unit took a step forward with the additions of Randy Moss and LaMont Jordan, along with the development of Robert Gallery and Jake Grove up front.

Regression: **Character**—Contrary to what people might say, character *is* a big component in the NFL and it *is* very critical to a team's success. The Raiders are drastically lacking in this department.

The Raiders offensive line has finally managed to get younger after three years of featuring a crop of players that resembled a Shoney's early-bird breakfast buffet crowd. The youth begins with a pair of second-year players in right tackle **Robert Gallery** and center **Jake Grove**.

Gallery—the second-overall draft pick out of Iowa last year—had a decent rookie season. He was not able to make the transition to the left side of the line like many assumed he would, but he was certainly adequate on the right. Gallery is a 6'7", 325-pound giant who has great natural quickness, good knee bend, and the strength to regularly put defenders on the ground. Best of all is that he is not only talented, but also a coachable player who is willing to learn.

Grove was a less heralded fourth-round pick last year who showed promise in starting eight games at guard. He has a nice feel for using his hands and getting out of his stance. He should continue to develop into a bang-up starter. One nice accessory to Groves's game is his ability to play anywhere in the interior front line.

Groves is replacing veteran **Adam Treu**, who will return to his traditional backup role in '05. (If it helps, Treu gets to be the designated long-snapper for this team in '05.) Groves's moving to the middle frees up one of the guard positions, which the Raiders will fill with fourth-year player **Langston Walker**. Walker has great size (6'8", 345 pounds), but he has started only 11 of the 48 games in his career. Walker has the tools to work with, but he must develop better technique.

Once minicamp opened up, the Raiders decided they wanted to refurbish the interior offensive line altogether. Utility lineman **Brad Badger** will start at right guard, replacing 12th-year veteran **Ron Stone**. Badger has limited skills but a broad range of experience. Stone played in just four games a year ago. He has outstanding power and the ability to dominate an opponent, but he doesn't consistently give a full effort. Essentially, what the Raiders are attempting to do here is become quicker on the offensive line,

Robert Gallery, last year's No. 2 overall draft pick, will likely be promoted to the left tackle position before this season is over—regardless of what the Raiders are saying right now.

in order to generate more movement up front.

Barry Sims rounds out the front five, starting at left tackle. In all likelihood, Sims will switch spots with Gallery before the season is over. The Raiders want to get their prized lineman, Gallery, at the prized position, and Sims's strength and ability to lock into defenders, coupled with his mediocre quickness, make him a natural fit on the right side anyway. However, the Raiders have been dogged in claiming that they have no intentions of moving Gallery over to the left side anytime soon.

Defense

Rob Ryan—son of notorious coach Buddy Ryan—took over the Raiders defense before last season and installed a unique array of schemes that covered both the 4–3 and the 3–4 variety. The experiment failed miserably; Oakland finished 31st in points allowed and 30th in yards given up. The Raiders are giving Ryan one more crack at it in '05, to see if maybe he can't right this ship.

However, it still remains to be seen whether Oakland will return to a more conventional 4–3 setup in '05. They list their depth chart with four defensive linemen and three linebackers, but this is also misleading because they will use three hybrid ends in **Derrick Burgess**, **Tyler Brayton**, and **Akbar Gbaja-Biamila**. Not to mention that big **Ted Washington** is still around, indicating that the nose tackle positions will likely be a necessary spot to fill (a tip-off that a 3–4 is in the plans).

The Raiders have the right type of players to operate in a 3–4. Burgess is a guy they signed over from Philadelphia in the offseason. He plays much lighter than his 266 pounds suggest and, in reality, possesses the skills of an outside linebacker. He is adept at playing in space and can be effective dropping into zone coverage. Last season, in the NFC Championship game, he was the key to Philadelphia's containing Michael Vick, because of his pass-rushing skills and, even more so, his discipline in backside containment.

Brayton is a player that is loved by some and lightly regarded by others. In just his third year out of Colorado, the 6'6", 280-pounder may actually be the key to Oakland's defensive front seven. Brayton is asked to do a whole list of things in this system, serving as something of a joker lineman. Besides lining up and playing his natural position, on occasion Brayton will work out of a two-point stance at linebacker. He'll cover keynote areas of the field in zone and he even does some work in man-to-man pass coverage. The reality is that Oakland is asking the man to play beyond himself, but when considering how young he is, Brayton does a fantastic job. Although he can be easy to block, he possesses good speed and acceleration, a brain for the game, and a motor that runs clear up until the whistle.

Burgess or Brayton may share part of their playing time with Gbaja-Biamila—just because the fourth-year pro has far too much speed to be left on the bench—but chances are that their breathers will come when opponents are in running situations. This is when veteran **Bobby Hamilton** is most effective. Of all the Raider linemen, Hamilton has the best grasp on his responsibilities in the system. He no longer has elite speed or explosion, but he takes on blocks well and is good in containment.

The captain of this front line is still Washington, simply because he weighs enough that it would make sense for him to travel to games by freight car. At 37 years of age, he can still attract double teams on a regular basis. The Raiders were expecting **Warren Sapp** to add more productivity to their pirate crew, but Sapp has really become more like the obnoxious squawking parrot on Long John Silver's shoulder. He can still be effective at times, but the bottom line is that Sapp's production drastically decreased in '04. This year, Oakland may use former Saint **Kenny Smith** or sixth-round draft pick **Anttaj Hawthorne** more often than Sapp would like. Hawthorne must stay drug-free and learn to play harder, though.

If the Raiders do indeed opt for the 3–4 often in '05, they'll have to rely heavily on their hybrid ends, because they do not have enough impact players at the linebacker position. Oakland, however, *does* have enough players to fit into a 4–3, beginning with middle linebacker **Danny Clark**. Clark led the team with 130 tackles a year ago. He is a stellar force who began his career as an unsung player in Jacksonville. As a Raider, Clark has made a living by dominating the middle of the field and making plays against the interior run. He is aggressive and willing to attack a pile.

A player Oakland would love to get on the field is rookie **Kirk Morrison**—who attended Bishop O'Dowd High School in Oakland and grew up in a family of die-hard Raiders fans. Morrison's dream to play in front of his fellow Silver and Black fans came true when the team selected him in the third round out of San Diego State. He does not have tremendous physical tools, but he has the smarts and toughness to be an NFL starter.

Morrison could start on the inside in 3–4, but if the team decides to go with more 4–3 alignments, it will be tough to find ways to get him in the starting lineup because neither he nor Clark really has the skills to play anywhere other than the middle.

The Raiders lack players who can fill the starting outside linebacker spots. Weakside starter **Travian Smith** is really more of a backup; he started just four games last year. Strongside starter **Sam Williams** is still developing (he is in his third season out of Fresno State), and although he has a nice football body and an okay feel for tackling, he is still too slow in reading and reacting to plays, and he is too methodical around the ball.

The Raiders will try to get something out of backup **DeLawrence Grant** (especially when they realize that Williams does not have any standout skills to offer), but it's almost no use. Grant does not have good presence as a tackler and he doesn't know how to take advantage of playmaking opportunities. He does a good job of using his hands to fight blocks, but often he allows himself to be in a position to get blocked in the first place.

The Raiders have taken the NFL's emphasis on illegal contact rules to heart, drafting a pair of cover corner rookies in rounds one and two. **Fabian Washington**, out of Nebraska, and **Stanford Routt**, out of Houston, each ran a 4.29 at the combine, one of the fastest times recorded over the past four years. Both have the skills to compete right away and eventually start, but Oakland will use them in nickel-and-dime packages for now.

The Raiders still have **Charles Woodson** and former first-round pick **Nnamdi Asomugha** (pronounced xqfn-d-jen-wam-cklq-zie-lgkd-x-tie-jqn-ieg). Woodson may have pulled off the greatest shocker in NFL offseason history when he signed his franchise player contract. Oakland was having trouble with their salary cap and decided to designate Woodson as their franchise player in order to buy themselves some time. Woodson—who has been hit with the tag before—was seeking a long-term deal or a

trade, and the Raiders figured he would be unhappy with the franchise tag and hold out. Instead, Woodson jumped all over an opportunity to get a guaranteed $10.5 million for just this year's work, so he signed the deal. The flabbergasted Raiders flew more than $15 million over the salary cap, which forces them to make several undesirable roster moves. They are now stuck with a lame-duck player for one more year. Oops.

There were some rumors about Woodson possibly switching to free safety this season, and yes, Ryan approached him about the idea. However, it did not go over well with Woodson, so such plans are likely still a few years away. Don't believe people who say that Woodson is overrated. He might be a little overhyped, but the bottom line is that he can cover anyone in the NFL man-to-man.

If the Raiders wanted to clear cap space, they should have continued to find a way to relocate Woodson, rather than trade cornerback Phillip Buchanon and his $800,000 contract to the Texans. The Raiders were concerned because Buchanon was not happy in silver and black, but since when has Woodson ever been pleased?

Oakland has good depth at the cornerback position. **Renaldo Hill**, a free agent from Arizona, is very physical and will be effective if he can get on the field, plus veteran **Denard Walker** is good at limiting a receiver's separation.

The starting safeties for the Raiders will be second-year man **Stuart Schweigert** and fifth-year man **Derrick Gibson**. Schweigert will play free safety. He is a physical player with decent run/pass recognition skills and an aptitude for getting near the ball. He still needs an entire season of full-time duty before he can begin to truly approach his potential, though.

Gibson missed virtually all of last year with a shoulder injury. He is a gifted player who packs a mean punch, but it remains to be seen how he'll bounce back. He is somewhat lucky that his backup, **Marques Anderson,** isn't more mature, because if he were, he would definitely supplant him as the starter.

Special Teams

Kicker **Sebastian Janikowski** remains one of the most powerful legs in the game. He has also become more consistent. **Shane Lechler** might be the league's most powerful punter, as well. Last year Lechler averaged a league-best 46.7 yards per boot. He could, however, do a better job of pinning the ball inside the 20-yard line. Phillip Buchanon was the return artist, but his absence likely means that either Washington or Routt will field punts in '05. Neither player has much experience in that department. Fargas or Curry can return kicks.

The Bottom Line

The Raiders certainly have a new roster to work with in '05, and when coming off a 5-11 season, that is almost always a good thing. But how much can this team really win with these guys? Talent is great, but it has been proven time and again that it can only take a club so far. Oakland will serve as the perfect example this season.

San Diego Chargers

Predicted: 2nd ▪ 2004: 12-4 (1st)

Draft

1	(12)	Shawne Merriman	OLB	Maryland
1	(28)	Luis Castillo	DT	Northwestern
2	(61)	Vincent Jackson	WR	Northern Colorado
4	(130)	Darren Sproles	RB	Kansas St.
5	(164)	Wesley Britt	OT	Alabama
6	(177)	Wes Sims	OG	Oklahoma
7	(242)	Scott Mruczkowski	C	Bowling Green

For the first time in ages, San Diego's draft was a measured quest for talent, not a desperate effort to bandage a wounded roster. They definitely upgraded their defense with the addition of Merriman, who will work nicely in their 3–4. Castillo tested positive for steroids at the combine, then "heroically" admitted his cheating. Both Jackson and Sproles offer raw talent in backup roles.

Head Coach: Marty Schottenheimer
Offensive Coordinator: Cam Cameron
Defensive Coordinator: Wade Phillips

Offense

QB:	Drew Brees*
RB:	LaDainian Tomlinson*
FB:	Lorenzo Neal
WR:	Keenan McCardell
WR:	Eric Parker
TE:	Antonio Gates*
LT:	Roman Oben
LG:	Toniu Fonoti
C:	Nick Hardwick
RG:	Mike Goff
RT:	Shane Olivea
QB:	Phillip Rivers
RB:	Jesse Chatman
WR:	Reche Caldwell
TE:	Justin Peelle
OL:	Courtney Van Buren

Defense

LDE:	Jacques Cesaire
NT:	Jamal Williams
RDE:	Igor Olshansky
LOLB:	Ben Leber
LILB:	Donnie Edwards
RILB:	Randall Godfrey
ROLB:	Steve Foley
CB:	Quentin Jammer
SS:	Terrence Kiel
FS:	Bhawoh Jue†
CB:	Drayton Florence
NB:	Sammy Davis
DL:	Luis Castillo‡
LB:	Shawne Merriman‡
K:	Nate Kaeding
P:	Mike Scifres

* Pro Bowler '04
† veteran acquisition
‡ rookie

Report Card

Quarterback	B+	Defensive Line	C+	Coaching	A–
Running Back	A+	Linebacker	B	Special Teams	B–
Receiver/Tight End	B–	Defensive Back	C+	Depth	C
Offensive Line	C+			Intangibles	C+

This past year, when tuning in to the NFL playoffs to watch the wildcard matchups, every football fan in America probably said aloud, "Hey, that looks like the Chargers! Gosh it *is*, but this is mid-January. What are *they* doing here?" Such reactions are more than understandable. After all, it almost seems like the arrival of great Portuguese explorer Juan Rodriguez Cabrillo at San Diego Bay in 1542 was more recent than the Chargers last 12–4 season.

The current issue is, what kind of legacy will the Chargers establish from this point forward? They set sail in 2004 and miraculously reached the land of the playoffs, where waiting for them were not Spanish natives but something equally as foreign: upper-echelon teams. However, San Diego's stay was cut short by a devastating overtime loss to the more experienced New York Jets. So, heading into the '05 season, what are people to believe about this team?

The Chargers have a good core of talented youth on offense. They also have a defense that was more than solid heading into the offseason and—thanks to the NFL draft—*much more* than solid coming out. Nevertheless, they still must prove to the skeptics that their playoff experience last year was not just a "once in a powder blue moon" event.

LaDainian Tomlinson

Offense

Normally, when someone speaks of the Chargers offense, the first name they bring up is that of superstar running back **LaDainian Tomlinson**. Tomlinson had been the only bright spot on this team for the first three years of his career—rushing for 4,564 yards in that span—but much of that has now changed, since quarterback **Drew Brees** won the NFL Comeback Player of the Year Award in '04.

Besides leading his team to a division title, Brees completed 65.5 percent of his throws and tossed 27 touchdowns (versus only seven interceptions), giving him an astounding rating of 104.8, the third best in the league. Most impressive of all was the fact that Brees did this while under the final year of his contract, with a rookie who was the No, 4 overall selection—**Phillip Rivers**—peering over his shoulder.

Brees's reward for his turnaround in '04 was a pat on the back, a one-year contract as the franchise player, and thus a chance to do it all again. The Chargers are in a very precarious spot with Brees and Rivers. People often remark that it is a nice situation to be in when a team has two good young quarterbacks under contract, but it's really not. San Diego is tying up a great deal of money in each quarterback, and they know that after this season they will have to decide which player they will build their franchise around. The Chargers made the right choice in bringing Brees back for another season; they have the cap space to pay him, they bought themselves another season to evaluate their situation and verify that Brees is legitimate, and oh yeah, coming off a 12-4 season, they are still trying to put themselves in a position to *win*.

One thing is certain: Brees has proven he is a leader who possesses high character and an ability to focus on the task at hand, despite obvious distractions. He is not a shoo-in to repeat his magic from a year ago, but he is a player who is worthy of that expectation. If Brees plays well in '05, he'll get a long-term deal with the organization and Rivers will be traded. If Brees fails, San Diego will let the 26-year-old walk and the Phillip Rivers Era will commence.

There should be no reason for Brees to fail when considering that Tomlinson is in the backfield. Tomlinson (or "LT") had another outstanding year in '04, rushing for 1,335 yards and 17 touchdowns (the most in the NFL), all while playing hurt for a good portion of the season. Overall, he is the best running back in the game of football right now. He can run for power or finesse. He can catch and block. And best of all, he is a good teammate with his mind set on making his club better. The only area in which Tomlinson truly needs to improve is holding onto the ball; he had six fumbles last season.

This season, the Chargers should be able to match their sixth-rated rushing attack from '04. In addition to Tomlinson, they have one of the best blocking fullbacks in all of football (**Lorenzo Neal**) and an explosive backup tailback (**Jesse Chatman**) who showed great speed in averaging six yards per carry a year ago. Chatman is entering his fourth season in the league and serves as a nice security blanket for "LT."

In '03, Tomlinson led all Charger players with 100 receptions, a number that spoke volumes about his versatility, emphasized Brees's discomfort in the passing scheme, and illuminated the lack of talent at the receiver position. In '04, Tomlinson's catch total dropped to 53, which, oddly enough, signified an improvement in the overall passing attack for San Diego. The Chargers improved by discovering the talents of tight end

Strengths

Running back

LaDainian Tomlinson is the best running back in the NFL, plain and simple. He can do anything that is asked of him. The Boltz also have nice depth here, with the speedy Jesse Chatman behind "LT."

Front seven

The starters for this unit have not changed since last year, meaning the Chargers should be able to maintain excellence against the run. The addition of rookie Shawne Merriman should help boost the pass rush, too.

Weaknesses

Pass defense

While Quentin Jammer has improved and the crop of third- and fourth-year players has been able to hold up, the Chargers still ranked 31st in this department last year and must elevate their play.

Credibility

Believe it or not, going 12-4 is still not enough evidence for this team to prove that they're for real. Drew Brees must put up good numbers for a second consecutive year, the offensive line must stick together, and the defense must get more out of its youth.

Antonio Gates and bringing in wide receiver **Keenan McCardell**. Both players are back this year.

A good many of the 47 passes that Tomlinson did not catch last year went to Gates. The 6'4", 260-pound target out of Kent State is in his third year and perhaps what could end up being his first as the most dominant player at his position. Gates, whose primary sport all the way through college was basketball (as a power forward, he even helped lead his Kent State Golden Flashes to a Sweet 16 appearance in '02), has an amazing collection of raw talent packed into his athletic frame. Coming off a season in which he caught 81 passes and led all tight ends with 13 touchdowns, Gates has good speed and strength, which allows him to be a force on third downs and in the red zone. He can even split out wide as a receiver. But Gates is by no means a finished product; he still needs to improve his blocking skills and mature enough to give a consistent effort in that department. The Chargers have another decent tight end in fourth-year player **Justin Peelle**, who can offer some support in run-blocking and use his soft hands to occasionally catch passes. Peelle must stay healthy, though.

Gates has worked wonders for San Diego's passing game, but equally as important is McCardell. After removing himself from the Bucs last year and joining the Chargers, McCardell may have become the first American in history to leave the Tampa region and actually *improve* the climate in which he lives.

McCardell gives the team their only genuine game-by-game receiving threat at wideout, presenting a nice blend of possession skills and downfield abilities. This will be McCardell's first full season with the Chargers (he did not arrive until October last year), but the team knows they cannot rely on a 35-year-old much longer.

The Chargers will most surely explore more receiving options through free agency and the draft after this season, but those future concerns will be slightly eased if receiver **Reche Caldwell** can stay healthy and live up to his billing. Caldwell is a well-built target who shows potential with his natural skills, but injuries have allowed him to start only 12 games in three years. He might start this season. It will depend on how things go in training camp.

Caldwell is likely the third-best receiver on the squad, though, because fourth-year target **Eric Parker** has continued to show

Write it Down:
In 2006, the Chargers will decide on Drew Brees as their long-term quarterback, making Phillip Rivers valuable trade bait.

This Season vs. Last Season

Progression: **Passing attack**—Having more confidence in Drew Brees and knowing that Antonio Gates is a star will generate more energy in the passing game early on. Plus, receiver Keenan McCardell will be here for the whole year.

Regression: **Expectations**—Without losing many players this offseason, this team is virtually the same squad as a year ago, except they won't be flying under anyone's radar anymore.

signs that he is a capable option. Parker is shifty and agile, plus he displays good body control and awareness. He started frequently last year because of a lack of depth, but he is clearly better designed to play in the slot.

San Diego features one of the most cohesive front fives in the NFL. Offensive line coach **Hudson Houck** was able to work miracles with this group. However, Houck is now in Miami, working under Nick Saban. Replacing Houck is **Carl Mauck**. Mauck is currently starting a pair of second-year players, both of whom started as rookies a year ago: center **Nick Hardwick** and right tackle **Shane Olivea**. What makes this an even better testament to the job Hudson is doing is the fact that Hardwick was a third-round pick and Olivea wasn't drafted until the seventh round. Both players must continue to improve this season, though. Hardwick desperately needs to enhance his athleticism with added power and strength. Olivea (who will likely move to guard at some point in his career) must continue to build on his knowledge and fundamentals in run-blocking, because he is already playing without NFL-quality quickness.

The best lineman that nobody has ever heard of is Chargers left guard **Toniu Fonoti** (*see* Ready to Breakout, page 75).

Fonoti joins left tackle **Roman Oben** and right guard **Mike Goff**. Oben turns 33 in October, but many scouts feel that he has plenty of years left in him. He has good quickness and natural athleticism, and has clearly relied on those elements—rather than fundamentals—to get him through his career. Goff is not a star, but, like most of these linemen, he works well as part of this group. He can get into guys and use his technique to power his way around.

Defense

In examining San Diego's situation on defense, it quickly becomes apparent that Chargers Executive Vice President and General Manager **A.J. Smith** has not received enough credit for the job he has done in patiently assembling talent that can play together. In his first year on the job—after taking over for the late John Butler in '03—Smith drafted three defensive backs and decided to make them the cornerstone of his team's secondary. While this has worked out to an extent—all three players (**Terrence Kiel**, **Drayton Florence**, and **Sammy Davis**) are still with the team—it has not necessarily been a walk on San Diego's placid Mission Beach. The Chargers still ranked 31st against the pass last year, allowing 253.3 yards per game. Granted, some of those yards had to do with the fact that teams had trouble running against their front seven—which allowed just 81.7 yards per game—so opponents attempted a league-high 607 passes against the Boltz. But most of the problem, which Smith recognized, had to do with the fact that the Chargers (who under defensive coordinator **Wade Phillips** run a very good 3–4) could not create enough pressure on the quarterback. They generated only 29 sacks last season, fourth fewest in the NFL.

So what San Diego did was go out and, with their two first-

round draft choices, select a pair of players who should immediately improve the pass rush from the front seven. The first is **Shawne Merriman**, who was taken No. 12 overall out of Maryland. Merriman is a great find; he has tremendous speed coming around the corner, and then he has more tremendous speed coming around the corner. San Diego will insert him into the lineup in passing situations and expect him to produce sacks right away.

However Merriman and the Chargers were at odds over the offseason, because after the draft, Merriman changed agents and hired Kevin Potson, who is one of the least respected and most illogical, agents who works with the NFL. Potson had Merriman hold out of the minicamps because of concerns about the injury clauses in the rookie's contract. A.J. Smith did not take it well—he declined to allow Merriman to sit in on the team meetings because of it, even though injuries rarely happen in the film room.

The second pick was a controversial move. The Boltz chose Northwestern's **Luis Castillo** late in the first round. Castillo drew attention for testing positive for the banned substance androstenedione at the combine. Andro is a form of steroid. However, Castillo drew praise for having the class to "admit to his mistake" by sending a letter to all 32 teams, confessing what he had done. Of course, this came *after* he learned of the positive test, which teams would have eventually found out about anyway. So before they stitch "Mother Theresa" onto the back of Castillo's jersey, let's consider the possibility that his agent, Rick Smith, made a rather clever PR move. Castillo's story sure doesn't sound too innocent; he claims he took steroids out of panic, needing to speed up the healing process of an injured elbow, yet he was on the drug for several weeks during January. Not too many people panic for weeks at a time. The bottom line is that, although he never tested positive while at Northwestern, Castillo benefited by cheating and got rewarded with another player's first-round money. But at least he can offer a lot in a backup role at nose tackle this year.

Castillo will play a backup role because starting nose tackle **Jamal Williams** (6'3", 348) is one of the best in the game. He has the size and strength to collapse any blocking scheme and thus allow San Diego's linebackers more room to operate.

In May, the Chargers showed their commitment to the well-respected Williams by signing him to a $27.5 million extension (with an $11.5 million signing bonus), which is designed to keep him around through 2010.

Williams is flanked up front by ends **Jacques Cesaire** and **Igor Olshansky**. Cesaire is a third-year player who does not have great features in any single aspect of his game; he even lacks ideal size. Fortunately for him, a 3–4 defense asks very little of its ends, and in the overall scheme of things, Cesaire does his job just fine. Olshansky is a second-year player who started as a rookie last season. At the age of 23, he is still learning on the fly and adjusting to his role in this defense. He won't break out this year, but he will be better all-around as he continues to build experience.

On third downs, the Chargers will likely go with ends **Adrian Dingle** and **DeQuincy Scott**, both of whom offer more quickness to not only rush the passer but also to defend sweeps and draws. Neither is a prominent sack artist, though; they combined for just 2 sacks in '04.

The fact that Merriman will be coming off the bench (at least early on) speaks well to the skills of the Chargers starting

San Diego's dynamic young pass-catching weapon, Antonio Gates, led all tight ends with 13 touchdown receptions last season.

Startling Statistics

37.3 Number of points higher that Drew Brees's quarterback rating in '04 was than it was in '03.

31 Age that LaDainian Tomlinson will be when he amasses 20,000 career rushing yards, if he continues at his current pace.

linebackers. The outside linebackers are **Ben Leber** and **Steve Foley**, both of whom are solid. Leber is a fast player who operates sideline to sideline. He is effective in pursuit and he's physical, but he could stand to improve his approach in taking on blocks. Foley is the veteran version of Merriman. He is used almost strictly as a pass-rusher, which, with his speed, is a good thing. Last season he recorded a team-high 10 sacks, thanks to his ability to not only blitz but also break down a blocker and use his agility and technique to get through.

San Diego's lack of a large stellar force on the outside would hurt them against the run if it weren't for the wide range of skills presented by inside linebacker **Donnie Edwards**. Edwards—a 10th-year player who is in his fourth season with the Chargers— is the heart and soul of this defense. He is a high-character man who exhibits leadership both in the way he carries himself and in his performance on the field. He will constantly lead the team in tackles by reaching triple digits (151 last year, second in the NFL), plus he may be the best pass-defending linebacker in the NFL. Last season, Edwards intercepted 5 passes and defensed 14 more.

Next to Edwards is another 10th-year veteran, **Randall Godfrey**. The book on him reads as it did last year (and likely will read that way until he retires): He is not the rangy player that he was while with the Cowboys and the Titans, but he has enough mobility—and certainly enough awareness—to be a sound starter. Godfrey must stay healthy because the only backup inside linebacker that San Diego can truly rely on is **Carlos Polk**, and they don't want to have to do that.

As previously alluded to, the Chargers secondary is still young and developing, but they have grown together for three years now. The "intentionally created clique" is headed by cornerback **Quentin Jammer**, who is in his fourth year out of Texas (he was

taken a year before most of his compadres). As his name suggests, Jammer is an aggressive corner who plays a physical game. He has drastically improved each season at timing his jumps on the ball and giving up little separation. This season, he could very well elevate his game to a Pro Bowl level and approach on the threshold of "shutdown" status.

Opposite Jammer is Florence, who has great range and an ability to get to the ball quickly, making him the secondary's best playmaker. Florence must hone his game, though; he tends to play with too little knee bend and he still needs to correct some of the bad habits that come with being a 24-year-old starter.

Florence was a second-round pick in '03 and Davis was a first-rounder, yet it is Davis who is coming off the bench three seasons later. Davis has good enough athletic skills, but he has simply had a tougher time adjusting to the NFL. The same can be said about **Jamar Fletcher**, another backup cornerback. Fletcher was taken by the Miami Dolphins in the first round back in '01, but has started just six games in his career.

The safety, Kiel, plays on the strongside, a role that fits him well. Although he is a little undersized for playing near the line of scrimmage, that is precisely where Kiel spends most of his time. He is a good tackler who hits with the courage of a lion— and not the kind that can be found in Detroit.

The only new veteran addition to this entire team in '05 is free safety **Bhawoh Jue**, who left Lake Michigan in Green Bay to settle on the Pacific Ocean in San Diego. Jue has been shuffled around the defensive backfield throughout his career, but with his range and flashes of playmaking skills, he seems to have found a home at free safety. It was an easy decision for the club to elect to go with him this year ahead of veteran **Jerry Wilson**.

Special Teams

Kicker **Nate Kaeding** had a good rookie season marred by a missed 40-yard field goal in the overtime playoff loss to the Jets, but the experience will be something he learns from. Punter **Mike Scifres** found a way to fit in with the team last season: He ranked third in the league in net punting yards at 38.4. Now that San Diego has traded Tim Dwight, the Chargers must find a new overrated player to return kicks. Eric Parker handled punts last year and could be a candidate for kicks as well.

The Bottom Line

Marty Schottenheimer and his coaching staff can be proud of the work they have put in toward making this franchise a success, but they are still far from satisfied. The electric boys in dark blue and gold (and occasionally powder blue and white) have not opened a season with so much optimism since, well, probably the days of the aforementioned explorer Juan Rodriguez Cabrillo. But with so many breakout players on offense last year and a slew of players on defense this year who are still young, San Diego has the burden of proof to show that they do not belong in the one-hit-wonder trash can with Bobby Bloom, Lou Bega, and John Rocker.

NFC East

Dallas
Cowboys

New York
Giants

Philadelphia
Eagles

Washington
Redskins

Looking Forward

Ready to Break Out

**Bradie James,
Dallas Cowboys**

Linebacker
6'2"–245
3rd year–24
Drafted: 4th round in '03 out of LSU

Of all the "Ready to Break Out" players, Bradie James may be the most hit-or-miss, simply because of the coach he plays for and the young talent that he has around him. The Cowboys drafted James with the intent of grooming him to be the replacement for Dexter Coakley. Coakley is now gone, and James—a man who has played sparingly in a backup role for the past two seasons—is in his place.

Bradie James

Dallas originally planned on having James play the weakside linebacker position, but those plans may have been altered when the team switched to a 3–4 and drafted outside linebackers Demarcus Ware and Kevin Burnett this year. James is still scheduled to start on the outside, but don't be surprised if he is shifted over to the middle.

James has the raw skills to succeed anywhere he lines up. He is a good athlete who shows a lot of natural talent. He has the size to play in traffic, and he is a good enough one-on-one tackler. His best feature, in fact, is his acceleration into making a hit. Of course, James plays for a man who is not too patient when it comes to fulfilling expectations. If James has a slow training camp, he could find himself in a limited role again this year. However, one thing is for sure: The potential for stardom in James is certainly there.

Hot Seat

**Tom Coughlin,
New York Giants**

Not too many people are talking about Tom Coughlin's future with the Giants, but consider the possibility of his team dropping a substantial number of games in a row, like they did last year. If this is the case, Coughlin could be on his way out of New York faster than a person can say "fuhgeddaboudit!"

There is already speculation that he has disconnected with his players, that they cannot tolerate his demeanor and big-stick policies. With a franchise quarterback like Eli Manning nearing his prime, the Giants may ultimately decide that it's just a better idea to find a more popular long-term solution right now. There has been speculation that defensive coordinator Tim Lewis (who is only 42) is the next in line and a great head coaching prospect. That said, Coughlin could erase all that by winning some games in '05.

Best Offseason Move

Giants signing right tackle Kareem McKenzie.

Worst Offseason Move

Redskins trading Laveranues Coles for Santana Moss.

Best Under-the-Radar Offseason Move

Cowboys signing nickel back Aaron Glenn.

Biggest Question

Given the circumstances in Philadelphia that have been created by Terrell Owens, how will his status affect the Eagles in '05?

QUICK HITS

TEAM BESTS		BEST PLAYERS	
Passing Game	Eagles	Pure Athlete	LaVar Arrington, Redskin
Running Game	Cowboys	Big Play Threat	Terrell Owens, Eagles
Offensive Line	Redskins	Best Use of Talent	Dat Nguyen, Cowboys
Pass Rush	Eagles	Worst Use of Talent	Terry Glenn, Cowboys
Run Defense	Redskins	On the Rise	Jason Witten, Cowboys
Pass Defense	Eagles		Julius Jones, Cowboys
Special Teams	Eagles		Osi Umenyiora, Giants
Coaching Staff	Eagles	On the Decline	Amani Toomer, Giants
Home Field	Eagles		Keyshawn Johnson, Cowboys
			Hugh Douglas, Eagles
		Best Leader	Brian Dawkins, Eagles
		Unsung Hero	Chris Cooley, Redskins
		Impact Rookie	Carlos Rogers, Redskins

Terrell Owens

Looking Back

Dallas Cowboys 2004

PASSING STATISTICS

PLAYER	CMP	ATT	YDS	CMP%	YDS/A	LNG	TD	TD%	INT	INT%	SACK	YDS	RAT
Vinny Testaverde	297	495	3532	60.0	7.14	53	17	3.4	20	4.0	35	186	76.4

RUSHING STATISTICS

PLAYER	ATT	YDS	AVG	LNG	TD	FUM	LST
Julius Jones	197	819	4.2	53	7	3	3
Eddie George	132	432	3.3	24	4	2	0
Richie Anderson	57	246	4.3	27	1	1	1

RECEIVING STATISTICS

PLAYER	REC	YDS	AVG	LNG	TD	FUM	LST
Keyshawn Johnson	70	981	14.0	39	6	1	1
Jason Witten	87	980	11.3	42	6	2	1
Terry Glenn	24	400	16.7	48	2	0	0
Antonio Bryant	16	266	16.6	48	0	1	1

RETURN STATISTICS

PLAYER	KICKOFFS ATT	YDS	FC	AVG	LNG	TD	PUNTS ATT	YDS	FC	AVG	LNG	TD
ReShard Lee	41	964	0	23.5	62	0	0	0	0	0.0	0	0
Terrance Copper	16	307	0	19.2	39	0	0	0	0	0.0	0	0

KICKING STATISTICS

PLAYER	1-20	20-29	30-39	40-49	50+	TOT	PCT	AVG	LNG	XPM/A	PTS
Billy Cundiff	1/1	6/6	4/4	9/13	0/2	20/26	76.9	35.3	49	31/31	91

PUNTING STATISTICS

PLAYER	PUNTS	YDS	AVG	LNG	TB	TB%	IN20	IN20%	RET	YDS	AVG	NET
Mat McBriar	75	3182	42.4	68	7	9.3	22	29.3	39	410	10.5	37

DEFENSIVE STATISTICS

PLAYER	TACKLES TOT	SOLO	AST	SACK	TLOSS	MISCELLANEOUS FF	BK	INTERCEPTIONS INT	YDS	AVG	LNG	TD	PD
Dat Nguyen	107	82	25	1.0	1.5	1	0	3	19	6.3	19	0	5
Roy Williams	88	72	16	0.0	3.5	1	0	2	53	26.5	33	0	10
Terence Newman	70	67	3	0.0	1	2	0	4	31	7.8	21	0	15
Dexter Coakley	68	57	11	0.0	0	0	0	0	0	0.0	0	0	6
Greg Ellis	59	49	10	9.0	2.5	1	1	0	0	0.0	0	0	9
Al Singleton	45	34	11	0.0	0.5	0	0	0	0	0.0	0	0	1
Leonardo Carson	43	34	9	0.5	3	0	0	0	0	0.0	0	0	0
La'Roi Glover	41	34	7	7.0	2.5	1	0	0	0	0.0	0	0	1
Lance Frazier	40	40	0	0.0	0	1	0	2	2	1.0	2	0	8
Marcellus Wiley	38	35	3	3.0	3	1	0	0	0	0.0	0	0	0

New York Giants 2004

PASSING STATISTICS

PLAYER	CMP	ATT	YDS	CMP%	YDS/A	LNG	TD	TD%	INT	INT%	SACK	YDS	RAT
Kurt Warner	174	277	2054	62.8	7.42	62	6	2.2	4	1.4	39	196	86.5
Eli Manning	95	197	1043	48.2	5.29	52	6	3.0	9	4.6	13	83	55.4

RUSHING STATISTICS

PLAYER	ATT	YDS	AVG	LNG	TD	FUM	LST
Tiki Barber	322	1518	4.7	72	13	5	2
Ron Dayne	52	179	3.4	15	1	0	0
Michael Cloud	21	90	4.3	26	3	0	0

RECEIVING STATISTICS

PLAYER	REC	YDS	AVG	LNG	TD	FUM	LST
Amani Toomer	51	747	14.6	48	0	1	1
Jeremy Shockey	61	666	10.9	38	6	1	0
Tiki Barber	52	578	11.1	62	2	0	0
Ike Hilliard	49	437	8.9	43	0	3	1

RETURN STATISTICS

PLAYER	KICKOFFS ATT	YDS	FC	AVG	LNG	TD	PUNTS ATT	YDS	FC	AVG	LNG	TD
Willie Ponder	36	967	0	26.9	91	1	0	0	0	0.0	0	0
Derrick Ward	16	436	0	27.3	92	1	0	0	0	0.0	0	0

KICKING STATISTICS

PLAYER	1-20	20-29	30-39	40-49	50+	TOT	PCT	AVG	LNG	XPM/A	PTS
Steve Christie	1/1	8/8	6/8	4/7	3/4	22/28	78.6	33.6	53	33/33	99

PUNTING STATISTICS

PLAYER	PUNTS	YDS	AVG	LNG	TB	TB%	IN20	IN20%	RET	YDS	AVG	NET
Jeff Feagles	74	3069	41.5	55	4	5.4	23	31.1	38	356	9.4	36.7

DEFENSIVE STATISTICS

PLAYER	TACKLES TOT	SOLO	AST	SACK	TLOSS	MISCELLANEOUS FF	BK	INTERCEPTIONS INT	YDS	AVG	LNG	TD	PD
Carlos Emmons	97	64	33	1.0	2	0	0	0	0	0.0	0	0	3
Kevin Lewis	88	64	24	1.0	4	0	0	0	0	0.0	0	0	3
Will Allen	81	75	6	1.0	2	1	0	1	11	11.0	11	0	19
Brent Alexander	80	57	23	2.0	1	1	0	3	3	1.0	2	0	7
Nick Greisen	72	53	19	2.0	2	1	0	0	0	0.0	0	0	6
Will Peterson	69	61	8	0.0	1	1	0	2	9	4.5	9	0	14
Osi Umenyiora	58	40	18	7.0	7	3	0	0	0	0.0	0	0	3
Gibril Wilson	55	49	6	3.0	2	1	0	3	39	13.0	39	0	5
Fred Robbins	40	30	10	5.0	4.5	2	0	1	13	13.0	13	0	2
Terry Cousin	39	33	6	0.0	0	0	0	1	6	6.0	6	0	3

2004 Team Stats (Dallas Cowboys)

OFFENSE

Scoring:	18.3 (25)
Yards per Game:	324.8 (14)
Pass Yards per Game:	214.0 (15)
Rush Yards per Game:	10.8 (20)
Sacks Allowed:	37 (t15)
3rd Down Percentage:	36.4 (17)
Punts:	76 (t18)
Giveaways:	33 (13)

DEFENSE

Scoring:	25.3 (t27)
Yards per Game:	330.3 (16)
Pass Yards per Game:	220.1 (21)
Rush Yards per Game:	110.3 (10)
Sacks:	33 (26)
3rd Down Percentage:	39.1 (22)
Takeaways:	18 (13)

2004 Team Stats (New York Giants)

OFFENSE

Scoring:	18.9 (22)
Yards per Game:	295.1 (23)
Pass Yards per Game:	176.1 (t26)
Rush Yards per Game:	19.0 (11)
Sacks Allowed:	52 (t29)
3rd Down Percentage:	29.5 (30)
Punts:	75 (20)
Giveaways:	22 (t14)

DEFENSE

Scoring:	21.7 (17)
Yards per Game:	324.2 (13)
Pass Yards per Game:	189.1 (8)
Rush Yards per Game:	135.1 (28)
Sacks:	41 (t7)
3rd Down Percentage:	41.8 (25)
Takeaways:	24 (t20)

Philadelphia Eagles 2004

PASSING STATISTICS

PLAYER	CMP	ATT	YDS	CMP%	YDS/A	LNG	TD	TD%	INT	INT%	SACK	YDS	RAT
Donovan McNabb	300	469	3875	64.0	8.26	80	31	6.6	8	1.7	32	192	104.7

RUSHING STATISTICS

PLAYER	ATT	YDS	AVG	LNG	TD	FUM	LST
Brian Westbrook	177	812	4.6	50	3	0	0
Dorsey Levens	94	410	4.4	45	4	0	0
Donovan McNabb	41	220	5.4	28	3	2	1

RECEIVING STATISTICS

PLAYER	REC	YDS	AVG	LNG	TD	FUM	LST
Terrell Owens	77	1200	15.6	59	14	2	1
Brian Westbrook	73	703	9.6	50	6	1	1
Todd Pinkston	36	676	18.8	80	1	0	0
Freddie Mitchell	22	377	17.1	60	2	0	0

RETURN STATISTICS

PLAYER	KICKOFFS ATT	YDS	FC	AVG	LNG	TD	PUNTS ATT	YDS	FC	AVG	LNG	TD
J.R. Reed	33	761	0	23.1	66	0	0	18	0	0.0	18	0
Roderick Hood	15	336	0	22.4	45	0	0	0	0	0.0	0	0

KICKING STATISTICS

PLAYER	1-20	20-29	30-39	40-49	50+	TOT	PCT	AVG	LNG	XPM/A	PTS
David Akers	0/0	4/4	6/7	15/18	2/3	27/32	84.4	39.8	51	41/42	122

PUNTING STATISTICS

PLAYER	PUNTS	YDS	AVG	LNG	TB	TB%	IN20	IN20%	RET	YDS	AVG	NET
Dirk Johnson	72	3032	42.1	62	6	8.3	20	27.8	34	221	6.5	39

DEFENSIVE STATISTICS

PLAYER	TACKLES TOT	SOLO	AST	SACK	TLOSS	MISCELLANEOUS FF	BK	INTERCEPTIONS INT	YDS	AVG	LNG	TD	PD
Michael Lewis	90	83	7	0.0	4	2	0	1	0	0.0	0	0	12
Sheldon Brown	89	73	16	3.0	2	1	0	2	33	16.5	33	0	16
Brian Dawkins	70	67	3	3.0	0	2	0	4	40	10.0	32	0	12
Dhani Jones	67	47	20	0.5	7	0	0	1	0	0.0	0	0	5
Jeremiah Trotter	61	57	4	1.0	9	0	0	0	0	0.0	0	0	1
Lito Sheppard	56	55	1	1.0	1.5	0	0	5	172	34.4	101	2	15
Mark Simoneau	49	38	11	1.5	1.5	1	0	0	0	0.0	0	0	1
Ike Reese	36	34	2	1.0	1	1	0	2	22	11.0	15	0	8
Roderick Hood	35	33	2	0.0	0	1	0	1	20	20.0	20	0	7
Keith Adams	34	30	4	0.0	2	1	0	0	0	0.0	0	0	1

Washington Redskins 2004

PASSING STATISTICS

PLAYER	CMP	ATT	YDS	CMP%	YDS/A	LNG	TD	TD%	INT	INT%	SACK	YDS	RAT
Patrick Ramsey	169	272	1665	62.1	6.12	51	10	3.7	11	4.0	23	137	74.8
Mark Brunell	118	237	1194	49.8	5.04	49	7	3.0	6	2.5	15	105	63.9

RUSHING STATISTICS

PLAYER	ATT	YDS	AVG	LNG	TD	FUM	LST
Clinton Portis	343	1315	3.8	64	5	5	4
Ladell Betts	90	371	4.1	27	1	0	0
Mark Brunell	19	62	3.3	21	0	2	1

RECEIVING STATISTICS

PLAYER	REC	YDS	AVG	LNG	TD	FUM	LST
Laveranues Coles	90	950	10.6	45	1	1	1
Rod Gardner	51	650	12.7	51	5	0	0
Chris Cooley	37	314	8.5	31	6	0	0
Clinton Portis	40	235	5.9	18	2	0	0

RETURN STATISTICS

PLAYER	KICKOFFS ATT	YDS	FC	AVG	LNG	TD	PUNTS ATT	YDS	FC	AVG	LNG	TD
Ladell Betts	23	528	0	23.0	70	0	0	0	0	0.0	0	0
Chad Morton	16	358	0	22.4	49	0	13	80	12	6.2	14	0

KICKING STATISTICS

PLAYER	1-20	20-29	30-39	40-49	50+	TOT	PCT	AVG	LNG	XPM/A	PTS
Jeff Chandler	0/0	4/4	0/0	1/1	0/1	5/6	83.3	29.0	49	6/6	21

PUNTING STATISTICS

PLAYER	PUNTS	YDS	AVG	LNG	TB	TB%	IN20	IN20%	RET	YDS	AVG	NET
Tom Tupa	103	4544	44.1	61	8	7.8	30	29.1	65	727	11.2	37.1

DEFENSIVE STATISTICS

PLAYER	TACKLES TOT	SOLO	AST	SACK	TLOSS	MISCELLANEOUS FF	BK	INTERCEPTIONS INT	YDS	AVG	LNG	TD	PD
Antonio Pierce	110	92	18	1.0	1.5	1	0	2	94	47.0	78	1	5
Marcus Washington	102	86	16	4.5	10.5	1	0	0	0	0.0	0	0	3
Sean Taylor	76	63	13	1.0	1	2	0	4	85	21.3	45	0	15
Ryan Clark	75	63	12	0.0	2	0	0	0	0	0.0	0	0	1
Cornelius Griffin	70	59	11	6.0	14.5	0	0	0	0	0.0	0	0	6
Lemar Marshall	65	49	16	1.5	3.5	0	0	0	0	0.0	0	0	1
Shawn Springs	64	55	9	6.0	2.5	1	0	5	117	23.4	38	0	12
Fred Smoot	61	56	5	0.0	0.5	2	0	3	17	5.7	17	0	13
Renaldo Wynn	38	33	5	3.0	2.5	0	0	0	0	0.0	0	0	0
Demetric Evans	26	18	8	2.5	3	0	0	0	0	0.0	0	0	1

2004 Team Stats (Philadelphia Eagles)

OFFENSE

Scoring:	24.1 (8)
Yards per Game:	351.1 (9)
Pass Yards per Game:	248.7 (7)
Rush Yards per Game:	102.4 (24)
Sacks Allowed:	37 (t15)
3rd Down Percentage:	36.9 (t15)
Punts:	73 (t21)
Giveaways:	16 (t5)

DEFENSE

Scoring:	16.2 (t2)
Yards per Game:	319.7 (10)
Pass Yards per Game:	200.8 (12)
Rush Yards per Game:	118.9 (16)
Sacks:	47 (2)
3rd Down Percentage:	35.8 (12)
Takeaways:	27 (13)

2004 Team Stats (Washington Redskins)

OFFENSE

Scoring:	15.0 (31)
Yards per Game:	274.8 (30)
Pass Yards per Game:	164.5 (29)
Rush Yards per Game:	10.3 (21)
Sacks Allowed:	38 (t18)
3rd Down Percentage:	31.7 (28)
Punts:	103 (2)
Giveaways:	22 (t14)

DEFENSE

Scoring:	16.6 (5)
Yards per Game:	267.6 (3)
Pass Yards per Game:	186.1 (7)
Rush Yards per Game:	81.5 (2)
Sacks:	40 (t9)
Takeaways:	24 (t20)

Dallas Cowboys

Predicted: 2nd ▪ 2004: 6-10 (2nd)

Players Added

QB	Drew Bledsoe (Buf)	
OL	Gennaro Di Napoli	
DT	Jason Ferguson (NYJ)	
CB	Aaron Glenn (Hou)	
CB	Anthony Henry (Cle)	
RB	Richard Lee (Buf)	
G	Marco Rivera (GB)	
RB	Anthony Thomas (Chi)	

Players Lost

RB	Richie Anderson
LB	Dexter Coakley (StL)
RB	Eddie George
QB	Vinny Testaverde
DE	Marcellus Wiley (Jax)
WR	Randall Williams
S	Darren Woodson (retired)

Draft

1	(11)	Demarcus Ware	DE	Troy St.
1	(20)	Marcus Spears	DE	LSU
2	(42)	Kevin Burnett	OLB	Tennessee
4	(109)	Marion Barber III	RB	Minnesota
4	(132)	Chris Canty	DE	Virginia
6	(208)	Justin Beriault	S	Ball St.
6	(209)	Rob Petitti	OT	Pittsburgh
7	(224)	Jay Ratliff	DT	Auburn

Dallas fielded a great draft—especially considering that they're transitioning into a 3–4 defense. They were torn between selecting Ware and Spears at No. 11 and wound up getting both in the first round anyway. Each is a versatile athlete. Burnett has star potential but may need a year to improve his awareness. Useful in the 3–4 will be Canty, who may have been the best bargain in the draft. Barber can be a legitimate backup to Julius Jones this year.

Head Coach: Bill Parcells (3rd year)

Offensive Coordinator: None

Defensive Coordinator: Mike Zimmer

Offense

QB:	Drew Bledsoe†
RB:	Julius Jones
FB:	Darian Barnes
WR:	Keyshawn Johnson
WR:	Terry Glenn
TE:	Jason Witten*
LT:	Flozell Adams*
LG:	Larry Allen*
C:	Al Johnson
RG:	Marco Rivera*
RT:	Kurt Vollers
QB:	Drew Henson
RB:	Anthony Thomas†
WR:	Quincy Morgan
TE:	Dan Campbell
OL:	Jacob Rogers

Defense

LDE:	Greg Ellis
NT:	Jason Ferguson†
RDE:	Marcus Spears‡
LOLB:	Bradie James
LILB:	Al Singleton
RILB:	Dat Nguyen
ROLB:	Demarcus Ware‡
CB:	Terrence Newman
SS:	Roy Williams
FS:	Keith Davis
CB:	Anthony Henry†
NB:	Aaron Glenn†
DL:	La'Roi Glover*
LB:	Kevin Burnett‡
P:	Mat McBriar
K:	Billy Cundiff

* Pro Bowler '04
† veteran acquisition
‡ rookie

Report Card

Quarterback	C+	Defensive Line	B	Coaching	A
Running Back	B	Linebacker	B–	Special Teams	C+
Receiver/Tight End	C+	Defensive Back	B+	Depth	B
Offensive Line	B+			Intangibles	B

Everything's big in Texas, especially when it comes to football, and especially when that football has to do with the Dallas Cowboys. And yes, the "everything's big in Texas" rule sure applies to the expectations placed on Bill Parcells's . . . errrr, Jerry Jones's club this year. The heat is on; the Cowboys aren't just Texas's team, they are America's team, which makes them (in the minds of Southerners) the football icon of *two* countries. Ever since the "America's team" label was established by Bob Ryan of NFL Films in 1978, the pressure has been put on this franchise. People want to see this club win because that makes it easier to either love them or hate them.

After a disappointing 6-10 season in '04, the good ol' boys from Valley Ranch loaded up the Ford truck and hit the highway in search of some help. What began as a free agent rodeo became another Parcells reunion, as he brought in his former quarterback from the Patriots (Drew Bledsoe), the nose tackle he drafted with the Jets (Jason Ferguson), and his one-time big-money Jets cornerback (Aaron Glenn).

The changes have not just come in personnel, either. A cranky 64-year-old Parcells is having his patience grow thin and is not about to tolerate any more losing; he has revamped several areas of his coaching staff and scouting department. In what many have guessed will be his final year in Big D, Parcells is finally getting the type of defense that he wants: His trademark

Roy Williams

3–4, which won him a Super Bowl with the Giants. Yes, the ol' sheriff is still in town, only now he's mad.

Offense

With the addition of **Drew Bledsoe**, the Cowboys will now be starting their third quarterback in as many years. Last season's attempt to continue on with the offense under Vinny Testaverde was a failed experiment; the 41-year-old led the league in interceptions and became consistently worse as games lingered on. With the 33-year-old Bledsoe under center, Dallas hopes to have a strong-armed pocket passer that they can rely on. However, one question that isn't being posed is this: Is there really that much difference between Testaverde and Bledsoe? Granted, nine years of age separate the two, but it's not as if Bledsoe is some young energetic speedster aglow with potential.

Nevertheless, Parcells is comfortable with the man who led his Patriot team to a Super Bowl appearance in '96, and that may be all that's needed to make the Cowboys offense click. While many will buy into the slogan that says "A good running game is a quarterback's best friend," the key for Bledsoe in '05 will actually be Dallas's receiving corps. Don't misconstrue this, though: The quarterback–running game adage is very much correct, but the bottom line is that Bledsoe is going to have to make throws if the Cowboys are to win. There are going to be plenty of third-down situations—there always are—and it was here that the Cowboys struggled a year ago.

Bledsoe's starting receivers will be **Terry Glenn** and **Keyshawn Johnson**, both of whom carry as much baggage as a Delta flight leaving the Dallas/Fort Worth International Airport. Glenn was on that same '96 Patriots team that went to the Super Bowl; problem is, that happened to be his best season as a pro. Doing the math, one quickly realizes that it occurred precisely one decade ago, leaving one to question how good Glenn really is. The answer is about as gray as the helmet he'll wear: Glenn has always been talented, but he has never fulfilled that talent. Part of this has been due to unfortunate health circumstances; in fact, Glenn missed the final 10 games last season with a broken foot. The other part of it, however, has been Glenn's selfishness and lack of courage. He is a quick player who can make spectacular catches, but only if he is assured ahead of time of not getting hit. Glenn's unwillingness to take a tough hit or go over the middle can be a drive killer.

Johnson, on the other hand, shows tremendous heart and valor in chasing receptions, but unlike Glenn, he doesn't have the speed and quickness to make big plays. Johnson must rely on his toughness and his 6'4" frame to be effective catching passes in traffic.

Dallas may have major shortcomings at the starting receiver position in '05. Glenn is 31 and coming off a foot injury, while Johnson is 33 and coming off an unpublicized broken ankle that was surgically repaired during the offseason. In reality, the Cowboys probably should have drafted a receiver this year, but instead they chose to roll the dice with what they have. They are also hoping that tight end **Jason Witten** and the team's backup receivers, **Quincy Morgan** and **Terrance Copper,** can step up.

In just his third year out of Tennessee, Witten—a former third-round pick—is already coming off a Pro Bowl season in which he caught a team-high 87 passes, for 980 yards and six touchdowns. Witten, 23, is one of the premier receiving tight ends in the game today. He has incredibly soft hands, and he is perhaps the league's best route runner at his position. Not since

Strengths

Left Offensive Line

Flozell Adams and Larry Allen can pave the way for Julius Jones (who, as it is, likes to run left) by creating holes large enough to drive a Hummer through.

Cornerbacks

Terrence Newman will bounce back from a subpar season. Anthony Henry and Aaron Glenn were both great finds; each possesses the one-on-one coverage skills, as well as the aptitude in zone, needed to run this defense. Plus, there are several starters from last season buried in the depth chart, giving Dallas great depth at this position.

Weaknesses

Front Seven Youth

The Cowboys have outstanding talent to operate in their 3–4, but let's not forget that they will be playing three rookies and a first-year starter on a regular basis. No matter how gifted a player is, he will still make rookie mistakes.

Passing Security

With a shaky right tackle up front and a quarterback like Drew Bledsoe—who moves about as well as a lazy mule on a hot day—the Cowboys may be under pressure more often than they'd like. Couple this with a pair of starting receivers (Keyshawn Johnson and Terry Glenn) who are aging and coming off of major injuries.

Jay Novacek (*see* Whatever Happened To, page 176) have the Boys had a tight end like this, and not since Ben Coates has Bledsoe had a tight end as good as Witten. Expect Witten—who will continue to improve as a blocker—to have another great year. He will be the best pass-catching option on this team.

Morgan is not among the elite No. 3 receivers in the NFL, mainly because he defines "average" the way Bobby Fischer defines "insane." Morgan does not explode off the line of scrimmage, he is not particularly fast, and he has trouble at times with getting separation. Part of his weakness may be the fact that teams have tried to force him into being a starter, which is something he's simply not. If Copper continues to surge like he did toward the end of last season, he could *maybe* sneak into the slot receiver job.

The passing game is all well and good, but with this being a Parcells team and second-year pro **Julius Jones** being the runner that he is, the Cowboys are going to eat clock and control games on the ground in '05.

After returning from a broken collarbone suffered in week 2, Jones started the final seven games of the year for the Cowboys, rushing for 803 yards and seven touchdowns during that time. His defining moment came in a four-day stretch, in which he carried the ball 30 times at Baltimore and 33 times just days later, on Thanksgiving, against his brother, Thomas Jones, and his Chicago Bears. In the Thanksgiving game, Jones produced 150 yards and a pair of touchdowns. It would have been a career-day for the former Notre Dame tailback, except that the next week he had 30 carries, for 198 yards and three touchdowns, in a Monday night victory over Seattle.

Jones—who began his rookie year inactive and in Parcells's doghouse for not showing enough toughness—has quickly learned what it takes to be a pro. He has the potential to be great. Not to say that he will become the best running back of all time, but with the naked eye, he looks like—*looks* like—Emmitt Smith with more speed and·quickness. Jones *does* need to improve in every facet of the passing game, though.

He is most effective when he lines up as the lone setback, because from there he can run draws. In fact, last year Jones averaged 3.4 yards per carry running out of a split-backs formation, 3.1 yards per carry running out of the I-formation, and 5.9 yards per carry running as a single back out of the backfield.

Write it Down:

No matter what areas are successful and what areas aren't, Bill Parcells is simply not going to allow his team to perform as poorly as they did last season.

This Season vs. Last Season

Progression: **Front seven**—After drafting three players to fill spots here with their first three picks, the Cowboys had better improve up front. They also added starter Jason Ferguson, giving the line more depth.

Regression: **Free safety**—This was a glaring weakness a year ago, but back then the team at least thought they might have Darren Woodson around. With Woodson now retired, this spot looks dangerously bleak heading into the season.

With this in mind, the Cowboys will likely use a lot of two-tight-end sets with Witten and blocking specialist **Dan Campbell**, in order to set up the delay handoff. When they do go with a fullback, they'll use fifth-year pro **Darian Barnes**, who lacks the athleticism to get consistent clean shots on opponents, but has the size and power to be effective when he *does* lock on. Speaking of power, the Cowboys improved their depth and ability in short-yardage situations by adding former Bear **Anthony Thomas**.

Jones didn't just have lopsided rushing statistics in certain formations, he also averaged far better numbers running to the left side. On powers and off-tackle runs to the left, he averaged 4.6 yards per carry, versus 2.7 to the right. On tosses and sweeps to the left, Jones gained an astounding 8.6 yards per carry, versus just 2.9 to the right.

These discrepancies wouldn't have anything to do with the fact that Dallas has a pair of Pro Bowlers over on the left in tackle **Flozell Adams** and guard **Larry Allen**, would they? To get back to the "everything's big in Texas" theme, these two weigh in at 343 pounds and 325 pounds, respectively. (To be fair, according to reports in May, Adams had lost some weight.) On the left, Dallas has two linemen who can absolutely dominate when playing at their fullest.

The rest of the line is not too bad, either. Center **Al Johnson** has recovered well from a knee injury that wiped out his rookie season. Johnson has the strength to neutralize defensive tackles (but not drive them), and he moves very well. However, he still must learn to connect better on blocks in the open field, and he needs to spend less time on the ground. All in all, the future is still very bright for this young guy.

When guard **Andre Gurode** first got to know Parcells, the coach harped on him but told him that he would not let him fail. Parcells has been true to his word, because he has benched the 314-pounder in favor of veteran acquisition **Marco Rivera**. (Hey, it's going to be hard for Gurode to fail when he's not in the game, right?) Gurode has very good natural talent, both as a run-blocker

and as a pass-blocker, but the Cowboys have grown impatient waiting for his mind to catch up to his skills. Parcells will no longer let Gurode play guard and has moved him to backup center. Rivera—who had been with the Packers his entire career—is returning from offseason back surgery, but the team still feels confident that the patient run-blocking master can be ready for training camp.

The only glaring weakness on this Cowboys offense (besides, potentially, the receiver position) is at right tackle. It will be a five-man competition for the job at this training camp, between leading candidate **Kurt Vollers**, **Torrin Tucker**, former guard Ben Noll, last year's second-round pick **Jacob Rogers**, and this year's sixth-round pick **Rob Petitti**. The winner gets 16 games' worth of Parcells's wrath for not being able to keep up this year.

Defense

As much change as has taken place on offense, it doesn't begin to compare to the amount of change that will be seen on Dallas's defense this year. The Cowboys have shuffled so many cards in their defensive deck that it's amazing they didn't find a way to just bulldoze the depth chart and begin from scratch. The only thing that has managed to stay the same for the Cowboys on defense is the uniform that the players will be wearing.

While a lot of teams are switching to a 3–4 (as many as 10 teams will run the defense this year), most of them, at the time the decision was made, had the personnel to do it. The Cowboys did not. Instead, they went out and signed a nose tackle, drafted a defensive end, and drafted three new linebackers, all of whom are expected to make serious contributions in '05. Just for good measure, the Cowboys will also start two new defensive backs and feature a new nickel back this season.

Defensive linemen and defensive backs are neat, but the real key to Parcells's 3–4 is the linebacker position. It has been well documented that Parcells favors big, strong linebackers, but until now, he has had to tolerate the speedy, undersized players that coordinator **Mike Zimmer** offered. Those undersized players helped lead the way toward a 27th-ranked scoring unit in '04 and, of course, the drafting of the aforementioned linebackers.

Those conservative Cowboy fans will have to get to know these rookies quickly, because all three will wind up playing a meaningful role this year. The first is outside linebacker **Demarcus Ware**, who was taken 11th overall out of Troy. As a collegiate player, Ware did not face premium competition in the Sunbelt Conference, but the Cowboys are so in love with his speed in turning the corner that they made him the starter the instant Paul Tagliabue called his name. Ware will start on the right side and is expected to help the team generate more than 33 sacks, which is all they managed a year ago.

The next linebacker is **Kevin Burnett**, who was taken in the second round out of Tennessee. Burnett is a big player (6'3", 237 pounds) with terrific upside. However, he may not start right away, because the Cowboys already have a young, emerging linebacker, who is getting his first chance at starting, in **Bradie James** (*see* Ready to Break Out, page 95).

The final rookie linebacker taken in the draft was **Chris Canty**, a prospect out of Virginia, who was projected to be taken some time in the second round, before he damaged the retina in his left eye during a fight at a club. The incident cost him about two months' worth of offseason preparation. Canty has also had reconstructive knee surgery in his career. If healthy, he is a player

Second-year running back Julius Jones is expected to be the driving force for Bill Parcells and the Cowboys offense this season.

© Jim Turner/WireImage.com

who can rush the quarterback from the linebacker or defensive end position.

What will likely happen is that Dallas will move James over to the middle, in place of veteran **Al Singleton**, who has lost a step, and start Burnett on the outside. Next to James will be **Dat Nguyen**, a small player (5'11", 238 pounds) who has survived the great shake-up at his position. Nguyen was a player that Parcells wanted to all but get rid of when he first arrived in Dallas, but the energetic seventh-year veteran has won over the coach's heart, thanks to his heady play and outstanding production. Nguyen is very good in pass coverage and he is a great tackler. Virtually every aspect of his situation seems to suggest that Dallas is sitting on the next Tedy Bruschi.

No single area on defense will feel the effects of the 3–4 shake-up more than the defensive line. The most notable difference is that Pro Bowl defensive tackle **La'Roi Glover** will likely get stuck on the second-string unit this season, just because he doesn't fit the mold to play end or tackle on a three-man front. Glover is Dallas's best defensive lineman, possessing deadly quickness and strength that attracts regular double teams, but it is true that he is more oriented to play in a 4–3.

The starting ends for the Cowboys will be rookie and 20th-overall draft pick, **Marcus Spears**, along with veteran **Greg Ellis**. The Cowboys will probably list either **Kenyon Coleman** or **Leonardo Carson** as the starter ahead of Spears when training camp opens up, but this will be a case of political correctness once again getting in the way. Everybody knows that Spears, a powerful 305-pound force out of LSU, will start immediately. Spears can anchor against the run and use his array of pass-rushing moves to beat blockers or attract the crucial double teams that make a 3–4 go. Having begun his college career as a tight end, Spears has the versatility and agility to be an impact player.

The much-needed nose tackle for the Cowboys is **Jason Ferguson**, a player whom Dallas targeted in free agency. The former Jet did not want to leave New York, but the Cowboys pampered him like a baby. Parcells and Jones eventually cornered Ferguson on the owner's plane and convinced him to sign a deal to wear blue and white. Don't think that just because the Cowboys paid Ferguson $21.5 million to join them ($9 million signing bonus, by the way) that they're getting an elite nose tackle. Ferguson can be effective through his power, but he is not particularly explosive or dynamic.

With a revamped front seven, the media and fans will overlook the importance of the secondary for the Cowboys, but in fact—as with just about any defense—it is the area most crucial to the team's success. In '03, when the Cowboys ranked first in yards allowed on defense, the secondary allowed opponents to complete just 48.6 percent of their passes. Last year that number rose to 61.8 percent, and the Cowboys fizzled. Zimmer lost confidence in his cornerbacks, and rightfully so. That forced Dallas to be more conservative in their blitz schemes. With the emphasis this year being on creative pass rushing from the front seven, the Cowboys need their cornerbacks to handle all coverage responsibilities.

With this in mind, they went out and paid big money to bring in **Anthony Henry**, who left the Browns after four years and 17 interceptions. Henry has terrific size (6'1", 205 pounds) for a corner, and he is very adept at playing one-on-one. He is not in

the upper echelon of players at his position, but he is athletic and, again, very gifted in man coverage.

Henry will likely be the No. 2 corner, with third-year pro **Terrence Newman** regaining his No. 1 job, despite a poor sophomore season last year. Newman actually took a step back in '04, giving up a load of passes and losing his shutdown status. However, he still has the best hips in the NFL, he is still fast, and he has learned a lot over the first two years of his career. There is no reason Newman cannot finish this season as one of the top five or six cover corners in the game.

Dallas's best acquisition this offseason may have been the signing of veteran cornerback **Aaron Glenn**. Glenn—who was cut by interstate foe Houston—is 33 years old, but he is still one of the 15 best cornerbacks in the league. He is a good tackler; he gives up virtually no separation, acting as a shadow for most receivers; and he is crafty, getting away with a lot of contact. The only reason he will play nickel this year is because his skills are ideal for the job.

The Cowboys' greatest weakness will be the free safety position. The team has not been able to find an adequate replacement for Darren Woodson. Little-known **Lynn Scott** has surprising speed and could develop nicely here, but he would require more years of experience than the Cowboys are willing to give him. **Keith Davis** has been mentioned as an option, but that's almost a last resort. Cornerback **Pete Hunter** is returning from an ACL injury and has great size, so a move would make sense, but the Boys have indicated that he will play safety only in nickel packages—if at all. Ultimately, Dallas may decide to sign a free agent to fill this void.

In saving the best for last, it is time to introduce **Roy Williams**. Picture everything that has been said about the Cowboys defense thus far. Now, add a fourth-year, rock-solid hitman from Oklahoma to the scene and imagine him flying around the field, drilling people with a sense of revenge, as if he were a demon hell-bent on creating carnage and destruction. Then multiply that by six, and you have Roy Williams.

Special Teams

Kicker **Billy Cundiff** has been adequate over the past two years and has done nothing to lose his job. Punter **Mat McBriar** did some nice things in '04, coming up with big plays as only a punter can, so the Cowboys feel all right about what they have in the Australian native. The kick returner for Dallas could be anyone, as they like to change it up. Don't be surprised if it's backup running backs **Marion Barber**, a fourth-round rookie out of Minnesota.

The Bottom Line

The offense will be counted on to score points by running the ball and committing a limited number of turnovers. The defense will be expected to generate more turnovers and also put the offense in better field position. Overseeing the whole thing is a high-rolling Jones and an angry Parcells. They say the hole in the roof of Texas Stadium is so God can look down and watch his favorite team play. This year, he might like what he sees.

Players Added

WR	Plaxico Burress	(Pit)
DT	Kendrick Clancy	(Pit)
K	Jay Feely	(Atl)
QB	Tim Hasselbeck	(Was)
OT	Kareem McKenzie	(NYJ)
LB	Antonio Pierce	(Was)
OT	Bob Whitfield	(Jax)

Players Lost

DT	Martin Chase	
CB	Terry Cousin	(Jax)
RB	Ron Dayne	(Den)
DT	Norman Hand	
WR	Ike Hilliard	(TB)
OT	Barry Stokes	(Atl)
DT	Lance Legree	(NYJ)
S	Omar Stoutmire	
QB	Kurt Warner	(Ari)
DE	Keith Washington	

Draft

2	(43)	Corey Webster	CB	LSU
3	(74)	Justin Tuck	DE	Notre Dame
4	(110)	Brandon Jacobs	RB	Southern Illinois
6	(186)	Eric Moore	DE	Florida St.

The Giants felt the side effects of getting Eli Manning in '04 after having their first-round pick this year go to San Diego. Webster is a risk/reward player: He was a lock to be a first-rounder before suffering a foot injury during his senior year; now there are durability concerns. Tuck has the pass-rushing skills and football IQ to be a good player; it's just a matter of helping him find his niche at the pro level. Jacobs can be the short-yardage specialist that Ron Dayne never became.

Head Coach: Tom Coughlin (2nd year)
Offensive Coordinator: John Hufnagel
Defensive Coordinator: Tim Lewis

Offense

QB:	Eli Manning
RB:	Tiki Barber*
FB:	Jim Finn
WR:	Plaxico Burress†
WR:	Amani Toomer
TE:	Jeremy Shockey
LT:	Luke Petitgout
LG:	David Diehl
C:	Shaun O'Hara
RG:	Chris Snee
RT:	Kareem McKenzie†
QB:	Tim Hasselbeck†
RB:	Mike Cloud
WR:	Jamaar Taylor
TE:	Visanthe Shiancoe
OL:	Jason Whittle

Defense

LDE:	Michael Strahan
DT:	Fred Robbins
DT:	William Joseph
RDE:	Osi Umenyiora
SLB:	Carlos Emmons
MLB:	Antonio Pierce†
WLB:	Barrett Green
CB:	Will Allen
SS:	Brent Alexander
FS:	Gibril Wilson
CB:	William Peterson
NB:	Corey Webster‡
DL:	Justin Tuck‡
HE:	Reggie Torbor
K:	Jay Feely
P:	Jeff Feagles

* Pro Bowler '04
† veteran acquisition
‡ rookie

Report Card

Quarterback	C	Defensive Line	B	Coaching	C+
Running Back	B+	Linebacker	C+	Special Teams	B+
Receiver/Tight End	B–	Defensive Back	B+	Depth	D+
Offensive Line	C+			Intangibles	C–

Michael Strahan

The notorious New York City media should get exactly what it wants out of the New York Giants in '05: Juicy storylines. There are just too many ways for the Giants (a team that gave the country a great harbinger last year by beginning the season at 5-2, before dropping eight consecutive games) to have this season erupt in their faces.

For starters, the fact that just about every player in the Giants locker room has a strong distaste for the head coach, Tom Coughlin, is perhaps the poorest kept secret since New York City's rat problem back in '00. Coughlin—the league's most stringent disciplinarian—has fallen out of favor with virtually every player he has coached. While the public will hear the tongues of political correctness and public relations claim that all of the rumors about the players' perception of Coughlin are overblown, the fact is, no—they're not. The rumors are like stereotypes: They must be true to some *extent*, otherwise what would cause anybody to think of them in the first place?

Whether or not Coughlin completely loses his team this year remains to be seen, but one thing's for sure: The Big Apple hopes he doesn't. This city wants to see the Giants do well. They are the football team that represents the five boroughs of America's largest town. The Jets have a healthy fan base, but for whatever reason, they don't have the same appeal. If the Jets are the Chrysler Building, the Giants are the Empire State Building. If the Jets are 42nd Street, the Giants are Broadway. The discrepancy is not as bad as that of the Mets and Yankees, but to sum things up, if the Jets are Ellis Island, the Giants are the Statue of Liberty that towers over it. So, what will these Giants give this city to cheer about in '05?

Offense

No player on this team has more of the big-city spotlight on him than quarterback **Eli Manning**. Manning will be charged with redirecting an offense that scored only 18.9 points per game and ranked 26th in passing in '04. Much of the team's struggles could be attributed to the mistakes and missed opportunities made by the overwhelmed Manning. In his eight starts, Manning went 1–7, completed just 48.2 percent of his passes, averaged only 5.3 yards per pass attempt, and had a quarterback rating so low that if it were his age, he would still be ineligible to receive Social Security benefits. However, last season was last season. It's in the books. Who cares whether or not the Giants squandered a chance at the playoffs? It's over. New York now enters this season led by their prized 24-year-old quarterback, who has eight starts' worth of onerous learning experience now in his back pocket.

Manning clearly has the tools to be a big-time quarterback at the professional level, there's no doubt about that. He can throw the deep ball, he was accurate in college, he has the mobility to move in the pocket, and—most important—he has that Manning desire to be great. However, the Giants must be concerned about him trying to take in too much information and trying too hard to outthink opponents. Everyone knows one quarterback who is like this, but, without naming names, let's just say that particular player is far, *far* more experienced than his younger brother . . . err, than Eli. Last season, Manning made a great deal of audibles on pre-snap reads at the line of scrimmage, but his success rate was somewhere around a Mario Mendoza batting average.

Pre-snap reads can be great, but they aren't something that can be learned quickly. The most crucial way for Manning to improve this season is going to be through his presence in the pocket and his ability to read a defense while dropping back with the ball in his hands. What's worrisome about this is that New York may not have adequate pass protection up front to allow Manning the proper time to process plays.

Last year the Giants' front five allowed 52 sacks, which tied for the fourth most in the NFL. Part of that can be attributed to Kurt Warner and his John Deere tractor–like elusiveness, but much of it can be attributed to the offensive line.

As a result, this past offseason the Giants walked around Central Park and other patches of Upper West Side Manhattan before bumping into right tackle **Kareem McKenzie**, who was out looking for work after not being re-signed by the Jets. With the two sides coming to agreement, the Giants now have a premier right tackle who is 6'6", 327 pounds, and just 26 years of age. McKenzie can anchor the line in run-blocking and handle any opponent, in facing both linemen up front and linebackers at the second level. The only problem is that, as a tackle, McKenzie tends to the right as naturally as Ann Coulter and, thus, cannot serve as a star pass-blocker. He is too good on the right side to even consider playing at left, which means that the man who *is* on the left is **Luke Petitgout**.

Petitgout is a major weakness as a left tackle; like McKenzie, he is a natural right tackle who can use his power to anchor in run-blocking. As a pass-blocker responsible for guarding Manning's blind side, though, Petitgout plays too high and lacks the lower-body strength to handle a bull rusher. He is also very susceptible to getting beat off the snap by quicker defensive ends.

Strengths	Weaknesses
Front Four With the return of Michael Strahan, the Giants now have a solid veteran who can be the focal point of their defensive line. They also have three young players in Osi Umenyiora, William Joseph, and Justin Tuck, all of whom could break out and have big years in '05.	**Pass blocking** The Giants have a stellar offensive line, but all five starters are better in run-blocking than they are in pass protection. New York needs to find a way to protect Eli Manning this year.
Secondary Cornerbacks Will Allen and William Peterson are very good in man-to-man, and each offers a contrasting set of skills. Second-year player Gibril Wilson is an emerging star safety in the league, and rookie Corey Webster can become a good nickel back over time.	**Wide receiver depth** Outside of Plaxico Burress and Amani Toomer, the Giants don't have any truly reliable receivers they can go to. The first four backups listed on the depth chart all combined to catch just 29 passes a year ago.

Write it Down:

Hybrid end Reggie Torbor has the potential to be a major impact player in the league.

With McKenzie now handling the right tackle duties, **David Diehl** moves inside to serve at left guard, a position he has not played since his senior season at Illinois, in '02. This is also Diehl's third relocation up front in as many years. Nevertheless, he is excited about finding a home at his new position, and he should be more effective there. Diehl will upgrade the interior run-blocking because of how well he angles his blocks to create holes. However, sticking with the theme of concern for Manning's well-being, Diehl does not have ideal power and struggled at times last year with blocking pass-rushing ends.

Second-year player **Chris Snee** likely knows all about being in Coughlin's doghouse. While at Boston College, Snee fathered the baby boy of a young woman named Katie Cough-l-in. Ooh. Not to worry, though; since then, the couple has gotten married, both families are happy, and Chris has become the starting right guard on his father-in-law's football team.

Of course, if Snee cannot keep defenders off of Coughlin's quarterback this year, the family gatherings may become more awkward and tense. It won't be easy, either. Snee offers impressive athleticism and is great at run-blocking when he's on the move, but he must drastically improve in pass protection. Snee fails to make any initial contact in pass-blocking, and as a result, he gets beat. There is no reason he can't get better this season, though.

The center for New York is **Shaun O'Hara**, a player who survives strictly on effort and sheer will. Over the past couple of years, the Giants have seemingly had trouble staying healthy up front. As a result, they have a lot of experienced players on the second string. Guard **Jason Whittle** started last season, as did **Wayne Lucier**. Even third-string guard **Rich Seubert** is a player who could potentially compete for a starting job, as long as he can rebound from injuries that have caused him to miss all but six games over the past two years.

Manning does not have one of the best offensive lines to work behind in '05, but he does have the benefit of being surrounded by decent skill-position players. The best player on the Giants offense is running back **Tiki Barber**, who had a career-year in '04, rushing for 1,518 yards and earning a starting spot in the Pro Bowl. There will always be the knock on Barber that he fumbles too much—and yes, he does; he had five last year—but who in their right mind would not take a player who last season averaged three touchdowns for every one turnover?

This Season vs. Last Season

Progression: **Offensive efficiency—**Although the Giants will still not be completely up to par as an offensive unit in '05, the maturation of Eli Manning and the addition of Plaxico Burress, among other things, should make this a much more respectable offense.

Regression: **Player/coach relationship—**Tom Coughlin's iron-fist tactics do not work with today's players, and his stringent policies and acrimonious approach are already wearing thin on this team.

Barber—who turned 30 in April—still has plenty of his quickness left, which makes him very effective, considering how well he times his runs and hits the holes. He is also a decent receiver out of the backfield. The Giants have never used the 5'10", 200-pound Barber much as a short-yardage back. That won't change this year, but instead of bringing in the underachieving Ron Dayne, they'll bring in rookie fourth-round pick **Brandon Jacobs**.

The passing game for New York will have a different outlook now that a broken-down Ike Hilliard is out and a 6'5" vertical threat like **Plaxico Burress** is in. Burress's arrival will open up the offense and pump some life into the aerial game. After five up-and-down seasons in Pittsburgh, Burress reluctantly settled on a six-year, $25 million deal to play with Manning in New York.

But there is some concern about how well he will fit in with the Giants. Although he did not give a young Ben Roethlisberger much grief about catching only 35 passes last season, some have speculated that Burress might hinder Manning's growth by demanding the ball too much. Also, how he will get along with Coughlin remains to be seen.

Veteran receiver **Amani Toomer** is slowing down, but is still capable of being a No. 2 wideout. He will likely be Manning's third option this year, behind Burress and tight end **Jeremy Shockey**. Shockey is clearly a player who raises concern when it comes to interacting with Coughlin. He already infuriated his coach during the offseason by refusing to work out with the team, opting instead to join his former Hurricane teammates down in Miami. Shockey is a gifted receiver who has improved as a blocker, and he is healthy for the first time in a while. However, in order to be effective, he must be allowed to play with flair and attitude, something that wasn't the case last year.

Defense

The Giants have a solid young defense that is attempting to build chemistry and order heading into '05. There are a lot of players who are inexperienced and at a point in their career where they need to step up and take on a bigger role. Just as much, there are several players who will be competing for playing time as key backups this season.

First and foremost is the status of team leader **Michael Strahan**. Strahan is the longest-tenured Giant on the squad, entering his 13th season in New York. But his days with the team could become numbered if the 31-year-old continues to suffer injuries like the torn pectoral muscle that ended his season at the halfway point last year. If that sounds like a difficult season, it's nothing compared to Strahan's offseason, in which he went through an embarrassingly public and ugly divorce with his *former* wife, Jean.

The Giants are hoping that the NFL single-season sacks record holder can find salvation on the field and reestablish himself as the dominant force that has made him a six-time Pro Bowler. Perhaps more than his sacks, New York needs Strahan for what he does against the run, as the team ranked 28th in that

department a year ago. The Giants have a good pair of young defensive ends in **Osi Umenyiora** and third-round rookie **Justin Tuck**, but both are more of the pass-rushing variety.

Umenyiora starts at end on the right side. Entering his third year out of Troy, Umenyiora appears to be a player capable of registering double digits in sacks; he has an extremely quick first move that can give slow-footed linemen headaches. Umenyiora weighs just 280, but he still attempts to play the run and is conscious of his backside responsibilities. However, he must improve his run/pass recognition and become quicker in diagnosing plays before he can become a complete threat.

The effectiveness of the Giants' defensive tackles may hinge on the development of third-year player **William Joseph**. Joseph is a former first-round draft choice who has not lived up to his billing, but entering this season, the 315-pounder out of Miami can still become the impact player that New York needs him to be. Joseph is extremely athletic for a man of his size, and his power helps him get penetration. However, defensive line coach **Pat Flaherty** has a lot to teach him about making an initial move and finishing plays. Joseph has the good fortune of playing beside 325-pound veteran **Fred Robbins**. Robbins can command a double team with his presence alone, and although his power and limited versatility make him a run-stuffing tackle, he still managed to get five sacks last year.

The Giants' major offseason acquisition on defense came in the signing of middle linebacker **Antonio Pierce**. While the team didn't necessarily give the fifth-year player Bloomberg quantities of money, they did pony up a $6.5 million signing bonus to a man who was unproven up until last year. Pierce was the leading tackler for the Redskins in '04, filling in for an injured Michael Barrow. He became a prized commodity in the free agent market for being a coachable player who does what is asked of him.

The Giants found a respectable player in Pierce, but they are kidding themselves if they think he can be their savior on defense. Pierce lacks ideal speed and has trouble moving in the box. His best feature, in fact, is his physicality in pass coverage.

The signing of Pierce was very similar to an acquisition of a year ago, when the Giants signed free agent strongside linebacker **Carlos Emmons**. They did not overpay the former Eagle, but a lot of people thought the team was getting more of a star. The reality is that Emmons is a big and powerful force near the line of scrimmage, but he does not have very much speed, making it difficult for him to chase down ball carriers. Emmons still led the club with 97 tackles last season. In fact, tackling is something that comes easy for him—as does taking on blocks—but at times Emmons does not appear to be doing either with the greatest intensity. But in fairness, it could very well just be his nature, too.

The weakside job could be up for grabs heading into training camp. The logical starter is the agile **Barrett Green**, who can operate in space and give this Giants linebacking unit some much-needed quickness. However, Green and Coughlin get along about as well as Kobe and Shaq. Last year the coach benched the sixth-year player after he was tardy to a team meeting during their bye week in October. Since then, their relationship has been distant.

Normally, such circumstances can be overlooked when it comes to a starter, but in this case, Green is dealing with a very strict coach, he's coming off an ACL injury, and he's playing in

After taking his licks as a rookie last year, the highly-touted Eli Manning enters the '05 season with expectations of being the unquestioned leader on the Giants offense.

Startling Statistics

4, 27   Number of completions and passing yards that Manning had in a week 11 loss at Baltimore.

0   Total number of touchdowns made by New York's starting wide receivers in '04.

front of a very good backup in **Nick Greisen**. The combination spells trouble for his chances of seeing quality action this season.

Coughlin (and, one could assume, the rest of the coaching staff) is fond of Greisen and the tempo at which he plays the game. Coming from the weakside, Greisen can blitz the quarterback, chase down the ball, and use his agility to make plays. However, he lacks ideal quickness and could be a better fit in the middle.

Reggie Torbor is a name that will be heard more and more around the New York/East Rutherford area this year. A second-year player who was a fourth-round pick out of Auburn, Torbor is listed as the No. 2 strongside linebacker behind Emmons, but last season Torbor saw a lot of work at defensive end in passing situations. He has speed that is remarkable enough to earn him a starting job this season; the only question is, at what position?

Torbor was not the only late-round draft pick who showed promise as a rookie in '04. Fifth-round pick **Gibril Wilson** had an outstanding year at strong safety, making 55 tackles, three sacks, and three interceptions. Wilson is a good athlete who can fly around the field, as well as blitz while playing near the line of scrimmage. He is a disciplined player who rarely misses tackles, and he is a hustler.

New York will move Wilson to the free safety position this year, partly because, as he weighs just 197 pounds, he doesn't have the size to hold up on the strongside over the course of an entire season. Wilson will develop into a very good free safety, but he must learn to do a better job at recognizing a pass play and rotating in coverage.

The Giants have to find a starter to replace Wilson at the strong safety position, especially after releasing Shaun Williams in June. The likely choice will be 12th-year veteran **Brent Alexander**, although he, too, is more of a natural free safety. Alexander still has a familiarity with the job, though; he is a good tackler who is active near the line of scrimmage.

Making it easier to experiment with the safety position is the fact that New York has one of the best cornerback tandems in the NFL, in **William Peterson** and **Will Allen**. Both players are entering their fifth year in the league. Peterson is a 6'0" cover corner who is outstanding at deflecting passes and tackling receivers. He is not a playmaker, but he will be physical while blanketing a receiver in coverage. Allen, on the other hand, allows more separation than Peterson but, in return, has the quickness that is more likely to generate big plays. New York will need more big plays out of each of these two in '05; last season they combined for just 3 of the team's 12 interceptions. The Giants have good depth at this position. The nickel back will be either the confident **Frank Walker** or this team's first draft pick, **Corey Webster**.

Special Teams

The Giants boasted the number one kickoff return game in the league last season, thanks to the performance of **Willie Ponder**. He averaged nearly 27 yards per runback and was consistent in doing so. New York has improved their kicking game by signing former Falcon **Jay Feely**, who had an off year in '04, but, nevertheless, is still an upgrade for this club. Punter **Jeff Feagles** is not spectacular, but since when has there been anything wrong with being an average punter?

The Bottom Line

The New York Giants are a lot like a tent pitched by a first-time camper: Sure, it stands up and appears just fine, but there is the sense that it's just seconds away from having one little thing cause it to collapse. The Giants have a nice collection of players, but it doesn't seem like they will necessarily work well as a unit. They cannot stand their head coach, the quarterback is a rookie, the defense is full of guys learning new roles, and the city for which the team plays in is the media capital of the United States, making it hard to distinguish between the muckrakers and the supporters. Of course, in comparison to the overall situation last year, things really don't look that bad.

Philadelphia Eagles

Predicted: 1st ▪ 2004: 13-3 (1st)

Draft

1	(31)	Mike Patterson	DT	USC
2	(35)	Reggie Brown	WR	Georgia
2	(63)	Matt McCoy	OLB	San Diego St.
3	(77)	Ryan Moats	RB	Louisiana Tech
4	(102)	Sean Considine	S	Iowa
4	(126)	Todd Herremans	OT	Saginaw Valley
5	(146)	Trent Cole	DE	Cincinnati
5	(172)	Scott Young	OG	BYU
6	(211)	Calvin Armstrong	OT	Washington St.
7	(247)	Keyonta Marshall	DT	Grand Valley St.
7	(252)	David Bergeron	ILB	Stanford

The defending NFC champs came away with a league-high 11 picks. Knowing Andy Reid, seven or eight are likely to go into a two-year developmental phase and emerge as big-time players in the future. Patterson was drafted for security in case Corey Simon leaves after this year. Brown can be the much-needed playmaking receiver opposite Owens, and McCoy has potential to one day start, but he must get bigger. Moats is a tough runner who can be solid in a backup role.

Head Coach: Andy Reid (7th year)

Offensive Coordinator: Brad Childress

Defensive Coordinator: Jim Johnson

Offense

QB:	Donovan McNabb*
RB:	Brian Westbrook*
FB:	Jon Ritchie
WR:	Terrell Owens*
WR:	Todd Pinkston
TE:	L.J. Smith
LT:	Tra Thomas*
LG:	Artis Hicks
C:	Hank Fraley
RG:	Shawn Andrews
RT:	Jon Runyan
QB:	Koy Detmer
RB:	Correll Buckhalter
WR:	Greg Lewis
TE:	James Whalen
OL:	Steve Sciullo

Defense

LDE:	Jevon Kearse
DT:	Corey Simon
DT:	Darwin Walker
RDE:	N.D. Kalu
SLB:	Dhani Jones
MLB:	Jeremiah Trotter*
WLB:	Keith Adams
CB:	Lito Sheppard*
SS:	Michael Lewis*
FS:	Brian Dawkins*
CB:	Sheldon Brown
NB:	Roderick Hood
DL:	Sam Rayburn
LB:	Mark Simoneau
K:	David Akers*
P:	Dirk Johnson

* Pro Bowler '04
† veteran acquisition
‡ rookie

Report Card

Quarterback	A	Defensive Line	B	Coaching	A+
Running Back	B	Linebacker	B	Special Teams	B
Receiver/Tight End	B–	Defensive Back	A+	Depth	B–
Offensive Line	A–			Intangibles	A–

"I did everything they asked me to do. I played every snap they allowed me to play. I wasn't even running until, like, two weeks before the game. But I made sure I was in the best shape possible. I wasn't the guy who got tired in the Super Bowl."
— Terrell Owens, April 2005

Only Terrell Owens is capable of spreading such acrimony in a town named after the Greek word for "the City of Brotherly Love." Coming off a season in which the franchise finally got over the NFC Championship hump—ending a 24-year Super Bowl drought—one would assume that all would be cheery and well in southeastern Pennsylvania. However, such is not the case. The man who, a year ago, was believed to be the one who had saved the town, the man whom coach Andy Reid thought he could trust, ruffled the Eagles' feathers over the offseason.

Owens hired superagent Drew Rosenhaus, demanded a new contract (despite signing a seven-year deal with the team only a year ago), and went on television crying about the injustice cast upon him. Worst of all, Owens made the statement that appears above in reference to his quarterback Donovan McNabb. He took on the heart and soul of the team. The nature of the comments made

© Drew Hallowell/WireImage.com

Donovan McNabb

many realize that McNabb is in that echelon of Philly icons that a man just doesn't touch. He is now held, it would seem, in the same regard as a Ben Franklin, a Rocky Balboa, or a Bill Cosby.

Sure, Owens will hold out for most, if not *all*, of training camp. But unlike other players who pull this stunt, this franchise frankly does not give a damn; they are as stable as the Roman arch. Owens's insecurity compares in magnitude to Reid's and McNabb's coolness. The impressive attitude of the coach and his quarterback rub off on the rest of the team. Owens can whine and pout all he wants, but the hard truth is that this team is going to be one of the best in the NFC, with or without him.

Offense

For argument's sake, let's just assume that **Terrell Owens** is going to amble back onto this team with his tail between his legs. He has no choice; Philly is not going to play "Let's Make a Deal" with him, and he is a lost man without football. When he returns, the team will continue on without missing a beat. Everyone will be glad to have each other back—after all, while this team does not hinge on having Owens, it is obvious that they're significantly better with him.

However, the Owens saga is nothing more than a moot issue, because this is still **Donovan McNabb**'s team. In fact, it has been that way for a long time. This became Donovan McNabb's team when he walked up on stage and smiled in the face of those senseless boobirds on draft day in 1999. This became his team when he threw four touchdown passes while playing on a broken ankle in 2002. This became his team when he stood firm in the face of asinine criticism from Rush Limbaugh, only to see the conservative icon crumble in the end. This became McNabb's team when he led the Eagles to three consecutive NFC championship appearances, despite having less help around him than a skydiver. This became McNabb's team when he produced the play of the year on a Monday night against the Cowboys last season, running around in the backfield for 14 seconds before rifling a 60-yard completion downfield. This became McNabb's team when he finally led the franchise to a Super Bowl. Lastly, this became McNabb's team when he responded to Owens's incisive jabs by saying that he is the leader of the squad and he doesn't play games in the media.

A person could talk about statistics all they want with McNabb, and after last season (31 touchdowns, eight interceptions, 8.3 yards per attempt, 104.7 rating) it would probably be a pretty interesting conversation. However, the overall issue with the seventh-year man out of Syracuse is that he is one of the greatest players in the game today because of feats like those mentioned here. Regardless of what Owens or anyone like him has to say, McNabb is the Liberty Bell of this Philly team.

Of course, no single man can do it alone; even William Penn had his supporting cast. Reid and coordinator **Brad Childress** run an offense that is so West Coast, officials at Lincoln Financial Field should consider turning the clocks back three hours when Philly has the ball. The Eagles do not like to run—they did so only 376 times last year, fewer than any team except the Raiders. Instead of rushing, they prefer to attack defenses with an array of short passes. This is where **Brian Westbrook** comes in. Westbrook—who is in his fourth season out of local Villanova—is considered the key to this offensive scheme. He is one of the best all-around weapons in the game, possessing great speed and

quickness, plus the receiving skills of a top-tier wideout. Westbrook's 812 rushing yards on 177 carries may not sound like Pro Bowl numbers, but tacked onto his 73 catches for 703 yards and six scores, they certainly are.

Due to concerns about his durability, the team did not offer the 5'10", 210-pound Westbrook the long-term deal he was seeking over the offseason. They instead tendered him a $1.43 million contract and told him that big money awaits him after this season. To this, Westbrook did the unthinkable: He wasn't pleased, but he vowed not to miss training camp because of it, deciding instead sign the deal and to wait patiently for his time to come. (Perhaps a certain Number 81 could learn from him?) Reid and the Eagles have made it clear that they are committed to going even further in this short-passing variation of the West Coast offense. The team drafted a Westbrook clone in running back **Ryan Moats**, who should capture most of backup **Correll Buckhalter**'s playing time.

The Eagles also drafted wide receiver **Reggie Brown** (out of Georgia) early in the second round. Brown is a natural athlete who can be tough to defend against. If he can avoid injuries and prove that he gives enough of a consistent effort throughout games, he could see some significant playing time, particularly if "TO" is gone for a long period of time.

The Eagles need Brown to step up because, regardless of whether Owens is around or not, Philly is still thin at the wideout position. No. 2 receiver, **Todd Pinkston**, should not be starting in the NFL. At 6'3", 180 pounds, Pinkston has a gossamer frame that resembles half an Olson twin. Even thinner is the man's courage. Frankly put, Pinkston's fear of getting hit has become such an issue that he is a serious threat to the success of McNabb and the rest of the offense. He cannot go over the middle of the field or extend his arms to catch a pass. The only thing that Pinkston is good for is reeling in balls downfield (last year Philly led the league with twenty 40-yard pass plays). However, a player cannot go through an entire season just running fly patterns, especially if he is a starting receiver.

Greg Lewis is a fast player who will be counted on in select situations this year. If Lewis has a good camp, it might not even be that bad of an idea to have him replace Pinkston in the starting 11. The Eagles finally got rid of Freddie Mitchell, after the talkative bust made more senseless comments than he did receptions in his career.

The tight end is a huge element in Philadelphia's offense, which means that third-year player **L.J. Smith** will have to formally step up in '05. With a 6'3", 258-pound frame, Smith is a

Write it Down:

The Terrell Owens mess will work itself out (if it hasn't already) because the Eagles are not going to play games with this perverse receiver.

This Season vs. Last Season

Progression: **Linebacker—**Jeremiah Trotter should be more effective now that he can go through an entire
offseason and training camp with the team, and weakside linebacker Keith Adams has a lot to offer as
a first-year starter.

Regression: **Passing chemistry—**Not only were Terrell Owens and Donovan McNabb *not* fighting a year ago,
but they were good friends. Not anymore.

great athlete who has a strong variety of skills to offer. He is fairly fast, he has decent hands, and his long arms serve him well as a blocker. Expect Smith to do a fine job at filling the starting role this season.

Veteran Chad Lewis has retired, partly because of a broken foot suffered in the NFC Championship game. His absence leaves a major void at the No. 2 tight end spot.

The Eagles have one of the grittiest front lines in all of football, starting with right tackle **Jon Runyan**. A 6'7", 330-pound veteran out of Michigan, Runyan is a throwback player. He is a mauler in the ground game, using his field vision and intensity to clear out space, plus he is an enforcer away from the ball, serving as a threat to lay a good, *clean*, unexpected shot at any time. Runyan *does* tend to struggle with quicker pass-rushing defensive ends, but his pride runs so deep that he will never allow any opponent to beat him play in and play out.

The other tackle for the Eagles was their only Pro Bowler up front in '04, **Tra Thomas**. Like Runyan, Thomas has tremendous size (6'7", 349 pounds) and power. He benefits from more athletic ability, too. He can get movement in run-blocking, and he has the rare ability to recover after getting beat. Thomas plays with a good base in pass protection and he is a Pro Bowler, but his main weaknesses center around his footwork and balance in blocking pass-rushers. He is by no means a liability—he's far from that—but he suffers minor lapses from time to time.

The interior line for the Eagles is led by **Hank Fraley**, a man who exemplifies the consequences of having eaten too many Philly cheesesteaks. However, the 6'2", 300-pound Fraley is not hampered by his girth—he has too great of a football mind not to thrive. Fraley is one of the upper-tier centers in the NFL.

Guard **Shawn Andrews** started as a rookie in week 1 last season, but he fractured his right fibula in the opener and was lost for the year. He is back and starting again, this time with more awareness and professionalism. Andrews is a mammoth man who can engulf defenders, but he has had problems controlling his weight, at one point ticking in at over 400 pounds. Part of that may have been related to polyps in his sinuses, which Eagles doctors removed last year.

The other guard is **Artis Hicks**, who played well in his 13 starts last season. Hicks is on the left side, where he should be a nice complement to Thomas because of his serviceable pass-blocking.

Defense

In much the same way that Thomas Jefferson wrote the Declaration of Independence in Philadelphia's Independence Hall, Eagles defensive coordinator **Jim Johnson** has crafted his own Philadelphia masterpiece. He has not written a scathing letter to the British Parliament, but rather, a concise and clear message to the rest of the NFL, saying that they can endure the atrocities of the typical 4–3 or the 3–4 defense, but that the real prosperity lies within the 46 defense.

While Johnson cannot claim the credit for being the father of the 46 defense (that was Buddy Ryan and the 1985 Bears), he can receive credit for perfecting the most consistent defense in the game today. Johnson's scheme is not too complex to learn, but it is very difficult to process during live action. It is basically a defensive alignment that features an eight-man front, with blitzes coming in all directions and without any sort of pattern.

Because of the jailbreak nature of the 46 defense, the secondary is the element most crucial to its success. It just so happens that Johnson has three returning Pro Bowlers in cornerback **Lito Sheppard**, free safety **Brian Dawkins**, and strong safety **Michael Lewis**. What's more, the only starter in the defensive backfield who was not a Pro Bowler last year—**Sheldon Brown**—may actually be the second-best player (behind Dawkins).

When the Eagles originally drafted their starting cornerbacks back in '02 (Sheppard in the first round, Brown in the second), they had Bobby Taylor and Troy Vincent on the team. Philadelphia caught heat for wasting such early picks on backup players, but it's funny what a little patience can bring. Today, those cornerbacks are a dynamic tandem. Sheppard makes up for a lack of size (5'10", 194 pounds) with his quickness and uncanny ability to follow a receiver; he can even face-guard a player. His quickness and energy led to five interceptions and two touchdowns last season. Brown is not much bigger than Sheppard, but he possesses more strength. His main skills relate to his physical nature; he is a good tackler who loves to hit; he can defend the slot receiver, play the ball, and even blitz the quarterback (he had three sacks in '04).

Dawkins is one of the prime reasons that Philadelphia was among the best playmaking defenses in all of football last season. He had 12 passes defensed, four interceptions, two forced fumbles, and three sacks. Such numbers are typical for the 10th-year pro. Dawkins is simply an animal who can intimidate opponents in the box or hassle receivers in pass coverage.

Finally, there are not a lot of safeties who are more rock-solid than Lewis. The fourth-year pro out of Colorado is a mean hitter who will decapitate a daydreaming receiver over the middle.

© Rich Gabrielson/WireImage.com

"Free lance safety" Brian Dawkins is a veteran leader and the most destructive force in football's best defensive backfield.

Injuries forced Lewis into the lineup at an early stage in his career, giving him a lot of responsibility without a lot of experience. The results are now beginning to show. The 25-year-old has good awareness and is rarely caught out of position.

Philly's only vulnerability in the backfield may be in its depth. However, third-year nickel back **Roderick Hood**—who struggled at times last year—is destined to improve, as are **Dexter Wynn** and former Boise State Bronco **Quintin Mikell**.

With so much pressure on the secondary to maintain single-man-coverage, it is vital not only that Johnson's blitzers reach the quarterback, but that the front four provide a healthy pass-rush, as well. That said, not a lot of players are better in these terms than end **Jevon Kearse**. While on paper it may not seem like Kearse's 7½ sacks are worthy of the $16 million signing bonus he received as a free agent last year, the reality is that the Eagles have no trouble handing him so many dead presidents just as long as he continues to command double teams. When Kearse is attracting two blockers, it makes it easier for the Eagles to execute their blitz packages.

With the subtraction of Derrick Burgess, the new starting end on the right side is **N.D. Kalu**, who is coming off an ACL tear. Assuming Kalu is fully recovered, he can help anchor the run defense, but as far as reaching the quarterback goes, the Eagles may have to bring third-year player **Jerome McDougle** off the bench. McDougle is undersized, but athletic and quick. He has not lived up to expectations since being taken in the first round out of Miami, but he has the talent to succeed. He just needs to find his niche on this team.

The tackles for the Eagles have been cogs in this winning machine for three years and change. **Corey Simon** is the high-profile name, and **Darwin Walker** is the consistent role player. While both players have had star moments, expect '05 to be the year that the position begins to transform for Philadelphia. Simon was slapped with the franchise tag this past offseason, meaning he will angrily hold out of training camp and then likely leave for a more lucrative free agent contract next season. With this in mind, Philly may start working in **Sam Rayburn** more often. Simon is a powerful player who can make himself disruptive by bull-rushing single blocking on a regular basis, but his stamina has not been consistent from year to year. With this in mind, plus the fact that Rayburn has the energy and power to be an above-average starter right now, Simon could see fewer reps in '05.

Walker's lack of natural speed limits him to defensive tackle (the team tried him at defensive end late last season), where he will be pushed for playing time by first-round rookie **Mike Patterson**.

The entire front four, as well as the linebacking crew, will all look brilliant if middle linebacker **Jeremiah Trotter** is able to pick up where he left off a year ago. After vowing never to play

for Andy Reid again, Trotter felt his career slipping out from under him midway through last season. Both he and the coach swallowed their pride (while regurgitating their class) and reunited. Trotter finished the year as the most ruinous linebacker in the NFC. He is a beast who has outstanding strength and the type of intensity that can scare the daylights out of someone.

Much like last year, Trotter's presence will elevate the entire run defense and allow other players to work out of more natural positions. One of those players is **Keith Adams**, who displayed enough speed and high energy on special teams to earn the starting weakside job over **Mark Simoneau** this year. Adams may struggle initially because he still needs some experience as a starter—particularly in honing his pass defense—but by mid-November, the move to a more athletic threat on the weakside will have paid off for the Eagles. Simoneau will still see time as a nickel linebacker in passing situations; he is one of the best coverage linebackers in the NFL.

Strongside linebacker **Dhani Jones** is a Renaissance man off the field, having hosted a television show on ESPN2 and performed as a guest conductor for Peter Nero and the Philadelphia Pops, among other things. On the field, Jones is nearly as well-versed. He has never gotten great playing time as a starter (neither here nor with his former Giants team), but he should this season. Jones has good quickness, which allows him to do a wide range of on-the-field activities such as blitz, play coverage, or chase the ball. With all of those skills, perhaps he is Philadelphia's new Ben Franklin.

Special Teams

A team that is constantly looking forward and adding young players for the future is always going to have good special teams, especially in punt and kickoff coverage. In the offensive spectrum, kicker **David Akers** has great range and tremendous composure under pressure, which is why he made his second Pro Bowl appearance last season. Punter **Dirk Johnson** is a middle-tier player. The Eagles constantly seem to be changing their kick and punt returners; at this point, even Pennsylvania governor Ed Rendell might get a shot.

The Bottom Line

The Eagles are every bit as strong as they were last season. The offense will click as long as McNabb and Westbrook can stay healthy. They have a defense that is capable of repeating (if not improving on) last year's dominating performance. In a lot of ways, the Eagles resemble a well-run college program. They redshirt their rookies, return their seniors, and hold on to their top assistant coaches. Now all they have to do is win the BCS that is the NFC and give themselves an opportunity to finally wear a Super Bowl ring.

Washington Redskins

Predicted: 4ᵗʰ ▪ 2004: 6-10 (4ᵗʰ)

Players Added

LB	Brian Allen	(Car)
LB	Warrick Holdman	(Cle)
WR	Santana Moss	(NYJ)
WR	David Patten	(NE)
S	Pierson Prioleau	(Buf)
C	Casey Rabach	(Bal)

Players Lost

WR	Laveranues Coles	(NYJ)
DB	Todd Franz	(GB)
DL	Jermaine Haley	
QB	Tim Hasselbeck	
KR	Chad Morton	
OL	Vaughn Parker	
LB	Antonio Pierce	(NYG)
CB	Fred Smoot	(Min)

Draft

1	(9)	Carlos Rogers	CB	Auburn
1	(25)	Jason Campbell	QB	Auburn
4	(120)	Manuel White, Jr.	FB	UCLA
5	(154)	Robert McCune	ILB	Louisville
6	(183)	Jared Newberry	OLB	Stanford
7	(222)	Nehemiah Broughton	FB	The Citadel

The Skins capped their foolish offseason with a poorly-thought-out draft. Needing to replace Fred Smoot, they were able to get a playmaker in Rogers. He'll be good. But it went downhill from there. In taking Campbell, they traded next year's first-round pick just to draft a quarterback who can do nothing but cause a controversy among the other two quarterbacks they are already overpaying. Also, who drafts fullbacks in the fourth round these days, especially when they already traded to select Chris Cooley last year?

Head Coach: Joe Gibbs (2nd season)

Offensive Coordinator: Don Breaux

Defensive Coordinator: Gregg Williams

Offense

QB:	Patrick Ramsey
RB:	Clinton Portis
HB:	Chris Cooley
WR:	Santana Moss†
WR:	Rod Gardner
TE:	Robert Royal
LT:	Chris Samuels
LG:	Derrick Dockery
C:	Casey Rabach†
RG:	Randy Thomas
RT:	Jon Jansen
QB:	Mark Brunell
RB:	Ladell Betts
WR:	David Patten†
WR:	Darnerien McCants
OL:	Ray Brown

Defense

LDE:	Renaldo Wynn
DT:	Brandon Noble
DT:	Cornelius Griffin
RDE:	Phillip Daniels
SLB:	Marcus Washington
MLB:	Lemar Marshall
WLB:	LaVar Arrington
CB:	Shawn Springs
SS:	Matt Bowen
FS:	Sean Taylor
CB:	Carlos Rogers‡
NB:	Walt Harris
DL:	Joe Salave'a
LB:	Brian Allen†
K:	John Hall
P:	Tom Tupa

* Pro Bowler '04
† veteran acquisition
‡ rookie

Report Card

Quarterback	C	Defensive Line	C	Coaching	C+
Running Back	B+	Linebacker	B	Special Teams	B–
Receiver/Tight End	B	Defensive Back	B	Depth	C–
Offensive Line	B			Intangibles	D

President Bush's inevitable Supreme Court nominations will undoubtedly further divide an already torn U.S. Congress in the near future, but such tension on Capitol Hill won't hold a candle to the chaos brewing at FedEx Way in nearby Landover, Maryland. Landover is the home of the Washington Redskins, a team that is coming off perhaps the worst offseason in the NFL.

After team owner Dan Snyder forked over $5 million a season last year to bring back head coach Joe Gibbs—only to see his team lose 10 games—one figured that things could only improve for the Skins. However, since their last game back in January, things have only gotten worse.

The team that plays in the nation's capital made a slew of horrendous legislative decisions, beginning with trading unhappy receiver Laveranues Coles. In exchange, Washington received an inferior wideout from New York in Santana Moss, and they had to pay the Jets a $5 million tariff on Coles's old signing bonus. Once Senator Moss became a Redskin, he initially refused to show up, protesting the insufficient grants appropriated to his Underachieving Receiver Act (i.e., his contract). That forced the team to pass a bill that gave the receiver a pricey new six-year contract.

After *paying* to trade one receiver for another, the Redskins fielded scathing criticism from their franchise player, LaVar Arrington (who was upset about the way the team handled his knee injury); endured the embarrassing episodes of star safety Sean Taylor going AWOL and running back Clinton Portis bragging about his partying during the offseason (while

Clinton Portis

campaigning for fewer workout requirements); watched leading tackler Antonio Pierce leave to join bitter division rival New York Giants; and pulled together a terrible draft, in which the team's Congress voted to select quarterback Jason Campbell, thus creating a three-man competition for the starting job this year. From here, it appears that many frustrated Redskin fans will be writing their congressman and asking for the impeachment of someone—*anyone*—this year.

Offense

When the Redskins traded their No. 1 draft pick in 2006 and two additional picks to the Broncos in order to draft Auburn quarterback **Jason Campbell** with the 25th overall pick this season, they caused many in the football world to question their direction. In sticking with the political theme, drafting a quarterback in Campbell was the football version of the Social Security debate; the same questions arose: Is it a smart idea to attack a potential problem at this moment? Just how severe is this problem? Are the immediate consequences worth the trouble?

Apparently Gibbs views his quarterback situation as a developing problem, because teams do not draft backups in the first round. However, considering that the Redskins have 26-year-old **Patrick Ramsey** returning, did they really need to bend over so far backward to get Campbell? What the Redskins have done now is add a monumental distraction to their season.

The long-term answers to this situation are fairly easy to figure out: The team is going to make Campbell their franchise quarterback and gradually phase Ramsey out of the picture, via either release or demotion. However, focusing on *this* season, it's hard to forecast what the team has in mind. First off, discard all rumors about veteran **Mark Brunell** re-earning the starting job—the Skins would be fools to go that route. What they'll likely do instead is start Ramsey in the initial stages of the season, lose some games, and then decide to give Campbell a chance. In fact, because he performed so well during the team's minicamps during the offseason, there is an outside possibility that Campbell will open the season as the starter. Nevertheless, Ramsey is approaching the season as if it were still *his* team, but he knows that if this were the case they would not have drafted Campbell to begin with.

Gibbs is correct to question whether Ramsey is his guy. Although the fourth-year quarterback has shown admirable toughness in taking hit after hit, he has also shown that he is a slow learner. In the pocket, he takes as long to read a defense and pass the ball as Congress does to read a bill and pass a law. Ramsey struggles against the blitz, he struggles in the second half of games, and he struggles with taking care of possession. He has the optimum skills to be a great No. 2 quarterback in the NFL, but as a starter he just isn't quite there.

Running back **Clinton Portis** is entering his second year in D.C. Portis struggled at times last season, averaging a career-low 3.8 yards per carry with five fumbles. His problems stem from the simple fact that he is not the right type of back to play in Gibbs's power-running, between-the-tackles system. Portis's greatest assets are his speed, quickness, and agility, each of which is limited when he has to wait for slow-developing counterplays.

Portis is still going to put up great numbers, for the simple reason that he is incredibly talented. However, he may not be the

Strengths

Run Defense

Washington was very strong in this department a year ago, and with their girth up front protecting players like LaVar Arrington and Marcus Washington in the middle, they should be tough to rush the ball against in '05.

Tackles

Chris Samuels is close to becoming an All-World player. He is certainly among the top five left tackles in the game. Jon Jansen is coming off a foot injury, but he has the character and passion for the sport to fully recover and have a good year.

Weaknesses

Offensive Scheme

Joe Gibbs has been a great coach in the past, but, unfortunately, right now he is flat-out running the wrong system with this offense.

Hurricanes

The former Miami Hurricane players are killing this team: Santana Moss caused a brief stir when he demanded a new contract, and Clinton Portis and Sean Taylor spent a majority of their offseason having fun on South Beach, rather than working to improve as professional athletes.

type of player that this team can win with. In addition to his skills being incompatible with the offense, Portis has not shown enough passion for the game or enough maturity as a professional. He made no bones about spending his offseason having fun and not working, and he has even preached an anti-workout message to his younger constituents on the team.

One player who is great in Gibbs's offense is halfback **Chris Cooley**, a second-year man out of Utah State. Cooley is a good short-yardage receiver; last year he had 37 receptions and six touchdowns. As a halfback, Cooley's responsibilities are similar to those of a fullback in running situations and a tight end in passing situations.

Washington is listing veteran **Mike Sellers** as their starting fullback, but he is a player who should tattoo the phrase "Yes, I'm still in the league" on his forehead. Expect the Redskins to use Cooley as their lead-blocker for Portis this year. As a blocker, Cooley isn't too powerful, but he has outstanding quickness and technique. At the tight end position, the Skins will go with third-year player **Robert Royal**. Royal would be a second-stringer on almost any other team in the NFL, but because he plays hard and can block, he starts in Gibbs's offense.

Royal caught eight passes last year, and although Cooley makes up for many of his receptions, this team still needs a bona fide short-yardage receiver. A dump-off target would serve Ramsey well and allow him to become more comfortable under pressure. The same can be said for helping Campbell—should he start.

This is where the offense begins to jumble. The Redskins *had* the perfect type of receiver in Coles, but they chose to deal him for fifth-year player **Santana Moss**. Moss is a tremendous big-play threat—averaging 18.6 yards per catch last year—but at 5'10", 185 pounds, he does not have the size (or, frankly, the toughness) to go over the middle.

Washington's other options don't really work, either. As of May, the Redskins were still trying to move receiver **Rod Gardner**. The starter could be former Patriot **David Patten**, a multitalented player who averaged 18.2 yards per catch in 2004, but he has "product of the New England system" written all over him. Gibbs has even indicated that third-year receiver **Taylor Jacobs** might start, although Jacobs has done absolutely nothing thus far in his career to show that he's worthy.

> **Write it Down:**
>
> Clinton Portis is an outstanding talent, but his success in Washington will be limited by his inability to fully utilize his skills in this offense. Furthermore, Portis still might put up great numbers, but he isn't a leader or the type of player who will win football games in the long haul.

Progression: **Front five—**The return of Jon Jansen, the improvement of the mediocre yet still respectable Derrick Dockery, and the addition of center Casey Rabach will all translate into a better offensive line this season.

Regression: **Team morale—**The Redskins simply had too many things go wrong over the offseason to make this thing work in '05.

Concerning the running back and receiver situation, Washington essentially has a very talented offense that is operating in the worst possible system for these players' skills. At this age, Gibbs should not be expected to change now, and, of course, he's not going to. However, this is going to make it very difficult for the Redskins to improve their 31st-ranked scoring output from a year ago.

One factor that will make matters much easier for Washington is their stellar offensive line, headed by left tackle **Chris Samuels**. Although he did not make the Pro Bowl last season, Samuels is still regarded as one of the best linemen in the NFL, and rightfully so. He has improved his toughness to become one of the most controlling run-blockers in the game today. The sixth-year pro out of Alabama also has outstanding athleticism, making him a standout pass-blocker.

The other keynote lineman for the Skins is **Jon Jansen**, a man who was considered one of the premium right tackles in the league, before going to Canton and rupturing his Achilles tendon in the NFL Hall of Fame game last year. If the 305-pound Jansen can return in full health in '05, the Redskins will have one of the best bookend tackle tandems in the game.

Free agent acquisition **Casey Rabach** takes over at starting center for **Cory Raymer**, who is a solid one-on-one player but is entering his 10th year in the league. The former Raven Rabach—who is approaching his fifth season—is a bright young center with Pro Bowl potential. Last year was his first season as a starter, and he showed a great feel for the game. Rabach boasts good athleticism and plays with great energy, making him a terrific fit in this system.

Right guard **Randy Thomas** is a powerful run-blocking force. Thomas can dominate opponents when he is going north and south, and he is adequate in pass protection, just as long as he can establish a solid base. The other guard is **Derrick Dockery**, a player who has improved his awareness enough that he should no longer be considered a liability up front. Dockery, however, still needs to build his confidence and become more aggressive.

Defense

Last season, despite all that went wrong, the Redskins were still able to generate some excitement for their fans by having one of the best defenses in the NFL. Washington ranked fifth in fewest points allowed (16.6 per game) and third in fewest yards allowed (267.6 per game). They also ranked second in both rush defense and third-down defense.

The main factor in the team's success in '04 was new defensive coordinator **Gregg Williams**. Williams has installed a more aggressive scheme that asks for extra energy from his front seven. Furthermore, on the sideline during games, he himself is a great source of energy, motivating his players with his passion and enthusiasm. Perhaps most remarkable about Williams and his defense (particularly with the job he did last season) is how it has

proven to work no matter who is executing it on the field. Last year the Redskins were missing about half of their starters for a good majority of the schedule, yet they still managed to play well.

One starter who missed a lot of playing time was weakside linebacker **LaVar Arrington**. Arrington played in only five games in '04, due to ongoing knee problems that were a result of torn cartilage. While Washington can play well without their key figures in the game, they cannot enjoy success over a sustained period of time if they do not have Arrington on the field. He is the motor on this defense—in fact, he is the prime superstar on this team. At 6'3", 253 pounds, the 27-year-old can do it all, whether it's rush the quarterback, stuff the run, chase down a ball carrier, or defend a pass. However, Arrington is not entering this season on the best of terms with the Redskins. In April he had a second surgery on his knee and later blasted the team for not showing him more support. He has since met with Gibbs, and in all likelihood, the two have patched things up. Arrington is an extremely intelligent and judicious man who is not afraid to speak out. But all in all, he understands the realm of professional sports and what it means to play for a proud franchise. In a sense, his public complaints about the team were really just something that the politicians around D.C. call a trial balloon.

With Arrington in the game, Washington's other linebackers—**Marcus Washington** and **Lemar Marshall**—should have more freedom to operate. Washington is coming off his best season as a pro, in which he had 102 tackles and $4\frac{1}{2}$ sacks. He is a well-sized strongside linebacker who plays the game with nice dexterity. He never gives up on a play and he never gets blown up by blockers. Marcus Washington does not have the raw talent to be considered a superstar (he makes a lot of his tackles too far downfield), but he is the type of player who works extremely well as part of a group. He'll help enhance the overall performance of the linebacking unit.

Marshall is a fourth-year player out of Michigan State. He is approaching his first year as a starting middle linebacker, although injuries in various other positions on defense allowed him to start 14 games a year ago. Marshall will definitely need the talent of Arrington and Marcus Washington around him. He doesn't quite have the skills to be a starting middle linebacker in

Finally healthy, All-World linebacker LaVar Arrington should return to dismantling opposing offenses in '05.

the NFL, lacking size, speed, and the strength to shed blocks. The Redskins may even opt to start veteran **Mike Barrow** (who missed all of last season with tendinitis in his knee) or free agent acquisition **Warrick Holdman**. They could then use the versatile Marshall as a utility backup off the bench.

With Arrington and Marcus Washington at linebacker, this team is going to be tough to run against in '05. Helping the cause is the situation at the defensive tackle position, which features a prospering young star in **Cornelius Griffin** and a rotation of enormous space-eaters. Griffin, in his sixth season out of Alabama, is a wide body who is explosive. He has an assortment of dynamic first moves and gets off blocks extremely well. He has superb lateral mobility, too, making him difficult to control as a run-stopper.

Next to Griffin is **Brandon Noble**, a 304-pound bull who can clog the middle. Noble does not have any skills to offer other than being a large man, which is why they will use the more active **Joe Salave'a** from time to time. Salave'a can move much better than Noble, although he does not have as much size (a small 295 pounds). The third man of the rotation could be **Cedric Killings**.

The Redskins have solid defensive ends on first and second down, but somewhat helpless options on third downs. Washington starts ninth-year veteran **Renaldo Wynn** on the left side. Wynn is not a particularly fast player, but he has crafty moves that he's constantly fighting to use, and the fact that he can slide over to defensive tackle to rush the passer makes him a versatile option. The Redskins need to upgrade their right defensive end because **Phillip Daniels** is a 32-year-old player who is coming off a wrist injury. While a wrist injury is not going to set a man's career back too much, a year away from football can. If Daniels can regain his fiber, he can be an adequate run-stopping end.

Although none of them—Noble, Salave'a, Wynn, or Griffin—is a viable pass-rushing option, Washington still ranked ninth in total sacks a year ago, thanks to the creativity of Williams. Williams finds time for backup threats like **Ron Warner** and linebacker **Chris Clemons** to get sacks out of special defensive packages. In fact, Williams's array of blitz schemes is so elaborate that the Redskins had 16 players record at least one sack and 9 players with at least two sacks last season.

One of those players was cornerback **Shawn Springs**, who didn't have just one or two—he actually tied with Griffin for the team lead with six. A cornerback in the NFL has not had six sacks since the last Roosevelt administration.

Springs didn't just sack quarterbacks last season, he also proved that despite having more hamstring problems than Ken Griffey, Jr., he could still be a valuable cover corner in the NFL.

Springs is now 30 years old, but if he can stay healthy, he still has good hips, technique, and an ability to close on a receiver.

Although Williams historically has avoided starting rookie players (particularly cornerbacks), opposite Springs will be ninth-overall pick **Carlos Rogers**, who is replacing star Fred Smoot. Rogers is a player who the Redskins believe can be a shutdown corner at the pro level. He was a superstar playmaker at Auburn, showing the speed and agility to dominate in one-on-one coverage.

Nickel back **Walt Harris** is a good talent at this position, although he might not have the agility to handle double moves and run with a player left or right. It would not be a bad idea to move Harris over to the outside and slide either Springs or Rogers over to cover the slot on third down.

No player epitomizes the immature pro more than free safety **Sean Taylor**. In his second season out of Miami, Taylor has the skills to be a superstar in every sense of the word. He hits hard, he's athletic, and he plays with great energy. However, Taylor infuriated his teammates and coaches by going AWOL during the offseason. The problem with him is that off the field he has been known to party more than one of the puppies in Snoop Dog's posse.

Matt Bowen is penciled in at the strong safety position, but he is coming off a knee injury and has limited abilities as it is. He could be pushed for playing time by **Ryan Clark**, who is really not much of an option himself.

Special Teams

The Redskins punted more than any team in the NFL last season, other than the Bears, which means that **Tom Tupa** might run the risk of becoming exhausted this year. Not to worry about Tupa, though: At the age of 39, he is coming off one of his best seasons as a pro. Kicker **John Hall** still has one of the most powerful legs in all of football, although he will have to beat out **Jeff Chandler** for a job this season. Backup running back **Ladell Betts** is an all-right kick returner. Last season punt return duties were split by **Chad Morton** (who was released) and **James Thrash**, but this year the electrifying Moss will take over.

The Bottom Line

With so much drama in D.C. this past offseason, the Redskins will probably be glad once September finally arrives. However, this is when the real losing starts to take place, something that neither Snyder nor Gibbs will tolerate. Washington's offense is full of talented players who will be working in the wrong type of system this year. The defense will be stellar, especially against the run. However, with so many areas of concern for this team, it is more likely that Ted Kennedy will be invited over to eat dinner and watch a ball game at 1600 Pennsylvania Avenue than it is that this team will rebound to contend for the division title in '05.

NFC North

Chicago
Bears

Detroit
Lions

Green Bay
Packers

Minnesota
Vikings

Looking Forward

How They'll Finish
1. Minnesota Vikings
2. Detroit Lions
3. Green Bay Packers
4. Chicago Bears

Ready to Break Out

**Tommie Harris,
Chicago Bears**

Defensive Tackle
6'3"—300
2nd year—22 years old
Drafted: 1st round in '04 out of Oklahoma

People said that Tommie Harris was one of those players who used the collegiate game as nothing more than a springboard to the NFL. They were right. A medium-impact player at Oklahoma, Harris has a rare combination of skills that make him ideal for the professional game.

Tommie Harris

He is one of the most explosive players in all of football, which gives him an extra half step on virtually every play. He has a diverse arsenal of moves, including a Michael Phelps–like swim move, a Pamplona-like bull-rush, and a powerful punch that would make the giant Kool-Aid guy jealous.

In addition to his mouthwatering raw talent, Harris shows the intelligence to diagnose plays (a rare trait for a player who has been athletically superior his entire life) and the type of passion for the game that greatness is made of. If he doesn't make the Pro Bowl this season, it will likely be due to a lack of publicity, not a lack of performance.

Hot Seat

**Joey Harrington,
Detroit Lions**

There isn't much that needs to be said about Harrington's situation this year. He is a former No. 2 overall pick who has not lived up to expectations in his first three seasons. His team has given him a one-year trial and plenty of help: He has more weapons around him than Fort Knox. Finally, the Lions have signed a proven veteran quarterback in Jeff Garcia, who came to town as a close friend of half of the coaching staff and brought with him a mind well-versed in Detroit's offense. Plus, in just his first minicamp in sky blue and silver, Garcia all but announced his intentions to pry Harrington's job away in '05.

Best Offseason Move

Vikings trading receiver Randy Moss for linebacker Napoleon Harris and a bounty of draft picks.

Worst Offseason Move

Vikings using a fourth-round draft pick on Florida running back Ciatrick Fason.

Best Under-the-Radar Offseason Move

Bears switching Mike Brown to strong safety and Mike Green to free safety.

Biggest Question

With passing attacks as potent as the ones in Minnesota, Detroit, and Green Bay, which team's secondary will step up in '05?

QUICK HITS

TEAM BESTS		BEST PLAYERS	
Passing Game	Packers	Pure Athlete	Daunte Culpepper, Viking
Running Game	Packers	Big Play Threat	Javon Walker, Packers
Offensive Line	Vikings	Best Use of Talent	Aaron Kampman, Packers
Pass Rush	Vikings	Worst Use of Talent	Cletidus Hunt, Packers
Run Defense	Bears	On the Rise	Roy Williams, Lions
Pass Defense	Vikings		Javon Walker, Packers
Special Teams	Bears		Lance Briggs, Bears
Coaching Staff	Lions	On the Decline	Earl Holmes, Lions
Home Field	Packers		Fred Miller, Bears
			Brad Johnson, Vikings
		Best Leader	Brett Favre, Packers
		Unsung Hero	Grady Jackson, Packers
		Impact Rookie	Troy Williamson, Vikings

Daunte Culpepper

Looking Back

Chicago Bears 2004

PASSING STATISTICS

PLAYER	CMP	ATT	YDS	CMP%	YDS/A	LNG	TD	TD%	INT	INT%	SACK	YDS	RAT
Chad Hutchinson	92	161	903	57.1	5.61	63	4	2.5	3	1.9	23	160	73.6

RUSHING STATISTICS

PLAYER	ATT	YDS	AVG	LNG	TD	FUM	LST
Thomas Jones	240	948	4.0	54	7	2	1
Anthony Thomas	122	404	3.3	41	2	1	1
Bobby Wade	12	76	6.3	14	0	0	0

RECEIVING STATISTICS

PLAYER	REC	YDS	AVG	LNG	TD	FUM	LST
David Terrell	42	699	16.6	63	1	0	0
Bobby Wade	42	481	11.5	40	0	2	1
Thomas Jones	56	427	7.6	45	0	0	0
Desmond Clark	24	282	11.8	31	1	1	1

RETURN STATISTICS

PLAYER	KICKOFFS					PUNTS				
	ATT	YDS	FC	AVG	LNG	TD	ATT	YDS	FC	AVG	LNG	TD
Jerry Azumah	42	924	0	22.0	73	0	0	0	0	0.0	0	0
Bernard Berrian	17	385	0	22.6	41	0	2	10	2	5.0	12	0

KICKING STATISTICS

PLAYER	1-20	20-29	30-39	40-49	50+	TOT	PCT	AVG	LNG	XPM/A	PTS
Paul Edinger	0/0	6/7	2/5	4/7	3/5	15/24	62.5	36.3	53	22/22	67

PUNTING STATISTICS

PLAYER	PUNTS	YDS	AVG	LNG	TB	TB%	IN20	IN20%	RET	YDS	AVG	NET
Brad Maynard	108	4638	42.9	58	5	4.6	34	31.5	55	363	6.6	39.6

DEFENSIVE STATISTICS

PLAYER	TACKLES					MISCELLANEOUS		INTERCEPTIONS				
	TOT	SOLO	AST	SACK	TLOSS	FF	BK	INT	YDS	AVG	LNG	TD	PD
Lance Briggs	126	104	22	0.5	8.5	0	0	1	38	38.0	38	1	10
Mike Green	107	89	18	1.5	4.5	2	0	2	0	0	0	0	9
Brian Urlacher	71	55	16	5.0	5.5	2	0	1	42	42.0	42	0	7
Hunter Hillenmeyer	70	54	16	2.0	6.5	1	0	0	0	0.0	0	0	2
Todd Johnson	68	58	10	0.0	1	0	0	0	0	0.0	0	0	2
R.W. McQuarters	67	56	11	0	0	0	0	2	85	42.5	45	1	9
Alex Brown	51	39	12	6.0	6	3	0	0	0	0.0	0	0	9
Jerry Azumah	50	42	8	1.5	2	2	0	4	128	32.0	70	1	9
Ian Scott	44	35	9	2.0	5.5	0	0	0	0	0.0	0	0	3
Tommie Harris	44	30	14	3.5	7	1	0	0	0	0.0	0	0	2

Detroit Lions 2004

PASSING STATISTICS

PLAYER	CMP	ATT	YDS	CMP%	YDS/A	LNG	TD	TD%	INT	INT%	SACK	YDS	RAT
Joey Harrington	274	489	3047	56.0	6.23	62	19	3.9	12	2.5	36	196	77.5

RUSHING STATISTICS

PLAYER	ATT	YDS	AVG	LNG	TD	FUM	LST
Kevin Jones	241	1133	4.7	74	5	2	1
Shawn Bryson	50	264	5.3	28	0	0	0
Joey Harrington	48	175	3.6	17	0	1	0

RECEIVING STATISTICS

PLAYER	REC	YDS	AVG	LNG	TD	FUM	LST
Roy Williams	54	817	15.1	46	8	1	1
Az-Zahir Hakim	31	533	17.2	39	3	0	0
Stephen Alexander	41	377	9.2	30	1	0	0
Shawn Bryson	44	322	7.3	30	0	1	1

RETURN STATISTICS

PLAYER	KICKOFFS					PUNTS				
	ATT	YDS	FC	AVG	LNG	TD	ATT	YDS	FC	AVG	LNG	TD
Eddie Drummond	41	1092	0	26.6	99	2	24	316	8	13.2	83	2
Reggie Swinton	18	410	0	22.8	43	0	16	104	9	6.5	18	0

KICKING STATISTICS

PLAYER	1-20	20-29	30-39	40-49	50+	TOT	PCT	AVG	LNG	XPM/A	PTS
Jason Hanson	0/0	9/9	10/11	5/8	0/0	24/28	85.7	31.9	48	28/28	100

PUNTING STATISTICS

PLAYER	PUNTS	YDS	AVG	LNG	TB	TB%	IN20	IN20%	RET	YDS	AVG	NET
Nick Harris	92	3765	40.9	60	7	7.6	32	34.8	46	441	9.6	36.1

DEFENSIVE STATISTICS

PLAYER	TACKLES					MISCELLANEOUS		INTERCEPTIONS				
	TOT	SOLO	AST	SACK	TLOSS	FF	BK	INT	YDS	AVG	LNG	TD	PD
Earl Holmes	111	91	20	0.0	7.5	0	0	0	0	0.0	0	0	2
Teddy Lehman	98	84	14	1.0	2	1	0	1	1	1.0	1	0	3
Brock Marion	88	77	11	0.0	0	0	0	3	43	14.3	24	0	8
James Davis	79	65	14	3.5	6.5	0	0	0	0	0.0	0	0	3
Bracy Walker	74	56	18	1.0	0	0	0	1	0	0.0	0	0	6
Shaun Rogers	68	53	15	4.0	7	0	3	0	0	0.0	0	0	5
Fernando Bryant	50	46	4	0.0	1	0	0	0	0	0.0	0	0	9
Alex Lewis	49	37	12	2.0	1	0	0	1	33	33.0	33	0	3
James Hall	48	40	8	11.5	3	4	0	1	30	30.0	30	0	5
Cory Redding	40	36	4	3.0	4.5	1	0	0	0	0.0	0	0	0

2004 Team Stats (Chicago Bears)

OFFENSE

Scoring:	14.4 (32)
Yards per Game:	238.5 (32)
Pass Yards per Game:	137.0 (32)
Rush Yards per Game:	101.5 (t25)
Sacks Allowed:	66 (32)
3rd Down Percentage:	25.1 (32)
Giveaways:	35 (t31)

DEFENSE

Scoring:	20.7 (13)
Yards per Game:	336.9 (21)
Pass Yards per Game:	208.8 (15)
Rush Yards per Game:	128.1 (25)
Sacks:	35 (23)
3rd Down Percentage:	30.5 (1)
Takeaways:	28 (t10)

2004 Team Stats (Detroit Lions)

OFFENSE

Scoring:	18.5 (24)
Yards per Game:	293.3 (24)
Pass Yards per Game:	182.3 (23)
Rush Yards per Game:	111.1 (19)
Sacks Allowed:	37 (t15)
Giveaways:	17 (t7)

DEFENSE

Scoring:	21.9 (t18)
Yards per Game:	337.6 (22)
Pass Yards per Game:	219.6 (20)
Rush Yards per Game:	117.9 (15)
Sacks:	38 (t14)
3rd Down Percentage:	42.4 (t27)
Takeaways:	23 (22)

🏈 Green Bay Packers 2004

PASSING STATISTICS

PLAYER	CMP	ATT	YDS	CMP%	YDS/A	LNG	TD	TD%	INT	INT%	SACK	YDS	RAT
Brett Favre	346	540	4088	64.1	7.57	79	30	5.6	17	3.1	12	101	92.4

RUSHING STATISTICS

PLAYER	ATT	YDS	AVG	LNG	TD	FUM	LST
Ahman Green	259	1163	4.5	90	7	6	4
Najeh Davenport	71	359	5.1	40	2	0	0
Tony Fisher	65	224	3.4	24	0	0	0

RECEIVING STATISTICS

PLAYER	REC	YDS	AVG	LNG	TD	FUM	LST
Javon Walker	89	1382	15.5	79	12	2	2
Donald Driver	84	1208	14.4	50	9	1	1
Robert Ferguson	24	367	15.3	48	1	0	0
Bubba Franks	34	361	10.6	29	7	0	0

RETURN STATISTICS

PLAYER	KICKOFFS						PUNTS					
	ATT	YDS	FC	AVG	LNG	TD	ATT	YDS	FC	AVG	LNG	TD
Antonio Chatman	25	565	0	22.6	59	0	32	245	27	7.7	28	0
Robert Ferguson	21	526	0	25.0	71	0	0	0	0	0.0	0	0

KICKING STATISTICS

PLAYER	1-20	20-29	30-39	40-49	50+	TOT	PCT	AVG	LNG	XPM/A	PTS
Ryan Longwell	0/0	8/8	8/9	6/8	2/3	24/28	85.7	35.5	53	48/48	120

PUNTING STATISTICS

PLAYER	PUNTS	YDS	AVG	LNG	TB	TB%	IN20	IN20%	RET	YDS	AVG	NET
Bryan Barker	66	2644	40.1	64	7	10.6	16	24.2	34	301	8.9	35.5

DEFENSIVE STATISTICS

PLAYER	TACKLES					MISCELLANEOUS		INTERCEPTIONS					
	TOT	SOLO	AST	SACK	TLOSS	FF	BK	INT	YDS	AVG	LNG	TD	PD
Nick Barnett	121	95	26	3.0	6	0	0	1	16	16.0	16	0	6
Na'il Diggs	80	63	17	1.0	8	0	1	0	0	0.0	0	0	0
Darren Sharper	72	61	11	0.0	1	2	0	4	97	24.3	43	2	7
Mark Roman	71	54	17	3.5	2.5	0	0	0	0	0.0	0	0	2
Aaron Kampman	68	54	14	4.5	4.5	1	0	0	0	0.0	0	0	3
Al Harris	62	57	5	0.0	1	0	0	1	29	29.0	29	0	20
Hannibal Navies	47	40	7	0.5	2.5	0	0	0	0	0.0	0	0	0
Kabeer Gbaja-Biamila	47	36	11	13.5	2	2	0	0	0	0.0	0	0	2
Ahmad Carroll	46	43	3	2.0	2	0	0	1	0	0.0	0	0	8
Michael Hawthorne	34	27	7	0.0	1	2	0	0	0	0.0	0	0	7

🏈 Minnesota Vikings 2004

PASSING STATISTICS

PLAYER	CMP	ATT	YDS	CMP%	YDS/A	LNG	TD	TD%	INT	INT%	SACK	YDS	RAT
Daunte Culpepper	379	548	4717	69.2	8.61	82	39	7.1	11	2.0	46	238	110.9

RUSHING STATISTICS

PLAYER	ATT	YDS	AVG	LNG	TD	FUM	LST
Onterrio Smith	124	544	4.4	38	2	2	1
Daunte Culpepper	88	406	4.6	16	2	5	3
Mewelde Moore	65	379	5.8	33	0	0	0

RECEIVING STATISTICS

PLAYER	REC	YDS	AVG	LNG	TD	FUM	LST
Nate Burleson	68	1006	14.8	68	9	0	0
Randy Moss	49	767	15.7	82	13	1	1
Jermaine Wiggins	71	705	9.9	39	4	1	0
Marcus Robinson	47	657	14.0	50	8	1	0

RETURN STATISTICS

PLAYER	KICKOFFS						PUNTS					
	ATT	YDS	FC	AVG	LNG	TD	ATT	YDS	FC	AVG	LNG	TD
Kelly Campbell	35	760	0	21.7	55	0	0	0	0	0.0	0	0
Mewelde Moore	20	386	0	19.3	33	0	4	28	1	7.0	17	0

KICKING STATISTICS

PLAYER	1-20	20-29	30-39	40-49	50+	TOT	PCT	AVG	LNG	XPM/A	PTS
Morten Andersen	1/1	8/8	5/7	4/6	0/0	18/22	81.8	31.7	48	45/45	99

PUNTING STATISTICS

PLAYER	PUNTS	YDS	AVG	LNG	TB	TB%	IN20	IN20%	RET	YDS	AVG	NET
Darren Bennett	57	2240	39.3	61	3	5.3	18	31.6	26	169	6.5	36.3

DEFENSIVE STATISTICS

PLAYER	TACKLES					MISCELLANEOUS		INTERCEPTIONS					
	TOT	SOLO	AST	SACK	TLOSS	FF	BK	INT	YDS	AVG	LNG	TD	PD
E.J. Henderson	94	73	21	1.0	6.5	1	0	0	0	0.0	0	0	3
Corey Chavous	79	63	16	0.0	1	1	0	1	0	0.0	0	0	6
Antoine Winfield	78	68	10	0.0	1	2	0	3	89	29.7	56	0	8
Brian Russell	78	64	14	0.0	0	0	0	1	41	41.0	41	0	7
Brian Williams	71	62	9	0.0	3.5	2	0	2	14	7.0	14	0	11
Kevin Williams	70	56	14	12.0	4.5	2	0	1	7	7.0	7	0	8
Chris Claiborne	57	40	17	1.0	0	1	0	1	15	15.0	15	1	5
Dontarrious Thomas	51	40	11	0.5	1	1	0	0	0	0.0	0	0	0
Keith Newman	47	39	8	3.0	0.5	0	0	0	0	0.0	0	0	3
Kenny Mixon	46	29	17	2.5	0	0	0	0	0	0.0	0	0	2

2004 Team Stats

OFFENSE

Scoring:	26.5 (5)
Yards per Game:	396.8 (3)
Pass Yards per Game:	277.6 (3)
Rush Yards per Game:	119.3 (10)
Sacks Allowed:	14 (t1)
3rd Down Percentage:	47.3 (2)
Giveaways:	28 (t23)

DEFENSE

Scoring:	23.8 (23)
Yards per Game:	346.3 (25)
Pass Yards per Game:	228.9 (25)
Rush Yards per Game:	117.4 (14)
Sacks:	4 (t9)
3rd Down Percentage:	35 (9)
Takeaways:	14 (t30)

2004 Team Stats

OFFENSE

Scoring:	25.3 (6)
Yards per Game:	396.2 (4)
Pass Yards per Game:	282.3 (2)
Rush Yards per Game:	113.9 (18)
Sacks Allowed:	46 (25)
3rd Down Percentage:	52.3 (1)
Giveaways:	21 (t10)

DEFENSE

Scoring:	24.7 (26)
Yards per Game:	368.4 (28)
Pass Yards per Game:	243.0 (t27)
Rush Yards per Game:	125.4 (21)
Sacks:	39 (t12)
3rd Down Percentage:	45.9 (30)
Takeaways:	19 (24)

Chicago Bears

Predicted: 4th ▪ 2004: 5-11 (4th)

Players Added

WR	Eddie Berlin (Ten)
K	Doug Brien (NYJ)
G	Roberto Garza (Atl)
RT	Fred Miller (Ten)
WR	Muhsin Muhammad (Car)
LB	LeVar Woods

Players Lost

K	Paul Edinger
OT	Mike Gandy (Buf)
OT	Aaron Gibson
CB	R.W. McQuarters
QB	Jonathan Quinn
WR	David Terrell (NE)
RB	Anthony Thomas (Dal)
OT	Rex Tucker (StL)

Draft

1	(4)	Cedric Benson	RB	Texas
2	(39)	Mark Bradley	WR	Oklahoma
4	(106)	Kyle Orton	QB	Purdue
5	(140)	Airese Currie	WR	Clemson
6	(181)	Chris Harris	S	Louisiana Monroe
7	(220)	Rodriques Wilson	S	South Carolina

Benson will be their plow horse on offense. The Bears continued their trend of reaching for receivers by taking Bradley and Currie. Bradley is very raw, but has a tremendous combination of size and speed. Size is what limits Currie, who is projected to become a No. 4 receiver in his career. Chicago likes their new backup quarterback, Orton, and they should; he was a great find on day 2 of the draft.

The city of Chicago seems to have, in recent years, become immune to losing. After all, the Cubs are the quintessential "lovable losers," approaching year 97 of their World Series drought. The lesser-known south-side brother of the Cubs—the White Sox—haven't won it all since 1917. The Bulls refreshed the city's heart for basketball by reaching the NBA playoffs this year, but '05 was still the first time the team has reached the postseason since Michael Jordan retired for the second and final time (before returning to play for the Washington Wizards, of course). And in hockey, the Blackhawks haven't been any more successful than the league they are currently *not* playing in.

With this in mind, perhaps it should not be too surprising that the Chicago Bears—the more grown-up version of those losers at Wrigley Field—have not made a splash in the NFL since 1985. What's more, outside of the organization and the Super Fans from the old *Saturday Night Live* skit, nobody seems too upset about it, either.

However, this isn't to say the Bears are not trying to turn things around in '05. After hiring Lovie Smith as their head coach a year ago, Chicago has added former University of Illinois head coach Ron Turner to the payroll, making him the offensive coordinator. The Bears have adjusted their personnel, changed their approach, and held on to their past draft picks. Now all they have to do in the Windy City is translate all this into more victories.

Head Coach: Lovie Smith (2nd year)
Offensive Coordinator: Ron Turner
Defensive Coordinator: Ron Rivera

Offense

QB:	Rex Grossman
RB:	Cedric Benson†
FB:	Bryan Johnson
WR:	Muhsin Muhammad*†
WR:	Justin Gage
TE:	Desmond Clark
LT:	John Tait
LG:	Ruben Brown
C:	Olin Kreutz*
RG:	Roberto Garza†
RT:	Fred Miller
QB:	Kyle Orton‡
RB:	Thomas Jones
WR:	Bernard Berrian
TE:	Dustin Lyman
OL:	Steve Edwards

Defense

LDE:	Adewale Ogunleye
DT:	Tommie Harris
NT:	Ian Scott
RDE:	Alex Brown
SLB:	Hunter Hillenmeyer
MLB:	Brian Urlacher
WLB:	Lance Briggs
CB:	Charles Tillman
SS:	Mike Brown
FS:	Mike Green
CB:	Jerry Azumah
NB:	Nathan Vasher
DL:	Michael Haynes
LB:	Joe Odom
K:	Doug Brien†
P:	Brad Maynard

* Pro Bowler '04
† veteran acquisition
‡ rookie

Report Card

Quarterback	C	Defensive Line	B	Coaching	B–
Running Back	B–	Linebacker	B+	Special Teams	B
Receiver/Tight End	C+	Defensive Back	B	Depth	A–
Offensive Line	C+			Intangibles	C–

Brian Urlacher

Offense

The Bears may have finally gotten it right when they hired **Ron Turner** to take over their offense this season. Watching last year's offensive coordinator, Terry Shea, try to execute a Kansas City–style system with this team was like watching William "The Refrigerator" Perry trying to wear one of those colorful old Mike Ditka sweaters: It didn't look good and it didn't fit.

This season, Turner will install a true Chicago offense, which is predicated on running the football, eating the clock, and wearing teams down late in games on cold and blustery afternoons. In other words, the Bears' offensive attack has been transformed from a Japanese karate match into a sumo-wrestling slugfest. The player that Chicago is hoping can ease this transition is rookie running back **Cedric Benson** (*see* Painting a New Picture, page 8).

The 5'10", 222-pound Benson will be a bell cow on offense, running the ball 30 times an outing and dictating the pace of the game. In an effort to augment their power-running scheme, the Bears will try to surround Benson with as much girth and strength as they can, but they may be strapped to find the ideal player to line up beside him in the backfield. Starting fullback **Bryan Johnson**—in his fifth season out of Boise State—is a respectable player, but he is better known for his consistency and pass-catching skills rather than his muscle in lead-blocking. Johnson, in fact, may wind up losing his job to fourth-year fullback **Jason McKie**, whose good technique and quickness make him a better run-blocker.

Last season's leading rusher, **Thomas Jones**, is still with the team, but he plays a more finessed style of game, which is not a great fit for Turner's offense. However, Jones will still have a valuable role on this squad, thanks to his abilities as a receiver (56 catches in '04). Jones also plays with very good vision and agility, making him a threat on draw plays.

The man throwing to Jones will be third-year player **Rex Grossman**, who last year saw his first season as a starter wiped out by an ACL tear in week 3. While a lot of people like to talk about Grossman's raw skills and his potential for stardom (he has good athleticism and a solid all-around arm), the fact of the matter is that the Bears are relying on a player who has a questionable reputation as a worker and only 156 career pass attempts to his name. Of course, after seeing the performances of players like **Chad Hutchinson**, **Craig Krenzel**, and Jonathan Quinn in Grossman's absence last year, Chicago's own Oprah Winfrey may look pretty good under center at this point. In order to avoid a future injury-inflicted meltdown at the quarterback position, the Bears drafted Purdue's **Kyle Orton** in the fourth round this year.

Perhaps the most significant change that will be noticed in Chicago's new offense in '05 is the passing game, which ranked dead last a season ago. Turner has replaced the "spread 'em out, air 'em out" method with the more logical "bunch 'em up and just hope like heck you can wedge the ball in there for a first down" approach.

The Bears are spending $30 million over the next six years on the perfect possession receiver to execute this approach: **Muhsin Muhammad**. Despite being 32, the former Panther is coming off a career-year in which he led the league with 1,405 receiving yards and six touchdowns. Muhammad is a strong 6'2", 217-pound target who shows great concentration hauling in catches. Chicago is right to assume that he can be their guy on

offense, but there must be some concern about whether they can get this kind of performance out of him when he's not playing for a new contract.

Prior to 2005, Muhammad's last great season came in 2000, when he caught 102 passes. It isn't fair to forebode that a player is going to fail once he has earned the last big paycheck of his career, but it would be naïve to think that he does not understand his own situation.

The Bears have a plethora of options throughout the rest of the receiving lineup. Wideout **Bobby Wade** entered the offseason as the projected No. 2 receiver in '05, but due to the various events that unfolded with the offense in spring, he could open week 1 as low as No. 5 on the depth chart. Wade has not done anything to harm the Bears or offend the franchise—his skills are just no longer as applicable to this team.

Instead, Chicago is opting to go with third-year man **Justin Gage**, who is a favorite of wide receivers coach **Darryl Drake** and the rest of the Bears coaching staff. Gage is a big, 6'4" target who plays the game with an all-out effort, showing a good ability to make tough catches.

The slot receiver will be second-year man **Bernard Berrian**, who had a disappointing rookie season (just 15 catches), but nevertheless possesses the size and speed to be an electrifying player. Rookie **Mark Bradley** is expected to earn the No. 4 job, leaving Wade and free agent acquisition **Eddie Berlin** on the bench or with the special teams. With an emphasis on being a power offense, one would think that the Bears would have a big, Sears Tower–like tight end who could anchor the rushing attack. However, such is not the case. The man actually filling the job is the more nimble and soft-handed **Desmond Clark**.

The Bears offensive line shuffled more people through it than Chicago-O'Hare International last year. Injuries depleted the front five, forcing the team to start 10 different blockers up front.

This year, the team hopes for more stability, particularly on the left side, where they have placed veterans **John Tait** (tackle) and **Ruben Brown** (guard). The 30-year-old Tait is shifting over from his career-long right tackle position. The move will downgrade Tait as an individual player, but upgrade the *team* at this position, in comparison to what they had with Mike Gandy

---

Write it Down:

If the Bears can get all of their young players on defense to rise up and play to their abilities, they will have one of the best units in the entire league.

This Season vs. Last Season

Progression: **Offensive scheme**—The change in game plan may not work wonders—after all, the Bears have been horrible on offense since they were mere cubs—but at least they have the right idea this time.

Regression: **Offensive line**—Strange as it sounds, getting healthier does not mean getting better—unless Ruben Brown and Fred Miller can halt their aging process this season.

and **Qasim Mitchell** at left tackle a year ago. Tait plays with good technique, excelling at keeping players in front of him and turning defenders. His inconsistency will cause him to give up a few sacks, though. Brown is a former Pro Bowl player who has begun to fall off the map in recent years. His power and strength are not where they once were, and he has never shown the most tremendous passion for the game.

The Bears signed former Falcon **Roberto Garza** to fill the other guard spot on the right side. Garza is not a great solo player, but lining up beside Pro Bowl star center **Olin Kreutz** will benefit him well. Kreutz is undersized, but still one of the premier centers in the game. He locks into any opponent and absolutely controls that player for the duration of the down. He is also fantastic at getting to the second level and helping out his teammates.

The Bears would be wise to slide Garza to the left side (where he played in Atlanta), move Brown to the bench, and start third-year player **Steve Edwards** at right guard. At 330 pounds, Edwards has the size and strength to dominate. He is very adept at pulling as a run-blocker, moving as well as just about any offensive lineman in the game today. If given the proper opportunity, he can evolve into a Pro Bowl player.

The right tackle duties will likely belong to **Fred Miller** in September, before his slow feet convince head coach **Lovie Smith** to let the 355-pound Mitchell step in there and finish out the year.

Defense

As lackluster as the Bears have been over the last couple of years, one area that has consistently improved is the defense. The Bears ranked 21st in "total defense" last season (336.9 yards per game), but in the *real* rankings—points given up—they ranked an adequate 13th. This season, Chicago has enough emerging young players in all three areas to catapult them into the top five.

Everything begins and ends with middle linebacker **Brian Urlacher**. In his sixth season out of New Mexico, Urlacher has become one of the game's most marketable stars. He roams around, enforcing his will on his enemies and dishing out punishment in a way that the city of Chicago has not seen since Al Capone. However, Urlacher is not a gangster helping distribute alcohol to a prohibition-stricken community, but rather, a star handing out big plays to what has recently been a deadbeat defense. He has amazing speed with an explosive burst and the ability to rush the quarterback, defend a pass, or destroy a ball carrier.

But Urlacher has his critics. In fact, last season *Sporting News* named him football's most overrated player. The carping about Urlacher has to do with the facts that he has not been able to stay healthy week in and week out and he does not play with the best football mind in the world. Both are fair complaints; Urlacher *does* need to improve his recognition skills and the angles he takes to the ball.

Next to Urlacher on the weak side is **Lance Briggs**, a player who has a load of raw talent. Briggs—who is coming off of a 126-tackle season—is in his third year out of Arizona. He is a fast player who possesses impressive agility and all-around athleticism. He can be a force against the run because of his quick change-of-direction skills and his dexterity in "getting through the trash" (scout speak for running around people). However, the Bears wouldn't mind seeing more big plays out of the 24-year-old.

The strong-side linebacker will likely be **Hunter Hillenmeyer**, although second-year player **Marcus Reese** and third-year man **Joe Odom** will get a look here, as well. Expect the Bears to ultimately choose to start the 24-year-old Hillenmeyer because of the playing experience that his teammates' injuries granted him a year ago. Hillenmeyer is not a great individual force, but he can be effective when he has a distinct role as part of a group. He's physical in how he takes on blocks, which is always a plus out of the strongside position.

If Urlacher can stay healthy, the Bears will be tougher to run against in '05; last season they gave up an unimpressive 128.1 yards per game. This year will be different, though, because in addition to a healthy Urlacher, Chicago also has a more mature pair of defensive tackles in 22-year-old **Tommie Harris** (*see* Ready to Break Out, page 115) and 23-year-old **Ian Scott**. Harris is destined to be a superstar in the NFL, maybe as early as this year. Scott is a portly 305-pound nose tackle who has no trouble getting by blocks and making tackles. Chicago also has a pair of meaty backups in **Alfonso Boone** and **Tank Johnson**, but each is a situational player at best.

The Bears may have some trouble stopping the run on the outside in '05, but it is nothing to be alarmed about. Chicago actually focuses their defensive ends on generating a pass-rush anyway. With this in mind, it was wise of the Bears to trade for end **Adewale Ogunleye** last year. Ogunleye gives them a solid all-around force on the outside, who can get by blockers with his first step or clever thinking, whichever is required. Now that he has forgotten all about the dreadful beaches and bikinis of Miami's Atlantic Ocean lifestyle and become better acclimated to the ice-covered shores and thick wool sweaters that accommodate Lake Michigan, Ogunleye should improve upon his 5½ sacks from '04.

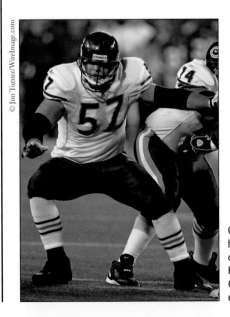

Olin Kreutz has established himself as one of the most complete centers in the NFL. He will play a key role in Chicago's power-running offense this season.

The Bears' other starting end is **Alex Brown**, a fourth-year player out of Florida. Brown mans the right side. He led the team with six sacks a season ago and is certainly capable of continuing that output this year. However, Chicago would be wise to move him to a backup role, in which he can specialize on third downs. Brown is a quick player who, at times, is explosive off the snap, but he is not physical enough to stop the run.

If the Bears were to use Brown as a situational pass-rusher, they could then find a way to get former first-round draft choice **Michael Haynes** on the field. Haynes—in his third season out of Penn State—is a more methodical player, but he has slightly better size than Brown (274 as opposed to 262) and he knows how to take on a blocker. Haynes is not a major threat to get to the quarterback, but that isn't to say he is a "Chicago breeze," either. All in all, Haynes still needs to hone his skills and give coaches a reason to think he can emerge in '05. If he doesn't, he may find himself out of the franchise's future plans.

What is a slightly above-average pass-rushing front four can become much better by benefiting from the coverage skills of Chicago's cornerbacks. The Bears have three players, all of whom are capable of starting for a lot of teams; one is veteran **Jerry Azumah** and the other two are young players **Charles Tillman** and **Nathan Vasher**.

The Bears will start Azumah and Tillman in week 1. Azumah is a player who thrives on speed and agility. Such skills have helped him gain notoriety as a kick returner (he averaged 22 yards per return last season) and made him a big-play threat on defense. Last year Azumah had four interceptions, averaging 32 yards per runback. He does not get as much publicity as some of the other Chicago defensive backs, but much of that has to do with the fact that quarterbacks do not challenge him quite as much.

Tillman's development last season was hampered by a right knee injury, but the 24-year-old was able to play late in the year, showing why he is one of the future stars in the game. At 6'1", Tillman has the size to match up with most receivers. He is very physical, and he can use his lanky frame to get his hands on the ball.

The nickel back duties will likely fall to Vasher, now that R.W. McQuarters is out of the picture. Vasher is an elite playmaker in the making, as his speed and five interceptions from a year ago indicate. At this stage of his career, though, Vasher still lacks the strength and physicality to control a receiver.

The starting safeties for the Bears will continue to be the colorful Mikes: **Mike Green** and **Mike Brown**. Bears defensive coordinator **Ron Rivera** is making a very interesting change with these two in '05; He is having them swap roles. Green is moving from the strong safety to the free safety and vice versa for Brown. Rivera's reasoning is simple: At 212 pounds, Brown is a more physical player who tackles better, while Green (192 pounds) is quicker and more adept in coverage. Rivera is 100 percent right; the only question is "Why in the world did it take him so long to realize this?"

Special Teams

After watching him miss 9 of his 24 field goal attempts in '04, the Bears replaced kicker Paul Edinger with former Jet **Doug Brien**. Brien does not have the greatest reputation at the moment himself, being remembered for his playoff meltdown in Pittsburgh last season. Punter **Brad Maynard** netted 39.6 yards per punt last year (second best in the NFL), a nice testament to his leg and to the team's coverage unit. The Bears must find a guy to replace McQuarters on kick returns, likely someone from the receivers department.

The Bottom Line

The Bears still have a lot to prove on offense, particularly with Grossman in the passing game, but also with Benson and the "new-look" rushing attack, which is really just a return to the old style. While Chicago is talented on defense, that does not excuse the fact that this unit is young and historically inconsistent. That said, the NFL is a league of shocking revelations. If this team can find a way just to move the ball well enough to compete offensively, they could be poised for a nice coming-out party. However, the rest of the NFC North will likely prove too tough.

Detroit Lions

Predicted: 2nd ▪ 2004: 6-10 (3rd)

Players Added

G	Rick DeMulling	(Ind)
QB	Jeff Garcia	(Cle)
WR	Kevin Johnson	(Bal)
S	Kenoy Kennedy	(Den)
G	Kyle Kosier	(SF)
TE	Marcus Pollard	(Ind)

Players Lost

TE	Stephen Alexander	(Den)
WR	Az-Zahir Hakim	
FS	Brock Marion	
OT	Stockar McDougle	(Mia)
QB	Mike McMahon	(Phi)
WR	Tai Streets	
KR	Reggie Swinton	(Hou)

Draft

1	(10)	Mike Williams	WR	USC
2	(37)	Shaun Cody	DT	USC
3	(72)	Stanley Wilson	CB	Stanford
5	(145)	Dan Orlovsky	QB	Connecticut
6	(184)	Bill Swancutt	DE	Oregon St.
6	(206)	Jonathan Goddard	DE	Marshall
7	(223)	Marcus Maxwell	WR	Oregon

The move to select another receiver in the top 10 was certainly questionable, considering the help they could use on defense, but when October rolls around, nobody will remember the defensive players the Lions passed on. The country will get caught up with what their trio of young wideouts will be doing to teams. Cody can play anywhere up front, and he will immediately improve Detroit's interior pass rush. Orlovsky had a prolific college career.

Head Coach: Steve Mariucci (3rd year)
Offensive Coordinator: Ted Tollner
Defensive Coordinator: Dick Jauron

Offense

QB:	Joey Harrington
RB:	Kevin Jones
FB:	Cory Schlesinger
WR:	Roy Williams
WR:	Charles Rogers
TE:	Marcus Pollard†
LT:	Jeff Backus
LG:	Rick DeMulling†
C:	Dominic Raiola
RG:	Damien Woody
RT:	Kelly Butler
QB:	Jeff Garcia†
RB:	Shawn Bryson
WR:	Mike Williams‡
WR:	Kevin Johnson†
OL:	Kyle Kosier†

Defense

DE:	Cory Redding
DT:	Dan Wilkinson
DT:	Shaun Rogers*
DE:	James Hall
SLB:	Boss Bailey
MLB:	Earl Holmes
WLB:	Teddy Lehman
CB:	Dré Bly*
SS:	Kenoy Kennedy†
FS:	Terrence Holt
CB:	Fernando Bryant
NB:	Keith Smith
DL:	Shaun Cody‡
LB:	James Davis
K:	Jason Hanson
P:	Nick Harris

* Pro Bowler '04
† veteran acquisition
‡ rookie

Report Card

Quarterback	C	Defensive Line	B–	Coaching	B+
Running Back	B	Linebacker	B–	Special Teams	A–
Receiver/Tight End	A	Defensive Back	C+	Depth	B
Offensive Line	C+			Intangibles	C–

The music will certainly be playing in Motown this season, and not just because the city is hosting Super Bowl XL in February. The people of Michigan (and a few spare Canadians) are anticipating a gigantic roar out of their Detroit Lions this year, after the past two potential breakout years produced a disappointing total of 11 wins. ·

The pressure is on the club's high-profile president, Matt Millen (no, seriously, this time, it really is). Since taking over the franchise in '01, Millen's Lions have posted the worst record in the NFL during that span (16-48). They are one of just eight teams to not reach the playoffs over the past four years, and they are the only team to have put together four consecutive double-digit-loss seasons.

Give Millen credit, though. He is at least piecing together a roster that has some cohesion and some sense of direction. Detroit is building a young offensive cast that includes a fourth-year quarterback, a third-year receiver, two second-year receivers, and a first-year receiver, all of whom are playing leading roles. On defense, they are putting their stock in young athletes who all seem to have that little thing known as "potential."

Essentially, the entire Detroit operation has been in one enormous rebuilding phase. However, this isn't the "Big Dig" of Boston—eventually, something's going to have to be built from all this. The people in the Motor City are expecting a nice, new, state-of-the-art playoff season. In fact, anything less may just result in the slaying of the club's lead Lion, Millen.

Roy Williams

Offense

Judging by the past three years, it appears as if Detroit is attempting to become the NFC version of the Indianapolis Colts. They have selected a blue-chip receiving prospect in the top 10 of each draft: **Charles Rogers** (No. 2 overall out of Michigan State in '03), **Roy Williams** (No. 7 overall out of Texas in '04), and **Mike Williams** (No. 10 overall out of USC in '05). In addition to their Harrison/Wayne/Stokley rendition, the team from Motown used another first-round draft choice a year ago on running back **Kevin Jones**, giving them their Edgerrin James. Couple this with a stellar offensive line and two new former Colts (guard **Rick DeMulling** and tight end **Marcus Pollard**) in the lineup, and Detroit's got themselves a pretty nice version of that high-powered offense a little to the east of them. There's just one problem: Quarterback **Joey Harrington** is *no* Peyton Manning.

This is where the story of the '05 Lions begins. A person could make the argument that no team in the NFL is counting on seeing their quarterback take a greater step forward than the Lions. Since drafting Harrington second overall out of Oregon four years ago, Detroit has seen more inconsistency than the U.S. General Accounting Office. Nobody questions the fact that Harrington is a prototypical NFL quarterback. At 6'4", 220 pounds, he has the perfect build to go with his picturesque throwing motion. There isn't a pass that Harrington can't make.

But for whatever reason, those skills have not translated into success on the football field. Harrington has struggled with his accuracy (56 percent completion rate last year), he has come up short at crucial junctures, and he has tailed off as time wears on (*see* Startling Statistics, page 125). In a sense, with Harrington at the helm, Lions head coach **Steve Mariucci** has an offense that's like owning one of neighboring Ford Motor Company's new Lincoln Navigators, equipped with all of the luxury features that make up a $50,000 SUV, but built with a faulty engine. Mariucci knows his Lincoln Navigator will look nice, but he cannot be sure about how far it can be driven.

With this in mind, the Lions signed quarterback **Jeff Garcia**, who is an insurance policy against the event that Harrington turns the Lincoln Navigator into an old Model T Ford. Harrington could not have been given a more direct wake-up call than this. Garcia is a 35-year-old veteran who knows how to play the game. He quarterbacked for Mariucci while at San Francisco, and the two became very close. **Ted Tollner**—the new offensive coordinator who was hired to replace the retiring Marvin Lewis—runs the same West Coast system that Garcia played in while with the 49ers. Oh yeah, Tollner was also Garcia's quarterback coach in '02.

Under these circumstances, one would assume that Harrington is done for in Detroit. But keep in mind that the team still wants him to be the starter in '05. He is entering the season as the No. 1 man, and the only way that will change is if he does not perform up to expectations. This may not seem like the best situation for a quarterback to succeed in, but perhaps it is the jolt that Harrington needs. Besides, after so many ups and downs in his career, what other option does the team really have?

Harrington will have a chance to play with a trio of receivers that could become the most dynamic group in the league before the season is over. At times last season, Roy Williams was brilliant as a rookie, but an ankle injury prevented him from operating at

(*see* Startling Statistics, page 125)

Write it Down:

He might play well enough to finish the season as the starter, but quarterback Joey Harrington is still going to be benched in favor of Jeff Garcia at some point in 2005.

Strengths	Weaknesses
Offensive Firepower	**Winning Mentality**
The receiving core, if healthy, can become the most dynamic in the NFL this season, regardless of how young everyone is. Charles Rogers, Roy Williams, and Mike Williams aren't just good players, they are also the type of players who are tough to match up against.	It may not seem like something that can be gauged, but when dealing with a young club that has lost more games in the past four years than the Washington Generals, it can be tough to teach these players how to win.
Front Seven Speed	**Leadership**
Defensive end James Hall can get past any blocker he faces and backup end Kalimba Edwards is not too slow, either. Three linebackers (Teddy Lehman, Boss Bailey, and James Davis) can all make plays just by using their speed.	Not only are the Lions young, but they are young in key areas, as well. Perhaps aside from middle linebacker Earl Holmes, there really isn't a great deal of seniority on this roster.

full strength during the second half of the year. The speedy 6'2" target is almost a lock to have a monstrous year in '05.

The man scheduled to split out on the other side of Roy Williams is Rogers, who at this point is a bit less of a sure thing. Rogers is extremely talented in virtually all phases of the game, but injuries to his collarbone have caused him to miss all but six games over his first two seasons as a pro. Now in his third season, Rogers's ability to stay healthy is certainly a concern. If he can do so, he should still become a star. His biggest challenge this year—especially early on—will simply be building the confidence and trust in his body to play all-out.

The Lions expect to use Mike Williams (*see* Painting a New Picture, page 9) in the slot this season, in order to generate as many mismatches as possible. The receiving options do not just dissolve after the big three: No. 4 receiver, **Kevin Johnson**, is a consistent weapon over the middle, and the tight end, Pollard, has a decade of pass-catching experience to fall back on. Pollard is a willing blocker, as well.

(*see* Painting a New Picture, page 9)

If having potentially three young superstars to throw to isn't enough for Harrington, he'll also have a second-year running back (Jones) who rushed for 1,133 yards as a rookie. After getting hurt and running the ball a total of just 57 times over the first two months of the season last year, Jones gained 554 yards in the month of December, showing the combination of power and speed that made him a first-round pick. This year, Jones should continue to build on his strong finish in '04. He's a smart runner who is learning how to set up his blocks and bait defenders into taking false steps. He is not superquick or agile, but he is a tough runner who has the ability to make something out of nothing.

Jones's fullback is tentatively **Cory Schlesinger**, although that could change at any moment. Schlesinger is in his 11th season in the league, and with his style of play, his career should be evaluated in dog years. He is an all-out fighter who has taken one pounding after another. On third downs, the Lions will bring in **Shawn Bryson**, who offers better hands and open-field speed than Jones. Bryson caught 44 passes last year.

With such a bounty of young skill-position players, it is almost remarkable that the team from Ford Field has still found room to offend such a solid assembly line . . . errr, assemble such a solid offensive line. A year ago, the team forked over the big money to

This Season vs. Last Season

Progression: **Playmaking—**The additions of Mike Williams on offense and Kenoy Kennedy on defense, plus the return of Boss Bailey, upgrade Detroit's big-play abilities.

Regression: **Interior front seven—**It is unlikely that Shaun Rogers will play as well this year as he did in '04, Dan Wilkinson is on his last fried chicken leg of life, and middle linebacker Earl Holmes is starting to slow down.

bring in guard **Damien Woody,** and this year they signed DeMulling.

Woody—a seventh-year pro who began his career with the Patriots—is a Pro Bowl–caliber player who can perform any task asked of him. In fact, there may not be a more fundamentally sound all-around lineman in the game. Woody does everything at a high level.

DeMulling will start on the right side this season. The fifth-year player out of Idaho is basically a poor man's Damien Woody. At 304 pounds, DeMulling is about three or four hamburgers smaller, but what he lacks in girth, he makes up for in mobility. Only time will tell how effective DeMulling will be in his new system, though.

The man stuck in the middle of these two solid guards is center **Dominic Raiola,** who is not impressive as an individual player, but can be adequate in Detroit's scheme. The Lions will not get anything special out of Raiola (he has the strength of a Ford Pinto), but at least he is aware of his duties.

Tackle **Jeff Backus** is somewhat overrated on the left side, but a man does not start all 64 games of his career for no reason. When he plays low (which is often), Backus has good power, which enables him to effectively angle his blocks. His only shortcomings are in his quickness and footwork in pass protection, which are not ideal but are certainly good enough.

The right tackle position is up for grabs, with **Kelly Butler** (who missed all of his rookie season in '04 with a shoulder injury), free agent acquisition **Kyle Kosier** (who is a better fit at guard), and **Victor Rogers** (who is a long shot) competing for the job.

This season, the chips are down for Joey Harrington. His play this year will determine whether he joins this offense on their path to future prosperity or finds work elsewhere.

Defense

A lot of focus is given to Detroit's youthful offense, but what many fail to realize is that the defense is not too many steps removed from graduating with the NFL's kindergarten class, either. While Detroit's defense does not boast the youthful superstars of the offense, they are counting on a fair number of youngsters to improve this 18th-ranked scoring unit from a year ago.

Most of the whippersnappers can be found in the Lions' pack of linebackers, which features second-year pro **Teddy Lehman** and third-year man **Boss Bailey.** Lehman is expected to start on the weakside in '05, although last year, as a rookie out of Oklahoma, he got his repetitions primarily in the strong and middle slots. Lehman was the only defensive rookie in the NFL to start in all 16 of his team's games last season.

The move to the weakside should benefit the sprightly Lehman. He plays at a Jeff Gordon pace, showing more energy and fire than anyone on the field. His awareness and decision-making skills are still developing, but working out of his new position, he will have more opportunities to use his instincts in reacting and giving chase versus having to diagnose plays and take more specific angles like he did last year.

Lehman spent his rookie year playing the strongside position because Detroit had to fill the void that was left when Bailey suffered a knee injury in the preseason. The 6'3", 235-pounder is back this year, though, and should resume at full strength. Bailey has good mobility, but only mediocre power. He may seem to have the type of skills that would make him a better weakside linebacker, but he started all 16 games on the strongside as a rookie in '03 and, at times, looked like a budding All-Pro.

Detroit's main weakness in the box this year will likely be middle linebacker **Earl Holmes,** which is ironic considering that the 10th-year pro has led this team in tackles in each of the past two seasons. However, Holmes turned 32 in April and is fast approaching the threshold of retirement. He does not fire into plays or get off blocks particularly well, and this wear and tear has left him looking slow and soft. Granted, Holmes has been able to put up the numbers (and he still *might* put up the numbers this year), but in terms of having the much-needed impact player in the middle, the Lions simply fall short here.

Detroit's best option for putting talent on the field would be to move Lehman to the middle—where he would be less effective but, nevertheless, just fine—and start third-year player **James Davis** on the weak side. Davis started at this position last year and thrived at times because of his speed and energy. He is a very fast tackler, quickly converging on a runner and promptly putting him on the ground.

However, the Lions will almost surely leave either Holmes or backup veteran **Wali Rainer** in at middle linebacker, because playing Lehman, Bailey, and Davis together would give the team three fast and energetic linebackers, but no veteran leadership or wisdom.

The front four features two of the largest collections of meat ever regarded as human beings. Fifth-year tackle **Shaun Rogers** weighs 345 pounds, and 12th-year tackle **Dan Wilkinson** weighs 335. The Lions obviously have such enormous tackles in order to clog against the run, which both players do. (It's challenging for runners to get around a couple of mail trucks parked in the middle of the line of scrimmage.) However, don't expect these players to work together much this season—this is likely the year that "Big Daddy" Wilkinson waddles out of the league. He is just too lazy to continue playing at a high level.

Rogers, on the other hand, had a Pro Bowl season in '04 and may finally have become the player everyone expected him to be. He can be a voracious force who is quick off the snap and outstanding in lateral movement. However, he has a history of gaining too much weight and not playing hard, two factors that might arise this year, since he got a long-term contract and $15 million in bonuses back in January.

It's almost certain that the Lions will look to get second-round rookie **Shaun Cody** into games this season. Cody—who won a national title at USC—will see time on third downs as a pass-rusher, where he can use his quickness and ability to penetrate.

The real pass-rusher for the Lions is end **James Hall**, who quietly had an $11\frac{1}{2}$-sack season in '04. Hall (who forced four fumbles, as well) is a pure sack artist with great quickness, both off the snap and in moving side to side. He has the athleticism to control a game, but he will never be an upper-echelon player if he does not learn to operate more within the system. Too often he overpursues and ignores the run.

Third-year player **Cory Redding** is the left defensive end. In an ideal world, the Lions would have a more potent starter at this spot and use the versatile Redding as a utility lineman off the bench. However, backup end **Jared DeVries** is exactly what his title implies—a backup—and the gifted **Kalimba Edwards** is more of an athlete than a football player.

The Lions secondary will have a new look in '05. Both starting cornerbacks (Pro Bowler **Dré Bly** and veteran **Fernando Bryant**) are back, but in centerfield, Detroit has a pair of new safeties in **Kenoy Kennedy** and **Terence Holt**.

Kennedy comes over from the Broncos, a team he both helped and hurt during his first five years there. The help comes from the fact that Kennedy is an absolute demon when it comes to drilling people; the hurt comes from the fact that, well, he is an absolute demon when it comes to drilling people. It is obvious that Kennedy is the type of safety who likes to lower his head and fly around the field looking for people to inflict pain upon. This approach has made him a good strong safety, but it has also earned him a surplus of disciplinary action by the league, not to mention crucial personal foul penalties. There is a way to coach Kennedy, though. Lions defensive coordinator **Dick Jauron** must find ways to put his talented strong safety near the action, where he can be physical in a dominant way, and defensive backs coach **George Catavolos** must work with Kennedy on fundamentals and playing with restraint, both of which will allow him to continue to grow.

It was surprising that the young free safety Holt did not get more playing time last year, something that the Lions may regret now that they are starting the 25-year-old. Holt does not have ideal skills, but he is a player who can get better with experience.

Bly is one of the more subtle cover corners in the NFL. He plays light on his feet and moves well, but his best features are his intelligence and understanding of how to play the game. No cornerback is better at reading a passer and baiting him into making poor throws.

Bryant is an athletic player who has never quite lived up to his abilities. If he has a down year and becomes a liability, Detroit is in trouble. The Lions have decent depth on paper, but upon closer examination of **Chris Cash**, **André Goodman**, and **Mike Echols**, a person realizes that not one has made any kind of impact in the league. The Lions will probably end up using second-year player **Keith Smith** and rookie **Stanley Wilson** in nickel-and-dime packages this year.

Special Teams

Kicker **Jason Hanson** seems like he has been around forever; playing indoors his entire career has really helped him. Last season he made 24/28 field goals. **Nick Harris** is the punter. He could stand to get better distance on his boots, but he is good at pinning opponents back near the goal line. **Eddie Drummond** was last year's version of Dante Hall, averaging 26.6 yards per kick return, with two touchdowns, plus 13.2 yards per punt return, with two more touchdowns. But Drummond must perform well again this year before he can be considered lethal.

The Bottom Line

If this team were a fruit, a shopper could spend hours staring at it in deliberation, knowing that it is definitely the right color and texture, but perhaps not quite ripe enough. However, Mariucci is the type of coach who can handle a young squad, and the system in which these players are operating fits them well. From this, one can conclude that the team from the Motor City has enough horsepower to emerge from the gutter; it's just a matter of how well they can actually drive.

Green Bay Packers

Predicted: 3ʳᵈ ▪ 2004: 10-6 (1ˢᵗ)

Players Added

S	Arturo Freeman	(Mia)
OL	Adrian Klemm	(NE)
FS	Earl Little	(Cle)
G	Matt O'Dwyer	(TB)
LB	Ray Thompson	(Ari)

Players Lost

P	Bryan Barker	
CB	Michael Hawthorne	(StL)
DB	Bhawoh Jue	(SD)
G	Marco Rivera	(Dal)
FS	Darren Sharper	(Min)
G	Mike Wahle	(Car)

Draft

1	(24)	Aaron Rodgers	QB	California
2	(51)	Nick Collins	CB	Bethune Cookman
2	(58)	Terrence Murphy	WR	Texas A & M
4	(115)	Marviel Underwood	S	San Diego St.
4	(125)	Brady Poppinga	DE	BYU
5	(143)	Junius Coston	C	North Carolina A & T
5	(167)	Michael Hawkins	CB	Oklahoma
6	(180)	Mike Montgomery	DT	Texas A & M
6	(195)	Craig Bragg	WR	UCLA
7	(245)	Kurt Campbell	S	Albany
7	(246)	Will Whitticker	OG	Michigan St.

Many thought the Packers needed immediate help from a first-round pick, which they won't get with Rodgers. However, it would have been foolish not to cash in their lottery ticket when he fell to them at No. 24. It was divine intervention. Collins was a reach in the second round; he is too raw to compete for right now. Murphy is a fast player who will finally give them a dangerous threat in the return game.

Head Coach: Mike Sherman (6th year)

Offensive Coordinator: Tom Rossley

Defensive Coordinator: Jim Bates

Offense

Brett Favre

RB:	Ahman Green*
FB:	William Henderson*
WR:	Javon Walker*
WR:	Donald Driver
TE:	Bubba Franks
LT:	Chad Clifton
LG:	Adrian Klemm†
C:	Mike Flanagan
RG:	Grey Ruegamer
RT:	Mark Tauscher
QB:	Craig Nall
RB:	Najeh Davenport
WR:	Robert Ferguson
TE:	David Martin
OL:	Kevin Barry

Defense

LDE:	Aaron Kampman
NT:	Grady Jackson
DT:	Cletidus Hunt
RDE:	Kabeer Gbaja-Biamila
SLB:	Hannibal Navies
MLB:	Nick Barnett
WLB:	Na'il Diggs
CB:	Ahmad Carroll
SS:	Mark Roman
FS:	Earl Little†
CB:	Al Harris
NB:	Joey Thomas
DL:	Cullen Jenkins
LB:	Ray Thompson†
K:	Ryan Longwell
P:	B.J. Sander

* Pro Bowler '04
† veteran acquisition
‡ rookie

Report Card

Quarterback	A–	Defensive Line	C	Coaching	B
Running Back	A	Linebacker	C+	Special Teams	C+
Receiver/Tight End	A–	Defensive Back	C–	Depth	C
Offensive Line	C+			Intangibles	A

Brett Favre

It is hard not to root for the Green Bay Packers. They represent everything that is right about football. They come from America's core, from Wisconsin's first town, which rests on Lake Michigan and boasts a population of barely 100,000. They come from a town that supports its players like PETA supports its furry heroes with tails. They come from a town that has a stadium that still has bleacher seats, that eternally immortalizes their much-loved figures with dedications like Lombardi Avenue and Ray Nitschke Bridge.

From the look of things, though, one might say that the gold-and-green team from America's Dairyland is losing its luster. They ranked an impressive fifth in scoring and third in total yards on offense last season, but they were just 23rd in scoring defense and 25th in yards allowed, and, in reality, their defense was probably much worse than those numbers indicate. Now they are coming out of an offseason in which they had to use two of their first three draft picks on future offensive weapons and struggled with a salary cap situation that left them empty when it came time to restock the defense. The only adjustment was bringing in Jim Bates to be the new defensive coordinator, a move that will help this unit, but not propel them into the upper echelon of the league.

Perhaps most alarming of all is that this could very well be Brett Favre's final year. This is enough to make the entire small farming town stop and lower its flags to half-mast. The Packers will undoubtedly be shooting for a Super Bowl this season, but with a downgraded offense and a less-than-stellar defense, it will take some midwestern magic to pull off one last hurrah in '05.

Offense

Anyone who argues that **Brett Favre** has lost a step or is no longer a superstar quarterback is simply out of his mind. Although Favre will turn 36 in October, he is still as active as ever, plus he still has an unprecedented 225-consecutive-starts streak (postseason included) intact. The Packers attempted a league-high 598 passes in '04, with Favre being the triggerman on all but 58 of them. Number 4 completed 64.1 percent of his throws (fifth-best in the NFL), tossing the fourth-highest total of touchdowns in the league (30) and finishing with a rating of 92.4. Slowing down? Please. Favre is *slowing* down as much as Hugh Hefner is *settling* down.

However, this could still very well be Favre's final season in the NFL, especially now that Green Bay used their first-round draft choice to snag his future replacement, **Aaron Rodgers**. There has been no shortage of coverage for Favre's off-the-field grief these past few years, which has included the deaths of his father and brother-in-law, plus his wife Deanna's battle against breast cancer. During the season, Favre misses his family—his daughters, Brittany and Breleigh, are now 16 and 6 years old—and the laid-back culture of Kiln, Mississippi, is looking better each year.

Favre seems to be realizing that his final chance at claiming his second Lombardi Trophy is right here and now, and that he is going to have to do it with the young weapons that he has around him. One of those young weapons is fourth-year receiver **Javon Walker**, who is coming off a breakout season in which he ranked third in the league in receiving yards (1,382) and tied for sixth, with 12 touchdowns. Walker is a tall speedster who can stretch the field and use his 39½-inch vertical leap (that's right—39½-inches) to elevate over any defender to snag a pass.

However, Walker has not failed to notice his value to the Packer franchise. Over the offseason he hired superagent Drew Rosenhaus, who promptly told his client to hold out for a better contract. Walker's decision to forgo the team's minicamps during the spring drew ire from Favre, who said that he hoped the team didn't give in to the receiver's demands. Walker is a player who is concerned about his relationship with his quarterback, but perhaps not concerned enough to decline a chance to take his team to the cleaners for a couple million more.

Walker is vital to Green Bay's chances of flourishing on offense, but it's not as if the Packers don't have other receivers who can get the job done. No. 2 wideout, **Donald Driver**, is a high-character team leader who—despite struggling once every warm Wisconsin winter day to hold onto the ball—can still be counted on to come up big. In fact, the 30-year-old is coming off what was by far his best season as a pro, in which he caught 84 passes, for 1,208 yards and nine touchdowns. Driver runs goods routes and can streak (in a football way) over the middle.

Slot receiver **Robert Ferguson** has not emerged as a big-time weapon; nevertheless, he has the combination of speed and strength to be effective. Having three top-tier wideouts would seem like enough for most passing games, but over the past few years, Green Bay has really seemed to need just one more

Strengths

Aerial Attack

Any team with Brett Favre at quarterback is going to throw the ball well, especially if they have two receivers like Javon Walker and Donald Driver, and running backs who can make catches out of the backfield.

Football Allure

No matter what their record is in early fall or how many players are performing poorly, these are the Green Bay Packers, the archetype of classic football. They always seem to be contenders in the end.

Weaknesses

Secondary

The Packers are still young at the cornerback position, and with the loss of Darren Sharper, they have downgraded at the free safety spot.

Defensive Leadership

Grady Jackson may be able to say some words from time to time, but in terms of having a wise and astute veteran presence on defense, the Packers come up empty.

effective wideout to run their offense. In an ideal world, second-round rookie **Terrence Murphy** would step up and become that fourth guy for this team. In the red zone, tight end **Bubba Franks** is very effective, showing soft hands and a consistency in running smart routes. Over the offseason, Green Bay made Franks their transition player (essentially their franchise player), which didn't please him, but, regardless, they kept him around for 12 more months.

Green Bay's passing attack does not hinge strictly on the thin guys wearing numbers in the 80s; it also includes a diverse set of screen passes and short-yardage dump-off throws. This is one area where the versatility of the running back position comes in handy for the Pack.

Running backs **Ahman Green**, **Tony Fisher**, and **William Henderson** combined for 112 receptions a year ago, helping give Green Bay one of the most well-rounded backfields in all of football. However, the bread and butter of Green Bay's offense (even with Favre) is their ability to move the football on the ground—something they did not do quite as well in '04.

This season, expect the Packers to rely on their rushing attack more often. They have a great situation with Green as the starter. The slithery eighth-year veteran has terrific vision and timing in hitting his holes. Factor in his ability to change direction and accelerate, and one begins to realize why Green has made four consecutive Pro Bowls. However, Green's tendency to fumble (7 last season and a total of 21 over the past four years) has been a detriment to the offense.

The Packers have an entire boardroom of running backs on their roster. At 250 pounds, backup **Najeh Davenport** is fast becoming one of the best downhill power runners in the game. He averaged 5.1 yards per carry in '04. Fisher, a third-string back, is used frequently on third downs because of his pass-blocking and receiving abilities.

The Packers have always asked for a lot out of fullback Henderson, who is coming off his first Pro Bowl. The 11th-year veteran is 34 years old, but, like his quarterback, he is not showing many signs of slowing down. Henderson has great tactics as a lead-blocker, showing tremendous strength and drive. He also has an uncanny ability to pick up a big first down with the ball in his hands. Backup fullback **Nick Luchey** somehow got fatter than his 273-pound playing weight over the offseason and has now likely lost his job to **Vonta Leach**.

The Packers offense will likely be up to standards this year simply because Favre is still around. However, if the offense is

Write it Down:

Nobody wants the moment to come, but it will: This will be Brett Favre's final season in the NFL.

This Season vs. Last Season

Progression: **Defensive structure**—With their younger players a year older and the tutelage of new defensive coordinator, Jim Bates, the Packers defense, while still second class, will at least be less vulnerable in '05.

Regression: **Interior offensive line**—Replacing Marco Rivera and Mike Wahle with Grey Ruegamer and perhaps Adrian Klemm (both playing out of position) is a significant step backward, no matter how it's spun.

not, the reason will be the changes made to the front line. Green Bay had been the icon of stability up front—starting virtually the same five men for three years. However, the team was unable to retain guards Marco Rivera and Mike Wahle in the offseason, resulting in a dramatic downgrade.

Longtime tackle **Adrian Klemm** left New England for a chance to start at left guard in front of 60,000-plus people in camouflage. However, Klemm has played tackle for all five years of his career. Not only that, but also injuries and various other factors have caused him to miss 34 games over that span.

The new guard on the right side is **Grey Ruegamer**, who started 11 games last season, but primarily at the center position. Ruegamer is a better center than guard, but the return of **Mike Flanagan**, who can be a force as long as he's healthy (he missed the entire '04 season with a patellar tendon injury) and the experience of backup **Scott Wells** (who is *only* a backup) leave him at the new position. Ruegamer should be fine in run-blocking, but if he isn't, veteran **Matt O'Dwyer** will likely take his job.

The tackles for Green Bay remain **Chad Clifton** on the left side and **Mark Tauscher** on the right. Clifton is an agile technician who is perhaps too polite as a blocker, but definitely very effective in pass protection. Tauscher is a 320-pound mudder who will just "out-nasty" people. The Packers also benefit from the services of tight end Franks, a hardworking run-blocker, and backup tackle **Kevin Barry**, who helps anchor the ground attack. Barry, in fact, might start at right tackle, in which case the Pack would move Tauscher over to replace Klemm at guard.

Defense

Offense is not going to be the problem for the Green Bay Packers in '05. Even if they are less productive because of the changes up front, offense still isn't going to be the problem. The problem is going to be on the defensive side of the football.

The Packers had a defense that, thanks to a lack of depth and general poor play from key figures, ranked 25th against the pass a year ago. Now, with a new season approaching, Green Bay will open up with the exact same personnel they had a year ago, with the exception of free safety Darren Sharper—who signed with division rival Minnesota, of all places. Replacing Sharper will be either **Earl Little**, who was signed from the Browns, or **Arturo Freeman**, a former Dolphin. Little is a decent option, considering that he has good enough range to cover the deep pass, which is an area that the Packers struggled mightily with last season. However, Freeman may win the job in training camp because his time in Miami gave him more familiarity with the system that Green Bay's new defensive coordinator, **Jim Bates**, runs. (Bates was the defensive coordinator and interim head coach for the Dolphins last year.) Neither player is as good as Sharper, though, and neither will provide any substantial help against the run.

Strong safety **Mark Roman** is returning for another year in Green Bay, which is as big of a shock as the ol' fiancée walking in

on the bachelor party. Roman joined the Packers in '04 and had an absolutely horrendous season, missing tackles, forgetting assignments, and becoming one of the few whipping boys in Lambeau history, as short-tempered fans showered him with boos.

It is said that Bates is very fond of rookie **Nick Collins** and could even start the third-round pick ahead of Roman at strong safety this year. However, doing so would make the Packers too young in the secondary, because they are already going to be relying heavily on second-year cornerbacks **Ahmad Carroll** and **Joey Thomas**.

The play of Carroll might be the deciding factor for this Packers defense in '05. A first-round pick out of Arkansas, Carroll is still adjusting to the professional game. He flashes positive signs from time to time, but until he becomes more comfortable with the illegal contact rules and learns to trust his fundamentals when matched up against elite competition, he is going to be a liability. Don't expect Carroll to struggle as terribly as he did a season ago, but at the same time, don't think he is going to blossom this early in his career, either.

Thomas will be the nickel back, a role he can thrive in because of his lanky frame and natural speed and agility. However, he must improve his technique and learn not to reach so much. This season should be full of more growing pains for the second-year player.

Al Harris is the No. 1 cornerback on this team, although the reality is that he is more of a No. 2. He is one of the few players in the game who literally defends receivers one-on-one each play. He'll give up a lot of catches, but considering the tasks he takes on and the plays he makes (20 passes defensed last year), he is an admirable veteran. However, Harris is very physical and he doesn't have elite speed, making him a penalty magnet. Bates needs to create coverages that will give Harris more help in '05.

One way to help a cover corner is to pressure the quarterback up front. During the offseason, a lot of people believed the Packers needed to find help for their defensive front four more than any single area, but the only move made by general manager **Ted Thompson** was the re-signing of starting left end **Aaron Kampman**. Kampman is a blue-collar player who is good in run support, but he is by no means a difference maker.

The other defensive end is **Kabeer Gbaja-Biamila**, who really has no business being an every-down player in the NFL. KGB (his nickname, not his affiliation with the Soviet Union's enforcer unit) is an outstanding pass rusher (49 sacks over the past four years), but at just 252 pounds, he gets eaten alive in run defense.

Nose tackle **Grady Jackson** might be the only difference maker to have just 23 tackles in a single season. At 340 pounds, the ninth-year veteran is so big that if a Wisconsin dairy farmer ever encountered him, Jackson just might mistakenly get milked. When he is in the game, offensive lines have to divert most of their interior attention to Jackson; if they don't, his explosive quickness and power will blow up a play.

Next to Jackson is **Cletidus Hunt**, a living example of the effects laziness can have on a talented athlete. Hunt has unusual athleticism for his size, but his vacillating effort and general disinterest in the game hurt this front four. A football team cannot depend on him; last year he was even benched for not playing hard.

When considering the one-dimensional skills of the ends and the inconsistent output at the tackle position, the Packers front

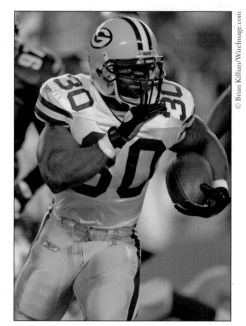

Ahman Green is every bit as important to this offense as Brett Favre. It will be up to him to produce big numbers for Green Bay's rushing attack in 2005.

Startling Statistics

15-1 Packers' two-year record at Lambeau Field prior to losing to Michael Vick and the Atlanta Falcons in the 2002 Wild Card game.

9-7 Packers' two-year record at Lambeau Field after losing to Michael Vick and the Atlanta Falcons in the 2002 Wild Card game.

In his third season out of Oregon State, Barnett has the speed to chase down a runner and the ability to shed blocks and overpower players in traffic. However, he must improve his eighth-grade-level maturity and learn to play under better control. If Barnett can improve as a football player mentally, he should earn some postseason trips to Hawaii in the near future.

Strongside linebacker **Hannibal Navies** does not play with enough aggression at his position. The Packers would benefit from a change here, but the only option is free agent acquisition **Ray Thompson**, who is fast but really only a nickel linebacker.

Weakside man **Na'il Diggs** has the ability to charge the ball and play sideline-to-sideline. If he and Barnett can step up their games, the Packers will be in pretty good shape at the linebacker position.

Special Teams

Kicker **Ryan Longwell** continues to kick like his name: Real long and real well. He is still only 30 years old, which in kicker years makes him, like, 11 or 12. Punter **B.J. Sander** was drafted in the third round last season, only to become a bust. He never even got an opportunity to punt in the regular season, but he will get a second chance this year. Everybody loves return man **Antonio Chatman**, but there are not a lot of weaker big-play threats in the entire league. After last season, Chatman ought to copyright the "fair catch." The rookie **Terrence Murphy** could wind up taking Chatman's job this year.

four is certainly weaker than most, but Bates absolutely loves this unit, because of what he perceives to be a deep pool of talent behind the starters. However, the only depth that he can cite truthfully is third-year tackle **Cullen Jenkins**, who will have a good season as an interior pass rusher in '05. Other than that, Bates is pretending to be giddy about ends **R-Kal Truluck**, who cannot create on his own, and **Kenny Peterson**, who has gotten limited playing time since joining the league in '03. However, Bates says that he has never seen such depth in all of his 15 years in the league (he's even excited about his third-string players), so perhaps he knows something that others don't.

The linebackers for the Packers are not *atrocious*—after all, the team gave up only 117.4 rushing yards per game last season, which isn't *too* bad. However, this unit will be only as good as its man in the middle, **Nick Barnett**.

The Bottom Line

Green Bay is a proud franchise, but it is hard to see this team being better than they were last season. Under Favre, the offense will be just fine, but the defense is the same vanilla unit that prevented this team from moving on in the postseason a year ago. With an improving division, a declining home-field advantage, and a paucity of playmakers on defense, it would be an accomplishment for this team to reach the playoffs in '05.

Minnesota Vikings

Predicted: 1st ▪ 2004: 8-8 (2nd)

Players Added

LB	Sam Cowart	(NYJ)
K	Paul Edinger	(Chi)
LB	Napoleon Harris	(Oak)
QB	Brad Johnson	(TB)
FS	Darren Sharper	(GB)
CB	Fred Smoot	(Was)
WR	Travis Taylor	(Bal)
NT	Pat Williams	(Buf)

Players Lost

LB	Chris Claiborne	(StL)
QB	Gus Frerotte	(Mia)
DT	Chris Hovan	(TB)
DE	Kenny Mixon	
WR	Randy Moss	(Oak)
S	Brian Russell	(Cle)
CB	Terrence Shaw	

Draft

1	(7)	Troy Williamson	WR	South Carolina
1	(18)	Erasmus James	DE	Wisconsin
2	(49)	Marcus Johnson	OT	Mississippi
3	(80)	Dustin Fox	S	Ohio St.
4	(112)	Ciatrick Fason	RB	Florida
6	(191)	C.J. Mosley	DT	Missouri
7	(219)	Adrian Ward	DB	Texas–El Paso

The Vikings made great use of their two first-round picks, doing their best to replace Randy Moss with the fast and incredibly gifted Williamson. He can become a superstar if all goes well. James had a great senior year, showing all-around ability; he only furthers Minnesota's efforts to build an empire on the defensive line. Johnson gives the offensive line great depth because of his versatility. Fason is a much better value than a typical fourth-round pick, although the Vikings still didn't need to take him.

Head Coach: Mike Tice (5th year)
Offensive Coordinator: Steve Loney
Defensive Coordinator: Ted Cottrell

Offense

QB:	Daunte Culpepper*
RB:	Michael Bennett
HB:	Jim Kleinsasser
WR:	Troy Williamson‡
WR:	Nate Burleson
TE:	Jermaine Wiggins
LT:	Bryant McKinnie
LG:	Adam Goldberg
C:	Matt Birk*
RG:	Chris Liwienski
RT:	Mike Rosenthal
QB:	Brad Johnson†
RB:	Moe Williams
WR:	Marcus Robinson
WR:	Travis Taylor†
OL:	Marcus Johnson‡

Defense

LDE:	Kenechi Udeze
DT:	Kevin Williams*
NT:	Pat Williams†
RDE:	Darrion Scott
SLB:	Napoleon Harris†
MLB:	Sam Cowart†
WLB:	Dontarrious Thomas
CB:	Antoine Winfield
SS:	Corey Chavous
FS:	Darren Sharper†
CB:	Fred Smoot†
NB:	Brian Williams
DL:	Lance Johnstone
LB:	Keith Newman
K:	Aaron Elling
P:	Darren Bennett

* Pro Bowler '04
† veteran acquisition
‡ rookie

Report Card

Quarterback	A	Defensive Line	B	Coaching	C+
Running Back	C+	Linebacker	C	Special Teams	C−
Receiver/Tight End	B	Defensive Back	A	Depth	A+
Offensive Line	B−			Intangibles	C−

After four or five years of annual late-season collapses, high-level drama, and unfulfilled expectations, the Minnesota Vikings decided that perhaps this year the time for a change was finally ripe. However, not too many people could have foreseen the purple team from the North Star State making as many adjustments as they did.

In January, Minnesota began to fall into new management. Having spent the past few years trying to escape the Great White North as if it were 1945 Dresden, owner Red McCombs finally appears to be leaving the picture. In early March, Minnesota pulled the trigger on a Paul Bunyan–sized deal, sending disgruntled receiver Randy Moss to Oakland in exchange for linebacker Napoleon Harris and draft picks.

After the Moss deal, the Vikings continued to get aggressive toward revamping a defense that ranked 26th in scoring a year ago. They turned the free agent market into their personal Mall of America, signing five new defensive starters, giving them seven in all.

Aside from a minor Mike Tice ticket-scalping scandal (a "knavery scam" that nobody could really ever muster up enough anger about), things went pretty well up in the Minneapolis–St. Paul region. Of course, it's impossible to suffer a late-season meltdown during the spring and summer.

Kevin Williams

Offense

With Randy Moss and his selfish ego now gone out west, this is officially **Daunte Culpepper**'s team. Culpepper has definitely earned the honor. After struggling to be a leader and play with consistency for much of the early part of his seven-year career, the 6'4", 265-pound superathlete from Central Florida has put together back-to-back strong seasons. (Strong on paper, anyway.) Last year, he was the second-best quarterback in the league in just about every fashion imaginable: 69.2 completion percentage, 4,717 yards, 39 touchdowns, only 11 interceptions! The list goes on, but most revealing may be Minnesota's league-best 52.3 third-down success rate, which was a direct result of Culpepper's poise and ability to improvise.

However, when all was said and done, the Vikings still wound up losing in the divisional round of the playoffs. Granted, it wasn't because of their quarterback; nevertheless, an undecorated ring finger will always be an undecorated ring finger. Just ask Dan Marino. But this year is different in that, as mentioned, Culpepper is in complete control. Anyone who believes that Moss is what made Culpepper is sadly mistaken. In fact, because he no longer has to deal with Moss's extracurricular nonsense, Culpepper will be the best he's ever been. He has all the tools needed to carry an offense: a great arm, amazing strength, an ability to scramble and avoid the rush, and the "it" that is required to make big plays.

The logical assumption is that Minnesota's second-ranked passing offense will drop a level in '05 now that (okay, his name has been printed enough) is gone. However, such is not the case. The Vikings still have an explosive collection of wide receivers, led by rookie **Troy Williamson**. The Vikings made Williamson the seventh overall draft pick this year, taking him ahead of the man everyone thought they would grab, Mike Williams.

While the team will never use the phrase "replace Moss," that is exactly what they are hoping the 6'1" Williamson can do. He has 4.34 speed to stretch the field, and while at South Carolina, he showed a fantastic balance of skills. The Vikings will make him their No. 1 wideout, which means third-year man **Nate Burleson** will once again be option numero dos. Either veteran **Marcus Robinson** or free agent acquisition **Travis Taylor** (a career underachiever) will be the first receiver off the bench.

Just because none of these names flashes a Pro Bowl flare does not mean Minnesota doesn't have a dynamic throng of weapons to throw to. Burleson has great speed and is one of the league's best at running after the catch. The Vikings will spread the field in order to help give him an opportunity to catch passes in full stride. He is also a great weapon on third down (22 catches, seven touchdowns last year) because of his awareness of how to get open when Culpepper is scrambling outside the pocket. Burleson likely will not have as much room to operate this year (Williamson, as good as he can be, will still not command the attention that Moss did), but he is still poised to build on his 1,000-yard, nine-touchdown season in '04.

Tight end **Jermaine Wiggins** had a breakout season in '04, catching a team-high 71 passes, but his production will likely decrease in this year's offense. Wiggins is a nice receiver in the flats, but the departure of—ahem—Moss, means the departure of the wide-open space that Wiggins has enjoyed. Wiggins is not the type of player who can create opportunities on his own, as his speed and agility are about as effective as a professional wrestler serving as governor.

Write it Down:
With Moss gone, the offense will not miss a beat.

Where the real speed can be found in Minnesota is in the Vikings backfield—specifically, in **Michael Bennett** and **Onterrio Smith**. Both running backs are part of a five-man group that head coach **Mike Tice** and new offensive coordinator **Steve Loney** will have to assort. In addition, the clan includes **Moe Williams**, **Mewelde Moore**, and rookie **Ciatrick Fason**. So far, the only player who has even been assured of a roster spot—let alone a starting job—is the 10th-year veteran Williams, because of his past history as the Vikings third-down back.

The rest of the lot comes with as many pros and cons as the Portland Trailblazers lineup. Both Bennett and Smith have tremendous open-field speed—which fits the Vikings' straight-ahead run-blocking scheme—but neither is a particularly viable third-down option. Furthermore, Bennett has had a history of injuries and Smith has a history of substance abuse–related problems. Smith, in fact, may have finally punched his ticket out of town when he was discovered by airport security officials to have in his possession a kit (called The Whizzinator) that is used to beat drug tests. Smith already served a four-game suspension last season as part of previous NFL substance abuse violations and in college he was kicked off the Tennessee Volunteers for smoking marijuana. This year, he may wind up serving a one-year suspension for a separate violation of the NFL drug policy.

If the talented Smith remains with the team, that leaves Moore—a fourth-round pick last season who averaged 5.8 yards per carry as a fill-in starter during October—and Fason, a fourth-round pick this year. It's impossible to say which player will make the roster and which will wind up on the practice squad, but one thing that's very possible is asking "Why in the world did the Vikings draft a running back this year to begin with?" A $10,000 prize for whoever can answer *that*.

The halfback is a key component in Minnesota's offense. **Jim Kleinsasser** has held the job since 1999, but he is coming off an ACL injury. Don't be surprised if third-year player **Sean Berton** takes over here at some point in '05.

The Vikings have a front five that can be very good, although it will be up to the offensive coordinator, Loney (who will also continue his duties as offensive line coach), to make it all come together this year. Pro Bowl center **Matt Birk** is one of the brightest and most effective linemen in the game, but his health is in doubt this year, after hip surgery in late May. Birk may not be ready for the start of the season in September, and if he is

This Season vs. Last Season

Progression: **Pass defense**—The improvements in what will be a more aggressive secondary—as well as the additions made up front that accompany the rising young stars—will make the Vikings much more potent against the pass in '05.

Regression: **Linebacker speed**—Although Minnesota has slightly improved at this position as a whole, they did sacrifice a lot of young speed to bring in Sam Cowart and Napoleon Harris.

ready, what kind of playing shape will he be in? The cornerstone of this group is fourth-year left tackle **Bryant McKinnie**. Minnesota—the Land of 10,000 Lakes—is said to actually have around 15,000 of them. McKinnie is bigger than half of them. At 6'8", 335 pounds, McKinnie has plenty of room to store his raging athleticism. However, the game comes so easily to him that he must consciously fight off lazy habits. As soon as McKinnie can develop a more aggressive game, he will be a fixture in the Pro Bowl.

Guard **Chris Liwienski** is moving from the left to the right side this year in order to allow second-year player **Adam Goldberg** a chance to start. (This relegates 12th-year veteran David Dixon to backup duties or retirement.) Liwienski has good initial quickness and he knows how to handle an opponent, but the Vikings need him to be more consistent in all phases of the game. Goldberg, on the other hand, does not have first-rate talent, but he was able to hold up as the starting right tackle for six games a year ago. He will be a different player once he develops better awareness and establishes more confidence.

The right tackle duties tentatively belong to **Mike Rosenthal**, who is returning from a broken foot. But in all likelihood, rookie second-round draft pick **Marcus Johnson** will steal this job before training camp ends. Johnson worked with the first unit for much of minicamp, and the Vikes loved what they saw.

Defense

The Vikings are out ice fishing on one of those 15,000 lakes in the same boat as other teams like the Chiefs and the Colts. They have a great offense and scoring is as easy for them as it was for Wilt Chamberlain (both on *and* off the court), but they will never succeed unless they can learn to defend. Last season the Vikings ranked 26th in points allowed, 28th in yards allowed, 27th against the pass, 21st against the run, and 30th on third downs. In other words, the picture was pretty clear, heading into the offseason, about which side of the ball the team needed to fix.

Tice and the front office have dialed in on the secondary and made it a major priority over the past two years. Last season they signed free agent **Antoine Winfield** to a big-money contract, and this year they forked over enough cash to bring in cornerback **Fred Smoot** (*see* Painting a New Picture, page 6) and free safety **Darren Sharper**. Factor these additions in with the return of strong safety **Corey Chavous** and the re-signing of nickel back **Brian Williams**, and Minnesota has gone from having a shoddy secondary to having one of the more well-rounded units in the league.

Smoot's presence will be great for the Vikes because, lining up opposite Winfield, he gives the team another cornerback who can thrive on playing genuine man-to-man coverage. What's more, each player's skills complements the other's extremely well. Winfield has long been one of the elite cover corners in the league because of his physicality and quickness in defending the underneath pass. He has not let his bantam size (5'9", 180 pounds) hinder his game—in fact, Winfield is probably the best

tackling cornerback in the entire NFL. Smoot, on the other hand, is more of a finesse playmaker who can run with fast receivers and take away the long ball. He, too, is a willing tackler, although he would much rather make a big interception.

With two cover corners pressing the outsides, the veteran safeties for Minnesota—Sharper and Chavous—will have more freedom in this defense. Sharper was on the decline when he left the Packers, but if he can be healthy throughout the season, he is capable of picking off six or seven passes, especially when considering that he will have far fewer responsibilities to worry about here. Chavous is a Pro Bowl–caliber safety who has similar circumstances; when healthy, he can be an interception machine. Chavous doesn't have tremendous size (which is why Minnesota may find ways to get the underrated **Willie Offord** more reps in '05), but he has one of the highest football IQs in the game.

The improvement of the secondary will be monumental for this club, especially when considering that young pass-rushers up front, such as ends **Kenechi Udeze** and rookie **Erasmus James**, plus tackle **Kevin Williams**, are only going to get better.

The Vikings made Udeze a first-round pick last season, a move the jury is still deliberating. Udeze has nice skills, but it is going to take the 22-year-old some time to build his awareness and translate his talents to the pro level. James was a first-round pick this season (18th overall). The 6'4" former Wisconsin Badger is not as pure a pass rusher as his fellow young teammate, but he possesses a broader range of skills. However, unlike Udeze, James won't start right away as a rookie; he is slated to come off the bench behind second-year man **Darrion Scott**. Scott is a wide-bodied end who has the explosiveness of a sparkler (rather than, oh, say a *bomb*, for example) but the power and tenacity to be disruptive against the run.

The team could slide Scott over to defensive tackle, but they already have Kevin Williams and free agent acquisition **Pat Williams** (*see* Painting a New Picture, page 7) locked in there. Kevin Williams is entering just his third year in the league, but has already established himself as one of, if not *the*, best interior defensive linemen in the game. He has superb athleticism and an active motor that makes him an absolute menace for opposing blockers. He totaled a rare 12 sacks last season, the highest total for a defensive tackle since Warren Sapp's $16\frac{1}{2}$ in 2000. It is

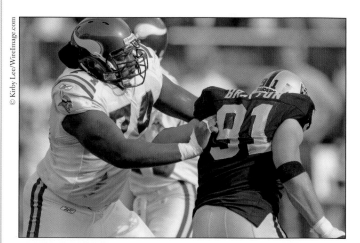

Left tackle Bryant McKinnie has the skills to flourish in the NFL, but Minnesota is still waiting for him to fully emerge this year.

frightening to imagine what Kevin Williams will be able to do this season, when blockers will have to double-team his neighbor Pat Williams.

When the Vikings sail their slender European warships around the Great Lakes region and visit clubs like the Lions and Packers and Bears (oh my!), they will be doing so with one of the deepest crews in all the land. In addition to the aforementioned James, Minnesota's bench includes pass-rushing ace **Lance Johnstone** (last season he had 11 sacks and five forced fumbles, most coming on third down), and tackles **Spencer Johnson** and **Steve Martin**. Johnson is a talented second-year player who can one day start, as long as he gets a better grasp on how to play the game. Martin is a run-stuffing veteran who can provide leadership, if nothing else.

The origin of the state name "Minnesota" is emblematic of theVikings' linebacking situation. "Minnesota" comes from the Sioux Indians, who occupied the region long before French fur trappers arrived in the early 19th century. In Sioux, it means "cloudy water." There is little doubt that the defensive backfield and front four are going to be better in '05, but nobody can convincingly say the same about the murky puddle that is the linebacking unit. Logistically, Minnesota—who had three different starting linebackers at this point last year—should be better here, but there are still uncertainties.

A good amount of those uncertainties lie behind middle linebacker **Sam Cowart**. Although he is only 30, Cowart has aged faster than Robin Williams in the movie *Jack*, as a result of various injuries throughout his career. Cowart is not the same star that he was in his early years as a Bill, but he is an experienced veteran who knows how to tackle. The addition of Cowart consigns third-year man **E.J. Henderson** to the bench. Henderson was once a second-round draft pick, but his poor decision making—both on and off the field—has cost him dearly.

Strongside linebacker **Napoleon Harris** came over as part of the Moss deal (there's that name again). Harris is not a huge upgrade for the defense—he possesses only average speed and strength in shedding blocks—but he is only 26 and his versatility in run support will be helpful. On third downs, Minnesota will bring in veteran **Keith Newman**, who specializes in pass defense.

The weakside job is up for grabs. **Dontarrious Thomas** did duty here as a rookie last season and he has a good NFL frame, but the Vikes remain lukewarm about him, which is why they will give fourth-year man **Raonall Smith** a chance. And don't forget about fourth-string rookie free agent **Sarth Benoit**, whose last name implies the sheer genius hidden somewhere deep in his soul.

Special Teams

The Vikings will not invite the 45-year-old kicker (yes, seriously, 45) Morten Andersen back this year, which means they will have to go with **Aaron Elling**—a guy they cut in the middle of last season—or some outside veteran. Either way, it doesn't look good. Punter **Darren Bennett** is also expected to be replaced before September. The Vikings' return unit will feature one of the running backs on kicks and one of the receivers on punts.

The Bottom Line

No team underwent more substantial improvements over the offseason than the Vikings. With Culpepper at the helm, they have enough playmakers and depth on offense to continue to put up huge numbers, even without that certain Number 84. Defensively, Minnesota will reap the benefits of their great free agent and draft day moves. If Tice can rally his players and keep them focused for the duration of the entire 2005 season, this team could contend for a title.

NFC South

Atlanta
Falcons

Carolina
Panthers

New Orleans
Saints

Tampa Bay
Buccaneers

Looking Forward

Ready to Break Out

**Will Smith,
New Orleans Saints**

Defensive End
6'3"—282
2nd year—24 years old
Drafted: 1st round in '04 out of Ohio State

Will Smith

Saints defensive end Will Smith will turn out to be the greatest thing since the Fresh Prince of Bel Air. Smith had 7¹/₂ sacks as a second-string rookie in '04, but his main contributions came in run defense.

The athletic 6'3", 282-pounder has the power and quickness to own the trenches in playing the run. He also has a great motor, showing the awareness and energy to make plays getting from one end of the field to the other. Smith is a lot like Michael Strahan, but with even more energy. He takes on blocks at the line of scrimmage and has an uncanny knack for diagnosing plays. Once he sniffs out a play, he has the raw skills to "outquick" a blocker in pass protection or get separation and clog the holes in run support.

The party doesn't stop once Smith reaches the ball, either. Last season he forced six—count 'em, *six*—fumbles. Simply put, this guy has the potential to be a 10-time Pro Bowler before the final chapter of his career.

Hot Seat

**Aaron Brooks,
New Orleans Saints**

This is a very tepid hot seat, because if the New Orleans Saints were really serious about laying down the law on their 29-year-old quarterback, Aaron Brooks, they would have done so long ago. Furthermore, Brooks's coach, Jim Haslett, deserves to be the one on the hot seat, but the team continues to show faith for the sixth-year head coach. All of the blame is shifted to the leadership (or lack thereof) on the field.

Brooks is a very gifted player, possessing all of the skills that a quarterback must have in order to succeed. However, he has not had the demeanor of a leader or shown the actions of someone who is learning from his mistakes. With a talented team that is expecting big things once again this season, Brooks is now in a position to shoulder the entire blame if things don't go well.

Best Offseason Move

Falcons replacing the incapable middle linebacker Chris Draft with Ed Hartwell.

Worst Offseason Move

Saints retaining head coach Jim Haslett.

Best Under-the-Radar Offseason Move

Carolina's signing of Ken Lucas allows cornerback Ricky Manning, Jr., to focus strictly on covering the slot defender in nickel defense.

Biggest Question

With the Carolina Panthers being a rejuvenated football team, do they have enough to overtake the one club that has had their number in recent years, the Atlanta Falcons?

QUICK HITS

TEAM BESTS		BEST PLAYERS	
Passing Game	Saints	Pure Athlete	Julius Peppers, Panthers
Running Game	Falcons	Big Play Threat	Michael Vick, Falcons
Offensive Line	Saints	Best Use of Talent	Jake Delhomme, Panthers
Pass Rush	Falcons	Worst Use of Talent	Boo Williams, Saints
Run Defense	Falcons	On the Rise	DeAngelo Hall, Falcons
Pass Defense	Buccaneers		Michael Clayton, Buccaneers
Special Teams	Saints		Chris Gamble, Panthers
Coaching Staff	Panthers	On the Decline	Joey Galloway, Buccaneers
Home Field	Falcons		Brentson Buckner, Panthers
			Mike Alstott, Buccaneers
		Best Leader	Derrick Brooks, Buccaneers
		Unsung Hero	Rod Coleman, Falcons
		Impact Rookie	Jammal Brown, Saints

Jake Delhomme

Looking Back

Altanta Falcons 2004

PASSING STATISTICS

PLAYER	CMP	ATT	YDS	CMP%	YDS/A	LNG	TD	TD%	INT	INT%	SACK	YDS	RAT
Michael Vick	181	321	2313	56.4	7.21	62	14	4.4	12	3.7	46	266	78.1

RUSHING STATISTICS

PLAYER	ATT	YDS	AVG	LNG	TD	FUM	LST
Warrick Dunn	265	1106	4.2	60	9	3	2
Michael Vick	120	902	7.5	58	3	3	0
T.J. Duckett	104	509	4.9	35	8	2	2

RECEIVING STATISTICS

PLAYER	REC	YDS	AVG	LNG	TD	FUM	LST
Alge Crumpler	48	774	16.1	49	6	1	1
Peerless Price	45	575	12.8	50	3	0	0
Dez White	30	370	12.3	54	2	0	0
Warrick Dunn	29	293	10.1	59	0	0	0

RETURN STATISTICS

PLAYER	KICKOFFS						PUNTS					
	ATT	YDS	FC	AVG	LNG	TD	ATT	YDS	FC	AVG	LNG	TD
Allen Rossum	58	1250	0	21.6	49	0	37	457	14	12.4	75	1
Stanley Pritchett	1	2	0	2.0	2	0	0	0	0	0.0	0	0

KICKING STATISTICS

PLAYER	1-20	20-29	30-39	40-49	50+	TOT	PCT	AVG	LNG	XPM/A	PTS
Jay Feely	1/1	7/7	7/9	3/6	0/0	18/23	78.3	30.8	47	40/40	94

PUNTING STATISTICS

PLAYER	PUNTS	YDS	AVG	LNG	TB	TB%	IN20	IN20%	RET	YDS	AVG	NET
Chris Mohr	76	3082	40.6	56	7	9.2	19	25.0	33	134	4.1	38.8

DEFENSIVE STATISTICS

PLAYER	TACKLES					MISCELLANEOUS			INTERCEPTIONS				
	TOT	SOLO	AST	SACK	TLOSS	FF	BK	INT	YDS	AVG	LNG	TD	PD
Keith Brooking	102	87	15	2.5	2	2	0	3	41	13.7	27	0	6
Bryan Scott	87	78	9	2.5	0	1	0	1	22	22.0	22	0	5
Matt Stewart	67	57	10	1.5	3.5	0	0	0	0	0.0	0	0	4
Patrick Kerney	66	58	8	13.0	4.5	1	0	1	0	0.0	0	0	9
Kevin Mathis	64	59	5	0.0	0.5	0	0	2	101	50.5	66	2	8
Chris Draft	57	47	10	0.0	3	1	0	1	33	33.0	33	0	3
Cory Hall	53	43	10	0.0	1.5	0	0	0	0	0.0	0	0	2
Demorrio Williams	45	39	6	2.5	1.5	0	1	0	0	0.0	0	0	0
Rod Coleman	41	34	7	11.5	5	3	0	1	39	39.0	39	1	6
Jason Webster	41	39	2	0.0	1	1	0	1	18	18.0	18	0	10

2004 Team Stats

OFFENSE

Scoring:	21.2 (16)
Yards per Game:	317.7 (20)
Pass Yards per Game:	150.7 (30)
Rush Yards per Game:	167.0 (1)
Sacks Allowed:	50 (t27)
3rd Down Percentage:	36.3 (18)
Giveaways:	26 (t20)

DEFENSE

Scoring:	21.1 (14)
Yards per Game:	325.4 (14)
Pass Yards per Game:	220.4 (22)
Rush Yards per Game:	105.1 (t8)
Sacks:	48 (1)
3rd Down Percentage:	36.0 (t13)
Takeaways:	29 (t8)

Carolina Panthers 2004

PASSING STATISTICS

PLAYER	CMP	ATT	YDS	CMP%	YDS/A	LNG	TD	TD%	INT	INT%	SACK	YDS	RAT
Jake Delhomme	310	533	3886	58.2	7.29	63	29	5.4	15	2.8	33	246	87.3

RUSHING STATISTICS

PLAYER	ATT	YDS	AVG	LNG	TD	FUM	LST
Nick Goings	217	821	3.8	57	6	1	1
DeShaun Foster	59	255	4.3	71	2	0	0
Brad Hoover	68	246	3.6	16	0	0	0

RECEIVING STATISTICS

PLAYER	REC	YDS	AVG	LNG	TD	FUM	LST
Muhsin Muhammad	93	1405	15.1	51	16	2	0
Keary Colbert	47	754	16.0	63	5	1	1
Ricky Proehl	34	497	14.6	34	0	0	0
Nick Goings	45	394	8.8	37	1	0	0

RETURN STATISTICS

PLAYER	KICKOFFS						PUNTS					
	ATT	YDS	FC	AVG	LNG	TD	ATT	YDS	FC	AVG	LNG	TD
Jamall Broussard	24	555	0	23.1	49	0	10	43	8	4.3	13	0
Brandon Bennett	8	177	0	22.1	43	0	0	0	0	0.0	0	0

KICKING STATISTICS

PLAYER	1-20	20-29	30-39	40-49	50+	TOT	PCT	AVG	LNG	XPM/A	PTS
John Kasay	0/0	11/11	4/4	1/2	3/5	19/22	86.4	31.5	54	27/28	84

PUNTING STATISTICS

PLAYER	PUNTS	YDS	AVG	LNG	TB	TB%	IN20	IN20%	RET	YDS	AVG	NET
Todd Sauerbrun	76	3351	44.1	65	8	10.5	25	32.9	38	303	8	40.1

DEFENSIVE STATISTICS

PLAYER	TACKLES					MISCELLANEOUS			INTERCEPTIONS				
	TOT	SOLO	AST	SACK	TLOSS	FF	BK	INT	YDS	AVG	LNG	TD	PD
Dan Morgan	102	85	17	2.0	1.5	1	0	2	20	10.0	11	0	6
Will Witherspoon	102	88	14	3.0	1.5	1	0	4	48	12.0	25	0	14
Mike Minter	83	64	19	2.0	2	3	0	0	0	0.0	0	0	10
Chris Gamble	66	61	5	0.0	1.5	1	0	6	15	2.5	13	0	14
Julius Peppers	65	56	9	11.0	4.5	4	1	2	143	71.5	97	1	9
Mark Fields	62	52	10	4.0	8	1	0	1	14	14.0	14	0	3
Ricky Manning Jr.	60	52	8	0.0	2	0	0	4	46	11.5	30	0	9
Colin Branch	54	43	11	0.0	2.5	0	0	3	79	26.3	76	0	8
Brentson Buckner	41	30	11	3.5	2	1	0	1	8	8.0	8	0	5
Brandon Short	40	31	9	0.0	3.5	1	0	0	0	0.0	0	0	0

2004 Team Stats

OFFENSE

Scoring:	22.2 (13)
Yards per Game:	326.6 (13)
Pass Yards per Game:	227.7 (9
Rush Yards per Game:	98.9 (28)
Sacks Allowed:	33 (11)
3rd Down Percentage:	40.3 (10)
Giveaways:	23 (15)

DEFENSE

Scoring:	21.2 (t15)
Yards per Game:	336.4 (20)
Pass Yards per Game:	217.4 (18)
Rush Yards per Game:	119.0 (17)
Sacks:	34 (t24)
3rd Down Percentage:	46.0 (31)
Takeaways:	35 (t1)

New Orleans Saints 2004

PASSING STATISTICS

PLAYER	CMP	ATT	YDS	CMP%	YDS/A	LNG	TD	TD%	INT	INT%	SACK	YDS	RAT
Aaron Brooks	309	542	3810	57.0	7.03	57	21	3.9	16	3.0	41	223	79.5

RUSHING STATISTICS

PLAYER	ATT	YDS	AVG	LNG	TD	FUM	LST
Deuce McAllister	269	1074	4.0	71	9	5	4
Aaron Stecker	58	244	4.2	42	2	1	1
Aaron Brooks	58	173	3.0	15	4	6	1

RECEIVING STATISTICS

PLAYER	REC	YDS	AVG	LNG	TD	FUM	LST
Joe Horn	94	1399	14.9	57	11	0	0
Donte' Stallworth	58	767	13.2	45	5	0	0
Jerome Pathon	34	581	17.1	38	1	1	1
Boo Williams	33	362	11.0	22	2	2	1

RETURN STATISTICS

PLAYER	KICKOFFS						PUNTS					
	ATT	YDS	FC	AVG	LNG	TD	ATT	YDS	FC	AVG	LNG	TD
Michael Lewis	51	1215	0	23.8	96	1	34	382	11	11.2	53	0
Aaron Stecker	18	469	0	26.1	98	1	0	0	0	0.0	0	0

KICKING STATISTICS

PLAYER	1-20	20-29	30-39	40-49	50+	TOT	PCT	AVG	LNG	XPM/A	PTS
John Carney	0/0	3/3	12/15	5/6	2/3	22/27	81.5	38.0	53	38/38	104

PUNTING STATISTICS

PLAYER	PUNTS	YDS	AVG	LNG	TB	TB%	IN20	IN20%	RET	YDS	AVG	NET
Mitch Berger	85	3704	43.6	63	4	4.7	28	32.9	43	310	7.2	39.9

DEFENSIVE STATISTICS

PLAYER	TACKLES					MISCELLANEOUS		INTERCEPTIONS					
	TOT	SOLO	AST	SACK	TLOSS	FF	BK	INT	YDS	AVG	LNG	TD	PD
Tebucky Jones	102	80	22	0.0	0	1	0	1	55	55.0	55	0	4
Jay Bellamy	92	75	17	0.0	3	2	0	0	0	0.0	0	0	1
Charles Grant	80	67	13	10.5	11.5	3	0	1	8	8.0	8	0	7
Orlando Ruff	74	54	20	0.0	1	0	0	1	0	0.0	0	0	3
Brian Young	59	43	16	2.5	5	0	0	0	0	0.0	0	0	0
Derrick Rodgers	55	44	11	0.0	0.5	1	0	0	0	0.0	0	0	3
Courtney Watson	55	40	15	2.0	2	0	0	0	0	0.0	0	0	3
Fakhir Brown	54	54	0	0.0	0	2	0	2	0	0.0	0	0	12
Darren Howard	46	38	8	11.0	2.5	4	0	0	0	0.0	0	0	1
James Allen	46	31	15	0.0	0	2	0	0	0	0.0	0	0	1

2004 Team Stats

OFFENSE

Scoring:	324.6 (15)
Yards per Game:	324.6 (15)
Pass Yards per Game:	224.2 (12)
Rush Yards per Game:	100.4 (27)
Sacks Allowed:	41 (21)
3rd Down Percentage:	33.3 (26)
Giveaways:	24 (16)

DEFENSE

Scoring:	25.3 (t27)
Yards per Game:	383.8 (32)
Pass Yards per Game:	243.0 (t27)
Rush Yards per Game:	140.8 (30)
Sacks:	37 (t17)
3rd Down Percentage:	38.1 (19)
Takeaways:	26 (t14)

Tampa Bay Buccaneers 2004

PASSING STATISTICS

PLAYER	CMP	ATT	YDS	CMP%	YDS/A	LNG	TD	TD%	INT	INT%	SACK	YDS	RAT
Brian Griese	233	336	2632	69.3	7.83	68	20	6.0	12	3.6	26	169	97.5

RUSHING STATISTICS

PLAYER	ATT	YDS	AVG	LNG	TD	FUM	LST
Michael Pittman	219	926	4.2	78	7	5	5
Mike Alstott	67	230	3.4	32	2	1	1
Charlie Garner	30	111	3.7	25	0	0	0

RECEIVING STATISTICS

PLAYER	REC	YDS	AVG	LNG	TD	FUM	LST
Michael Clayton	80	1193	14.9	75	7	0	0
Joey Galloway	33	416	12.6	36	5	0	0
Michael Pittman	41	391	9.5	68	3	1	1
Ken Dilger	39	345	8.8	45	3	0	0

RETURN STATISTICS

PLAYER	KICKOFFS						PUNTS					
	ATT	YDS	FC	AVG	LNG	TD	ATT	YDS	FC	AVG	LNG	TD
Torrie Cox	33	866	0	26.2	59	0	0	0	0	0.0	0	0
Frank Murphy	8	208	0	26.0	54	0	0	0	0	0.0	0	0

KICKING STATISTICS

PLAYER	1-20	20-29	30-39	40-49	50+	TOT	PCT	AVG	LNG	XPM/A	PTS
Martin Gramatica	0/0	6/7	3/6	1/5	1/1	11/19	57.9	31.1	53	21/22	54

PUNTING STATISTICS

PLAYER	PUNTS	YDS	AVG	LNG	TB	TB%	IN20	IN20%	RET	YDS	AVG	NET
Josh Bidwell	82	3472	42.3	60	7	8.5	23	28.0	31	279	9	38.9

DEFENSIVE STATISTICS

PLAYER	TACKLES					MISCELLANEOUS		INTERCEPTIONS					
	TOT	SOLO	AST	SACK	TLOSS	FF	BK	INT	YDS	AVG	LNG	TD	PD
Derrick Brooks	137	109	28	3.0	3.5	2	0	1	3	3.0	3	0	6
Shelton Quarles	104	72	32	3.5	3	0	0	0	0	0.0	0	0	3
Ronde Barber	92	78	14	3.0	5.5	2	0	3	23	7.7	23	0	13
Dwight Smith	83	72	11	0.0	3.5	3	0	3	13	4.3	13	0	13
Ian Gold	71	54	17	0.5	4	0	0	1	31	31.0	31	0	3
Greg Spires	61	47	14	8.0	6.5	3	0	0	0	0.0	0	0	3
Brian Kelly	58	52	6	0.0	1	0	0	4	101	25.3	75	0	22
Chartric Darby	50	40	10	0.0	3	1	0	0	0	0.0	0	0	0
Jermaine Phillips	42	31	11	1.0	1.5	0	0	1	0	0.0	0	0	4
Simeon Rice	40	35	5	12.0	2.5	1	0	0	0	0.0	0	0	5

2004 Team Stats

OFFENSE

Scoring:	18.8 (23)
Yards per Game:	310.2 (22)
Pass Yards per Game:	217.1 (14)
Rush Yards per Game:	93.1 (29)
Sacks Allowed:	44 (23)
3rd Down Percentage:	37.7 (14)
Giveaways:	28 (t23)

DEFENSE

Scoring:	19.0 (t9)
Yards per Game:	284.5 (5)
Pass Yards per Game:	161.2 (1)
Rush Yards per Game:	123.3 (19)
Sacks:	45 (t3)
3rd Down Percentage:	35.3 (11)
Takeaways:	26 (t14)

Atlanta Falcons

Predicted: 2nd ▪ 2004: 11–5 (reached NFC Championship)

Head Coach: Jim Mora, Jr. (2nd year)

Offensive Coordinator: Greg Knapp

Defensive Coordinator: Ed Donatell

Players Added

S	Rich Coady (StL)
P	Toby Gowin (NYJ)
LB	Ed Hartwell (Bal)
S	Ronnie Heard (SF)
OL	Matt Lehr (StL)
DL	Brandon Mitchell (Sea)
K	Todd Peterson (SF)
LB	Ike Reese (Phi)
OT	Barry Stokes (NYG)

Players Lost

LB	Chris Draft (Car)
LB	Jamie Duncan
K	Jay Feely (NYG)
G	Roberto Garza (Chi)
S	Cory Hall (Was)
DE	Travis Hall
NT	Ed Jasper (retired)
P	Chris Mohr
LB	Matt Stewart (Cle)
LB	Artie Ulmer

Draft

1	27(27)	Roddy White	WR	Alabama–Birmingham
2	27(59)	Jonathan Babineaux	DT	Iowa
3	26(90)	Jordan Beck	OLB	Cal Poly
4	27(128)	Chauncey Davis	DE	Florida St.
5	24(160)	Michael Boley	OLB	Southern Mississippi
5	27(163)	Frank Omiyale	OT	Tennessee Tech
6	27(201)	DeAndra Cobb	RB	Michigan St.
7	27(241)	Darrell Shropshire	DT	South Carolina

The Falcons needed a playmaker at receiver to match Michael Vick, and that is exactly what they got in the speedy White. He is not a sure fire pick, though. Considering the dilatory development of last year's first-round pick Michael Jenkins, it's fairly important that White pan out. Babineaux only makes the defensive line that much more of a pass-rushing threat; he should do well next to Rod Coleman on third downs. Both Beck and Davis are developmental players with the potential to fly around on defense.

Offense

QB:	Michael Vick*
RB:	Warrick Dunn
FB:	Justin Griffith
WR:	Peerless Price
WR:	Dez White
TE:	Alge Crumpler*
LT:	Kevin Shaffer
LG:	Mookie Moore
C:	Todd McClure
RG:	Kynan Forney
RT:	Todd Weiner
QB:	Matt Schaub
RB:	T.J. Duckett
WR:	Brian Finneran
WR:	Michael Jenkins
OL:	Barry Stokes†

Defense

LDE:	Patrick Kerney*
UT:	Rod Coleman
NT:	Chad Lavalais
RDE:	Brady Smith
SLB:	DeMorrio Williams
MLB:	Ed Hartwell
WLB:	Keith Brooking*
CB:	DeAngelo Hall
SS:	Keion Carpenter
FS:	Bryan Scott
CB:	Jason Webster
NB:	Kevin Mathis
DL:	Brandon Mitchell†
LB:	Ike Reese*†
K:	Todd Peterson†
P:	Toby Gowin†

* Pro Bowler '04
† veteran acquisition
‡ rookie

Report Card

Quarterback	A–	Defensive Line	B+	Coaching	B+
Running Back	B	Linebacker	B+	Special Teams	B
Receiver/Tight End	C	Defensive Back	C+	Depth	C
Offensive Line	C–			Intangibles	A

Michael Vick, Michael Vick, Michael Vick, Michael Vick. Now that that's out of the way, let's talk about the Atlanta Falcons.

The Falcons are one of the premier up-and-coming teams in the NFL, thanks to that young and electrifying quarterback (can't remember his name at the moment) who leads their budding offense. The defense is getting more talented by the week, the coaching staff is upbeat and fresh-faced (headed by 43-year-old Jim Mora, Jr.), and owner Arthur Blank has already put himself in the same class as Jerry Jones and Dan Snyder. In fact, Blank—who made his fortune as one of the founders of Home Depot and bought the Falcons four years ago—is one of the biggest reasons why the franchise has prospered. He has brought sports to life in Georgia's capital, serving as a likable and more proactive Ted Turner.

It is hard to imagine a person who doesn't enjoy the way Atlanta plays, simply because of the excitement that Vick and company (well, maybe just Vick) bring to the table on game days. If such a person *does* exist, then he or she may want to take a break from football, because this team is going to be in front of America all season long. The Falcons will play three of their eight home games on Monday night. They will also be featured

Michael Vick

on a Sunday night matchup in Chicago, as well as a trip to Detroit on the holiest of football days, Thanksgiving.

Clearly, the population is not the only thing growing in the horizontal city of Atlanta. From Five Points in the heart of the city to the historical Auburn Avenue, clear west to the Appalachian Mountains, the buzz in the southeast will be directed toward the Georgia Dome in downtown "Hotlanta." This climbing franchise is in a position to take the NFL by storm in '05.

Well, Vick is, anyway.

Offense

Anyone who says that the Falcons offense does not hinge at least 95 percent on **Michael Vick** is flat-out wrong. There are no ifs, ands, or buts about it: The fifth-year quarterback out of Virginia Tech is relied upon by his team more than any other player in the game. Period. For anyone who wants to argue that Atlanta's thunder-and-lightning combination at running back (**T.J. Duckett** and **Warrick Dunn**) is as critical to this offense—and, specifically, the rushing attack—as Vick is, read the *Startling Statistics* on page 141.

But not to put any pressure on Vick. After all, he is still only 24 years old—something that is often forgotten. Vick may very well be a unique player in the history of the NFL, simply because nobody has ever seen such amazing speed and athleticism at the quarterback position. Vick's unparalleled combination of skills is always going to be heavily scrutinized because it is human nature to be cautious of something that's different.

The criticism that many cast upon Vick is that he does not deliver as a passer for this offense. This is true *to an extent* (Vick completed just 56.4 percent of his throws last year and Atlanta ranked 30th in passing yards per game), but it has not proven to be a catastrophic blemish on his game. Vick is never going to be a "true quarterback" from a passing standpoint—he's too gifted for that. Sure, his arm strength is incredible and he shows pinpoint accuracy that only Red Ryder himself could match (granted, Vick's a little inconsistent here), but that doesn't mean he has to become a "pocket passer."

The term "pocket passer" may in fact be the only thing on this planet that can truly prevent Vick from having a marvelous career. Many believe that Vick cannot reach his full potential until he becomes more of a traditional drop-back quarterback. Why? He is most lethal as a runner. Why would someone take the most lethal weapon the game has to offer and tell him to be careful not to do what he does best too often? Because it's not how the game is supposed to be played? It's not safe? It's not in the team's best long-term interest? Telling that to Vick would be like telling Albert Einstein to stop studying science so much because he needs to become better in grammar and penmanship, like his fellow classmates.

So much was said about Vick's health and longevity after his 120 rushing attempts in '04, the "experts" seem focused on the injury risk rather than the fact that he averaged 7.5 yards for each of those runs (which gave him an NFL-quarterback-record 902 rushing yards on the season). When Vick is a threat to run the ball, he attracts the attention of the defense like Halle Berry attracts the attention of the Y chromosome. Teams cannot play true man coverage against Atlanta receivers because Vick will torch the defense with his feet. They cannot blitz like they normally would because if Vick escapes, he's gone. They cannot

even attack him with the highest level of intensity because Vick might dart right past them as they overpursue.

Don't misinterpret this, though; *of course* the Falcons need Vick to improve as a passer—why in the world wouldn't they want their best player to become better in one of his weakest areas? But **Jim Mora, Jr.,** and the coaching staff would be absolute fools to start limiting Vick's rushing attempts just to protect his future. After all, what's better—having *the* most exciting and dominant player in the game for 12 years and losing him when he turns 32 or having a player for about 16 years and having him enjoy only a few Pro Bowl appearances because the team protected him in order to ensure that he can continue to play when he's in his mid-30s and no longer as fast? Here's a hint: Option 2 isn't what wins Super Bowls.

If Atlanta is to improve their passing attack in '05, they'll have to get more catches and fewer drops out of the wide receivers. Don't misinterpret this, either; it's not like the Falcons aren't trying to improve at this position. In '03 they traded away a first-round draft pick and spent big money to bring in what they thought would be a star wideout in **Peerless Price**. But the 5'11", seventh-year veteran is coming off a lowly 45-catch season, proving that, despite his quickness, he really is better suited to be a complementary option rather than a No. 1 target. Last year, the team drafted receiver **Michael Jenkins** in the first round, only to see the former Buckeye total a measly seven receptions as a rookie. This year, the team spent another first-round pick on a wideout, taking the athletic and speedy **Roddy White**, out of UAB. However, White is as raw as "war" spelled backward. He likely won't contribute much in '05.

This leaves Atlanta with the same crop of receivers that struggled to make plays last season, with Price starting on one side and **Dez White** on the other. It is far too early to shun Jenkins; he has good size (6'4", 217 pounds) and plays with nimble feet. However, he is still expected to come off the bench with **Brian Finneran** in '05.

Thank goodness Vick has tight end **Alge Crumpler** to throw to. In his fifth year out of North Carolina, Crumpler may benefit from the league's new emphasis on illegal contact more than

> **Write it Down:**
>
> Michael Vick is at risk when he is scrambling, but every player is at risk when he's on the field. It is insane to limit Vick's best feature simply because of what might happen. If Vick doesn't run, he's not worth protecting anyway.

This Season vs. Last Season	
Progression:	**Linebacker**—What was a glaring weakness with Chris Draft and Matt Stewart has now become a strength, thanks to the addition of Ed Hartwell and the insertion of DeMorrio Williams into the lineup.
Regression:	**Defensive backfield**—Cory Hall is gone, leaving a weak safety tandem behind. The Falcons also lost some depth here, assuming they were unable to re-sign Aaron Beasley or bring in Lance Schulters.

anyone in the NFL. He doesn't have great strength (which shows in his run-blocking), but as an athletic target who can operate in space, Crumpler is very effective. Atlanta loves to stretch the field with him, because Crumpler not only can be potent in this sense, but can also force linebackers to follow him, which leaves more rushing lanes for Vick.

Rushing lanes are exactly what the running back duo that was previously alluded to needs in '05. Dunn is a shifty veteran who operates well within a system (1,160 yards last year) and takes advantage of big-play opportunities. Duckett is the freight train barreling through an eight-man box in short-yardage situations. Duckett is also Atlanta's Mariano Rivera—last year, 49 of his 104 carries came in the fourth quarter. It should also be mentioned that Duckett is a former first-round draft pick himself, who, over his previous three years in the NFL, has shown true class and a genuine "team-first attitude" by not complaining about his role as the backup runner in this offense.

The Falcons aren't likely to use veteran fullback **Fred McCrary** as often this year as they are third-year man **Justin Griffith**. McCrary is a classic lead-blocker who offers more for the running game, but Griffith's soft hands, adept footwork, and solid quickness make him a perfect fit for Vick and this offense's agile style of play.

When examining the individual blockers for the Falcons up front, it becomes even clearer that longtime offensive line guru **Alex Gibbs** is to coaching what the city of Atlanta's local company, Coca-Cola, is to soda pop. This year, Gibbs has stepped down in order to become a consultant, leaving **Jeff Jagodzinski** to take his place. However, we've seen this before from Gibbs—he'll be back if the front five struggles.

This past April, Atlanta was contemplating using their first-round draft pick on a linemen who could help prevent Vick from

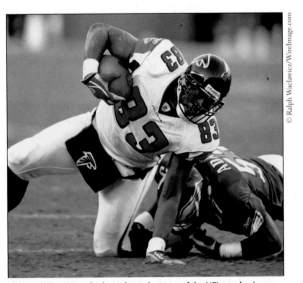

Tight end Alge Crumpler has taken advantage of the NFL emphasis on the illegal contact rule and become Michael Vick's favorite target on this team.

taking 46 sacks (like he did last year), but Gibbs told the team that all he needs is a fifth-round talent in order to make things work. After watching this group in '04, one is compelled to believe him.

Aside from center **Todd McClure**—who is fantastic in run-blocking, showing an ability to drive defenders and get to the second level—Atlanta has nothing to work with. Right guard **Kynan Forney** is fundamentally sound, but he has less power than a handheld fan. Right tackle **Todd Weiner** guards the blind side of the left-handed Vick, but Weiner lacks quickness, plus he plays with the type of ferocity that his last name would suggest. (Okay, that wasn't fair: It's pronounced Why-ner.)

Left tackle **Kevin Shaffer** is a serviceable run-blocker, but he doesn't necessarily have a stranglehold on his job, considering the team signed veteran **Barry Stokes** in the offseason. And finally, new starter **Michael Moore** (an ironic name, considering that he too weighs 318 pounds and works on the left side) may not be able to keep his job from either backup, **Matt Lehr** or **Martin Bibla**. But with all that said, Gibbs's offensive line still played well as a unit last season and they look poised to do the same in '05.

Defense

As great as Vick and the offense can be, the true reason why the Falcons are a threat to repeat as NFC South champions—and maybe even compete for a chance to play in Super Bowl XL—is their high-energy defense. The hiring of Mora signified the beginning of a resurgence for a unit that had previously struggled in all phases of the game. Last year, Atlanta managed to rank a respectable 14th in both scoring and yards allowed. However, they lit up opponents by leading the league in sacks, with 48, and forcing 29 turnovers, which was good for third best in the NFC.

This year, the Falcons defense (which is actually coordinated by **Ed Donatell**, who, after getting run out of Green Bay unfairly, revived himself in his first season down south last year) will be even better, thanks to the increase in speed and athleticism up front. The improvements will be headlined by new middle linebacker **Ed Hartwell** (*see* Painting a New Picture, page 6), who left the Ravens' nest and migrated south to join the more powerful Falcon brood. Hartwell should have a Pro Bowl–caliber season.

Hartwell's decision to leave the wharfs of Baltimore for the nightlife of Buckhead or Atlanta Underground will significantly boost the linebacking unit this year. But he isn't the only star at this spot; weakside linebacker **Keith Brooking** is one of the premier players in the game, as well. The eighth-year veteran Brooking is not in the top echelon of linebackers, but his awareness and speed in pursuit place him firmly in the next-closest level. Brooking is a sound player who always puts up big numbers in the tackling department. He plays with a great center of gravity, showing the ability to get through the "trash" and make plays in traffic.

With Hartwell and Brooking manning two of the linebacker spots, the transition from nickel linebacker to starting strongside linebacker for **DeMorrio Williams** should be smoother in '05. Williams is a second-year player who was taken in the fourth round out of Nebraska last year. His speed and frame (6'0", 232 pounds) would probably make him a better fit on the weakside, but this is the only spot where the Falcons were able to fit him on the field this year. And make no mistake about it—they *must* get this guy on the field.

Williams will have to learn how to take on blocks and play with more strength, but considering the veterans he is flanked by (including his backup, **Ike Reese**, a special-teams ace who came over from the Eagles), he should only help improve the playmaking abilities of the front seven, particularly in pass coverage.

Atlanta's prime source of pass defense will not come from the secondary, but rather the front four, a unit that can put espresso machine–like pressure on the quarterback. The focal point of this group is **Rod Coleman**, a utility tackle (i.e., a defensive tackle who has more freedom in how he lines up) who registered $11^1/_2$ sacks in '04. Coleman has great quickness and power, showing a good jump off the snap and a broad foundation that often draws double teams.

The nose tackle will be first-year starter **Chad Lavalais**, who, like Williams, was drafted in the fourth round last year. Lavalais (out of LSU) will be an upgrade for Atlanta at this spot because of his combination of size and quickness, which spell potential ascendance as a run defender. Lavalais is also 26 years old, so he should have the maturity and confidence to be comfortable from the get-go. He won't have to be confident on passing downs, though, because in those situations the team will substitute newly acquired **Brandon Mitchell**, a converted end who should be fair in a backup role at tackle this year.

The Falcons boast one of the game's most unheralded Pro Bowlers in end **Patrick Kerney**. Kerney was fourth in the league, with 13 sacks, a year ago, marking the third time in four years that the 29-year-old has tallied double digits in this department. Kerney is a versatile threat who can play on either side of the defensive line. Although he is a tad slender (6'5", 273 pounds), he still plays under control and is therefore effective against the run.

The other defensive end is **Brady Smith**, a 10th-year veteran who can rush the passer and use his quickness to make plays. Smith, however, is inconsistent from down to down, plus he's 32 and nearing his decline. Fortunately for Atlanta, they have drafted well and secured great depth up front, most of which can contribute toward the team's effort to become faster in '05.

Second-round rookie **Jonathan Babineaux** can play anywhere on the defensive line, with his role in '05 likely being as a third-down tackle. Fourth-round pick **Chauncey Davis** plays with great energy and could earn a job as Brady's primary backup.

When it comes to their secondary, the Falcons may want to take **Arthur Blank** up on his Home Depot promise, "You can do it. We can help." The team is going to need a little help at the safety position. To begin with, third-year player **Bryan Scott** is moving from strong safety to free safety, in order to make room for veteran **Keion Carpenter**. Scott is a respectable player, but he lacks the range to play free safety (especially in this scheme) and

he is far more effective near the box, where he can employ his solid tackling skills. Carpenter is a questionable option, due to the fact that he has been slow to recover from an ACL tear suffered early last season. If Carpenter is unable to perform, the Birds will have to use one of their free agent acquisitions, **Ronnie Heard** from the 49ers or **Rich Coady** from the Rams. Either would be a liability in pass coverage. If Atlanta is able to sign Tennessee's Lance Schulters, the entire dynamic of the safety position would change because he could step into a starting role.

Atlanta's cornerbacks are **DeAngelo Hall** and **Jason Webster**, a hearty young duo who can generate big plays if needed. Hall is only 21 years old (he'll turn 22 in November), but he can already be one of the best defensive backs in the NFL, just as long as he avoids injuries like the fractured hip that cost him six games as a rookie last year. Hall is living proof that God plays favorites. He has tremendous speed, but even more impressive are his change-of-direction skills and quickness in making jumps on the ball. This season, Hall will continue to grow more comfortable with the scheme, meaning he'll become more consistent and less vulnerable to giving up separation.

With Hall about ready to emerge as a bona fide star, Webster's play may slightly decline in '05, for the simple reason that he will be challenged more often and, inevitably, give up more catches. Of course, he'll also have more chances to improve his interception total from last year, which equaled the number of noses that he has on his face. Veteran **Kevin Mathis** will be a good nickel back because he has such a great feel for making his presence known once he steps on the field. Overall, however, Atlanta still lacks tremendous depth in this area.

Special Teams

The Falcons have welcomed in two fresh legs this year. The first is kicker **Todd Peterson**, who was a curious addition considering that the team was looking to *upgrade* when they deliberately replaced Jay Feely. Punter **Toby Gowin** is also a step back for Atlanta; Gowin has been inconsistent throughout his entire career, shanking punts like Charles Barkley shanks with his 3-wood. The return and coverage units for Atlanta, however, may be the best in the league, thanks to the work done by special-teams coach **Joe DeCamillis**, who is the son-in-law of former head coach Dan Reeves. Punt returner **Allen Rossum** made the Pro Bowl last year.

The Bottom Line

This is a team that has improved since their 11-5 season a year ago. As long as Vick keeps getting better, the offense is going to keep getting better. The real strides will be made on defense, now that the Falcons have gotten faster up front. With as much talent as these birds down in "Hotlanta" have, one must still be careful when penciling them in as the favorites in the NFC, for the simple reason that they still lack the experience and winning mentality of those other birds in Philadelphia. Also, Atlanta has an alarming amount of stock invested in one player: Michael Vick.

Carolina Panthers

Predicted: 1st ▪ 2004: 7-9 (3rd)

Draft

1	(14)	Thomas Davis	S	Georgia
2	(54)	Eric Shelton	RB	Louisville
3	(79)	Evan Mathis	OG	Alabama
3	(89)	Atiyyah Ellison	DT	Missouri
4	(121)	Stefan LeFors	QB	Louisville
5	(149)	Adam Seward	ILB	Nevada–Las Vegas
5	(169)	Geoff Hangartner	C	Texas A & M
5	(171)	Ben Emanuel II	S	UCLA
6	(189)	Jovan Haye	DE	Vanderbilt
6	(207)	Joe Berger	OG	Michigan Tech

The Panthers may choose to play Davis at the linebacker position; he is a definite tweener. He is most effective in run support and has the size and strength to take on blocks. Shelton is not a superstar prospect, but he can be nearly impossible to bring down once he gets momentum running downhill; he could one day replace Stephen Davis. Mathis is a good athlete who can start, though probably not immediately. LeFors and Ellison both add to Carolina's depth.

Head Coach: John Fox (4th year)
Offensive Coordinator: Dan Henning
Defensive Coordinator: Mike Trgovac

Offense

QB:	Jake Delhomme
RB:	Stephen Davis
FB:	Brad Hoover
WR:	Steve Smith
WR:	Keary Colbert
TE:	Freddie Jones†
LT:	Travelle Wharton
LG:	Mike Wahle†
C:	Jeff Mitchell
RG:	Tutan Reyes
RT:	Jordan Gross
QB:	Chris Weinke
RB:	DeShaun Foster
WR:	Ricky Proehl
TE:	Kris Mangum
OL:	Bruce Nelson

Defense

LDE:	Julius Peppers*
DT:	Brentson Buckner
DT:	Kris Jenkins
RDE:	Mike Rucker
SLB:	Brandon Short
MLB:	Dan Morgan*
WLB:	Will Witherspoon
CB:	Ken Lucas†
SS:	Mike Minter
FS:	Idrees Bashir†
CB:	Chris Gamble
NB:	Ricky Manning, Jr.
DL:	Kindal Moorehead
LB:	Chris Draft†
K:	John Kasay
P:	Tom Rouen†

* Pro Bowler '04
† veteran acquisition
‡ rookie

Report Card

Quarterback	B	Defensive Line	A+	Coaching	A–
Running Back	B–	Linebacker	B–	Special Teams	B–
Receiver/Tight End	C+	Defensive Back	B	Depth	C
Offensive Line	C+			Intangibles	A–

Not much has gone right for the Carolina Panthers since their Super Bowl XXXVIII loss to the New England Patriots. Since that day in February of 2004, the team from the largest city in the Piedmont Plateau region of North Carolina (better known as Charlotte) has seen their program crumble.

Last year they began the season 1-7, thanks to a slew of injuries that seemed to leave even the equipment manager on the shelf. They were able to finish strong with a 6-2 record over the second half of the year; nevertheless, the result was no playoffs—just an extended offseason. Since then, the Panthers have been entangled in a steroid scandal involving three of their cheaters . . . er, *players* rather from the NFC champion team. Carolina has dealt with the death of linebackers coach Sam Mills (*see* In Memory Of, page 145), and, just weeks later, the team learned that Pro Bowl linebacker Mark Fields would not be back in '05, due to the return of his Hodgkin's disease, which had sidelined him during the entire '03 season.

But despite all that's gone on, this team is still leaps and bounds ahead of where they were in the middle of last season. They added help on both sides of the ball, via free agency and the draft. They are finally healthy this year, and because of the

Julius Peppers

experience gained by backups replacing injured starters in '04, they are also deeper.

Overall, the football-loving southerners from the Tar Heel State—and let's not forget, the Palmetto State, which shares a border and name—should be pleased with their team's chances heading into the season. Wherever it is in the Carolinas, the pigskin morale is relatively high at the moment.

Offense

A Carolina offense without an adequate rushing attack is like a foreign film without subtitles: It's useless. The Panthers were decimated by injuries in '04, bearing a closer resemblance to the North Carolina Confederate Army—which lost a southern record 120,000 soldiers during the Civil War—than a defending NFC champion team. Just about every running back in baby blue seemed to get hurt. Workhorse **Stephen Davis** went down in November to microfracture surgery on his right knee, in order to correct the problem that had hampered him all season up to that point. Prior to that, Carolina lost their No. 2 running back, **DeShaun Foster**, to a shoulder injury (his second season-ending injury in three years). The result of all this was a ground game that mustered just 98.9 yards per contest, good for 28th in the NFL. Other injuries that littered the offense left players like **Nick Goings** and **Brad Hoover** to carry the load.

All seems to be well now in Carolina, or at least not so outrageously bad. Offensive coordinator **Dan Henning** will have a crop of running backs to choose from in '05, headed by what he hopes to be a healthy Davis. However, such is wishful thinking when considering that Davis is 31, has played a rough-and-tumble brand of football for 10 years, and is stilling easing back into action after knee surgery. This doesn't sound like a 1,400-yard back anymore.

The Panthers will likely slide Davis back into a flow by mitigating his role early in the season. This should ultimately lead to a balanced rushing attack that is executed by committee in '05. Foster appears to be 100 percent, although he is a player whom teams can never again assume will stay healthy.

Because of these concerns about Davis and Foster, expect the Panthers to go Dolly-sheep on everyone and produce a pair of clones in rookie second-round pick **Eric Shelton** and fifth-year player **Nick Goings**. Shelton is simply Davis with more power (but less agility). He is a downhill runner who is punishing when he can get his forward momentum going. Goings—who, in filling in as the starter in eight games last year, rushed for a team-best 821 yards—will take over Foster's duties. While the tendency with the 27-year-old former Pitt Panther is to think that he might be a surprising star, the reality is that he is simply just a good third-down back. However, with his soft hands and feel for making plays as a receiver (45 catches last season), not to mention the 225-pound frame he puts to good use in pass-blocking, Goings has all of the tools needed to be great in this role.

Nothing is a bigger indicator of how hopelessly desperate the Panthers were last season than the fact that the fullback Hoover ran the ball 24 times in a week 7 game against San Diego. (Hoover actually had 99 yards in that game.) Although he is a fine player with underrated skills as a ball carrier—particularly after catching a pass in the flats—it will become obvious once again this year that Hoover is in the game to lead-block—and lead-block he will.

It is unfortunate that quarterback **Jake Delhomme** plays on an offense that has such a reputation for grinding it out on the

ground. Despite the fact that he tossed 29 touchdowns (fifth highest in the league) and threw for 3,886 yards last season, the first topic of discussion this year still focuses on all of the running backs returning from injury. However, the seventh-year Cajun from Louisiana realizes that this is the type of team he plays on—and he also realizes that Carolina did not get anywhere by attempting 33 passes per game in '04.

This season should be different in two positive ways for the Panthers: The first is that they will indeed throw less; the second is that the return of speedy receiver **Steve Smith** should equal more open passing lanes for when they do throw this season. Smith is coming back from a devastating broken leg that cost him the entire '04 season, but he is said to be at 100 percent now.

Smith's presence means a lot for Carolina. At just 5'9", 185 pounds, the fifth-year pro out of Utah does not have the size and power to muscle in tough receptions, but he has the breakaway speed and shifty quickness to create better separation in the passing game. Smith's skills will put more pressure on defenses and force opposing coaches to think twice about playing aggressively.

At the other receiver hole is second-year pro **Keary Colbert**, who at 5'10", 193 pounds, is the slightly inflated version of Smith. Colbert, out of USC, is poised to do good things in '05. He has the ideal set of skills and style of play to be a consummate No. 2 target in the NFL. He runs superb routes, especially for a 23-year-old, and he displays a solid ability to catch passes away from his body.

Having two smaller—yet quicker—receivers will help open up the passing game this season, but Carolina is still going to have to get something out of the tight end position. Although they ranked 10th in third-down percentage last year (40.3), the Panthers will struggle in this area if they cannot find a big, short-yardage target over the middle. They are hoping that veteran **Freddie Jones** (who was signed from the Cardinals over the offseason) can be that guy, but in reality Jones is not much better than what they had in **Kris Mangum** a year ago. Furthermore, the depth at the wide receiver position should more accurately be referred to as "shallowness." Slot receiver **Ricky Proehl** has made a living off this job, but he is approaching an age when lunch becomes dinner. Additionally, the No. 4 wideout, **Karl Hankton**, is on the roster strictly because of his contributions on special teams.

Write it Down:

Running back Stephen Davis will see his role dwindle in 2005.

This Season vs. Last Season

Progression: **Speed**—The health on offense and in the front seven on defense and, more specifically, the additions in the secondary have made the Panthers an all-around faster football team.

Regression: **Punting**—Getting rid of Todd Sauerbrun is great for this club, but from a pure kicking standpoint, the punting game will suffer a minor shank.

Perhaps the best indicator of a better offense in '05 is a sturdier front line, which has added the services of left guard **Mike Wahle**. The eighth-year veteran comes over from Green Bay, where he developed his reputation as a hard-nosed mauler who thrives off his intensity and Jack the Ripper–like mean streak. Wahle's ability to get out and pull (and generate movement in run-blocking) will add to the flexibility that had been lacking up front for the Panthers.

Early in spring, offensive line coach **Mike Maser** decided to move third-year tackle **Jordan Gross** back to the right side, where Gross played during his rookie season. The decision was made in order to maximize the talent up front, regardless of position. However, the change is still a little curious, simply because Gross is a budding young star who excelled on the left side a year ago. However, he is comfortable with the move and has the athleticism and all-around skills to perform well no matter where he lines up.

The talent that the coaching staff had in mind when moving Gross back to the right side was second-year man **Travelle Wharton**, who will occupy the left tackle position in '05. Wharton started 11 games at left guard last season, showing adequate natural ability but an evident lack of awareness. The 6'4", 312-pounder out of South Carolina is still very raw; he will need to be coached up and given an opportunity to take full advantage of his preseason experience in '05. In reality, the Panthers may be forcing things just a bit when considering that they relocated their best lineman (Gross) in order to get Wharton on the field.

The player who is in the middle of the steroids scandal is center **Jeff Mitchell**. To sum it up, Carolina must decide if they are prepared to suffer through a witch hunt like the one baseball has had to endure, because the possibility *is* there. If they aren't, they would be wise to just get rid of the 10th-year veteran,

Second-year player Keary Colbert will step into the more significant No. 2 receiver role for this offense in 2005.

because, when considering that backup **Bruce Nelson** is an up-and-coming player, Mitchell really isn't worth the trouble.

Right guard **Tutan Reyes** must have pulled off a Frank Abagnale–like imposter job, because it is hard to believe that he's actually starting in the NFL. He has his strengths, but none emphatic enough to make him a first-string player. Reyes can play multiple positions, making him a better option as a utility lineman off the bench.

Defense

The Panthers have a defense that is based on a dominant front four, a great idea considering that the return of tackle **Kris Jenkins** gives Carolina the best interior defensive lineman in the NFC, to go along with the best defensive end in the NFC: **Julius Peppers**.

After missing most of the '04 season with a shoulder injury, the 6'4", 335-pound Jenkins (who is only 26) is healthy, meaning he'll be dismantling opponents once again. In addition to his jumbo size, Jenkins has a great first step that carries a powerful punch. His most important impact will be attracting the double teams that allow other starters up front to work one-on-one. This process is also augmented by the fact that Jenkins's quickness allows him to collapse a double team, which further breaks down opponents' blocking schemes. Jenkins is very glad to be back on the field in 2005. Over the offseason, not playing football left him depressed, and he turned to alcohol. Jenkins's problems appear to be behind him now, and his appreciation and love for the game have grown.

On Jenkins's right is **Mike Rucker**, a seventh-year pro who possesses a sturdy balance of skills, making him one of the most complete ends in all of football. Without Jenkins's presence, Rucker is not much more than an average lineman, as his $3\frac{1}{2}$ sacks from last year prove. But with Jenkins around, Rucker is allowed to face single blocking and is much more dynamic, as his 12 sacks from '03 make clear. Rucker is also very adept in rush defense.

On the left of Jenkins is defensive tackle **Brentson Buckner**. Buckner relies on Jenkins like Steinbeck's Lenny relied on George. While the 12th-year pro is a respected vocal leader for the Panthers, it is almost certain that his days as a starter are numbered. Buckner no longer has elite skills, plus his decline is exacerbated by his lazy habits and inconsistent effort. Although he will be listed as the starter throughout most of training camp, expect this to be the season that third-year player **Kindal Moorehead** officially takes over. Moorehead was able to get the experience he needed while filling in for Jenkins last year. He has outstanding quickness and can get great penetration. His only weakness is how he struggles to get off blocks. However, with Jenkins next to him in '05, Moorehead should have no trouble.

Jenkins or no Jenkins, Carolina is going to have the best defensive end—and maybe the most versatile all-around defensive *player*—in the NFC as long as Peppers is in the game. The 6'6", 283-pounder (who started in both football and basketball down the road at Chapel Hill, for the University of North Carolina) is just 25 and in his fourth season in the league. The superathlete not only has outstanding speed, but also a vertical leap that could convince many in the state of North Carolina that it was he, and not the Wright Brothers, who was actually first in flight.

In Memory of Sam Mills

On April 18, the football community lost one of its best when Carolina linebackers coach Sam Mills died after a two-year battle with intestinal cancer. He was 45. After spending the better half of his career in the USFL and with the New Orleans Saints, Mills came to Carolina in 1995, the franchise's first year of existence. After three years in Carolina, Mills retired and joined the team's coaching staff. A statue of Mills stands outside the Bank of America Stadium, and he is the only player in the club's Ring of Honor. He played an integral role in helping the 2003 Panthers, when he continued his coaching duties while undergoing chemotherapy. However, Mills is remembered much more for the impact he had on others off the field. Mills is survived by his wife, Melanie, and four children: sons Sam III and Marcus and daughters Larissa and Sierra.

Last year Peppers had 11 sacks and forced four fumbles as a pass rusher, made 65 tackles as a run defender, and registered nine passes defensed and two interceptions (with returns off those picks totaling 143 yards) as a pass defender. His football IQ is very high, as seen in his recognition skills and ability to smother slow-developing plays (like screen passes and delayed handoffs).

Peppers's presence makes the linebackers' jobs much easier, but if they want to improve upon the team's 17th-ranked run defense from a year ago, Carolina is still going to need their young outside forces to step up in '05. The first name that comes to mind is weakside linebacker **Will Witherspoon**, who may develop into a Pro Bowl–level player before the year is over. Witherspoon has great agility, which allows him to do a wide range of things in the box. His biggest contributions come in pass defense, where he is one of the best at his position. The 25-year-old had 14 passes defensed and four interceptions in '04.

After losing Mark Fields for the season, the Panthers will surely suffer a setback with **Brandon Short** stepping into the strongside role. The sixth-year player has primarily been a backup throughout his career and it is unlikely that he will provide the blitzing power that Fields did.

Middle linebacker **Dan Morgan** can be one of the best in the game, just as long as he stays healthy. Morgan is a smart player who can diagnose a play better than most doctors can diagnose a rash. He has the speed to go sideline to sideline, and most notable of all is his ability to play in traffic and shed blocks.

Carolina's secondary will feature at least two new players in cornerback **Ken Lucas** and free safety **Idrees Bashir**. There may even be *three*, if first-round rookie **Thomas Davis** is able to supplant **Mike Minter** at strong safety. If such is the case, then the team would likely make Minter the starting free safety, ahead of Bashir. Considering that second-year player **Chris Gamble** should be much more fine-tuned at the cornerback position this

Startling Statistics

7-0 Panthers record in games decided by three points or less in '03.

0-4 Panthers record in games decided by three points or less in '04.

year, it becomes apparent that last season's 18th-ranked pass defense is irrelevant when analyzing this team in '05.

The addition of Lucas is huge for Carolina because it not only gives them a solid starting cornerback who is athletic and physical, but also allows last year's starter, **Ricky Manning, Jr.**, to slide over to the No. 3 spot, which is a much better fit for him. Lucas can make plays (he had an astounding 21 passes defensed to go with his six interceptions in Seattle last year), but he must improve his technique. It seems as if for every pass that he breaks up, he earns an illegal-contact flag later, in exchange. Manning's 5'8" size was a hindrance to his performance as a starter, but as a slot defender he'll have better opportunities to use his quickness and face-guarding skills.

As for Gamble, he is coming off a rookie season in which he led the club with six interceptions. He has great size (6'1", 181 pounds) and versatility. He can defend the deep pass extremely well, and he continues to improve as a tackler. Expect Gamble to only get better and more consistent in '05.

Carolina has a young defensive backfield, which is why it would be wise for the club to continue to start the eighth-year veteran Minter and use the rookie Davis in select packages. Minter has done nothing to lose his job, and he gives this unit the physical mind-set that is needed. Davis will likely be a rover in the NFL, anyway—meaning he'll spend most of his time as a freelance linebacker. Such a role can be easy to learn, but it is a risky decision for **John Fox** and defensive coordinator **Mike Trgovac** to make.

Bashir, who is in his fifth season after coming over from Indianapolis, should be much better as a role player in Carolina. As a Colt, he was forced, at times, to play a bigger part than he was capable of. As a Panther, Bashir can use his speed and quickness to play centerfield in pass defense, leaving the tackling duties to those around him. Of course, he'll have to beat out returning Panther **Colin Branch** for playing time.

Special Teams

Punter Todd Sauerbrun was good, but the Panthers will be much happier with the lesser **Jason Baker**, simply because Sauerbrun might be the most intolerable jerk in the entire NFL. Kicker **John Kasay** was his usual self in '04, making 19 of 22 field goal attempts. The 35-year-old still has over 50-yard range. **Rod Smart** can be a solid kick returner, just as long as he's healthy. The Panthers returned only 28 punts last season, which was among the fewest in the NFL. This must mean that anyone who can catch a falling football is a candidate for the job in '05.

The Bottom Line

Because their key players are healthy and they added fresh new faces, last season's 7-9 performance really has no bearing on this team whatsoever. Defensively, the Panthers are fierce up front and improved in the backfield. All of the drama that has gone on in Carolina does not have to be a negative. This team was in similar circumstances in '03, when Mark Fields and Sam Mills were both diagnosed with cancer and the franchise was still recovering from a major public image problem. The Panthers came together that year and found hidden strengths to carry them to the Super Bowl. While that might be too lofty for this season, there at least seems to be a similar feeling in the air.

New Orleans Saints

Predicted: 3rd ⬥ 2004: 8-8 (2nd)

Players Added

G	Jermane Mayberry	(Phi)
TE	Shad Meier	(Ten)
RB	Antowain Smith	(Ten)
S	Dwight Smith	(TB)
CB	Jimmy Williams	(SF)

Players Lost

CB	Ashley Ambrose	
FS	Tebucky Jones	(Mia)
WR	Jerome Pathon	(Sea)
OT	Victor Riley	(Hou)
LB	Orlando Ruff	
LB	Darrin Smith	
DT	Kenny Smith	(Oak)

Draft

1	(13)	Jammal Brown	OT	Oklahoma
2	(40)	Josh Bullocks	S	Nebraska
3	(82)	Alfred Fincher	ILB	Connecticut
4	(118)	Chase Lyman	WR	California
5	(152)	Adrian McPherson	QB	Florida St.
6	(193)	Jason Jefferson	DT	Wisconsin
7	(232)	Jimmy Verdon	DE	Arizona St.

The Saints had a chance to draft a quarterback in the first round who could challenge Aaron Brooks, but they didn't go through with it. Instead, they took the extremely talented McPherson in the fifth. He is fresh off a nice campaign in the Arena League. They traded up to get their guy Brown, who is a genuine right tackle who can more than hold up in pass-blocking. Bullocks was a risky pick in the second round, and Fincher has limited upside.

Head Coach: Jim Haslett (6th year)
Offensive Coordinator: Mike Sheppard
Defensive Coordinator: Rick Venturi

Offense

QB:	Aaron Brooks
RB:	Deuce McAllister
FB:	Mike Karney
WR:	Joe Horn*
WR:	Donté Stallworth
TE:	Ernie Conwell
LT:	Wayne Gandy
LG:	Montrae Holland
C:	LeCharles Bentley
RG:	Jermane Mayberry†
RT:	Jammal Brown‡
QB:	Todd Bouman
RB:	Aaron Stecker
WR:	Devery Henderson
TE:	Shad Meier†
OL:	Kendyl Jacox

Defense

LDE:	Charles Grant
DT:	Howard Green
DT:	Brian Young
RDE:	Darren Howard
SLB:	James Allen
MLB:	Courtney Watson
WLB:	Derrick Rodgers
CB:	Mike McKenzie
SS:	Jay Bellamy
FS:	Dwight Smith†
CB:	Fakhir Brown
NB:	Jason Craft
DL:	Will Smith
LB:	Orlando Ruff
K:	John Carney
P:	Mitch Berger*

* Pro Bowler '04
† veteran acquisition
‡ rookie

Report Card

Quarterback	C+	Defensive Line	A–	Coaching	D
Running Back	A–	Linebacker	C	Special Teams	A–
Receiver/Tight End	B–	Defensive Back	C+	Depth	B+
Offensive Line	B			Intangibles	C–

America's conflict with the British in the War of 1812 is a great narrative in this country's history. One of its monumental moments came when Major General Andrew Jackson and his soldiers victoriously defended against a British invasion in the Battle of New Orleans. But what if it had been a different man leading the way at that time? What if Jackson's makeshift crew, which included pirates and Creoles among the regular troops, had been led by, say, Sergeant Bilko? That team of men would have been a lot like New Orleans's current team, the Saints, who are under the direction of head coach Jim Haslett.

While the present situation in New Orleans is not quite this dire—Haslett is more capable at his job than Sergeant Bilko—there are still major problems in the Big Easy. For starters, that's exactly what Haslett has been with this franchise—a Big Easy. The Saints have not made the playoffs since 2000 (Haslett's first year with the team), yet they have had one of the league's most talented rosters year in and year out.

The cold, hard truth is that this team needed to fire Haslett in the offseason, not only because he hasn't gotten his players to perform, but because this entire organization needed a jolting wake-up call. New Orleans has had (and still does have) the same talented skill players on offense, and they play behind a mammoth front five. Defensively, they have drafted every highly touted lineman ever to grace the earth, tried more linebackers than Ozzy Osbourne tried drugs, and signed one freeagent defensive back after another, hoping to find the right answer. Sometimes they do, sometimes they don't—but whatever they find almost always turns out mediocre in the end.

Joe Horn

There are two constants in New Orleans. One is that each year the town is going to be the only major city in America that is a few feet *below* sea level; the other is that the Saints are going to be one of the few professional football teams in America that are a game or two *below* a play-off berth. For verification, look at their record in each of the last four seasons: 8-8 in both '04 and '03, 9-7 in '02, and 7-9 in '01.

Offense

The Saints have the type of offense that can put up big numbers on any given Sun . . . errr (that was a terrible movie), any given game day. The only problem is that they can falter on any given game day, as well. The reason for the inconsistency lies mainly behind the team's seventh-year quarterback **Aaron Brooks**. Brooks is one of those players who makes people wonder aloud how in the world he isn't a superstar. At 6'4", 220 pounds, he has a great frame, is very athletic, and possesses the speed and agility to make plays with his feet (heck, he's a second cousin of Michael Vick). What's more, the man can throw. Brooks has a terrific arm that is capable of passing for 3,810 yards (coincidentally, the exact amount he threw for last year).

But there have always been elements that are missing from Brooks's game. For starters, he doesn't have whatever the "It" is that has made legends out of players like Joe Montana and John Elway. Even more noticeable, Brooks doesn't have the mentality of a natural leader or the poise and awareness to be great. Too often he settles for less. Then again, too often he forces things and unsuccessfully tries to make something out of nothing.

Anyone can live in the past, and it's never great to offer analysis in the form of hindsight, but New Orleans really should have found another quarterback during the offseason. The team drafted the talented but troubled **Adrian McPherson** in the fifth round, but for a player who was kicked out of Florida State for a variety of reasons (including an alleged gambling problem), being rich and knowing he's not going to play this season could be a terrible combination—especially when he's living near Bourbon Street. But McPherson has his chance to show how much he's grown.

The Saints are not going to be a joke on offense; don't forget that Brooks *does have* his share of moments. Another reason why this offense will not draw too many laughs is because running back **Deuce McAllister** is healthy this year. After rushing for 1,641 yards in '03, McAllister limped his way to just 1,074 last season, thanks to a sprained ankle that never really "unsprained."

With the fifth-year player out of Mississippi (which is just a riverboat ride away from the Big Easy) operating at full force, the Saints have an offense that can once again hurt teams on the ground—something they didn't do when averaging just 100.4 yards per game last season (27th in the league). McAllister is a strong, 232-pound runner who has more power than a man with his speed ought to have. He sees the field well and is a load between the tackles.

Helping McAllister's cause is second-year fullback **Mike Karney**. Karney is a bright young player who has a solid grasp on his assignments within the offense. McAllister does not require a top-rate backup, because he has the receiving skills and pass-blocking abilities to play third down. However, the Saints still have a very adequate backup in **Aaron Stecker**. Plus, former Patriot Antowain Smith (remember him?) is somewhere on the bench, as well.

Strengths

Offensive Line

Having five players who all weigh over 315 pounds and are very skilled in their particular roles is a huge plus for New Orleans. Furthermore, they enjoy splendid depth in this area.

Defensive Line

The trio of ends—Charles Grant, Darren Howard, and Will Smith—alone can post 35 sacks this year, while the tackles Howard Green and Brian Young can control the middle running lanes.

Weaknesses

Coaching

With so much talent falling so short each year, what else could it possibly be other than an inept coaching staff? Watching Jim Haslett's team play is like watching the high school valedictorian smoke crack: too much wasted potential.

Leadership

This is a topic that falls into the weakness box every year. The closest thing this team has to a leader is Joe Horn, who is still paying the long-distance charges for his cell phone celebration a few years ago.

Jim Haslett has already stated that he is counting on McAllister rushing for 1,600 or 1,700 yards this season (goodness, *Jim*), mainly because the team has worked hard to slap together what they believe to be one of the best offensive lines in all of football. In the offseason, the Saints signed former Eagle guard **Jermane Mayberry** and told him he was moving to right tackle. But then in April, they pulled the old "never mind" on the 6'4", 325-pound Mayberry, when they traded up in the draft to get Oklahoma's **Jamaal Brown**. Brown (a 6'5", 316-pound right tackle) is a very skilled lineman who should be able to make an immediate impact. He has good all-around mobility and agility, both of which will be helpful in run-blocking (assuming he continues to improve his strength). However, offensive line coach **Jim Pyne** will have some work to do, because Brown is considered to be a risk/reward pick, due to the fact that he does not hold a reputation for having the greatest work ethic.

It is a much better idea to have Mayberry play right guard—that's where he's been for most of his previous nine years in the league. Mayberry is a player who has the natural power to always be in control. He will do a lot to open up more running lanes for McAllister & Company in '05.

The Saints have a shiny new steamboat in center **LeCharles Bentley** (fourth year out of Ohio State), but so far they have refused to load it with cargo and haul it up the Mississippi, instead opting to just leave it sitting near the bank of the river. Bentley is another enormous force (6'2", 313 pounds) up front, possessing amazing size and strength for a center. The game is as natural to Bentley as beads are to Mardi Gras. However, he seemed to almost get bored with his role in the offense last year. The promotion of quarterbacks coach **Mike Sheppard** to offensive coordinator (a move that is questionable at best) will likely simplify the system as well, meaning it's not likely that Bentley will see his role expand.

What the Saints need to do with Bentley is utilize his rare skills by making him their personal Kevin Mawae. New Orleans needs to have Bentley pull, so they can take advantage of his strength and know-how to get to the second level in run-blocking. This would generate more energy and options for the entire front five.

The left guard position is going to go to **Montrae Holland**, even if the team acts as if **Kendyl Jacox** might win the job. Holland is five years younger than the powerful Jacox, he offers the same size (6'2", low-320s), and he has been consistent since first coming into the league three years ago. Jacox should pray for

Write it Down:

The Saints may look good on paper, but so does Communism. They will not succeed until they undergo a major change in the organization, starting at the top.

Progression: **Front five**—New Orleans should connect on their attempt to bolster the run-blocking. Drafting Jamaal Brown will likely pay off, and veteran Jermane Mayberry still has a lot left.

Regression: **Receiver**—It seems like a moot issue, but losing Jerome Pathon and filling the hole with Devery Henderson is not a good move for this offense. Pathon was the toughest and most reliable over-the-middle weapon this passing game had.

a trade because he is definitely good enough to start for most teams.

Left tackle **Wayne Gandy** rounds out the offensive line, and yes, like the rest of his peers up front, he weighs a healthy amount (315). Gandy is in his 12th season, but he still possesses the speed and quickness to serve in pass protection, something the Saints need when considering how much focus they are putting on run-blocking this year.

As for that pass-blocking, it will go toward helping receivers like **Joe Horn** and **Donté Stallworth** make plays in '05. Horn should be pleased entering this season—he signed a new six-year, $42 million contract in May. The deal (which the 33-year-old Horn will not stick around long enough to finish out) is a nice reward for his 94-catch, 1,399-yard, 11-touchdown performance in 2004. Horn is one of the brashest personalities in the game, but unlike so many players (hmmm . . . Freddie Mitchell?), his speed, quickness, and precise rout-running abilities have backed up his mouth.

Injuries have plagued the 23-year-old Stallworth, who—now in his fourth season—has yet to live up to expectations. Do not give up on Stallworth yet; he has far too much breakaway speed to be written off. He just needs to be more consistent in holding onto the football.

The No. 3 receiver is second-year man **Devery Henderson**, a track burner out of LSU. Haslett has called Henderson out, saying the offense is relying heavily on his stepping up. Henderson still might be too unpolished to be consistent in '05, though.

Tight end **Boo Williams** finally got demoted this year, after four seasons of having his God-given receiving talents produce very little. In fact, Williams has been knocked all the way down to No. 3 on the depth chart. This is to allow veteran **Ernie Conwell** and free agent acquisition **Shad Meier** to provide the run-blocking support that Williams can't offer.

Defense

As many problems as Brooks and the inconsistent offense have given this team, there is absolutely no debating the fact that New Orleans's struggles on defense have been what ultimately keeps them from achieving success. Since their last playoff appearance in '00, the Saints have drafted one surefire defensive stud after another, only to see the group falter in the long run, due to injuries or general poor play.

Despite his group ranking dead last in yards allowed in '04, defensive coordinator **Rick Venturi** is back in '05, hoping to have a crop of talented athletes who for once can stay healthy and on the same page. The defensive line has to be the primary focus at all times this season; it is the Jackson Square to the team's French Quarter. The Saints boast a three-man rotation at the end position that is arguably the best in the league: **Charles Grant** stars on the left side, **Darren Howard** stars on the right side, and Will Smith starred in the movie *I, Robot* last summer. Oh yeah, in addition to Grant and Howard, the Saints also have their own

Will Smith (*see* Ready to Break Out, page 135), a second-year player who stars as the first man off the bench.

In only his fourth season out of Georgia, Grant is already among the elite players at his position. He registered 10½ sacks last year, but also showed his Renaissance football skills by posting 80 tackles in run support and defensing seven passes. Out of New Orleans's three ends, Grant sees the most playing time. He is not as quick as the other ends, but he has better power and discipline.

After tagging Howard as their franchise player in March (a $7.8 million move), the Saints spent a good portion of the offseason shopping him around. Unable to find any suitors, New Orleans will just have to keep the sixth-year veteran, which is not too much of a punishment. Howard is happy down in Louisiana, and he can be one of the best pass-rushers in the NFL if he chooses to (he had 11 sacks in '04, which was the most he has had since his rookie season in 2000).

Besides not wanting to pay such a high rate for an end who is fairly one-dimensional, New Orleans also tried to deal Howard because they need to somehow find a way to get Smith on the field. It does not matter what the situation is—Smith is too good of a player to designate as a backup. The fact that he will not be starting when the season opens is close to inexcusable, because it represents the franchise's idiocy either when it comes to constructing their depth chart or when it comes to orchestrating a draft, because they clearly picked up a player last year at a position that they did not really need to address. Drafting for talent over need is great, but not when that idea is taken *too far*.

The Saints thought they were getting an annual Pro Bowler when they traded up and drafted defensive tackle **Jonathan Sullivan** with the sixth-overall pick in '03, but the way it stands now, Sullivan is fifth—*fifth*—on the depth chart. The starters are **Howard Green** and **Brian Young**, two players who are round anchors used to clog the middle of the line.

Defensive end Charles Grant is the most complete all-around player on the Saints' talented front four.

The Saints' linebacker situation is the antithesis of the front four. New Orleans has been trying desperately to draft the right player at this spot, but they have yet to do so. Middle linebacker **Courtney Watson** could prove to break this trend, though it would take a better output than he had as a rookie last year. Watson is a poor man's Kendrell Bell, showing adequate thickness and strength to size up the middle in run defense. However, Haslett and the Saints coaching staff would like to see him become more consistent in 2005.

The man currently holding down the strongside duties is **James Allen**, although with his quickness and shyness from contact, Allen is really a misplaced weakside linebacker. It is hard to say exactly what the Saints are doing with him on the strongside, because the only way he is going to be effective is if he can operate in space and not have to be preoccupied with taking on blocks.

The assumption one would make is that Allen is on the strongside because New Orleans already has a talented weakside linebacker that they like. However, they don't. They have a very sound linebacker in **Derrick Rodgers**, who has developed good awareness from his eight years of experience. However, Rodgers is not even a true weakside player. In fact, he would make a much better utility linebacker off the bench.

Speaking of the bench, the Saints have a decent set of options to refer to. Sedrick Hodge is an experienced backup who possesses decent versatility. Colby Bockwoldt is a high-energy guy who can thrive as a chaser. Bockwoldt does not have the raging skills to be a starter, but he'll contribute well in small doses.

After seeing his former team, the Packers, struggle in the defensive backfield once he left the club high and dry, cornerback **Mike McKenzie** thinks he is the greatest thing to hit Bourbon Street since the cameramen for *Girls Gone Wild 2*. However, McKenzie was not able to help New Orleans's 27th-ranked pass defense last year. But it may not be fair to rag on him; after all, he is the best defensive back on this roster. In fact, McKenzie could be the difference maker for this defense in '05, just as long as he continues to become more comfortable in this scheme while thriving off his speed and physicality in man coverage.

It isn't likely that opposing quarterbacks will challenge McKenzie too often in '05, because the corner playing opposite him (**Fakhir Brown**) has a tendency to give up separation. The sixth-year veteran Brown actually had a surprising season in '04, defensing 12 passes and making a handful of good tackles. All in all, Brown is a typical No. 2 corner who will not give up big plays.

The Saints will use **Jason Craft**, **Jimmy Williams**, or **Fred Thomas** as their No. 3 cornerback, an area that may prove to be a soft spot on this defense. (Gosh, surely someone is renting out Terrell Buckleys again this year.)

Free safety **Dwight Smith** left division rival Tampa Bay to join the Saints for when they come marching in this season. Because he had a good showing in the Super Bowl a few years ago, there is the perception that Smith is an elite ball hawk who will change a game. While he is an above-average playmaker, Smith is not going to single-handedly upgrade this pass defense. He is fairly weak in run support, and even worse, he has serious character flaws—something Haslett and this team do not need any more of than they already have.

Strong safety **Jay Bellamy** is not a horrendous player, but he is not worthy of the praise he receives, either. Bellamy is overrated because of his inconsistent tackling skills, his poor angles of pursuit, and his inability to succeed regularly as a one-on-one player.

It must be mentioned that New Orleans's lack of aggressiveness with their safeties is a major weakness for this entire defense. They play their safeties way too deep, which forces the linebackers to play too prominent a role in pass coverage.

Special Teams

Kicker **John Carney** can pay his two bucks and reach for the big stuffed-animal prize every now and then, but being 41, he may soon have to consider leaving the county fair. Nevertheless, Carney has still not done enough to suggest that he is in a serious decline. Punter **Mitch Berger** made the Pro Bowl last season—which, for a punter, really requires no further explanation. Finally, the Saints benefit from the services of return specialist **Michael Lewis**, who had another strong outing in '04, averaging 23.8 yards per kick return and 11.2 yards per punt return.

The Bottom Line

When looking at the upgraded front five on offense and the skilled players who work behind it, this may seem like a fairly competitive team. On defense, things look somewhat sound as well, thanks largely to an explosive front four. However, do not fall for this team's Tom Sawyer–like tricks. The Saints are no more legit than the mime posing as a statue down on Canal Street. They have been talented year in and year out since Haslett arrived, but each season they've screwed it up. This year will be no different than all the others.

Tampa Bay Buccaneers

Predicted: 4ᵗʰ ▪ 2004: 5-11 (4ᵗʰ)

Players Added

TE	Anthony Becht	(NYJ)
CB	Juran Bolden	(Jax)
K	Matt Bryant	(NYG)
WR	Ike Hilliard	(NYG)
DT	Chris Hovan	(Min)
QB	Luke McCown	(Cle)

Players Lost

DL	Chidi Ahanotu	
WR	Tim Brown	(retired)
LB	Keith Burns	(Den)
G	Cosey Coleman	(Cle)
DL	Chartric Darby	(Sea)
TE	Ken Dilger	
TE	Ricky Dudley	
CB	Mario Edwards	(Mia)
LB	Ian Gold	(Den)
S	John Howell	
DB	Corey Ivy	(StL)
QB	Brad Johnson	(Min)
WR	Joe Jurevicius	(Sea)
WR	Charles Lee	
G	Matt O'Dwyer	(GB)
S	Dwight Smith	(NO)

Draft

1	(5)	Carnell Williams	RB	Auburn
2	(36)	Barrett Ruud	ILB	Nebraska
3	(71)	Alex Smith	TE	Stanford
3	(91)	Chris Colmer	OT	North Carolina St.
4	(107)	Dan Buenning	OG	Wisconsin
5	(141)	Donte Nicholson	S	Oklahoma
5	(155)	Larry Brackins	WR	none
6	(178)	Anthony Bryant	DT	Alabama
7	(221)	Rich Razzano	FB	Mississippi
7	(225)	Paris Warren	WR	Utah
7	(231)	Hamza Abdullah	S	Washington St.
7	(253)	J.R. Russell	WR	Louisville

The Bucs had an outstanding draft, especially considering how much Gruden likes Williams, how NFL-ready Ruud is, and how helpful a tight end like Smith will be to the passing attack. Tampa Bay's offense hinges on having receiving talent at the tight end position; Smith is the only player who has fit the bill since Gruden arrived from Oakland. Nicholson may be better than most think, and even Russell has the potential to make the roster if he can mature.

Jon Gruden, captain of the Tampa Bay Buccaneers, will once again have a new crew to work with in '05. It seems like the Bucs have rotated every veteran player the NFL has ever had into their system at some point since Gruden arrived back in '02. This year is no different—the Bucs have overhauled much of their backup talent from last year, and in week 1 this year they are expected to start no fewer than eight players who did not start in week 1 last year.

One very positive sign for the Buccaneers has been the productivity they've pulled from the draft over the past two years. After trading most of their '03 draft picks to obtain Gruden, the Bucs found three starters in last season's rookie class. This year, they had a total of 12 draft choices and likely found at least three more starters.

Head Coach: Jon Gruden
Offensive Coordinator: none
Defensive Coordinator: Monte Kiffin

Offense

QB:	Brian Griese
RB:	Cadillac Williams‡
FB:	Mike Alstott
WR:	Michael Clayton
WR:	Joey Galloway
TE:	Anthony Becht
LT:	Derrick Deese
LG:	Matt Stinchcomb
C:	John Wade
RG:	Jeb Terry
RT:	Kenyatta Walker
QB:	Chris Simms
RB:	Michael Pittman
WR:	Ike Hilliard†
TE:	Alex Smith‡
OL:	Sean Mahan

Defense

LDE:	Greg Spires
DT:	Anthony McFarland
DT:	Ellis Wyms
RDE:	Simeon Rice
SLB:	Jeff Gooch
MLB:	Shelton Quarles
WLB:	Derrick Brooks*
CB:	Ronde Barber*
SS:	Jermaine Phillips
FS:	Will Allen
CB:	Brian Kelly
NB:	Torrie Cox
DL:	Dewayne White
LB:	Barrett Ruud‡
K:	Matt Bryant
P:	Josh Bidwell

* Pro Bowler '04
† veteran acquisition
‡ rookie

Report Card

Quarterback	C+	Defensive Line	B	Coaching	B+
Running Back	B−	Linebacker	B	Special Teams	C−
Receiver/Tight End	C	Defensive Back	B	Depth	C
Offensive Line	C			Intangibles	C−

Derrick Brooks

That said, the Bucs are still competing in one of the toughest divisions in all of football. Gruden's system is complex and cannot easily be learned right away. And unless there are a few hidden gems in the depth chart, this team is still behind the competition offensively. But at least Gruden is excited again.

Offense

Jon Gruden—who serves as his own offensive coordinator—runs a system that is so West Coast, it often seems out of place in an eastern state like Florida. However, whether it's in the San Francisco/Oakland region or the St. Petersburg/Tampa region, the emphasis is going to be placed on controlling drives via the run and even "more via" the short-yardage pass.

To orchestrate this scheme requires a serviceable running back with versatility. After ranking 29th in rushing, at 93.1 yards per game last season, the Bucs feel that eighth-year veteran **Michael Pittman** is no longer the guy they can count on to carry the load. Although Pittman, 30, still has quickness and an ability to catch the ball, his demotion to the second string has been warranted by his off-the-field issues and on-the-field inconsistency (which included six fumbles last year).

With Pittman now joining veteran **Charlie Garner** (who is all but finished after a season-ending knee injury in '04), the Bucs are prepared to start rookie **Carnell "Cadillac" Williams** (see Painting a New Picture, page 8) in '05. After coaching the former Auburn star during the Senior Bowl, Gruden fell in love with Williams like a boxer dog falls in love with a strong left leg. At 5'11", 217 pounds, the 23-year-old Williams has a solid foundation of running skills, which include the toughness and leg drive to run inside and the fluidity to get around the corner and find space. The knock on him is that he did not carry a full load at Auburn and he doesn't have the frame to do so in the NFL. However, playing in Tampa Bay's system (which called for less than 400 rushing attempts all season last year) means he shouldn't have to worry about being a workhorse; instead, he can focus on just adding a few pounds and expanding his receiving skills.

Tampa Bay fullback **Mike Alstott** has declined in recent years, partly because he's been such a physical player for nearly a decade, and partly because the 31-year-old has not been the same since suffering a neck injury in '03. As unfortunate as it is, the 248-pound hammer may soon be getting nailed. Alstott does not have the agility or quickness to excel as a pass catcher, he has never been much of a lead-blocker, and his role as the third-down power runner is receding. This year, it is very likely that the Bucs will work backup fullback **Jameel Cook** more into the offense.

The Bucs system has been great for quarterback **Brian Griese**, who completed 69.3 percent of his passes last year, while averaging 7.8 yards per attempt and posting a rating of 97.5. However, the 30-year-old Griese has always been one of those players who can put up great stats but never lead a team to victory. After all, was Tampa Bay not 5-11 last season?

This year Griese will enter the season as the starting quarterback, with third-year man **Chris Simms** right behind him. This means that for the third year in a row, there will be talk about whether Gruden is ready to go to Simms—his "man of the future." The problem is, nobody ever knows for sure whether Gruden will elect to start Simms or whether he'll put his faith in a veteran, because Gruden's quarterback pattern has been as predictable as serving jury duty: You speculate as to when your

Strengths

Pass Rush

Simeon Rice is one of the premier defensive ends in football, and surrounding him is a plethora of versatile linemen who can all reach the quarterback from the inside or outside.

Pass Defense

The Bucs ranked No. 1 in fewest passing yards allowed last year. They're younger at the safety position, but they're also more athletic. Ronde Barber and Brian Kelly are excellent in this scheme, and Tampa Bay gets good pass coverage help out of their linebackers.

Weaknesses

Receiver

Michael Clayton will be a star and rookie tight end Alex Smith will have his moments in '05, but the Bucs can't rely on a pair of 22-year-olds to carry their passing game. The depth here is shoddy, and with Joey Galloway and Ike Hilliard at the No. 2 and 3 spots, the complementary options are inadequate.

Blocking Stability

The offensive line seems fragmented. Each of the five starters is the type of player who could fill in on a good front five, but none of them seem like they can star on a shaky one.

name will next be called, you ponder the likely scenarios and weigh the various logistics, but when the notice actually arrives, you're still somehow caught off guard.

Gruden could surprise everyone this year. What is known are the criteria for quarterbacking this offense: A player must have a great grasp of the terminology, he must understand his reads, and he must have the patience and discipline to be consistent and methodical when need be. Maybe now it becomes more clear why the 25-year-old Simms is likely to continue to wait his turn.

Tampa Bay's focus on having a controlled passing attack puts a heavy emphasis on the tight end position. After suffering through players like Ken Dilger and Ricky Dudley, the Bucs finally went out and tried to find an adequate weapon to fill this role. What they got were two good fits in rookie **Alex Smith** (not that Alex Smith—this one is a 6'4", 258-pound man from Stanford) and former Jet **Anthony Becht**. If Becht is listed as the starter (as he was throughout the offseason), it means the Bucs are lying, because there is no way they are going to just gradually work Smith into the system. Gruden is elated about what he has in his third-round draft pick. Smith gives the Bucs offense a reliable receiving threat who has the quickness and speed to turn upfield and make plays after the catch.

Smith is also an intelligent player who learns quickly (in case the previous mention that he was educated at Stanford didn't jump out enough), making it all the more likely that he'll promptly find a role in this offense.

Don't assume that Becht won't contribute this season, though. The sixth-year veteran has a solid ability to run routes and make plays as a pass catcher, but at 6'5", 272 pounds, Becht's main contributions will come as a blocker. He is the prototype No. 2 tight end.

It is almost certain that Tampa Bay's 14th-ranked passing game from a year ago will produce fewer than 217 yards per contest in '05, because the receiving core is about as thin as a Republican majority vote in Florida. No. 1 receiver **Michael Clayton** is in his second year out of LSU, but already has 80 catches to his name. The 6'4" Clayton is a big target who seems to always be just a notch or two better than one would expect. He's a playmaker who will only get better for this team. However, after Clayton, the list includes **Joey Galloway** and **Ike Hilliard**, two veteran players who have both been hit with a hurricane of

Write it Down:

The Bucs roster is so up in the air right now that by the time the season is over, they will have found at least five new starters on either side of the ball.

This Season vs. Last Season

Progression: **Running back—**Getting a clear-cut featured back like Cadillac Williams in the draft is the right move for this team, even if he takes a while to develop.

Regression: **Passing game—**Despite the help that rookie tight end Alex Smith will provide, the Buccaneers cannot rely on Brian Griese or his receivers to build on what they managed to do through the air last year.

Defense

Although the Bucs defense is certainly not what it was when they won the Super Bowl three years ago, they still allowed just 19 points per game last season and ranked fifth in yards given up.

injuries in recent years. Galloway will almost certainly catch three passes a game, with one of them having merely the *potential* to become a big play. Hilliard likes how his skills fit in this offense, which is understandable, but fitting what's left of his skills into such a widespread system is like fitting one more pea into a casserole: It won't make a difference.

The Bucs front five is shaky at best. One can infer its potential volatility from the simple fact that 35-year-old **Derrick Deese** is the starting left tackle. Nothing against Deese—in fact, he's still capable of performing at a very high level. However, one would be just as inclined to believe that he actually moved to Tampa to buy a beach house and kick back.

It would be easy to take shots at the 35-year-old **Todd Steussie** (who was part of the Panthers' steroid scandal), but Steussie has already been relegated to backup, where he'll play behind 26-year-old **Kenyatta Walker**. Walker has struggled throughout most of his career, but entering his fifth season out of Florida, the former first-round pick finally seems to be getting the idea. Walker has cut down on his penalties and has vastly improved his awareness. He'll likely move to left tackle after this season, but for now he must become more aggressive playing on the right side.

Between the tackles are guards **Matt Stinchcomb** and **Jeb Terry**, and center **John Wade**. Stinchcomb is a nice weapon on the left side; he is used to execute the pulls in run-blocking, and at 6'6", he has extremely long arms, which are critical to his success. In reality, Stinchcomb is more of a tackle playing the inside. Terry is a relatively unknown second-year player who will succeed if he can just fit in. As for Wade—he lacks the ideal power in the middle, and it would make sense for the team to replace him with third-year lineman **Sean Mahan**, who started half of the games last season.

They also surrendered the fewest yards through the air, at just over 160 a game.

With virtually the same group of players from last season returning in '05, there's no reason to believe that they cannot repeat their performance from a year ago. Up front, Tampa Bay is led by end **Simeon Rice**, who is as much of a lock to finish with a double-digit sack total as the neighboring Devil Rays are to finish with a double-digit deficit in the American League East. Rice has recorded at least 10 sacks in seven of the nine seasons in his career. The 6'5", 268-pound lightning bolt has made 53½ sacks over his four years in Tampa Bay.

With Rice holding down one end on the front line, the other end duties will be shared by **Greg Spires** and **Dewayne White**. Spires, an eighth-year veteran out of Florida State, recorded eight sacks himself last year, thanks to his nice technique for beating one-on-one blocks. White is a third-year player who is still getting acclimated to the professional game. He shows positive signs from time to time, but he has far too many nonimpact plays between those signs.

The Buccaneers are very flexible up front because in addition to their traditional spots at end, both Spires and White can line up at defensive tackle. With 300 pound blocker-eater **Anthony McFarland** being as susceptible to getting hurt as he is, and with fifth-year tackle **Ellis Wyms** coming back from a shoulder injury, a crowded rotation is almost certain to form on the defensive line.

Everyone assumes that McFarland is the talented young tyro who will one day replace Warren Sapp's contributions, but the "rising star" is now in his *seventh* year in the league; he'll turn 28 before the season is over. McFarland is not a developing star—he's the star that Pinocchio, in the nearby Walt Disney kingdom, is wishing upon. Anyone who says that the gifted—and he *is* gifted—McFarland is to this team what Sapp once was will only see their nose grow.

Another name to throw into Tampa Bay's rotation up front is **Chris Hovan**, who was once a rising young player himself. Hovan came to Tampa after falling out of favor in Minnesota. He is one of the more mysterious figures in the game. He was on the brink of being a Pro Bowler, but the mental side of the game seemed to leave him. Hopefully, Hovan will be able to regain his confidence in Tampa Bay; he is a quick player, but more important, he's a passionate player who wants to succeed.

Success comes naturally for weakside linebacker **Derrick Brooks**. Brooks has been around since the dreadful days of white helmets with bright orange pirate logos that resembled an inverted pimp more than a dangerous buccaneer sailing the high seas. Brooks has suffered through the hard times, and he has played an integral role in this organization's winning its first Super Bowl. He is entering his 11th year in the league, but he is still only 32 and going as strong as ever. Brooks does it all for the Bucs, mainly because he has such great awareness and is so comfortable as the leader of this defense.

Next to Brooks will be middle linebacker **Shelton Quarles**, a ninth-year veteran who has played at a professional level for

© Reinhold Matay/WireImage.com

Second-year receiver Michael Clayton has the size, speed, and hands to be a Pro Bowler in the very near future.

12 years. Quarles is 34 and his career is beginning to close, but he restructured his contract over the offseason to help improve the team's salary cap situation and increase his chances of sticking around. Quarles's chances of remaining as a meaningful part of this team will continue to be good if he posts a third consecutive 100-plus tackle season in '05. The 6'1", 225-pound Quarles has good awareness and the upper body strength to take on blocks.

However, the Bucs drafted linebacker **Barrett Ruud** in the second round this year. Ruud left the Nebraska Cornhuskers as the program's all-time leading tackler. Although he is not a first-class athlete, Ruud is a classic football player who has the recognition skills to start right away in the NFL. Tampa Bay is going to have him begin as the backup to strongside linebacker **Jeff Gooch**, then they'll see where things go from there.

The logical move would be to push Gooch back to the second string—where he has spent much of his career anyway—and start both Quarles and Ruud. This very well may be what the Bucs wind up doing. However, they like Quarles in the middle—partly because it is easier for him to call out the defensive assignments from that spot. Furthermore, defensive coordinator **Monte Kiffin** and linebackers coach **Jon Barry** are bent on making Ruud their long-term answer at middle linebacker, meaning they will almost certainly not waste his rookie season ingraining the strongside duties into his mind.

Tampa Bay's outstanding pass defense from '04 was aided by the pressure that the front line and its 45 sacks put on quarterbacks. But it also had much to do with the play of cornerbacks **Ronde Barber** and **Brian Kelly**. Barber, in his ninth season, has become a fixture in the Pro Bowl. Playing in Kiffin's zone coverage scheme, he has grown like oranges grow in Florida. If this were basketball, Barber would be Oscar Robertson, because he can do it all. He covers any position on the field (especially the slot receiver, which is his forte), he deflects passes, intercepts balls, tackles in run support, gets sacks as a blitzer—the list goes on.

Kelly, who is 29, has improved each year in the defensive scheme, as well. He is not as physical or productive as Barber, but he is the team's most capable weapon when it comes to making a play on the ball. His inclination to go for the leather rather than the receiver certainly has its pros and cons, but the bottom line is that Kelly can make interceptions; he also had a monstrous 22 passes defensed in '04.

With Barber playing the slot in nickel situations, it means that No. 3 cornerback **Torrie Cox** is responsible for covering the outside. Cox is very raw, however, and it would make better sense for the Bucs to go with physical free agent acquisition **Juran Bolden** in this role.

The Bucs have been very high on safety **Jermaine Phillips** since he came into the league in '02. This year they are moving him to strong safety, in order to ease the pressure on his pass coverage and also to allow him to become more physical in the box. The move should benefit Phillips well.

That leaves the free safety job open. The men competing for it will be second-year player **Will Allen** and former Super Bowl MVP **Dexter Jackson**. Expect Allen to get the nod, simply because he has the better athleticism and the "upside" factor working to his favor.

Special Teams

Starting the season without Martin Gramatica as the kicker must feel to Gruden a lot like a quiet break with his three sons (ages 10, 7, and 3) spending the weekend at Grandma's—only this time, the peace is permanent. Of course, the man kicking for Tampa Bay is now the mediocre **Matt Bryant**. The Bucs' punter is **Josh Bidwell**, who had one of his best seasons last year, netting nearly 39 yards per boot. Anyone who has ever watched a Bucs game knows that the team has never once in its history returned a kickoff for a touchdown. The man charged with changing that in '05 will likely be Cox.

The Bottom Line

Let's face it: This team is in a rebuilding process. They show all the signs that the experts say to look out for. The offensive line is fairly unknown, the quarterback is (tentatively) Griese, there are broken-down veterans blended with unproven youngsters in the receiving game, and the starting tailback is a rookie. Defensively, Tampa Bay looks all right, though that is not going to be enough to allow this team to make much noise in the NFC South.

NFC West

Arizona
Cardinals

San Francisco
49ers

Seattle
Seahawks

St. Louis
Rams

Looking Forward

How They'll Finish
1. St. Louis Rams
2. Arizona Cardinals
3. Seattle Seahawks
4. San Francisco 49ers

Ready to Break Out

**Jamie Winborn,
San Francisco 49ers**

Outside Linebacker
5'11"—242 pounds
5th year—26 years old
Drafted: 2nd round in '01 out of Vanderbilt

Jamie Winborn

Many probably think that a 26-year-old would have already "broken out" by now. However, such is not the case with San Francisco's Jamie Winborn. He is a rising star with great natural talent.

Winborn's likelihood of finding success this year is augmented by the arrival of Mike Nolan in San Francisco; for the first time in his career, Winborn will have an opportunity to work in a 3–4. He should be excellent in this role because it encourages energy and tenacity, two traits he has in spades.

Winborn possesses outstanding athletic skills, most evident in his tremendous speed. He is also a versatile weapon: Last year he had 63 tackles, $4\frac{1}{2}$ sacks, two forced fumbles, an interception, and eight passes defensed. Winborn's attributes (coupled with those of star Julian Peterson) will give the 49ers great flexibility in their defensive approach in '05.

Hot Seat

**Mike Holmgren,
Seattle Seahawks**

Since arriving in Seattle in 1999, Mike Holmgren has taken his team to the playoffs just three times. He is also 0-3 in those appearances. Many fail to recognize this flimsy showing by Holmgren's clubs over the past six years because they are still enamored with what he did for Brett Favre in Green Bay.

But in Seattle, even without "Favre the Great," Holmgren has had very adequate talent to work with, most of which he personally selected when he was the general manager for the Hawks. However, that talent has proven to be immature, undisciplined (both on and off the field), and inconsistent, all characteristics which reflect poorly on the head coach.

After last season's disappointing conclusion, in which Holmgren almost seemed to be rooting along with the fans for his wavering team (rather than organizing them), the pressure is on to lead them deep into January this season. Holmgren was already stripped of his GM duties following the '02 season—could that have been a foreshadowing of what's to come?

Best Offseason Move

St. Louis Rams naming Steven Jackson their starting running back.

Worst Offseason Move

St. Louis's general inability to find a free safety to replace Aeneas Williams.

Best Under-the-Radar Offseason Move

Seattle re-signing both quarterback Matt Hasselbeck and left tackle Walter Jones to long-term deals.

Biggest Question

Armed with more talent than any other team in the NFC West, how can the Seattle Seahawks finally make it all come together in 2005?

QUICK HITS

TEAM BESTS		BEST PLAYERS	
Passing Game	Rams	Pure Athlete	Orlando Pace, Rams
Running Game	Seahawks	Big Play Threat	Torry Holt, Rams
Offensive Line	Seahawks	Best Use of Talent	Robbie Tobeck, Seahawks
Pass Rush	Cardinals	Worst Use of Talent	Koren Robinson, Seahawks
Run Defense	49ers	On the Rise	Marcus Trufant, Seahawks
Pass Defense	Rams		Steven Jackson, Rams
Special Teams	Seahawks		Adrian Wilson, Cardinals
Coaching Staff	Seahawks	On the Decline	Marshall Faulk, Rams
Home Field	Rams		Kurt Warner, Cardinals
			Rex Tucker, Rams
		Best Leader	Marshall Faulk, Rams
		Unsung Hero	James Darling, Cardinals
		Impact Rookie	Antrel Rolle, Cardinals

Torry Holt

🏈 Arizona Cardinals 2004

PASSING STATISTICS

PLAYER	CMP	ATT	YDS	CMP%	YDS/A	LNG	TD	TD%	INT	INT%	SACK	YDS	RAT
Josh McCown	233	408	2511	57.1	6.15	48	11	2.7	10	2.5	31	263	74.1
Shaun King	47	84	502	56.0	5.98	40	1	1.2	4	4.8	6	42	57.7
John Navarre	18	40	168	45.0	4.20	33	1	2.5	4	10.0	1	8	25.8

RUSHING STATISTICS

PLAYER	ATT	YDS	AVG	LNG	TD	FUM	LST
Emmitt Smith	267	937	3.5	29	9	4	1
Troy Hambrick	63	283	4.5	62	1	0	0
Obafemi Ayanbadejo	30	122	4.1	23	3	0	0

RECEIVING STATISTICS

PLAYER	REC	YDS	AVG	LNG	TD	FUM	LST
Larry Fitzgerald	58	780	13.4	48	8	1	0
Anquan Boldin	56	623	11.1	31	1	1	1
Bryant Johnson	49	537	11.0	40	1	1	0
Freddie Jones	45	426	9.5	40	2	0	0

RETURN STATISTICS

PLAYER	KICKOFFS ATT	YDS	FC	AVG	LNG	TD	PUNTS ATT	YDS	FC	AVG	LNG	TD
Josh Scobey	32	723	0	22.6	71	0	0	0	0	0.0	0	0
Larry Croom	16	314	0	19.6	35	0	0	0	0	0.0	0	0

KICKING STATISTICS

PLAYER	1-20	20-29	30-39	40-49	50+	TOT	PCT	AVG	LNG	XPM/A	PTS
Neil Rackers	0/0	6/6	5/7	6/7	5/9	22/29	75.9	38.0	55	28/28	94

PUNTING STATISTICS

PLAYER	PUNTS	YDS	AVG	LNG	TB	TB%	IN20	IN20%	RET	YDS	AVG	NET
Scott Player	98	4230	43.2	57	7	7.1	32	32.7	56	486	8.7	38.2

DEFENSIVE STATISTICS

PLAYER	TACKLES TOT	SOLO	AST	SACK	TLOSS	MISCELLANEOUS FF	BK	INTERCEPTIONS INT	YDS	AVG	LNG	TD	PD
Adrian Wilson	100	82	18	1.0	10	2	0	3	62	20.7	27	0	11
James Darling	88	75	13	1.0	6.5	2	0	1	65	65.0	65	0	6
Ronald McKinnon	74	57	17	0.0	5.5	0	1	0	0	0.0	0	0	0
David Macklin	71	64	7	0.5	1	1	0	4	18	4.5	16	0	16
Ifeanyi Ohalete	64	53	11	0.0	0	1	0	0	0	0.0	0	0	9
Duane Starks	58	54	4	1.0	0	1	0	3	46	15.3	41	1	12
Karlos Dansby	54	38	16	5.0	2.5	1	0	1	2	2.0	2	0	5
Russell Davis	50	39	11	1.0	1.5	1	0	0	0	0.0	0	0	3
Bertrand Berry	49	39	10	14.5	4	4	0	0	0	0.0	0	0	4

🏈 San Francisco 49ers 2004

PASSING STATISTICS

PLAYER	CMP	ATT	YDS	CMP%	YDS/A	LNG	TD	TD%	INT	INT%	SACK	YDS	RAT
Tim Rattay	198	325	2169	60.9	6.67	65	10	3.1	10	3.1	37	211	78.1
Ken Dorsey	123	226	1231	54.4	5.45	59	6	2.7	9	4.0	13	94	62.4

RUSHING STATISTICS

PLAYER	ATT	YDS	AVG	LNG	TD	FUM	LST
Kevan Barlow	244	822	3.4	60	7	2	2
Maurice Hicks	96	362	3.8	35	2	3	3
Terry Jackson	26	101	3.9	13	0	2	1

RECEIVING STATISTICS

PLAYER	REC	YDS	AVG	LNG	TD	FUM	LST
Eric Johnson	82	825	10.1	25	2	1	1
Cedrick Wilson	47	641	13.6	39	3	0	0
Brandon Lloyd	43	565	13.1	52	6	0	0
Curtis Conway	38	403	10.6	37	3	0	0

RETURN STATISTICS

PLAYER	KICKOFFS ATT	YDS	FC	AVG	LNG	TD	PUNTS ATT	YDS	FC	AVG	LNG	TD
Maurice Hicks	31	623	0	20.1	35	0	0	0	0	0.0	0	0
Jamal Robertson	25	560	0	22.4	37	0	0	0	0	0.0	0	0

KICKING STATISTICS

PLAYER	1-20	20-29	30-39	40-49	50+	TOT	PCT	AVG	LNG	XPM/A	PTS
Todd Peterson	1/1	3/3	7/8	5/6	2/4	18/22	81.8	35.9	51	23/23	77

PUNTING STATISTICS

PLAYER	PUNTS	YDS	AVG	LNG	TB	TB%	IN20	IN20%	RET	YDS	AVG	NET
Andy Lee	96	3990	41.6	81	8	8.3	25	26.0	51	445	8.7	36.9

DEFENSIVE STATISTICS

PLAYER	TACKLES TOT	SOLO	AST	SACK	TLOSS	MISCELLANEOUS FF	BK	INTERCEPTIONS INT	YDS	AVG	LNG	TD	PD
Derek Smith	109	86	23	1.5	4.5	0	0	0	0	0.0	0	0	3
Jeff Ulbrich	90	73	17	1.0	6.5	1	0	1	19	19.0	19	0	3
Tony Parrish	82	61	21	0.5	2	1	0	4	64	16.0	26	0	8
Ronnie Heard	68	57	11	0.0	1	0	0	1	14	14.0	14	0	6
Shawntae Spencer	67	62	5	0.0	2	0	0	0	0	0.0	0	0	7
Jamie Winborn	63	55	8	4.5	2.5	2	0	1	1	1.0	1	0	8
Bryant Young	48	39	9	3.0	8.5	1	0	0	0	0.0	0	0	1
Anthony Adams	48	42	6	0.0	7	1	0	0	0	0.0	0	0	2
Dwaine Carpenter	48	44	4	2.0	0	0	0	1	31	31.0	31	0	5
John Engelberger	45	30	15	6.0	3.5	4	0	0	0	0.0	0	0	5

2004 Team Stats

OFFENSE

Scoring:	17.8 (26)
Yards per Game:	284.4 (27)
Pass Yards per Game:	180.1 (24)
Rush Yards per Game:	104.3 (22)
Sacks Allowed:	39 (20)
3rd Down Percentage:	34.9 (23)
Giveaways:	26 (t20)

DEFENSE

Scoring:	20.1 (12)
Yards per Game:	321.3 (12)
Pass Yards per Game:	189.8 (9)
Rush Yards per Game:	131.6 (27)
Sacks:	38 (t14)
3rd Down Percentage:	31.6 (4)
Takeaways:	25 (t17)

2004 Team Stats

OFFENSE

Scoring:	16.2 (30)
Yards per Game:	286.6 (26)
Pass Yards per Game:	196.0 (20)
Rush Yards per Game:	90.6 (30)
Sacks Allowed:	52 (t29)
3rd Down Percentage:	32.4 (27)
Giveaways:	34 (t29)

DEFENSE

Scoring:	28.2 (32)
Yards per Game:	342.6 (24)
Pass Yards per Game:	217.9 (19)
Rush Yards per Game:	124.7 (20)
Sacks:	29 (t29)
3rd Down Percentage:	40.3 (23)
Takeaways:	17 (t27)

Seattle Seahawks 2004

PASSING STATISTICS

PLAYER	CMP	ATT	YDS	CMP%	YDS/A	LNG	TD	TD%	INT	INT%	SACK	YDS	RAT
Matt Hasselbeck	279	474	3382	58.9	7.14	60	22	4.6	15	3.2	30	155	83.1

RUSHING STATISTICS

PLAYER	ATT	YDS	AVG	LNG	TD	FUM	LST
Shaun Alexander	353	1696	4.8	44	16	4	3
Mack Strong	36	131	3.6	11	0	2	1
Maurice Morris	30	126	4.2	12	0	0	0

RECEIVING STATISTICS

PLAYER	REC	YDS	AVG	LNG	TD	FUM	LST
Darrell Jackson	87	1199	13.8	56	7	2	1
Bobby Engram	36	499	13.9	60	2	1	1
Koren Robinson	31	495	16.0	33	2	0	0
Jerry Rice	25	362	14.5	56	3	0	0

RETURN STATISTICS

PLAYER	KICKOFFS						PUNTS					
	ATT	YDS	FC	AVG	LNG	TD	ATT	YDS	FC	AVG	LNG	TD
Maurice Morris	47	994	0	21.1	34	0	15	75	4	5.0	22	0
Kerry Carter	21	448	0	21.3	36	0	0	0	0	0.0	0	0

KICKING STATISTICS

PLAYER	1-20	20-29	30-39	40-49	50+	TOT	PCT	AVG	LNG	XPM/A	PTS
Josh Brown	1/1	7/7	8/9	6/7	1/1	23/25	92.0	34.0	54	40/40	109

PUNTING STATISTICS

PLAYER	PUNTS	YDS	AVG	LNG	TB	TB%	IN20	IN20%	RET	YDS	AVG	NET
Tom Rouen	26	1093	42	60		3.8	10	38.5	10	91	9.1	38.5

DEFENSIVE STATISTICS

PLAYER	TACKLES					MISCELLANEOUS		INTERCEPTIONS					
	TOT	SOLO	AST	SACK	TLOSS	FF	BK	INT	YDS	AVG	LNG	TD	PD
Marcus Trufant	93	84	9	1.0	2	0	0	5	141	28.2	58	0	20
Isaiah Kacyvenski	81	63	18	1.0	4	1	0	0	0	0.0	0	0	0
Ken Hamlin	79	63	16	2.0	0.5	1	0	4	48	12.0	24	0	9
Terreal Bierria	69	47	22	0.0	1	1	0	1	10	10.0	10	0	5
Ken Lucas	67	60	7	0.0	3	1	0	6	46	7.7	25	1	21
Chike Okeafor	53	40	13	8.5	5.5	3	0	0	0	0.0	0	0	0
Michael Boulware	53	40	13	1.0	0	2	0	5	69	13.8	63	1	6
Orlando Huff	51	41	10	1.0	1.5	0	0	0	0	0.0	0	0	3
Cedric Woodard	49	29	20	1.0	2	1	0	0	0	0.0	0	0	0
Rashad Moore	46	32	14	2.0	1	0	0	0	0	0.0	0	0	2

2004 Team Stats

OFFENSE

Scoring:	23.2 (11)
Yards per Game:	352.1 (8)
Pass Yards per Game:	221.2 (13)
Rush Yards per Game:	130.9 (8)
Sacks Allowed:	34 (12)
3rd Down Percentage:	36.2 (19)
Giveaways:	25 (t18)

DEFENSE

Scoring:	23.3 (22)
Yards per Game:	351.3 (26)
Pass Yards per Game:	224.3 (23)
Rush Yards per Game:	126.9 (23)
Sacks:	36 (t21)
3rd Down Percentage:	42.4 (t27)
Takeaways:	32 (t3)

St. Louis Rams 2004

PASSING STATISTICS

PLAYER	CMP	ATT	YDS	CMP%	YDS/A	LNG	TD	TD%	INT	INT%	SACK	YDS	RAT
Marc Bulger	321	485	3964	66.2	8.17	56	21	4.3	14	2.9	41	302	93.7
Chris Chandler	35	62	463	56.5	7.47	75	2	3.2	8	12.9	7	54	51.4

RUSHING STATISTICS

PLAYER	ATT	YDS	AVG	LNG	TD	FUM	LST
Marshall Faulk	195	774	4.0	40	3	1	1
Steven Jackson	134	673	5.0	48	4	1	1
Marc Bulger	19	89	4.7	19	3	0	0

RECEIVING STATISTICS

PLAYER	REC	YDS	AVG	LNG	TD	FUM	LST
Torry Holt	94	1372	14.6	75	10	3	1
Isaac Bruce	89	1292	14.5	56	6	5	4
Shaun McDonald	37	494	13.4	52	3	1	0
Kevin Curtis	32	421	13.2	41	2	1	1

RETURN STATISTICS

PLAYER	KICKOFFS						PUNTS					
	ATT	YDS	FC	AVG	LNG	TD	ATT	YDS	FC	AVG	LNG	TD
Arlen Harris	47	951	0	20.2	29	0	0	0	0	0.0	0	0
Aveion Cason	14	310	0	22.1	31	0	0	0	0	0.0	0	0

KICKING STATISTICS

PLAYER	1-20	20-29	30-39	40-49	50+	TOT	PCT	AVG	LNG	XPM/A	PTS
Jeff Wilkins	0/0	7/7	5/6	3/6	4/5	19/24	79.2	36.6	53	32/32	89

PUNTING STATISTICS

PLAYER	PUNTS	YDS	AVG	LNG	TB	TB%	IN20	IN20%	RET	YDS	AVG	NET
Kevin Stemke	28	1115	39.8	56	3	10.7	12	42.9	11	44	4	38.3
Sean Landeta	40	1733	43.3	63	3	7.5	9	22.5	24	372	15.5	34

DEFENSIVE STATISTICS

PLAYER	TACKLES					MISCELLANEOUS		INTERCEPTIONS					
	TOT	SOLO	AST	SACK	TLOSS	FF	BK	INT	YDS	AVG	LNG	TD	PD
Pisa Tinoisamoa	92	75	17	1.5	8	0	0	0	0	0.0	0	0	4
Adam Archuleta	83	73	10	2.0	4	1	0	0	0	0.0	0	0	3
Tommy Polley	78	67	11	2.0	4.5	1	0	0	0	0.0	0	0	6
Jerametrius Butler	78	75	3	0.0	0	0	0	5	15	3.0	10	0	19
Robert Thomas	54	40	14	0.0	3.5	0	0	0	0	0.0	0	0	1
Aeneas Williams	48	41	7	0.0	0.5	2	0	0	0	0.0	0	0	2
Leonard Little	46	38	8	7.0	3.5	1	0	0	0	0.0	0	0	2
Bryce Fisher	46	38	8	8.5	3	2	0	0	0	0.0	0	0	1
Ryan Pickett	46	42	4	2.0	3.5	1	0	0	0	0.0	0	0	2
Rich Coady	40	34	6	0.0	1	1	0	0	0	0.0	0	0	4

2004 Team Stats

OFFENSE

Scoring:	19.9 (19)
Yards per Game:	367.3 (6)
Pass Yards per Game:	265.8 (5)
Rush Yards per Game:	101.5 (t25)
Sacks Allowed:	50 (t27)
3rd Down Percentage:	42.2 (9)
Giveaways:	35 (t31)

DEFENSE

Scoring:	19.6 (11)
Yards per Game:	334.6 (17)
Pass Yards per Game:	198.4 (12)
Rush Yards per Game:	136.2 (29)
Sacks:	34 (t24)
3rd Down Percentage:	36.4 (16)
Takeaways:	14 (t30)

Arizona Cardinals

Predicted: 2nd ▪ 2004: 6-10 (3rd)

Players Added

S	Robert Griffith	(Cle)
LB	Orlando Huff	(Sea)
WR	Charles Lee	(TB)
FB	Harold Morrow	(Bal)
DE	Chike Okeafor	(Sea)
OT	Oliver Ross	(Pit)
CB	Raymond Walls	(Bal)
QB	Kurt Warner	(NYG)

Players Lost

OT	Anthony Clement	(Den)
CB	Renaldo Hill	(Oak)
TE	Freddie Jones	(Car)
QB	Shaun King	
LB	Ronald McKinnon	
OT	L.J. Shelton	
RB	Emmitt Smith	(retired)
OL	Cameron Spikes	(Den)
CB	Duane Starks	(NE)
LB	Ray Thompson	(GB)
DE	Kyle Vanden Bosch	(Ten)
WR	Karl Williams	
LB	LeVar Woods	(Chi)

Draft

1	(8)	Antrel Rolle	CB	Miami, Fla.
2	(44)	J.J. Arrington	RB	California
3	(75)	Eric Green	CB	Virginia Tech
3	(95)	Darryl Blackstock	OLB	Virginia
4	(111)	Elton Brown	OG	Virginia
5	(168)	Lance Mitchell	ILB	Oklahoma
7	(226)	LeRon McCoy	WR	Indiana Pa.

The Cardinals may have had the best draft in the entire league. They got a corner in Rolle who can step right in and be an above-average starter, plus another corner in Green who adds more raw playmaking abilities. Green will likely play nickel this year. Arrington will push for a starting job right away. With a good training camp, Blackstock can start, but he must show he can live up to his abilities. Brown fell far after getting injured and not working out for scouts, but he was the best guard in this draft.

Head Coach: Dennis Green (2nd year)
Offensive Coordinator: none
Defensive Coordinator: Clancy Pendergast

Offense

QB:	Kurt Warner†
RB:	J.J. Arrington‡
FB:	James Hodgins
WR:	Anquan Boldin
WR:	Larry Fitzgerald
WR:	Bryant Johnson
LT:	Leonard Davis
LG:	Reggie Wells
C:	Alex Stepanovich
RG:	Jeremy Bridges
RT:	Oliver Ross†
QB:	Josh McCown
RB:	Marcell Shipp
WR:	Reggie Newhouse
TE:	Eric Edwards
OL:	Elton Brown‡

Defense

LDE:	Chike Okeafor†
NT:	Russell Davis
UT:	Darnell Dockett
RDE:	Bertrand Berry*
SLB:	Karlos Dansby
MLB:	Gerald Hayes
WLB:	Orlando Huff†
CB:	Antrel Rolle‡
SS:	Adrian Wilson
FS:	Robert Griffith†
CB:	David Macklin
NB:	Eric Green‡
DL:	Calvin Pace
LB:	James Darling
K:	Neil Rackers
P:	Scott Player

* Pro Bowler '04
† veteran acquisition
‡ rookie

Report Card

Quarterback	C–	Defensive Line	C+	Coaching	B
Running Back	C	Linebacker	B–	Special Teams	C+
Receiver/Tight End	B+	Defensive Back	B	Depth	C–
Offensive Line	B			Intangibles	B

If the Arizona Cardinals were not stranded all by their lonesome out in the middle of a southwestern desert, surrounded by the giant saguaro cactuses and long-nosed leopard lizards, it is very likely that it would be *they*, and not the Cincinnati Bengals, the Kansas City Royals, or the Los Angeles Clippers, who serve as icons for losing professional sports programs everywhere. As it is, the Cardinals almost get a free pass, because it's too hard to find one of their games on television, it's too hard to remember who plays for them, or maybe it's just too darn hot to care.

The last time the Cardinals seemed to be much of anything, the state's prized geographic treasure, the Grand Canyon, was still under water. The Cardinals have reached the playoffs just once since 1975. To put that in perspective, since then America has had six different presidents. Eight new NFL franchises have been established (either from teams relocating and starting over or from expansion) and half of those eight teams have reached the Super Bowl. Heck, in this span, the Cardinals themselves have been known as the St. Louis Cardinals, the Phoenix Cardinals, and, now, the Arizona Cardinals.

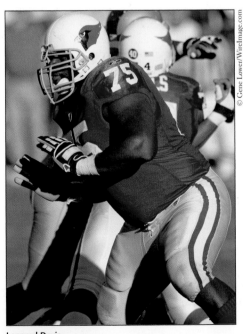

Leonard Davis

But once again, nobody notices the sorry Red Birds melting in the blistering southwestern heat. However, people may soon start to take note of this team. Head coach Dennis Green has marched into town with a big stick and, believe it or not, a plan. Thus far, he is executing his plan to near perfection, as the Cardinals have had the best class of new talent accumulated in the draft over the past two years. But this team doesn't have what it takes to rise to the top of the league, do they? *Come on!* The old tan and wrinkled people who shun daylight savings time don't care about football—how could they ever play host to a winning team?

Offense

Like Jon Gruden and Bill Parcells, **Dennis Green** acts as his own offensive coordinator, something that makes perfect sense when considering how involved he has always been with this aspect of his team. Whether it was his days in Minnesota during the '90s or last year in Arizona, Green orchestrates the offense to his own liking.

The first note that conductor Green has queued is that he does not believe **Josh McCown** can be his quarterback. McCown, a player in his fourth year out of Sam Houston State, was initially Green's guy last season. He was supposed to be the work in progress who had the potential to maybe turn out to be pretty good. However, toward the end of the year, with the Cardinals in the heat of the playoff race, Green benched his quarterback, electing instead to go with players like Shaun King or even seventh-round rookie **John Navarre** (who is back in an emergency quarterback role this season).

Green is not an idiot; he wouldn't just bench his best quarterback for no reason. Something happened over the course of last season that led Green to believe that if he wanted to get this sorry franchise back into a winning position (or rather, finally *into* a winning position), he would have to find an outside source to lead his offense in '05. The man he found was two-time MVP and one-time Super Bowl champion **Kurt Warner**.

After bagging groceries and working in the arena league . . . ah, forget it—everybody knows the Kurt Warner story by now. To sum things up, Warner came from nowhere, played in the Arena League, went to St. Louis, did well, hurt his thumb, started struggling, went to the Giants, and kept struggling. Now he's here, and nobody knows for sure if he's any good anymore. Unfortunately, the honest answer is, "No, Warner is not too good anymore."

Warner is by no means a one-hit wonder (considering his production in St. Louis from '99 through '02, he's at least a *three-* or *four*-hit wonder), but being 33 and as injury prone as he is, common sense says that Warner does not have much left. He initially played well with the Giants last season, but what they found out was that he isn't able to sustain a high performance for more than one or two games. A lot of people will argue that New York faltered once Warner (who was 5-4 as a starter) was benched, but his demotion had little to do with New York's demise. The man can no longer move in the pocket (he's seen more sacks in the past two seasons than he ever did bagging groceries), and he doesn't have a big, strong arm anymore. Most troublesome and peculiar is how, despite his experience in St. Louis, Warner really doesn't seem to have the confidence or decision-making skills to thrive, either.

<table>
<tr><th>Strengths</th><th>Weaknesses</th></tr>
</table>

Strengths

Potential

On offense, the receivers are young and talented, and there is nothing that says Arrington can't soon be good. Furthermore, the front five features two third-year players and a second-year player. On defense, Zona has Darnell Dockett and Karlos Dansby (both in their second year), plus three rookies (Antrel Rolle, Eric Green, and Darryl Blackstock), all of whom will contribute this season.

Coaching

While Dennis Green has never been regarded as a top-of-all-tiers coach, one must certainly admire the job he has done so far, both in arranging his personnel and getting his message through to this team.

Weaknesses

Quarterback

It is not a pleasure to dub Kurt Warner as a weakness, but he hasn't been able to finish out an entire season as a starter since his last MVP in '01. Furthermore, if Warner does get hurt, Dennis Green has already shown that he doesn't trust backup Josh McCown.

Fullback/Tight End

These can be two critical elements on a football team, particularly for a player like Warner, who needs a dump-off outlet. However, fullback James Hodgins is returning from a shoulder injury, and tight end Eric Edwards has only one career start to his name.

The Cardinals will go with Warner this year because it is their best chance of winning. Green must feel that he has a better chance of stumbling upon some old Warner magic than he does relying on McCown.

It won't be hard to make magic with the young receivers that Warner will have available to him this year. Green has always run a lot of three-receiver sets, dating back to his days with the Vikings. This season, the Cards will have a trio that features second-year stud **Larry Fitzgerald**, star **Anquan Boldin**, and the potentially solid **Bryant Johnson**.

Arizona is hoping that Fitzgerald, whom they drafted No. 3 overall out of Pitt last year, can be a top-five receiver in the pro game. Being a lanky 6'3", 223 pounds, and possessing the maturity, character, and natural feel for the game that he does, he is in pretty good shape to pan out for this franchise. Fitzgerald had a stellar rookie season, catching 58 passes (8 for touchdowns), but with a presumably more stable quarterback situation this year, he should see his development excel and his output flourish in '05.

If Fitzgerald can indeed become the No. 1 target that he is capable of being, Boldin will be in line for some huge accomplishments in the very near future. As a third-year player out of Florida State, Boldin has already caught more passes over the course of the first 26 games of his career (157) than anyone in NFL history. As a No. 2 receiver, Boldin would be able to use his strength and all-around skills against single coverage, something that not even Deion himself could stop.

There is one area of concern with Boldin: He is extremely underpaid. His agent is Drew Rosenhaus (the same agent who represents Terrell Owens), and he could very well tell his star to make some very distracting noise.

Johnson can be a potent slot receiver in the NFL if he establishes himself as a possession target who can move the chains on third down. He does not have great speed, but he shows the consistency in catching the ball that is needed to play this part. Arizona's tight end will not play a prominent role in '05, which is why all that needs to be said about **Eric Edwards** is . . . well, that's probably enough right there. (Edwards could actually be replaced by **Bobby Blizzard** who was tremendous in NFL Europe this year.)

Progression: **Defense**—The entire defense is getting better by the second. The front four added end Chike Okeafor, the linebackers are young, and the team drafted cornerback Antrel Rolle to help the secondary.

Regression: **Power running**—With both Marcell Shipp and James Hodgins being question marks heading into this season, the Cardinals may not be too effective in running for tough yards.

With Warner and the threesome of receivers expected to help improve Arizona's 24th-ranked passing attack from a year ago, the Cardinals used their second-round pick to draft a running back to help improve the 22nd-ranked rushing attack. The man they found was **J.J. Arrington**, a 5'9", 214-pound slasher out of California. Arrington will likely step into the starting role this season, because 230-pound veteran hammer **Marcel Shipp** has been slow to recover from a fractured foot that wiped out his entire season last year. Also, the team's other veteran (**Troy Hambrick**) has been slow to recover from an attack of offseason bingeeating, suffered a few years back when he blew his opportunity to become Emmitt Smith's long-term replacement in Dallas.

Arrington will start and, because of the system he ran with the Golden Bears, he should be comfortable enough to catch on right away in Arizona. However, his smaller size and unfamiliarity with playing a 16-game schedule will allow plenty of opportunities for Shipp this year. Whoever is in will be running behind either lead-blocker **James Hodgins** (who is trying to prove himself after a season-ending shoulder injury last year) or the less effective lead-blocker **Obafemi Ayanbadejo**.

The Cardinals offensive line was dubbed the Big Red Machine three years ago, but with tackle Anthony Clement now in Denver and the other tackle, L.J. Shelton, in Cleveland, it is time for a new nickname for the front five. But perhaps this young group should prove they're worthy of their own epithet first. They have a daunting task ahead of them—they must be able to keep pass-rushers off of Warner, something no line has been able to do for quite some time.

One man who will likely be worthy is the athletic and, therefore, dominant left tackle **Leonard Davis**, who at 6'6",

381 pounds, is large enough to declare himself to be his own province, if he so chooses. Next to Davis will be third-year player **Reggie Wells**. After starting all 16 games last season, Wells continues to get better each time he takes the field. He is not great in pass-blocking, but he can be very good as a run-blocker, thanks to his dexterity in how he uses angles.

The center is **Alex Stepanovich**, who probably should not have started so soon in his rookie season last year. Nevertheless, Stepanovich is growing and will be better in '05 because he'll be more comfortable with his assignments.

Right guard **Jeremy Bridges** will have to fight off fourth-round rookie **Elton Brown**, a former Virginia Cavalier who easily would have been drafted in the second round had he been healthy enough to work out for the scouts in February. The decision of whom to start may have to be made on the eve of the team's opening Sunday of the season, because it is impossible to forecast which player will beat out the other. Both are good athletes who have plenty of upside, but lack experience.

Finally, the right tackle is **Oliver Ross**, a former Steeler who is a load to match up against. The seventh-year veteran gets out of his stance well and naturally dominates weaker opponents. Overall, the most critical element for Arizona's success this season will be whether the front line can improve as a group in pass protection.

Defense

While the offense should be at least a little better in '05 than they were in '04, if the Cardinals are to propel into serious playoff contention this season, it's going to be a result of what they do on the defensive side of the football. Defense is where it's at these days, and with the progression the team has made here, it isn't too far of a stretch to think this team can emerge to do big things in '05.

Arizona actually ranked 12th in both points and yards allowed last season, plus they were a bang-up fourth in one of the most underrated categories of all: Third-down defense. However, the Cards allowed 131.6 yards per game on the ground, which explains why they had trouble hanging around against better teams throughout an entire game.

The most important element to the run defense is the linebacker position. Arizona's linebacking unit is headed by second-year player **Karlos Dansby**, who, as a rookie last season, really pumped a lot of life into this defense by making plays in pursuit and blitzing the quarterback. Dansby is a great talent who has a lot of potential. He is still learning how to be a professional, but the 23-year-old is a high-character individual who can be counted on.

Arizona signed former Seahawk **Orlando Huff** over the offseason. Huff was expected to start at the middle position (where he played in Seattle) and, thus, leave ninth-year veteran **James Darling** firmly implanted at his weakside spot. However, reports in May said the team would likely move Huff to the weakside and plug third-year player **Gerald Hayes** (another former Pitt Panther on this team) in the middle. Hayes had limited production last season, but the team likes his abilities as a run-stopper between the numbers.

This is all nice, and Huff *does* have the energy and burst, as well as ability in underneath pass coverage, to play the weakside, but to start Hayes would mean benching Darling, a move that

Arizona's head coach, Dennis Green, is only in his second year with the franchise, but already has his club on the fast track towards prosperity.

Cardinals defensive coordinator **Clancy Pendergast** and company cannot possibly justify. Although Darling, 30, is not as attractive in the long term as Dansby or Hayes, the man was simply too good last season (ranking second on the team in tackles, with 88) not to start this year. Darling is extremely fast, he plays hard, and he has the kind of strength that allows him to put ball carriers on the ground just by looking at them funny. He'll likely have a role as a nickel linebacker this season, but it would be a huge mistake not to find a way to put him on the field on a more regular basis. Pendergast may use some 3–4 looks, as well, which would get Darling on the field.

Arizona drafted Virginia's **Darryl Blackstock** in the third round this year. Blackstock was somewhat of an underachiever in college, but if Green and the Cardinals coaching staff can get him to maximize his potential, they may just have a player capable of starting at strongside linebacker—in which case Dansby would likely move over to the middle.

The dreadful football atmosphere (*yes*, there *is* a football atmosphere in Phoenix—you just can't *feel* it, that's all) and pathetic win/loss history of the team must have made Arizona feel as if it was still under control of Imperial Spain (or at least a later independent Mexico). It's seemed as if every good defensive lineman that this team has had (from Eric Swann to Simeon Rice) wanted out, while, at the same time, every good free agent wanted no part of the desert. In fact, Arizona has long been thought of as the Bermuda Triangle of football careers.

However, the recently acquired defensive ends for the Cards have changed the team's fortune. Last year, Denver's pass-rushing ace, **Bertrand Berry,** was available and he signed with the Cardinals—on *purpose*, too. Berry went on to post 14½ sacks (second-highest total in the league), earning a trip to the Pro Bowl, in which he got to debut the Cards' new, snazzier, angrier bird logo that will be seen on the team's helmets this year.

This year, Arizona signed one of Seattle's best pass-rushers in end **Chike Okeafor**. Okeafor is undersized (6'4", 265 pounds), but what he lacks in stature he makes up for in tenacity. He gets a good jump off the snap and is mobile around the line of scrimmage.

The Cardinals may have some trouble stopping teams from rushing on the outside. Berry is a stout force who can at least hold up against the run, but Okeafor gets overpowered. Furthermore, the team's first option off the bench is **Calvin Pace**, who was relegated to the second-string role because, being 6'4" and weighing in the low 260s himself, he was overmatched in run defense. One option could be backup **Peppi Zellner**, but he has been too inconsistent over his seven-year career.

Inside, the Cardinals shouldn't have as much trouble against the run. Nose tackle **Russell Davis** is not a particularly viable weapon, but he is wide-bodied and he works hard. If only his backup, **Wendell Bryant** (a first-round pick in '02), could be the same. Next to Davis is **Darnell Dockett**, a second-year player who was a bit of a pleasant surprise last year. Dockett has the capability of being a good player in the NFL, but for crying out loud, will somebody please teach him some methods for getting off blocks?

Green recognizes that the best way to improve a defense is to upgrade the secondary, particularly at the cornerback position. This is why he used the eighth-overall pick on Miami's **Antrel Rolle**. Rolle will step in and start right away for the Cardinals. He is not a speed burner with electrifying athleticism, but he is an excellent cover corner who is physical and willing to make a play on the ball. He can thrive in Arizona's defensive scheme, which relies on blitzing up front and, thus, man coverage (with a hint of some Cover 2) in the defensive backfield.

Opposite Rolle will be **David Macklin**, a sixth-year player whose contributions really go unnoticed. Macklin is a sound corner who is comfortable with his job. He shows great anticipation and has a good knack for getting between the receiver and the ball. The nickel back will be third-round rookie **Eric Green**, a man whose draft status fell because of character concerns. If Green can focus in the pros, he has the type of speed that could allow him to excel.

Strong safety **Adrian Wilson** may be the best defensive player on the Cardinals roster, which is a bold statement considering that not too many people are familiar with him. Wilson is a versatile safety who flies all over the field. He led the team in tackles last season, thanks to his comfort in playing in the box and his keen run/pass recognition. Wilson is always going to be the first guy to the ball, flying in at full speed.

The addition of veteran safety **Robert Griffith** will go a long way toward helping fifth-year pro Wilson. Griffith was once like Wilson, but injuries and 11 years of wear and tear have made him a mere shadow of his old self. That shadow, however, is still better than most players.

Special Teams

Kicker **Neil Rackers** was a mediocre 22/29 last season, although four of his seven misses were from 50-plus yards out—which shows the confidence that Green has in Rackers's leg. Punter **Scott Player** is one of the few players left in the league who still has a single bar on his face mask. It's sad, really, because with Gary Anderson gone and Player now 35, the funny-looking helmets will soon be extinct. Fourth-string running back **Josh Scobee** will serve as the kick returner. Arizona is hurting for a punt returner—they'll likely decide on one after the preseason.

The Bottom Line

It is too bad that the Cardinals are starting a shaky veteran (Warner) at quarterback and an unproven rookie (Arrington) at tailback. If not for these crucial elements being the way they are, this team could make a very serious run at the division title. The defense is young and on the rise, and Arizona finally has a capable coaching staff, led by Green. Furthermore, teams hate visiting the hot and boring desert, which can be a great home-field advantage for the Cards.

San Francisco 49ers

Predicted: 4th ▪ 2004: 2-14 (4th)

Draft

1	(1)	Alex Smith	QB	Utah
2	(33)	David Baas	C	Michigan
3	(65)	Frank Gore	RB	Miami, Fla.
3	(94)	Adam Snyder	OG	Oregon
5	(137)	Ronald Fields	DT	Mississippi St.
5	(174)	Rasheed Marshall	WR	West Virginia
6	(205)	Derrick Johnson	CB	Washington
7	(215)	Daven Holly	CB	Cincinnati
7	(248)	Patrick Estes	TE	Virginia
7	(249)	Billy Bajema	TE	Oklahoma St.

Perhaps the 49ers wanted to trade the No. 1 pick, but they didn't—and now Smith is their guy. Not a bad situation, though. Baas will step in and start immediately at guard. Because so many people in the organization can't stand Kevan Barlow, don't be surprised to see Gore, as long as his surgically repaired knee continues to hold up, push him for carries this year. Fields can be the nose tackle in Mike Nolan's new 3–4, but his poor conditioning will likely leave him in a backup role.

Head Coach: Mike Nolan (1st year)

Offensive Coordinator: Mike McCarthy

Defensive Coordinator: Billy Davis

Offense

QB:	Alex Smith‡
RB:	Kevan Barlow
FB:	Fred Beasley
WR:	Brandon Lloyd
WR:	Arnaz Battle
TE:	Eric Johnson
LT:	Jonas Jennings†
LG:	Justin Smiley
C:	Jeremy Newberry
RG:	David Baas‡
RT:	Kwame Harris
QB:	Tim Rattay
RB:	Terry Jackson
WR:	P.J. Fleck
TE:	Aaron Walker
OL:	Adam Snyder‡

Defense

LDE:	Bryant Young
NT:	Anthony Adams
RDE:	John Engelberger
LOLB:	Julian Peterson
LILB:	Derek Smith
RILB:	Jeff Ulbrich
ROLB:	Jamie Winborn
CB:	Ahmed Plummer
SS:	Tony Parrish
FS:	Mike Rumph
CB:	Shawntae Spencer
NB:	Dwaine Carpenter
DL:	Marques Douglas†
LB:	Andre Carter
K:	Joe Nedney†
P:	Andy Lee

* Pro Bowler '04
† veteran acquisition
‡ rookie

Report Card

Quarterback	C–	Defensive Line	C+	Coaching	C
Running Back	C+	Linebacker	B	Special Teams	C–
Receiver/Tight End	D–	Defensive Back	C	Depth	D–
Offensive Line	C+			Intangibles	D

Julian Peterson

The miners in the San Francisco area have not exactly enjoyed a gold rush in recent years when it comes to their beloved 49ers. Heck, they haven't even found pyrite. Simply put: This franchise is a dud right now.

To begin with, San Francisco lacks direction at the top: The Carmen Policy days are over—even Bill Walsh got out of town before this inevitable earthquake of losses begins to do even *more* serious damage this year. The 49ers have managed the salary cap about as well as MC Hammer has managed his credit card.

Enter Mike Nolan (*see* Painting a New Picture, page 5), an unheralded first-year head coach who left behind the halcyon life of coordinating Ray Lewis's defense in Baltimore to take over the most downtrodden franchise in the NFL. In the Bay Area, Nolan is a lot like a new janitor on his first day stumbling upon a toilet that overflowed in the men's room.

The Niners lack talent in a variety of ways, specifically at the offensive skill positions. However, at the age of 45, Nolan is relatively young and inexperienced as a head coach—which is where the false hope and optimism come from. He is returning the offense to its West Coast roots and installing a 3–4 scheme on the defensive side of the ball. Nolan is so giddy, in fact, that he even requested permission from the NFL to wear a suit during games—à la Tom Landry or Nolan's father, Dick, who coached the 49ers from 1968 to 1980. (The NFL rejected Nolan's request.)

During Nolan's first few days with the Niners, he addressed the topic of this team winning the NFC West division in '05, asking, "Why not us?" Well, Coach, because your team is terrible. Awful. Just plain bad. This team won all of two games last season, a total that they would be lucky to more than double this year.

Offense

It's hard to condemn Nolan's sorry lip service about this team having a chance to win—what else is he supposed to say? However, when a man starts claiming that (a) there *is* a competition for the starting quarterback job and (b) that competition includes not only No. 1 overall pick **Alex Smith** (*see* Painting a New Picture, page 8) and incumbent **Tim Rattay** but also second-year player **Ken Dorsey**, then at that point the political correctness has gone too far. Nolan can tease fans—but he shouldn't mock them.

Smith is going to be the starting quarterback for the Niners in '05. Why? Because there isn't enough of a sense of humor left in the Bay Area for the team to explain how either of their former *seventh*-rounders (Rattay or Dorsey) is better than this season's top overall pick. A job should be won or lost on the field and in practice, even in Smith's case, but San Francisco's quarterback situation is perfect proof that a little politics can be a good thing.

Considering the talent that Smith will have around him in '05, at times he'll probably wonder if he isn't stuck out on Alcatraz. The receiver outlook in San Francisco is as positive as the living conditions at Pelican Bay. The only wideout with any sort of credentials is third-year player **Brandon Lloyd**. Lloyd is a 6'0", 192-pound target out of Illinois. He possesses great playmaking abilities and has a knack for making a spectacular *SportsCenter*-worthy catch. However, as a No. 1 receiver, Lloyd is far too inadequate to give anyone reason to believe that the 49ers can improve upon their 20th-ranked passing attack from last season (a passing attack that ranked a much-lower 27th in yards per passing attempt, by the way). Lloyd had just 43 catches in this role last year, and there are certain players on this team who do not like his "young pup" attitude (namely **Fred Beasley**, who seems to be grouchy toward everyone anyway). The No. 2 receiver is **Arnaz Battle**. (Who?) Battle was a sixth-round draft pick in '03 and has played in 16 games since then, working mainly as a punt returner. Battle has a whopping eight receptions in his career—or, in other words, three-quarters of a single game of what Niner fans grew used to seeing out of Jerry Rice.

Speaking of Rice, he campaigned as hard as John Kerry for an opportunity to come back and play one final season with his longtime team. However, like Kerry, Rice's efforts didn't pay off. The Niners felt they needed to look forward, not backward, and politely refused the 43-year-old. The problem is, Rice would have been the No. 2 receiver on this team.

The depth at the wideout position is horrendous, to say the least. **P.J. Fleck** and **Derrick Hamilton** will compete for the No. 3 job, with the winner earning a chance for fans to actually learn his name. Last year's first-round draft choice **Rashaun Woods** has done little to impress since coming to the Bay Area, and with **Mike Nolan** and his new coaching staff taking over this year, Woods may find himself riding the bench as if it were a cable car.

Nolan's coaching staff includes offensive coordinator **Mike**

Strengths

Outside Linebacker

Julian Peterson is one of the most pliable weapons in all of football, Jamie Winborn has star potential, and Andre Carter is talented enough in some areas to contribute as a pass-rusher this season.

Offensive Line

This is not a particularly strong group compared to others in the league, but sometimes with the gold and red, a stretch has to be made. Jeremy Newberry will once again help anchor this group at center, Jonas Jennings is a top-ten left tackle, and the young guards (Justin Smiley and David Baas) will get better over time.

Weaknesses

Wide Receiver

The word *weakness* probably gives too much credit to this group. Brandon Lloyd is No. 1 on the depth chart—he would be no higher than No. 3 on most teams. A football nut should reward himself if he or she is able to identify at least *one* other receiver on this team.

Depth

As is the case with most bad teams, San Francisco lacks options off the bench. They are thin on offense and inexperienced on defense.

McCarthy, who was with New Orleans for the past five years. It may not be fair, but it must be said: If McCarthy could not make anything out of the talented players that he had with the Saints, then how in the name of Tony Bennett will he be able to do anything with *these* guys?

McCarthy's focus will be on returning to the West Coast system that made this team successful during the '80s and '90s. This is the right idea because it should give Smith a chance to utilize tight end **Eric Johnson** as often as possible. Johnson led this club with 82 catches for 825 yards last season. He is a 6'3", 256-pounder, who is in his fifth season out of Yale. Johnson is a short-yardage receiver in the truest fashion, with excellent hands and an acute ability to catch passes away from his body. He is not a threat to improve upon San Francisco's dismal number of big plays from a year ago (which included just 28 passes that went for more than 20 yards and only three completions over 40 yards), but he can help improve the club's 27th-ranked third-down success rate of 32.4.

Johnson is not often used as a blocker, which means that backup **Aaron Walker** will likely see some action in running situations this season. The real blocking support will come from fullback Beasley, who is one of the best all-around players at his position. Beasley is in his eighth year out of Auburn, and being a throwback purist from the back roads of Alabama, he is becoming fed up with the flashy young talent that surrounds him in the locker room. However, he is a proud man who likely won't let it affect his performance any more than it already has. But just know that Beasley might empathize with the underchallenged Silicon Valley computer technician who hates going to work. One of the "young punks" whom Beasley has made no secret about disliking is 26-year-old running back **Kevan Barlow**, who comes from inner-city Pittsburgh, where he grew up and played his college ball. Barlow is the pride and joy of the Pitt Panthers. After the miserable season that Barlow had last year, averaging only 3.4 yards per carry to lead San Francisco's 30th-ranked rushing attack, chances are Beasley is not alone in his distaste for the tailback.

Barlow can be a decent runner for this team—he has a respectable combination of speed and power. But he is inconsistent and unproven as a featured back, meaning he will likely never be too far above average. Barlow really needs someone to push him for his job this season, but none of the

Write it Down:

This team will be the greatest feel-good story since the Mighty Ducks if they win five games this year.

This Season vs. Last Season

Progression: **Offensive line**—Adding Jonas Jennings and getting Jeremy Newberry back healthy gives the Niners two very good veterans that they didn't have last year.

Regression: **Punting**—Getting rid of Todd Sauerbrun is great for this club, but from a pure kicking standpoint, the punting game will suffer a minor shank.

players behind him appear up to the challenge. Those players include third-down specialist **Terry Jackson**, the unproven **Maurice Hicks**, and the often-injured third-round rookie **Frank Gore**.

As terrible as this offense will be in '05, the 49ers are fortunate that they have a front line that can be stellar for them throughout the year. It's sort of like how, on even the cloudiest, most dreary San Francisco days, there will always be something fun to do down at Fisherman's Wharf.

Left tackle **Jonas Jennings** was this team's fresh catch over the offseason. Jennings, a fifth-year player out of Georgia, left the Buffalo Bills as a free agent. He is 6'3", 325 pounds, which partly explains why blocking appears so easy for him. Jennings is excellent at firing out of his stance and establishing a good, strong base. Although his game is predicated on strength more than quickness, Jennings plays with enough balance to handle most pass-rushers around the edge.

Next to Jennings will be second-year player **Justin Smiley**, who had a bright future while playing for the man who drafted him (Dennis Erickson) but now finds himself having to reaffirm his skills to a new coaching staff. Smiley will most likely win the starting job in '05 because he has good all-around quickness and—as long as he gets his weight forward—power.

Eighth-year veteran **Jeremy Newberry** missed 15 games last season because of knee and back injuries, and this year he may not be much better off. He told doctors that he's 50-50 right now, after having to surgically adjust his unstable kneecap. Newberry is one of the smartest players in the league, and when considering his duties on this offensive line (which include a vast amount of pre-snap reads), he is one of the most important, too.

The right side of the front five could showcase a pair of rookies in guard **David Baas** and tackle **Adam Snyder**, or it could feature a pair of young veterans in **Eric Heitmann** and **Kwame Harris**. Expect a combination of both: The team loves Baas (who was a center at Michigan) and will likely start him. Harris is a former first-round pick who is finally starting to become a capable player. He will probably start on the right side, where his improved strength and potency in run-blocking should serve him well.

Defense

Nolan, who (as previously noted) made his living as the coordinator of one of the best defenses in football (the Ravens), is stamping his name on this defense in '05, in the form of the 3–4. He'll have to stamp hard, because he is inheriting a unit that a year ago ranked 32nd (that's last) in points allowed, giving up 28.2 per game.

In fairness to the 49ers, this defense was derailed by injuries last season. It would be a surprise to see this group struggle so mightily again in '05. The prime luminary of this 3–4 will be outside linebacker **Julian Peterson**, who missed most of last season with a torn Achilles heel. (Those darn Greeks!) Despite the injury, the Niners made Peterson their franchise player for the second consecutive year, meaning there is a possibility that he could hold out. Peterson has one of the least-respected, most overly dollar-driven agents in all of football, Kevin Potson. Last year, Potson had Peterson reject the largest contract offer in 49ers history, a deal that would have made Peterson the second-highest-paid linebacker in football, behind only Ray Lewis. As it turned out, Peterson wound up getting tagged as the franchise player. He held out, then joined the team right before week 1, only to suffer his Achilles injury soon after. The injury likely decreased his market value, thus making the lucrative long-term deal that he had turned down just months before a far more enticing way to go.

Assuming Peterson is on the field in '05, the 49ers will have one of the most versatile weapons in the game. He can play at a high level anywhere in this defense. Yes, *anywhere*. Of course, should Peterson be unavailable for whatever reason, San Francisco still has two very viable options to plug in at the outside linebacker slots. The first is fifth-year pro **Jamie Winborn** (*see* Ready to Break Out, page 155), who is slated to start on the right.

The other option for the Niners is former defensive end **Andre Carter**, who missed 10 games with a back injury last season. In his fifth year in the league, Carter began his career as one of the up-and-coming pass-rushers in football. It will be in this role that he'll have a chance to resume his image in '05. But Carter will come off the bench (behind Peterson and Winborn) because his skills don't fit the linebacker position too well (namely in first- and second-down situations). But when Carter *is* in the game, Nolan and defensive coordinator **Billy Davis** will find ways to have him blitz the quarterback, much like Nolan did with Terrell Suggs in Baltimore.

The middle linebackers for the 49ers are sixth-year pro **Jeff Ulbrich** and ninth-year veteran **Derek Smith**. Both are stout run-stoppers who play hard, but neither quite has the athleticism needed to dominate sideline to sideline. Ulbrich is okay in pass coverage (and he does have *admirable* pursuit skills), but Smith is not too adept in this area, meaning fourth-year man **Saleem Rasheed** will see good playing time in '05. Rasheed can be a nickel linebacker because of his agility and serviceability in coverage.

The talented but injury-prone Andre Carter will have to find his niche in San Francisco's new 3–4 defense this year. Expect that niche to be that of the situational linebacker.

The 49ers front three will be headed by nose tackle **Anthony Adams**. Adams, a third-year player out of Penn State, was supposed to materialize into a solid starter a year ago, but he was never able to establish himself in a 4–3 scheme. Now, playing as a nose tackle, the 25-year-old 300-pounder is poised to become a force. Adams plays with absolutely great leverage, which is perhaps the most important characteristic of a nose tackle. Furthermore, he can occasionally draw double teams, through his ability to get penetration.

The ends for San Francisco will likely be 12th-year veteran **Bryant Young** and sixth-year player **John Engelberger**. Young has been slowing down the past couple of seasons, but he is the perfect fit for a 3–4; he has seen his career essentially extend another three years. At 268 pounds, Engelberger's skills seem to fit as well in his new run-stopping role as a semitruck loaded with Napa Valley wine careening down Lombard Street. Engelberger is a high-energy player who has sound awareness and is a good tackler, but his frame and his penchant for finesse almost guarantee that he won't be able to adequately take on blocks on the outside.

Free agent acquisition **Marques Douglas**, a defensive end, will likely find his way into the starting lineup this season. Douglas is in his sixth year in the league and has spent his entire career with the Ravens, meaning he is very familiar with Nolan and his scheme. Douglas is not explosive, but playing this gig, he doesn't need to be. The important thing is that he can anchor against the run and occasionally make his presence felt as a pass-rusher when attacking the inside.

In the same way that Marin County and the rest of the Bay Area need the Golden Gate Bridge in order to have any chance of getting to work, the 49ers need their defensive backs to stay healthy in order to have any chance of succeeding. The key figures will be cornerbacks **Ahmed Plummer** and **Shawntae Spencer**.

Plummer was once a surefire star as a cover corner, but inconsistency and instability in his surroundings have altered his fate. Now in his sixth season out of Ohio State, he seems constantly to be making up for his mistakes or trying too hard to outplay his opponents, which is what causes his problems. Plummer is a good player; he just needs to have less pressure on him in order to succeed. He also needs to stay healthy.

"Spencer is the No. 2 corner, a job that he held for a good part of last season, after **Mike Rumph** was lost for the year in September with a broken forearm. Rumph is moving to free safety in '05, leaving the second-year player Spencer to take over the cornerback assignments on a full-time basis.

Spencer has good agility and shows fluid change-of-direction skills, but he probably isn't ready to start at this point in his career. Furthermore, with him starting, San Francisco will have to go with one of the untested (and, frankly, unqualified) rookies, **Derrick Johnson** (a sixth-round pick) or **Daven Holly** (a seventh-round pick) in nickel packages. A better option would be playing

Dwaine Carpenter at nickel corner. Carpenter played cornerback last season and was a major liability, giving up far too much separation in man coverage and showing inconsistent awareness. However, he at least has some form of playing experience to fall back on. Either way one views it, the Niners are obviously in a bind.

The beginning of the fourth-year player Rumph's career was as disastrous as the 1906 San Francisco fire. In his rookie year, Rumph was arrested for a DUI, cruelly picked on by opposing offenses, and lambasted by fans and the media. However, in '03 he seemed to rediscover himself, showing the feel for getting his hands on passes and reading routes that made him a first-round pick. But his broken forearm last season presented a huge setback.

Now, the Niners have made Rumph a free safety, where he'll have to focus less on defending receivers in man coverage and more on reading offenses from centerfield. He should do well in his new role—most players who move from cornerback to safety find the transition simple and career boosting. However, by transforming one of their cornerbacks into a safety, San Francisco is sacrificing some depth in the secondary.

Strong safety **Tony Parrish** is a solid veteran for this club, but he is not as good as his numbers seem to indicate. The eighth-year pro will amass some interceptions (he has 20 over the last three years), but in terms of all-around presence, Parrish is not a star. What he is, though, is a consistent veteran who has the toughness to be a leader on this defense.

Special Teams

It seems the 49ers have been trying to solve their kicking woes since the California gold rush—or at least the days of Mike Cofer. This year they have found **Joe Nedney**, who has missed all but one game over the past two seasons with (boy, what luck) *leg* injuries. Punter **Andy Lee** came out of nowhere last year (though, come to think of it, what punter actually comes out of *somewhere*?) and did an okay job, averaging 41.6 yards per boot. The return man for the 49ers will likely be Maurice Hicks on kicks and Arnaz Battle on punts. One other note: This team's only Pro Bowler in '04 was long snapper **Brian Jennings**.

The Bottom Line

It is tough to find many nice things to say about San Francisco's offense, other than that Smith will learn a lot this year and the torture of the season is guaranteed to cease in January. Defensively, Nolan has his squad headed in the right direction, though many of these players have been unable to stay healthy over time. Overall, people in west-central California should just relax and enjoy the nice marine climate and beautiful bay water—because those will be San Francisco's only highlights this fall.

Seattle Seahawks

Predicted: 3rd ▪ 2004: 9-7 (1st)

Offensive Coordinator: Gil Haskell

Defensive Coordinator: Ray Rhodes

Players Added

LB	Kevin Bentley	(Cle)
DT	Chartric Darby	(TB)
CB	Andre Dyson	(Ten)
DE	Bryce Fisher	(StL)
CB	Kelly Herndon	(Den)
WR	Joe Jurevicius	(TB)
WR	Jerome Pathon	(NO)
LB	Jamie Sharper	(Hou)
DE	Joe Tafoya	(Atl)

Players Lost

LB	Chad Brown	(NE)
QB	Trent Dilfer	(Cle)
FB	Heath Evans	(Mia)
LB	Orlando Huff	(Ari)
CB	Ken Lucas	(Car)
DE	Brandon Mitchell	(Atl)
DE	Chike Okeafor	(Ari)
WR	Jerry Rice	(Den)
S	Damien Robinson	
WR	Koren Robinson	
P	Tom Rouen	(Car)
LB	Anthony Simmons	
CB	Bobby Taylor	
T	Chris Terry	

Draft

1	(26)	Chris Spencer	C	Mississippi
2	(45)	Lofa Tatupu	ILB	USC
3	(85)	David Greene	QB	Georgia
3	(98)	LeRoy Hill	ILB	Clemson
4	(105)	Ray Willis	OT	Florida St.
5	(159)	Jeb Huckeba	DE	Arkansas
6	(196)	Tony Jackson	TE	Iowa
7	(235)	Cornelius Wortham	OLB	Alabama
7	(254)	Doug Nienhuis	OT	Oregon St.

With 35-year-old Robbie Tobeck aging at the center position, taking Spencer was the right way to go. However, Seattle might have been able to acquire him by trading up in the second round instead of trading down in the first. Tatupu is limited in terms of potential, but he has starter skills playing behind a beefy Seahawk front five. Greene is supposedly a poor man's Tom Brady, which spells a respectable backup career. Willis gives them more breathing room in filling the empty right tackle position.

Offense

QB:	Matt Hasselbeck
RB:	Shaun Alexander*
FB:	Mack Strong
WR:	Darrell Jackson
WR:	Bobby Engram
TE:	Itula Mili
LT:	Walter Jones*
LG:	Steve Hutchinson*
C:	Robbie Tobeck
RG:	Chris Gray
RT:	Floyd Womack
QB:	Seneca Wallace
RB:	Maurice Morris
WR:	Jerome Pathon†
TE:	Jerramy Stevens
OL:	Jerry Wunsch

Defense

LDE:	Bryce Fisher†
DT:	Cedric Woodard
DT:	Rashad Moore
RDE:	Grant Wistrom
SLB:	Jamie Sharper†
MLB:	Niko Koutouvides
WLB:	D.D. Lewis
CB:	Marcus Trufant
SS:	Michael Boulware
FS:	Ken Hamlin
CB:	Andre Dyson
NB:	Kelly Herndon†
DL:	Rocky Bernard
LB:	Lofa Tatupu‡
K:	Josh Brown
P:	Donnie Jones

* Pro Bowler '04
† veteran acquisition
‡ rookie

Report Card

Quarterback	B−	Defensive Line	B−	Coaching	B
Running Back	B+	Linebacker	C−	Special Teams	B−
Receiver/Tight End	B−	Defensive Back	B	Depth	B+
Offensive Line	B			Intangibles	D+

Walter Jones

There are intense cumulonimbus clouds hovering over Elliott Bay in the Puget Sound. However, this is not one of those typical thunderstorms in Seattle's marine climate. While this growing city in the Pacific Northwest will undoubtedly see its share of rain this fall, this particular thunderstorm is nothing more than a metaphor to describe the current state of the Seattle Seahawks.

The Seahawks are in a position to flash a quick light, rumble a monstrous boom, and "reign" over the rest of the NFC West division in '05. The forecast of a possible late-afternoon downpour has become an annual event for Mike Holmgren's club, but thus far Seattle's dominance in the NFL has been nothing more than "partly cloudy with scattered showers."

The Seahawks are just about as talented as any team in the NFC, given that their offense has developed together as a unit and the defense is young, talented, and laced with new starters at all three prime locations. However, this is similar to last season, when they went a disappointing 9-7 (although Holmgren seemed upbeat all year) and lost at home in the Wild Card round of the playoffs.

After re-signing virtually all of their vital figures and welcoming a few new birds to their nest (or whatever the heck a *seahawk*—if there is such a thing—lives in), this club is poised to capitalize in '05. The Hawks certainly have the talent to step in line behind Boeing, Microsoft, and Starbucks and become the city's next big franchise, but do they have the will?

Offense

The Seahawks return all 11 starters to an offense that ranked 11th in scoring and eighth in total yards last season. With this in mind, there isn't a lot of mystery to unfold with this unit—there are simply a few things to sort out. The factors that have prevented **Mike Holmgren**'s team from maximizing their full potential seem to culminate on this side of the ball. For example, this past offseason, receiver Koren Robinson sought professional help for unspecified personal problems. (Robinson has had run-ins with the law, he served a four-game suspension for violating the league's substance abuse policy last year, and he has been benched in the past for violating team rules.) After seemingly striving to overcome his demons by swearing off alcohol, Robinson was arrested on DUI charges in May. Seattle finally gave up on the troubled star, releasing him in early June. In addition to Robinson's drama, running back **Shaun Alexander** held out of minicamps, protesting his franchise tag. Tight end **Itula Mili** did not attend all of the team functions, either, and when he *was* around, he weighed in at 290 pounds, a solid doughnut or two above his 260-pound playing weight. Also, receiver **Darrell Jackson** held out of minicamp, saying that he wants the team to keep the promise that was made to him by former club president Bob Whitsitt (whatever the hell that means).

Again, it's not that this offense—or *team*, for that matter—isn't gifted enough. It's that little things like this have hindered them year in and year out. This offseason was rather light on distractions, compared to previous years. A shortage of self-sacrifice and accountability has been rampant on this team, and until Seattle finds a totalitarian-like leader who will not tolerate any more of this nonsense, this is going to continue to be a problem for the Birds.

After signing a $48 million long-term contract in February, 30-year-old quarterback **Matt Hasselbeck** has indicated that he may be the man to step up and tighten the reins on this group; after a minicamp in May that drew "less than perfect attendance," he called out his absent teammates. Hasselbeck is a player who has taken his lumps since becoming Seattle's starter five seasons ago, but he is qualified to assume the leadership position on this team. Hasselbeck has progressed enough in Seattle's variation of the West Coast offense that he should be considered a finished product—from a skills standpoint. In other words, his good—but not great—accuracy, his decent—but not dangerous—mobility, and his solid—but not dynamic—arm strength will not progress too much from here.

What *will* make Hasselbeck a better player is improving his consistency and shoring up his decision making. A perfect illustration of the type of improvements he must make can be seen in the contrast of his performance at home versus on the road last year. At home, Hasselbeck completed 65 percent of his passes, threw only three interceptions, and had a rating of 98.8. But when traveling, Hasselbeck's completion percentage dropped to 54.4, he tossed 12 picks, and his rating number was a plebeian 71.7.

It's not as though Hasselbeck isn't capable of improving in '05, but if he is to get better, he will need his talented—yet underachieving—receivers to stop dropping so many passes. For some time now, senseless mistakes by receivers have been as common in Seattle as an Ichiro base hit. In order to improve the quality of the entire wideout position, over the offseason the Seahawks signed two tough, well-established, veteran slot receivers in **Jerome Pathon** and **Joe Jurevicius**. Both players will add depth to the passing options, while at the same time serving as a new possibility for Holmgren and offensive coordinator **Gil Haskell** to resort to if the men from last year don't come ready to play.

Those men would include 26-year-old Jackson and 10th-year veteran **Bobby Engram**. Jackson's heart is clearly in the right place, and his teammates understand that he will give them his best effort (when he is around). Last year, he caught 87 passes for 1,199 yards, but his lack of focus during games prevented him from leading Seattle's 13th-ranked passing attack to bigger things.

With Robinson's release, Engram will likely find himself in the starting lineup. Engram has been as inconsistent as any of the Seahawks receivers, but at this point, Holmgren does not have much choice about whom to turn to. Seattle must hope that Engram's slashing quickness and solid route-running skills can translate into *consistent* production in '05.

Despite expanding to the size of a Boeing 747 over the offseason, ninth-year veteran Mili will have a chance to retain his starting tight end duties in '05. Mili has better speed and agility than some might think, he runs nice routes, and he plays with good enough technique to survive in run-blocking. The man that should have stolen Mili's job long ago is fourth-year player **Jerramy Stevens**, a 6'7", 260-pound rock who played his college ball at the nearby University of Washington. However, Stevens has been unable to find his niche in the league, thanks to off-the-field problems and an apparent lack of passion for the game. When he's ready, Seattle will be ready for him. Stevens has a great frame that's highlighted by his long arms, plus he's strong, versatile, and willing to block.

Alexander had been considered the likable star on this offense, before his disappointing and unprecedented display of selfishness late last season. Alexander rushed for 1,696 yards and

Write It Down:
This team will fail to reach the playoffs in '05, prompting the removal of head coach Mike Holmgren.

This Season vs. Last Season

Progression: **Receiver—**Although Seattle lost Koren Robinson and Jerry Rice, the additions of Joe Jurevicius and Jerome Pathon will provide some much needed toughness at this position, while at the same time pushing the starters to play better.

Regression: **Linebacker—**Jamie Sharper is not as good as Chad Brown because he cannot blitz to help Seattle's mediocre pass-rush like Brown could. Furthermore, this team is without Anthony Simmons, who, when healthy, was a speedy force for them.

16 touchdowns in '04—gaudy numbers that suggest pure superstar. However, it was the 1,697th yard that he wanted, because it would have given him the NFL rushing title. It doesn't matter who it is or what the context of the situation is; any player who pouts after his team wins a division title because *he* didn't get his individual accolades is a raging "me-first" jerk. Alexander even poured gasoline on the fire by bellowing to the media that he was "stabbed in the back."

This year, Alexander is unhappy because he did not receive a long-term contract from the team (hmm . . . wonder why?). He'll still play in '05, but it will most likely be for himself. This will be a problem for the Hawks. Alexander will put up his usual big numbers (for negotiating purposes, of course), but he cannot be counted upon to sustain drives or come up big in crunch time, because he will be reaching for too many home runs and, thus, doing things like ignoring the direction in which a play is supposed to go, snubbing the little things that make a team great, and being a distraction in the locker room.

The polar opposite of Alexander is 13th-year veteran **Mack Strong**, who provides hard-nosed lead-blocking from the fullback position. Strong will likely be lead-blocking for backup tailback **Maurice Morris** more often in '05 than in recent years.

On the offensive line, left tackle **Walter Jones** and left guard **Steve Hutchinson** make up a Northwest duo that is second in power to only Bill Gates and Paul Allen. Both Jones and Hutchinson are coming off Pro Bowl seasons and both are firmly planted in the prime of their careers.

For the first time since '01, Jones will not hold out of training camp in reaction to being slapped with the franchise tag. Over the offseason, the 31-year-old All-World player signed a well-

deserved long-term deal. Jones has every attribute that a good left tackle can have; the man has no major weaknesses. Hutchinson is a fifth-year run-blocking force out of Michigan. His mobility and athleticism are superb, and his comfort in the blocking scheme is very evident.

Center **Robbie Tobeck** is in his 12th year and will be pushed by rookie first-round draft choice **Chris Spencer**. Expect Tobeck to still open the season as the team's starter, with Spencer being his understudy. Tobeck is a great leader who is crafty and has the ability to neutralize whomever he faces.

The right side of the line features 35-year-old guard **Chris Gray** (who probably should have retired this year) and 27-year-old tackle **Floyd "Pork Chop" Womack**, who probably should be playing Gray's position. Womack is a versatile blocker who gets great initial pop and drive in run-blocking, but his mediocre pass-blocking makes him a guard out of position.

Defense

The Seahawks defense is to the offense what *Friends* was to *Seinfeld*: The same thing, only watered down in terms of quality. Seattle has their share of young and talented defensive weapons and a handful of those players have been, well, a handful off the field. But then again, this unit was far less impressive than the offense in '04, ranking 22nd in points allowed and 26th in yards given up.

With this in mind, Seattle approached the offseason with an eye toward reshuffling their defense. They added a defensive end in **Bryce Fisher**, a linebacker in **Jamie Sharper**, and a cornerback in **Andre Dyson**. However, considering that Fisher is replacing leading sacker Chike Okeafor, Sharper is replacing the team's best linebacker over the years (Chad Brown), and Dyson is replacing the team's leader in interceptions last year (Ken Lucas), the changes made are closer to being mild downgrades than they are improvements.

This is where the Hershey's slogan "Change is bad" has some credibility. However, after failing again last season, a little change couldn't hurt, could it? Let's look at it, starting up front. It's not like Fisher is a bad player; in fact, now in his fifth year in the league, the onetime Ram is among some of the brightest up-and-coming ends in the game. Fisher does not have the explosiveness of a potentially active Mount Rainier, but he is still a very respectable athlete who is solid in all aspects of the game. He is great in backside pursuit, and he had enough ability to post 8½ sacks in a backup role with the Rams last season. One concern with Fisher is that he always has to be on the move in order to make plays.

Opposite Fisher at the right defensive end position is another former Ram, **Grant Wistrom**. After becoming one of the highest-paid athletes in all of sports last year, Wistrom struggled in his first season as a Seahawk, thanks to a slew of injuries that bounced him in and out of the lineup. Now that he's completely healthy, the 29-year-old Wistrom should resume his status as one of the best all-around defensive linemen in the game. Wistrom is phenomenal against the run, he's quick and can take on blocks as a pass-rusher, and he plays with a motor that never stops, much like that one bunny on television that has become the focal point of the lamest, most predictable, and most overused jokes since the 2000 election recount.

© Joseph Rogate/WireImage.com

The Seahawks were able to retain both potential free agents, quarterback Matt Hasselbeck (left) and running back Shaun Alexander, over the offseason.

The Seahawks have the kind of depth up front to which only Lake Union can compare. They love to rotate their young, run-stuffing tackles, **Rashad Moore** (324 pounds, third season), **Rocky Bernard** (293 pounds, fourth season), and **Marcus Tubbs** (320 pounds, second season). All three players are capable two-gap defenders.

The only defensive tackle who can offer more than a wide body in run support (though at 310 pounds, he can offer that, too) is **Cedric Woodard**. Woodard starts, but only because he has slightly more quickness than his three peers. He is not a pass-rushing threat, but rather, just a change-of-pace tackle—if such exists. Backup defensive end **Antonio Cochran** (who could start if he didn't play so tall and get dismantled against the run) had 6½ sacks off the bench last year.

The men who are supposed to benefit from the "clogging" services of the defensive tackles are, of course, the linebackers. This is by far the weakest area on this Seahawks team, because aside from the strongside starter Sharper, nobody is quite sure of what to expect from these guys.

Ninth-year veteran Sharper joined Seattle after being cut by Houston, a team where he was the most consistent tackler for each of his three years there. Seattle is not getting a superstar in Sharper, but they are getting a smart veteran who has great experience and can lead this younger unit. From a skills standpoint, Sharper is more than adequate; he attacks the inside well and has good power when closing. However, Sharper lacks the speed, quickness, and change-of-direction abilities to dominate—he is not stricken with paralyzing limitations in these areas, but he is definitely a straight-line player.

The middle linebacker will be **Niko Koutouvides**, who got this opportunity after the man he split time with in '05 (Orlando Huff) left the team, Niko Kou . . . uh . . . thiduski-tiders? (tough job that the public address announcer at Seattle's Qwest Field has) may not have the position locked up, though—the club drafted middle linebacker **Lofa Tatupu** in the second round this year. Tatupu comes in with championship experience from his days at USC. He is not an athletic specimen, but he has the heart, brains, and leadership ability that defensive coordinator **Ray Rhodes** loves. When considering that Kouv-acl . . . uh . . . ta-biddles? struggles in pass coverage and Tatupu can become an effective blitzer, more split responsibilities at the middle linebacker position appear imminent in Seattle.

The weakside linebacker is **D.D. Lewis**, who missed all of last season with a shoulder injury. If he is unable to bounce back, third-year player **Solomon Bates** could push him for playing time. Neither has great experience.

The secondary's free agent acquisition Dyson is a player who has the smooth agility and catch-up speed to help build on Seattle's impressive 20 team interceptions from last year. Dyson does not have the size to be dominant in bump-and-run coverage, but he is certainly adequate—plus, he can be fabulous in zone coverage.

The real story is cornerback **Marcus Trufant**, who may soon be as big in Seattle as Kelsey Grammer's Dr. Frasier Crane, or maybe *even Starbu*—dah, no, no—ju-just Frasier. In his third season out of Washington State, Trufant is already one of the elite cover corners in the NFL. He is a solid tackler who has fluid hips, amazing change-of-direction abilities, and, of course, the speed and all that other good athletic stuff that a superstar has. At his current rate, Trufant (who had five picks, 20 passes defensed, and 93 tackles a year ago) will soon be a shutdown corner who can shadow receivers to the point of insanity.

Seattle also added the soft but agile **Kelly Herndon**, from Denver. He will beat out **Kris Richard** as the nickel back. The safeties for the Seahawks are very intriguing. Strong safety **Michael Boulware** is a former college linebacker who hits with great energy and pop, but he defends passes with suspect awareness and dexterity. Boulware will not fully blossom until later in the season *next* year, but in the meantime he can provide some big plays in run support. If Boulware becomes too much of a liability in pass coverage, Seattle can always go back to **Terreal Bierria**, who had a surprisingly good season in '05.

Bierria actually warranted much of the playing time that free safety **Ken Hamlin**, a third-year man out of Arkansas, was supposed to get last year. The gifted Hamlin is a stout hitter who has improved into an above-average pass defender. As long as he can continue to grow more comfortable in this scheme and prove that he is mature enough to handle the responsibilities of a professional, he will be excellent.

Special Teams

Kicker **Josh Brown** is coming off a great season, in which he made all but two of his 25 field goal attempts. After Tom Rouen and Ken Walter struggled in '04, Seattle decided to go with second-year punter **Donnie Jones** in '05. The kick returner for the Hawks will be one of their two backup running backs, Maurice Morris or **Kerry Carter**. Finally, Seattle is the only team in the entire league that can honestly say that their punt returner is also their backup quarterback. The man who has been given such honors is the elusive **Seneca Wallace**.

The Bottom Line

The natural tendency is to pick this team to win the NFC West, but a lower finish is equally as likely. True, Seattle has a talented squad, and yes, it would not be a shock to see them win this division. However, they tripped last year because of inconsistent play, poor chemistry, immaturity, and mediocrity on defense. Heading into this season, these sorts of issues continue to plague them; in fact, things may even have gotten a bit worse.

St. Louis Rams

Predicted: 1ˢᵗ ▪ 2004: 8-8 (2ⁿᵈ)

Players Added

LB	Chris Claiborne	(Min)
LB	Dexter Coakley	(Dal)
S	Michael Hawthorne	(GB)
CB	Corey Ivy	(TB)
S	Michael Stone	(Ari)
OG	Rex Tucker	(Chi)
TE	Roland Williams	(Oak)

Players Lost

QB	Chris Chandler	
S	Rich Coady	(Atl)
DB	Antuan Edwards	(NE)
DE	Bryce Fisher	(Sea)
OL	Matt Lehr	(Atl)
LB	Tommy Polley	(Bal)
OT	Kyle Turley	
DB	Aeneas Williams	

Draft

1	(19)	Alex Barron	OT	Florida St.
2	(50)	Ronald Bartell, Jr.	CB	Howard
3	(66)	Oshiomogho Atogwe	S	Stanford
3	(81)	Richie Incognito	C	Nebraska
4	(117)	Jerome Carter	S	Florida St.
4	(134)	Claude Terrell	OG	New Mexico
5	(144)	Jerome Collins	TE	Notre Dame
6	(192)	Dante Ridgeway	WR	Ball St.
6	(210)	Reggie Hodges	P	Ball St.
7	(250)	Ryan Fitzpatrick	QB	Harvard
7	(251)	Madison Hedgecock	FB	North Carolina

St. Louis was hoping to get a more natural right tackle like Oklahoma's Jammal Brown, but instead they had to settle on a left tackle in Barron. He can start at the right side, but it will be up to the coaches to help him work harder and maximize his potential. Bartell is a project who probably won't be ready to start for at least two years. They needed a safety who is truly adept in coverage; Atogwe is not that type of player.

Head Coach: Mike Martz (6ᵗʰ year)
Offensive Coordinator: Steve Fairchild
Defensive Coordinator: Larry Marmie

Offense

QB:	Marc Bulger
RB:	Steven Jackson
FB:	Joey Goodspeed
WR:	Torry Holt*
WR:	Isaac Bruce
TE:	Brandon Manumaleuna
LT:	Orlando Pace*
LG:	Rex Tucker†
C:	Andy McCollum
RG:	Adam Timmerman
RT:	Alex Barron‡
QB:	Jamie Martin
RB:	Marshall Faulk
WR:	Kevin Curtis
WR:	Shaun McDonald
OL:	Blaine Saipaia

Defense

LDE:	Leonard Little
NT:	Ryan Pickett
DT:	Jimmy Kennedy
RDE:	Anthony Hargrove
SLB:	Brandon Chillar
MLB:	Chris Claiborne†
WLB:	Dexter Coakley†
CB:	Jerametrius Butler
SS:	Adam Archuleta
FS:	Michael Stone*
CB:	Travis Fisher
NB:	Ronald Bartell‡
DL:	Damione Lewis
LB:	Pisa Tinoisamoa
K:	Jeff Wilkins
P:	Reggie Hodges†

* Pro Bowler '04
† veteran acquisition
‡ rookie

Report Card

Quarterback	B	Defensive Line	C+	Coaching	C
Running Back	B+	Linebacker	C+	Special Teams	D+
Receiver/Tight End	A	Defensive Back	B	Depth	B
Offensive Line	B–			Intangibles	C–

After countless injuries, ongoing funny ball bounces, and nonstop complaining from around the league, the St. Louis Rams are finally replacing their notorious Astroturf with the new-age FieldTurf, which is essentially synthetic grass. However, the days of this circus-like offense being the "greatest show on turf" are not quite dead yet in St. Louis. Sure, ringmaster Kurt Warner is long gone and the team's best bearded lady, Marshall Faulk, is now a backup, but this club still has speed and explosion—it's just in the form of different players.

One item that is far too often forgotten—including within the Rams organization—is that the offense isn't the only show on turf; the defense plays there as well. This season, St. Louis renovated their linebacker position and revamped much of their secondary. However, it seems as if virtually every other team in the NFL has done the same, so how can these guys really be anything special?

The underlying issue for the Rams is head coach Mike Martz and his ability to oversee a club that hopes to get it right for once. In other words, no more burning time-outs as if they were kindling needed to save a campfire, no more rushing droughts on offense, no more senseless penalties, no more players fee—ah! Just no more inconsistency, okay?

© Peter Newcomb/WireImage.com

Orlando Pace

Much the way the St. Louis Arch is the gateway to the American West, a smoother all-around football operation can be this team's gateway to the top of the NFC West. But will this club finally stay on the right trail?

Offense

French fur traders established St. Louis in 1764. Those Frenchmen named the city in honor of Louis IX, a 13th-century French king. In reaching for a connection, there are many around the NFL who believe that **Mike Martz** would love to have the high-octane St. Louis offense named in honor of *him*. Martz has drawn heavy criticism over his coaching career for his stubbornness in play-calling, his shaky game management, and his cavalier attitude in dealing with certain players.

Most of the criticism has been warranted. Typically, the Rams have been a careless football team, particularly on offense—as evidenced by their NFC-high 35 giveaways last season. But a person could make a strong argument that this is simply who the Rams are. Although they put up big numbers, much of what St. Louis does is style over substance. Case in point: The Rams had 67 passing plays that went for over 20 yards last season, the second highest in the NFL. They also ranked sixth in the league at 367.3 total yards of offense per game (style). Of course, despite these gaudy numbers, the Rams still averaged only 19.9 points per game, which was 19th in the NFL (substance).

The St. Louis offense is very good, there's no question about that, but in order to be a winning unit (i.e., to showcase more substance and less style), they must establish a better grasp on the basics. This includes doing a better job of controlling the momentum of a game and setting the tone through physical play. The best way to do both is by running the football, something Martz and the Rams have done with far too little regularity.

Very rarely does a team improve by replacing a future first-ballot Hall of Famer with a second-year player, but that is precisely what is going to happen with St. Louis's backfield this year. After 11 previous seasons in the NFL and 6 in the Show Me State, **Marshall Faulk** has begun to show the people in the Edward Jones Dome what a breaking-down, 32-year-old running back looks like. However, in '05, Faulk will also show those fans what a classy, intelligent, first-rate team player looks like.

Faulk has willingly accepted a demotion to the change-of-pace (aka backup) duties this season, in order to allow the 6'2", 233-pound **Steven Jackson** to step into the starting role. This day has been on the horizon for quite a while now, and it couldn't have come at a better time.

Jackson averaged five yards per attempt last season (as opposed to Faulk's four), showing a great burst of speed and power. With Faulk as his mentor, Jackson should be able to post 1,500 yards on the ground this season—assuming that Martz gives him enough carries. Last year, St. Louis ran the ball less often than all but two teams. However, a more energetic ground game (which will still benefit from the services of Faulk) should give Martz more incentive to keep the football closer to the carpet in '05.

Of course, the emphasis is on the word *should*, because if history has shown anything, it's that you can't teach an old dog new tricks; Martz will throw first and pass second. It must be noted that Faulk's versatility helped create this offense, meaning that whoever is in the backfield this season (especially if it *is*

Strengths

Passing

Until Isaac Bruce shows any signs of slowing down (which isn't likely to happen this year) or until Torry Holt loses a leg, the Rams aerial attack is going to be tough to stop. St. Louis also has a strong-armed quarterback in Marc Bulger and solid depth at the receiver position.

Cornerback

The complementary skills of Travis Fisher and Jerametrius Butler provide the only true stability on this entire defense.

Offensive Line Security

Not counting superstar Orlando Pace, the Rams front five could suffer a collapse this season. Guard Rex Tucker has been hurt so much in the past three years that he should have a couple of Illinois health care benefit agencies on his speed dial. Additionally, tackle Alex Barron is a rookie who will have a tough time developing this year, and both Adam Timmerman and Andy McCollum are veterans who could soon wear down. Unlikely, yes—but still possible.

Little Things

St. Louis does not do the little things that winning teams do. They don't have good special teams, Martz is too liberal in his play-calling, and the club plays with sloppy habits (burning time-outs, turning the ball over, etc.).

Faulk) will have to be adept at catching the ball. This is an element of Jackson's game that is still developing, although it is much further along than many think.

That said, the pressure in the passing game will continue to rest on quarterback **Marc Bulger**. Bulger had a better season last year, throwing for 3,964 yards and completing 66.2 percent of his passes, all while limiting his interception total to a respectable 14. However, the fifth-year quarterback out of West Virginia has still not proven that he is the type of player who can be relied upon to single-handedly lead a team to victory. Bulger simply has too many of his moments, both good and bad. The word commonly used to describe this is *inconsistent*.

To help improve Bulger's consistency, St. Louis has made a conscious effort to put him behind a better offensive line in '05. Last year Bulger was sacked 41 times. This was the result of a combination of things, including Bulger's tendency to hold the ball too long, the offense's design—which forces the receivers to run long, slow-developing routes—and some glaring weaknesses on the offensive line.

While the first step to improvement is always identifying the problem (or problems), the only thing that really matters in the NFL is fixing the problems—something the Rams still have not quite done. Bulger is always going to be somewhat hit-or-miss with the ball in his hands and the receivers in this offense are always going to run longer routes, so nothing there will change. That leaves the spotlight on the front five.

The Rams have an all-world player in left tackle **Orlando Pace**, who finally received a long-term contract this past offseason (seven years, $52.9 million—$15 million signing bonus). In recent years, Pace had been hit with an annual franchise tag, which caused him to make a habit of avoiding training camp like Mark McGwire avoids steroid allegations (70, huh?). But Pace isn't here to talk about the past; this year he's here to dismantle opponents from the left tackle position.

Pace can dominate anywhere with ease—his most difficult task may be helping offensive line coach **John Matsko** teach rookie **Alex Barron** (the 19th-overall pick) to perform at right tackle. Barron, out of Florida State, is expected to help upgrade a

Write It Down:

This team cannot advance far in the playoffs because they do not have enough consistent defensive weapons to carry them.

This Season vs. Last Season

Progression: **Rushing Attack**—Not only is it the perfect time to start Steven Jackson, but Marshall Faulk will be fresher and, thus, more effective coming off the bench in '05.

Regression: **Safety**—The Rams weren't great at this spot a year ago, but at least they weren't having to choose from career backups like Michael Stone and Michael Hawthorne, or a rookie like O.J. Atogwe.

makes tough grabs and runs well after the catch. Finally, No. 4 receiver **Shaun McDonald** is a speedy player who can have a big game if he is able to create and exploit mismatches.

position that has absolutely plagued the Rams for the past two years. He is a gifted lineman who has outstanding natural skill, but a reputation for lacking a serious passion for the game. At first, Barron wasn't big on the idea of playing right tackle (which, unlike his natural position on the left side, requires more physicality and run-blocking skills), but after suffering through **Grant Williams** and **Blaine Saipaia** at this spot last season, the Rams couldn't care less about his preferences.

Barron will likely struggle for most of his rookie season. Fortunately for St. Louis, right guard **Adam Timmerman**, who is in his 11th season out of South Dakota State, is very crafty in run-blocking and is as dependable as the sun setting in the west. Next to Timmerman is center **Andy McCollum**. While the 35-year-old McCollum does not quite have a Barron-like future, he is still more than adequate for the time being. One would never know he is a 12th-year veteran; he has great hands, he is robust—especially in run-blocking—and he doesn't often get beat.

Newly acquired left guard **Rex Tucker** has spent the past three seasons on the injured reserve, which rightfully leads a person to wonder how he can possibly be counted on this year.

The bread and butter of this offense is still the receivers. **Torry Holt** and Isaac Bruce are viewed almost as twin brothers, and seldom as individuals. This makes sense—last year Holt (age 29) had 94 catches for 1,372 yards (fourth in the league) and 10 scores, while his "older twin" Bruce (age 33) had 89 receptions for 1,292 yards (fifth in the league) and 6 touchdowns. Both players are quick, experienced, and smart. They know how to execute this high-powered offense by running good routes, setting up their quick cuts, and getting great separation.

The complementary receivers are all very good in their own way. Tight end **Brandon Manumaleuna** (say that *one* time fast) is used as more of a blocker, but he is a capable short-yardage target. Slot receiver **Kevin Curtis** is remarkably quick. He

Second-year running back Steven Jackson has supplanted legend Marshall Faulk as the starter in the Rams' backfield this season. Jackson offers more explosiveness, power, and breakaway speed.

Defense

The Rams defense has, in recent years, been the evil foil to the offense. With their plethora of young and talented players over the past two or three seasons, St. Louis thought they had something going, but over time those players have become not so young and apparently not so talented.

The Rams are attempting to revamp their 25th-ranked scoring defense from a year ago by featuring proven veterans like **Chris Claiborne** and **Dexter Coakley** at the linebacker position. St. Louis hopes that substituting pure athleticism for more intelligence and experience can do the trick, specifically against the run, where the Rams allowed 136.2 yards per game last season (fourth-worst in the NFL). Additionally, they gave up an embarrassing 327 yards in the divisional-round playoff loss at Atlanta. Overall, the personnel adjustments at the linebacker position are purely experimental, because there are absolutely no guarantees that St. Louis has even upgraded. They've just rolled the dice on some changes.

Last season's starting middle linebacker, **Robert Thomas,** has been sent to the second string. Thomas has good tackling skills, but he lacks awareness the way Paris Hilton lacks respect for subtle decency. Claiborne will fill in at middle linebacker this year. However, Claiborne is not a savior or even close to a star, for that matter. The seventh-year veteran who came over from Minnesota is reliable, though, and can work well when surrounded by better talent.

The question, considering that Coakley turns 33 in October, is this: Is the former Cowboys sparkplug a better talent? The 5'10", 231-pound Coakley is certainly a career overachiever and will definitely play with great energy, but the Rams are not making a smart decision in having him replace third-year man **Pisa Tinoisamoa**. Although Tinoisamoa was part of the undisciplined linebacking unit last season—contributing his own share of mistakes—St. Louis seems to be making a change at the weakside position just for the sake of making a change. The athletically gifted Tinoisamoa, from (guess where) Hawaii, is the type of player who would flourish with veteran talent around him. He has all of the skills to play in space on the weakside. He's only 24 years old, which means the Rams are foolish to demote him now. This is where his learning experiences as a starter for the past two years begin to pay off.

Making this even more egregious is the fact that St. Louis is starting second-year player **Brandon Chillar**, who, as a fourth-round draft choice last season, made a minimal impact outside of special teams. Chillar was great there (when healthy), and there is certainly nothing to say that he can't be effective in his starting role this year—at 6'2", 253 pounds, he has the right skills to succeed on the strongside. But what justification can the team give for purposely promoting *him* while at the same time purposely *demoting* Tinoisamoa?

The original plan was to move Tinoisamoa to strong safety in '05, but as time wore on, the Rams wisely thought better of that. Instead, they'll once again start **Adam Archuleta** at this position. Now in his fifth year, Archuleta is no longer a developing talent, but rather, a 27-year-old veteran who will be responsible for leading this secondary now that Aeneas Williams has retired. Archuleta is coming off a back injury that last season hounded him to the point where he could not even bend over to tie his shoe. However, he claims to be "6,000 percent better," which, factoring in his exaggeration, is still at least 3×10^3 percent better. In keeping Archuleta at strong safety, the Rams avoid having to rely heavily on his shaky pass coverage skills, while at the same time, they get to enjoy his hard-hitting, freelancing destruction in the box. Archuleta is a tough player who can mix it up with anyone, but in keeping him at strong safety and leaving Tinoisamoa at weakside linebacker, the Rams are left with a gaping hole at the free safety spot.

Much the way Meriwether Lewis and William Clark left St. Louis to explore the unknown, veteran free agent acquisitions **Michael Stone** and **Michael Hawthorne** are setting off to explore the foreign free safety position. Don't expect either of them to discover vast new horizons and aspirations on their journey, though—both have been career backups, making it almost certain that they will serve as utility defensive backs off the bench this year.

The man who is most likely to take over the free safety duties is third-round rookie **Oshiomogho Atogwe** (he goes by O.J., though one would think he would know to steer clear of that nickname). The problem with Atogwe is that he is a player who would likely be more comfortable in run support, something that the Rams don't need from him.

Fortunately for St. Louis, they have two solid cornerbacks who can hold down the fort in pass coverage. They are fourth-year player **Travis Fisher** and fifth-year veteran **Jerametrius Butler**. Fisher is a lot like Minnesota's Antoine Winfield: At 5'10", 189 pounds, he is somewhat undersized. Also, he plays a lot of one-on-one coverage, has a great ability to close on a receiver, and—oh yes—he tackles extremely well. Butler is the antithesis of Fisher in that, while virtually the same size (5'10", 181 pounds), he plays a game that is predicated more on playing off a receiver and reaching for the big play. Fisher had five interceptions and 19 passes defensed last season.

The nickel back will likely be second-round pick **Ronald Bartell, Jr.**, simply because defensive coordinator **Larry Marmie** will want to get his youngster experience in the system. It is too bad that third-year player **DeJuan Groce** will not be given an adequate chance to play this season. Groce is an athletic force who has good technique and has shown continuous improvements since joining the league out of Nebraska in '03.

St. Louis has invested in their defensive line like Bill Gates has invested in microchips. They spent a pair of first-round picks in '01 on tackles **Ryan Pickett** and **Damione Lewis**, they drafted tackle **Jimmy Kennedy** in the first round in '03, and last season

they started third-round rookie **Tony Hargrove** at end. The only problem for the Rams is that aside from Hargrove, these players have been in the NFL just long enough to establish reputations as letdowns.

Be that as it may, the Rams are relying heavily on all of these players in '05. St. Louis will start Pickett at nose tackle and Kennedy at the other tackle position, giving them a pair of run-stuffers who are as big as the city's famed Budweiser Clydesdales. Pickett is a 310-pound force who has the strength to be destructive against the run. At 320 pounds and possessing the pass-rushing skills of a parked car on Market Street, Kennedy would probably be the more viable option to line up over the center. Kennedy has the lateral mobility to stop the run in the middle—he just won't rush the quarterback.

Hargrove will once again start at end this season. The Rams like his first-step and his potential, plus he looks like he can play the run. But overall, Hargrove needs to continue to elevate his game if he is going to become dynamic in this role.

Pressuring the quarterback is what end **Leonard Little** does best. Little had seven sacks last season and is capable of more this year. But it was a tough spring for him: Over the offseason, Circuit Judge Emmett O'Brien ordered Little to refrain from drinking while he serves a two-year probation for his speeding arrest last year (he has a previous vehicular manslaughter conviction). Backup **Tyoka Jackson** is not a starter anymore, but he could team with Lewis at the tackle position on third downs and be a decent pass-rushing option there.

Special Teams

Kicker **Jeff Wilkins** has been of Pro Bowl caliber for all 12 years of his career. He has upper-echelon range, especially playing indoors. The Rams drafted punter **Reggie Hodges** in the sixth round this year, giving him the job without any competition. St. Louis tied for last in kickoff returns a year ago, and they were 31st in punt returns, averaging a pitiful 4.8 yards. With this in mind, it is hard to speculate who might get the return duties this year.

The Bottom Line

On offense, the Rams will be slightly better than they were a year ago, thanks primarily to the changes made at the running back position. However, defense is the key for this circus act, and it remains to be seen how good they will be at linebacker and in the secondary. The Rams can win the NFC West (and nothing more) if they find a way to make opponents play to their style, while at the same time reducing the negative elements that impede their game.

The Schedules

NFC East

Dallas
Sept. 11	at San Diego	4:15*
Sept. 19	Washington	9:00* (Mon)
Sept. 25	at San Francisco	4:05
Oct. 2	at Oakland	4:15*
Oct. 9	Philadelphia	4:15*
Oct. 16	N.Y. Giants	1:00
Oct. 24	at Seattle	4:05
Oct. 30	Arizona	1:00
Nov. 6	BYE	
Nov. 14	at Philadelphia	9:00* (Mon)
Nov. 20	Detroit	1:00
Nov. 24	Denver	4:15* (Thur)
Dec. 4	at N.Y. Giants	1:00
Dec. 11	Kansas City	4:15*
Dec. 18	at Washington	1:00
Dec. 24	at Carolina	1:00 (Sat)
Jan. 1	St. Louis	8:30*

New York Giants
Sept. 11	Arizona	4:15
Sept. 18	at New Orleans	1:00
Sept. 25	at San Diego	8:30*
Oct. 2	St. Louis	1:00
Oct. 9	BYE	
Oct. 16	at Dallas	1:00
Oct. 23	Denver	4:15*
Oct. 30	Washington	1:00
Nov. 6	at San Francisco	4:05
Nov. 13	Minnesota	1:00
Nov. 20	Philadelphia	1:00
Nov. 27	at Seattle	4:15
Dec. 4	Dallas	1:00
Dec. 11	at Philadelphia	4:05
Dec. 17	Kansas City	5:00* (Sat)
Dec. 24	at Washington	1:00 (Sat)
Dec. 31	at Oakland	8:00* (Sat)

Philadelphia
Sept. 12	at Atlanta	9:00* (Mon)
Sept. 18	San Francisco	1:00
Sept. 25	Oakland	1:00
Oct. 2	at Kansas City	1:00
Oct. 9	at Dallas	4:15*
Oct. 16	BYE	
Oct. 23	San Diego	1:00
Oct. 30	at Denver	4:15*
Nov. 6	at Washington	8:30*
Nov. 14	Dallas	9:00* (Mon)
Nov. 20	at N.Y. Giants	1:00
Nov. 27	Green Bay	4:15*
Dec. 5	Seattle	9:00* (Mon)
Dec. 11	N.Y. Giants	4:05
Dec. 18	at St. Louis	4:15*
Dec. 24	at Arizona	4:05 (Sat)
Jan. 1	Washington	4:15

Washington
Sept. 11	Chicago	1:00
Sept. 19	at Dallas	9:00* (Mon)
Sept. 25	BYE	
Oct. 2	Seattle	1:00
Oct. 9	at Denver	4:15
Oct. 16	at Kansas City	1:00
Oct. 23	San Francisco	1:00
Oct. 30	at N.Y. Giants	1:00
Nov. 6	Philadelphia	8:30*
Nov. 13	at Tampa Bay	1:00
Nov. 20	Oakland	1:00
Nov. 27	San Diego	1:00
Dec. 4	at St. Louis	4:05
Dec. 11	at Arizona	4:05
Dec. 18	Dallas	1:00
Dec. 24	N.Y. Giants	1:00 (Sat)
Jan. 1	at Philadelphia	4:15

NFC North

Chicago
Sept. 11	at Washington	1:00
Sept. 18	Detroit	1:00
Sept. 25	Cincinnati	1:00
Oct. 2	BYE	
Oct. 9	at Cleveland	1:00
Oct. 16	Minnesota	1:00
Oct. 23	Baltimore	4:15
Oct. 30	at Detroit	1:00
Nov. 6	at New Orleans	1:00
Nov. 13	San Francisco	1:00
Nov. 20	Carolina	1:00
Nov. 27	at Tampa Bay	1:00
Dec. 4	Green Bay	1:00
Dec. 11	at Pittsburgh	1:00
Dec. 18	Atlanta	8:30*
Dec. 25	at Green Bay	5:00*
Jan. 1	at Minnesota	1:00

Detroit
Sept. 11	Green Bay	4:15
Sept. 18	at Chicago	1:00
Sept. 25	BYE	
Oct. 2	at Tampa Bay	1:00
Oct. 9	Baltimore	1:00
Oct. 16	Carolina	1:00
Oct. 23	at Cleveland	1:00
Oct. 30	Chicago	1:00
Nov. 6	at Minnesota	1:00
Nov. 13	Arizona	1:00
Nov. 20	at Dallas	1:00
Nov. 24	Atlanta	12:30* (Thur)
Dec. 4	Minnesota	1:00
Dec. 11	at Green Bay	8:30*
Dec. 18	Cincinnati	4:05
Dec. 24	at New Orleans	1:00 (Sat)
Jan. 1	at Pittsburgh	1:00

Green Bay
Sept. 11	at Detroit	4:15
Sept. 18	Cleveland	4:15*
Sept. 25	Tampa Bay	4:15
Oct. 3	at Carolina	9:00* (Mon)
Oct. 9	New Orleans	1:00
Oct. 16	BYE	
Oct. 23	at Minnesota	1:00
Oct. 30	at Cincinnati	1:00
Nov. 6	Pittsburgh	4:15*
Nov. 13	at Atlanta	4:15*
Nov. 21	Minnesota	9:00* (Mon)
Nov. 27	at Philadelphia	4:15*
Dec. 4	at Chicago	1:00
Dec. 11	Detroit	8:30*
Dec. 19	at Baltimore	9:00* (Mon)
Dec. 25	Chicago	5:00*
Jan. 1	Seattle	4:15*

Minnesota
Sept. 11	Tampa Bay	1:00
Sept. 18	at Cincinnati	1:00
Sept. 25	New Orleans	1:00
Oct. 2	at Atlanta	4:15
Oct. 9	BYE	
Oct. 16	at Chicago	1:00
Oct. 23	Green Bay	1:00
Oct. 30	at Carolina	1:00
Nov. 6	Detroit	1:00
Nov. 13	at N.Y. Giants	1:00
Nov. 21	at Green Bay	9:00* (Mon)
Nov. 27	Cleveland	1:00
Dec. 4	at Detroit	1:00
Dec. 11	St. Louis	1:00
Dec. 18	Pittsburgh	1:00
Dec. 25	at Baltimore	8:30*
Jan. 1	Chicago	1:00

NFC South

Atlanta
Sept. 12	Philadelphia	9:00* (Mon)
Sept. 18	at Seattle	4:05
Sept. 25	at Buffalo	1:00
Oct. 2	Minnesota	4:15
Oct. 9	New England	1:00
Oct. 16	at New Orleans	1:00
Oct. 24	N.Y. Jets	9:00* (Mon)
Oct. 30	BYE	
Nov. 6	at Miami	1:00
Nov. 13	Green Bay	4:15*
Nov. 20	Tampa Bay	1:00
Nov. 24	at Detroit	12:30* (Thur)
Dec. 4	at Carolina	1:00
Dec. 12	New Orleans	9:00* (Mon)
Dec. 18	at Chicago	8:30*
Dec. 24	at Tampa Bay	1:00 (Sat)
Jan. 1	Carolina	1:00

Carolina
Sept. 11	New Orleans	1:00
Sept. 18	New England	1:00
Sept. 25	at Miami	1:00
Oct. 3	Green Bay	9:00* (Mon)
Oct. 9	at Arizona	4:15
Oct. 16	at Detroit	1:00
Oct. 23	BYE	
Oct. 30	Minnesota	1:00
Nov. 6	at Tampa Bay	1:00
Nov. 13	N.Y. Jets	4:05
Nov. 20	at Chicago	1:00
Nov. 27	at Buffalo	1:00
Dec. 4	Atlanta	1:00
Dec. 11	Tampa Bay	1:00
Dec. 18	at New Orleans	1:00
Dec. 24	Dallas	1:00 (Sat)
Jan. 1	at Atlanta	1:00

New Orleans
Sept. 11	at Carolina	1:00
Sept. 18	N.Y. Giants	1:00
Sept. 25	at Minnesota	1:00
Oct. 2	Buffalo	1:00
Oct. 9	at Green Bay	1:00
Oct. 16	Atlanta	1:00
Oct. 23	at St. Louis	1:00
Oct. 30	Miami	1:00
Nov. 6	Chicago	1:00
Nov. 13	BYE	
Nov. 20	at New England	1:00
Nov. 27	at N.Y. Jets	8:30*
Dec. 4	Tampa Bay	1:00
Dec. 12	at Atlanta	9:00* (Mon)
Dec. 18	Carolina	1:00
Dec. 24	Detroit	1:00 (Sat)
Jan. 1	at Tampa Bay	1:00

Tampa Bay
Sept. 11	at Minnesota	1:00
Sept. 18	at Buffalo	:00
Sept. 25	at Green Bay	1:00
Oct. 2	Detroit	1:00
Oct. 9	at N.Y. Jets	1:00
Oct. 16	Miami	1:00
Oct. 23	BYE	
Oct. 30	at San Francisco	4:15
Nov. 6	Carolina	1:00
Nov. 13	Washington	1:00
Nov. 20	at Atlanta	1:00
Nov. 27	Chicago	1:00
Dec. 4	at New Orleans	1:00
Dec. 11	at Carolina	1:00
Dec. 17	at New England	1:30* (Sat)
Dec. 24	Atlanta	1:00 (Sat)
Jan. 1	New Orleans	1:00

NFC West

Arizona
Sept. 11	at N.Y. Giants	4:15
Sept. 18	St. Louis	4:05
Sept. 25	at Seattle	4:05
Oct. 2	vs San Francisco (at Mexico)	8:30*
Oct. 9	Carolina	4:15
Oct. 16	BYE	
Oct. 23	Tennessee	4:15
Oct. 30	at Dallas	1:00
Nov. 6	Seattle	4:05
Nov. 13	at Detroit	1:00
Nov. 20	at St. Louis	1:00
Nov. 27	Jacksonville	4:05
Dec. 4	San Francisco	4:05
Dec. 11	Washington	4:05
Dec. 18	at Houston	1:00
Dec. 24	Philadelphia	4:05 (Sat)
Jan. 1	at Indianapolis	1:00

St. Louis
Sept. 11	at San Francisco	4:15
Sept. 18	at Arizona	4:05
Sept. 25	Tennessee	4:05
Oct. 2	at N.Y. Giants	1:00
Oct. 9	Seattle	1:00
Oct. 17	at Indianapolis	9:00* (Mon)
Oct. 23	New Orleans	1:00
Oct. 30	Jacksonville	1:00
Nov. 6	BYE	
Nov. 13	at Seattle	4:15
Nov. 20	Arizona	1:00
Nov. 27	at Houston	1:00
Dec. 4	Washington	4:05
Dec. 11	at Minnesota	1:00
Dec. 18	Philadelphia	4:15*
Dec. 24	San Francisco	1:00 (Sat)
Jan. 1	at Dallas	8:30*

San Francisco
Sept. 11	St. Louis	4:15
Sept. 18	at Philadelphia	1:00
Sept. 25	Dallas	4:05
Oct. 2	vs Arizona (at Mexico)	8:30*
Oct. 9	Indianapolis	4:05
Oct. 16	BYE	
Oct. 23	at Washington	1:00
Oct. 30	Tampa Bay	4:15
Nov. 6	N.Y. Giants	4:05
Nov. 13	at Chicago	1:00
Nov. 20	Seattle	4:05
Nov. 27	at Tennessee	:00
Dec. 4	Arizona	4:05
Dec. 11	at Seattle	4:05
Dec. 18	at Jacksonville	1:00
Dec. 24	at St. Louis	1:00 (Sat)
Jan. 1	Houston	4:05

Seattle
Sept. 11	at Jacksonville	1:00
Sept. 18	Atlanta	4:05
Sept. 25	Arizona	4:05
Oct. 2	at Washington	1:00
Oct. 9	at St. Louis	1:00
Oct. 16	Houston	8:30*
Oct. 23	Dallas	4:05
Oct. 30	BYE	
Nov. 6	at Arizona	4:05
Nov. 13	St. Louis	4:15
Nov. 20	at San Francisco	4:05
Nov. 27	N.Y. Giants	4:15
Dec. 5	at Philadelphia	9:00* (Mon)
Dec. 11	San Francisco	4:05
Dec. 18	at Tennessee	1:00
Dec. 24	Indianapolis	4:15 (Sat)
Jan. 1	at Green Bay	4:15*

*nationally televised game, all times are EST

Postseason
Wild Card Weekend–January 7-8   Divisional Playoffs–January 14-15   Conference Championships–Sunday, January 22   Super Bowl XL–February 5, Fords Field in Detroit

AFC East

Buffalo
Sept. 11	Houston	1:00
Sept. 18	at Tampa Bay	1:00
Sept. 25	Atlanta	1:00
Oct. 2	at New Orleans	1:00
Oct. 9	Miami	1:00
Oct. 16	N.Y. Jets	4:15
Oct. 23	at Oakland	4:15
Oct. 30	at New England	8:30*
Nov. 6	BYE	
Nov. 13	Kansas City	1:00
Nov. 20	at San Diego	4:15
Nov. 27	Carolina	1:00
Dec. 4	at Miami	1:00
Dec. 11	New England	1:00
Dec. 17	Denver	8:30* (Sat)
Dec. 24	at Cincinnati	1:00 (Sat)
Jan. 1	at N.Y. Jets	1:00

Miami
Sept. 11	Denver	1:00
Sept. 18	at N.Y. Jets	4:15
Sept. 25	Carolina	1:00
Oct. 2	BYE	
Oct. 9	at Buffalo	1:00
Oct. 16	at Tampa Bay	1:00
Oct. 23	Kansas City	1:00
Oct. 30	at New Orleans	1:00
Nov. 6	Atlanta	1:00
Nov. 13	New England	1:00
Nov. 20	at Cleveland	1:00
Nov. 27	at Oakland	4:05
Dec. 4	Buffalo	1:00
Dec. 11	at San Diego	4:15
Dec. 18	N.Y. Jets	1:00
Dec. 24	Tennessee	1:00 (Sat)
Jan. 1	at New England	1:00

New England
Sept. 8	Oakland	9:00* (Thur)
Sept. 18	at Carolina	1:00
Sept. 25	at Pittsburgh	4:15*
Oct. 2	San Diego	1:00
Oct. 9	at Atlanta	1:00
Oct. 16	at Denver	4:15*
Oct. 23	BYE	
Oct. 30	Buffalo	8:30*
Nov. 7	Indianapolis	9:00* (Mon)
Nov. 13	at Miami	1:00
Nov. 20	New Orleans	1:00
Nov. 27	at Kansas City	1:00
Dec. 4	N.Y. Jets	4:15*
Dec. 11	at Buffalo	1:00
Dec. 17	Tampa Bay	1:30* (Sat)
Dec. 26	at N.Y. Jets	9:00* (Mon)
Jan. 1	Miami	1:00

New York Jets
Sept. 11	at Kansas City	1:00
Sept. 18	Miami	4:15
Sept. 25	Jacksonville	1:00
Oct. 2	at Baltimore	4:05
Oct. 9	Tampa Bay	1:00
Oct. 16	at Buffalo	4:15
Oct. 24	at Atlanta	9:00* (Mon)
Oct. 30	Oakland	
Nov. 6	San Diego	1:00
Nov. 13	at Carolina	4:05
Nov. 20	at Denver	4:15*
Nov. 27	New Orleans	8:30*
Dec. 4	at New England	4:15*
Dec. 11	Oakland	1:00
Dec. 18	at Miami	1:00
Dec. 26	New England	9:00* (Mon)
Jan. 1	Buffalo	1:00

AFC North

Ravens
Sept. 11	Indianapolis	8:30*
Sept. 18	at Tennessee	1:00
Sept. 25	BYE	
Oct. 2	N.Y. Jets	4:05
Oct. 9	at Detroit	1:00
Oct. 16	Cleveland	1:00
Oct. 23	at Chicago	4:15
Oct. 31	at Pittsburgh	9:00* (Mon)
Nov. 6	Cincinnati	1:00
Nov. 13	at Jacksonville	1:00
Nov. 20	Pittsburgh	4:15
Nov. 27	at Cincinnati	1:00
Dec. 4	Houston	1:00
Dec. 11	at Denver	4:15
Dec. 19	Green Bay	9:00* (Mon)
Dec. 25	Minnesota	8:30*
Jan. 1	at Cleveland	1:00

Cincinnati
Sept. 11	at Cleveland	1:00
Sept. 18	Minnesota	1:00
Sept. 25	at Chicago	1:00
Oct. 2	Houston	1:00
Oct. 9	at Jacksonville	8:30*
Oct. 16	at Tennessee	1:00
Oct. 23	Pittsburgh	1:00
Oct. 30	Green Bay	1:00
Nov. 6	at Baltimore	1:00
Nov. 13	BYE	
Nov. 20	Indianapolis	1:00
Nov. 27	Baltimore	1:00
Dec. 4	at Pittsburgh	1:00
Dec. 11	Cleveland	1:00
Dec. 18	at Detroit	4:05
Dec. 24	Buffalo	1:00 (Sat)
Jan. 1	at Kansas City	1:00

Cleveland
Sept. 11	Cincinnati	1:00
Sept. 18	at Green Bay	4:15*
Sept. 25	at Indianapolis	1:00
Oct. 2	BYE	
Oct. 9	Chicago	1:00
Oct. 16	at Baltimore	1:00
Oct. 23	Detroit	1:00
Oct. 30	at Houston	1:00
Nov. 6	Tennessee	1:00
Nov. 13	at Pittsburgh	8:30*
Nov. 20	Miami	1:00
Nov. 27	at Minnesota	1:00
Dec. 4	Jacksonville	1:00
Dec. 11	at Cincinnati	1:00
Dec. 18	at Oakland	4:05
Dec. 24	Pittsburgh	1:00 (Sat)
Jan. 1	Baltimore	1:00

Pittsburgh
Sept. 11	Tennessee	1:00
Sept. 18	at Houston	1:00
Sept. 25	New England	4:15*
Oct. 2	BYE	
Oct. 10	at San Diego	9:00* (Mon)
Oct. 16	Jacksonville	1:00
Oct. 23	at Cincinnati	1:00
Oct. 31	Baltimore	9:00* (Mon)
Nov. 6	at Green Bay	4:15*
Nov. 13	Cleveland	8:30*
Nov. 20	at Baltimore	4:15
Nov. 28	at Indianapolis	9:00* (Mon)
Dec. 4	Cincinnati	1:00
Dec. 11	Chicago	1:00
Dec. 18	at Minnesota	1:00
Dec. 24	at Cleveland	1:00
Jan. 1	Detroit	1:00

AFC South

Houston
Sept. 11	at Buffalo	1:00
Sept. 18	Pittsburgh	1:00
Sept. 25	BYE	
Oct. 2	at Cincinnati	1:00
Oct. 9	Minnesota	1:00
Oct. 16	at Seattle	8:30*
Oct. 23	Indianapolis	1:00
Oct. 30	Cleveland	1:00
Nov. 6	at Jacksonville	1:00
Nov. 13	at Indianapolis	1:00
Nov. 20	Kansas City	8:30*
Nov. 27	St. Louis	1:00
Dec. 4	at Baltimore	1:00
Dec. 11	at Tennessee	1:00
Dec. 18	Arizona	1:00
Dec. 24	Jacksonville	1:00 (Sat)
Jan. 1	at San Francisco	4:05

Indianapolis
Sept. 11	at Baltimore	8:30*
Sept. 18	Jacksonville	1:00
Sept. 25	Cleveland	1:00
Oct. 2	at Tennessee	1:00
Oct. 9	at San Francisco	4:05
Oct. 17	St. Louis	9:00* (Mon)
Oct. 23	at Houston	1:00
Oct. 30	BYE	
Nov. 7	at New England	9:00* (Mon)
Nov. 13	Houston	1:00
Nov. 20	at Cincinnati	1:00
Nov. 28	Pittsburgh	9:00* (Mon)
Dec. 4	Tennessee	1:00
Dec. 11	at Jacksonville	1:00
Dec. 18	San Diego	1:00
Dec. 24	at Seattle	4:15
Jan. 1	Arizona	1:00

Jacksonville
Sept. 11	Seattle	1:00
Sept. 18	at Indianapolis	1:00
Sept. 25	at N.Y. Jets	1:00
Oct. 2	Denver	1:00
Oct. 9	Cincinnati	8:30*
Oct. 16	at Pittsburgh	1:00
Oct. 23	BYE	
Oct. 30	at St. Louis	1:00
Nov. 6	Houston	1:00
Nov. 13	Baltimore	1:00
Nov. 20	at Tennessee	1:00
Nov. 27	at Arizona	4:05
Dec. 4	at Cleveland	1:00
Dec. 11	Indianapolis	1:00
Dec. 18	San Francisco	1:00
Dec. 24	at Houston	1:00 (Sat)
Jan. 1	Tennessee	4:05

Tennessee
Sept. 11	at Pittsburgh	1:00
Sept. 18	Baltimore	1:00
Sept. 25	at St. Louis	1:00
Oct. 2	Indianapolis	1:00
Oct. 9	at Houston	1:00
Oct. 16	Cincinnati	1:00
Oct. 23	at Arizona	4:15
Oct. 30	Oakland	1:00
Nov. 6	at Cleveland	1:00
Nov. 13	BYE	
Nov. 20	Jacksonville	1:00
Nov. 27	San Francisco	1:00
Dec. 4	at Indianapolis	1:00
Dec. 11	Houston	1:00
Dec. 18	Seattle	1:00
Dec. 24	at Miami	1:00 (Sat)
Jan. 1	at Jacksonville	4:05

AFC West

Denver
Sept. 11	at Miami	1:00
Sept. 18	San Diego	4:15
Sept. 26	Kansas City	9:00* (Mon)
Oct. 2	at Jacksonville	1:00
Oct. 9	Washington	4:15
Oct. 16	New England	4:15*
Oct. 23	at N.Y. Giants	4:15*
Oct. 30	Philadelphia	4:15*
Nov. 6	BYE	
Nov. 13	at Oakland	4:05
Nov. 20	N.Y. Jets	4:15*
Nov. 24	at Dallas	4:15* (Thur)
Dec. 4	at Kansas City	4:15
Dec. 11	Baltimore	4:15
Dec. 17	at Buffalo	8:30* (Sat)
Dec. 24	Oakland	4:15* (Sat)
Dec. 31	at San Diego	4:30* (Sat)

Kansas City
Sept. 11	N.Y. Jets	1:00
Sept. 18	at Oakland	8:30*
Sept. 26	at Denver	9:00* (Mon)
Oct. 2	Philadelphia	1:00
Oct. 9	BYE	
Oct. 16	Washington	1:00
Oct. 23	at Miami	1:00
Oct. 30	at San Diego	4:05
Nov. 6	Oakland	1:00
Nov. 13	at Buffalo	1:00
Nov. 20	at Houston	8:30*
Nov. 27	New England	1:00
Dec. 4	Denver	4:15
Dec. 11	at Dallas	4:15*
Dec. 17	at N.Y. Giants	5:00* (Sat)
Dec. 24	San Diego	1:00 (Sat)
Jan. 1	Cincinnati	1:00

Oakland
Sept. 8	at New England	9:00* (Thur)
Sept. 18	Kansas City	8:30*
Sept. 25	at Philadelphia	1:00
Oct. 2	Dallas	4:15*
Oct. 9	BYE	
Oct. 16	San Diego	4:15
Oct. 23	Buffalo	4:15
Oct. 30	at Tennessee	1:00
Nov. 6	at Kansas City	1:00
Nov. 13	Denver	4:05
Nov. 20	at Washington	1:00
Nov. 27	Miami	4:05
Dec. 4	at San Diego	8:30*
Dec. 11	at New York Jets	1:00
Dec. 18	Cleveland	4:05
Dec. 24	at Denver	4:15* (Sat)
Dec. 31	N.Y. Giants	8* (Sat)

San Diego
Sept. 11	Dallas	4:15*
Sept. 18	at Denver	4:15
Sept. 25	N.Y. Giants	8:30*
Oct. 2	at New England	1:00
Oct. 10	Pittsburgh	9:00* (Mon)
Oct. 16	at Oakland	4:15
Oct. 23	at Philadelphia	1:00
Oct. 30	Kansas City	4:05
Nov. 6	at N.Y. Jets	1:00
Nov. 13	BYE	
Nov. 20	Buffalo	4:15
Nov. 27	at Washington	1:00
Dec. 4	Oakland	8:30*
Dec. 11	Miami	4:15
Dec. 18	at Indianapolis	1:00
Dec. 24	at Kansas City	1:00 (Sat)
Dec. 31	Denver	4:30* (Sat)

*nationally televised game, all times are EST

Postseason

Wild Card Weekend–January 7-8   Divisional Playoffs–January 14-15   Conference Championships–Sunday, January 22   Super Bowl XL–February 5, Fords Field in Detroit

What Ever Happened To ...

When fans watch their favorite players compete on Sundays, they are living in the blissful moment, enjoying the first-class skills of some of the country's premier athletes. They root for a group of guys who make up a team, and they follow their stories each year as if they belonged to the royal family. Memories are formed, particularly when a team enjoys success. As time goes on, special players begin to find their way into people's hearts, and before anyone notices, fans subconsciously regard these athletes as something like close friends, without ever actually having known them.

But what about the key players who do not occupy the limelight during their careers—but, rather, carry the title of "role player"? Fans love these players while they are around, but once they're gone, they are often forgotten. They do not have enormous retirement press conferences, their numbers are never enshrined in a ring of honor, and they are very rarely seen on a Sunday morning pregame show. They often register good—even Pro Bowl–level— seasons during their careers, but teams don't venerate their play after they hang 'em up.

Instead, these men simply fade out of the league and quietly join the rest of society in going about their lives. Every once in a while a fan will see a clip from an old game on ESPN2 or pick up on a vaguely familiar name that rings a bell. Somehow, in some way, these role players are randomly remembered for a brief moment, and the comment that always accompanies this moment is: "Oh yeah! I remember (insert name)! Whatever happened to him?"

Believe it or not, these players do not simply cease to exist once their playing days are over. In fact, many of them go on to lead unique and interesting lives away from the game. Here are seven players whom fans can stop wondering about.

Jay Novacek, Tight End (1985–95)

When remembering the Dallas Cowboys dynasty of the early 1990s, most people first think of the triplets: Aikman, Emmitt, and Irvin. But few will deny the significance of tight end Jay Novacek. Novacek spent the first five years of his NFL career playing for the Los Angeles Rams and the Phoenix Cardinals, before joining the Boys in 1990. During his time with Dallas, he made five consecutive Pro Bowls and won three Super Bowls. Due to recurring back problems, Novacek retired after his third Super Bowl in 1995, which marked the beginning of the slow and painful end to the Cowboys' dominance. Today Novacek is a spokesman for Sport Clips, a male-haircut chain. He owns three Sport Clips in the Dallas–Fort Worth area.

If it is surprising to see a classic hard-nosed Texan in the haircut industry, do not be alarmed—Novacek also runs his Upper 84 Ranch, which is located near Brady, Nebraska, not far from his hometown of Gothenburg. From there he distributes precooked Upper 84 Brand Beef to grocery stores like Wal-Mart and Kroger.

Novacek has not completely left the game of football behind him. Last year, he spent time working with current Cowboys tight end Jason Witten. He has also continued the Jay Novacek Football Camp for Kids in Commerce, Texas—something that he has been doing since 1991.

Ken Harvey, Linebacker (1988–98)

Former Arizona Cardinals and Washington Redskins linebacker Ken Harvey has made a nice transition from being a four-time NFL Pro Bowler to being a full-time retired NFL player. Harvey has dedicated his post-football life to improving his community and the lives of young people. He has become a children's author, writing books such as *Life in the Fridge* and *When Chocolate Milk Moved In*, among others, designed for kids age eight and under.

Harvey is currently working for Ikoya, a television production company in Virginia. Harvey has also done some work with Ikoya in creating children's programs. When he is not writing stories or working with cameras, Harvey is spending time making appearances around the D.C. community, acting as a spokesman for drug awareness programs. He has given speeches and visited schools; during Red Ribbon Week, he was even a special guest at an antidrug event held at the Pentagon. Harvey has also been involved with the Central Union homeless shelter.

On the football side of things, Harvey has not drifted far from the Redskins organization. He works for Comcast Sports doing the team's postgame shows and is the president of the Washington Redskins Alumni Association.

Steve Atwater, Safety (1989–99)

It may not be fair to classify Steve Atwater as a role player. After all, with two Super Bowl titles and eight Pro Bowls to his name, the man is a legitimate Hall of Fame contender. However, Atwater's final days in the NFL were somewhat inauspicious (say, spending his final season with the New York Jets?), and his retirement, albeit with a ceremonial one-day contract with the Broncos, went fairly unnoticed.

It didn't take Atwater long to move his life in a different direction after his final season in 1999. Atwater moved to Duluth, Georgia (a suburb of Atlanta), and joined Keller Williams Realty in 2000. He is now a full-time real estate professional who specializes in marketing. Atwater works directly with buyers and sellers and is a former HomeVestors franchise owner. In his Realtor bio, he pledges to his clients honest pricing and respect, and strives for hassle-free transactions.

Andre Rison, Wide Receiver (1989–2000)

During his playing days, it was no secret that Andre Rison was a head case. After all, why would a man who had good enough speed and hands to finish his career with over 700 catches and 10,000-plus yards play for seven different clubs? Rison, who was drafted by the Indianapolis Colts, had his best years in Atlanta, where he made four Pro Bowls in five seasons. In 1997 he won a Super Bowl with the Green Bay Packers—but out of disgust for the franchise, he later threw his ring into an unspecified river.

Maybe it should be no surprise that Rison's life after football has been anything but smooth. In fact, Rison still is not technically retired; he has simply been out of the league for four years. After he left the Raiders and became a free agent in 2001, Rison was suspended for four games because of his repeated violations of the league's substance-abuse program. Not wanting to serve his suspension, Rison never signed with a team, which resulted in the unprecedented case of a player dwindling out of the league.

Rison has not dwindled out of the *game*, though. In August of last year, the 37-year-old was a receiver for the CFL Grey Cup Champion Toronto Argonauts, where he made a minimal impact.

Rison's football career may have officially been killed in early January 2005, when he was released from jail, after serving almost a month for failing to pay child support in 2003.

In January, Rison began touring the country, selling his new autobiography, *Wide Open*. Clearly, his playing options these days are anything but.

Merton Hanks, Safety (1991–99)

In December 2004, Redskins running back Clinton Portis was fined a total of $15,000 by the NFL over weeks 13 and 14 for wearing red socks, which differed from the rest of his team's white woolies. The man in charge of dealing with Portis's situation was former San Francisco 49ers safety Merton Hanks.

Hanks, who may have been best known for his awkward "Chicken Dance" celebrations, retired from the NFL after the 1999 season. That year was his only year out of the red and gold,

as he signed off as a Seattle Seahawk. Today he is the NFL's director of uniform compliance, a job that has certainly earned him his share of grief from former teammates. Fines for uniform violations, as one might imagine, are considered by players to be among the league's pettiest disciplinary actions.

Hanks also serves as the NFL's director of consumer products and compliance, which makes him responsible for eliminating copyright infringements on the league's logo. Hanks earned his new gig as a league executive with the help of former 49ers head coach and consultant Bill Walsh and team owner John York. His office is located at the NFL headquarters on Park Avenue in New York City.

Jeff Hostetler, Quarterback (1985–97)

Former NFL quarterback Jeff Hostetler made the Pro Bowl as a member of the Los Angeles Raiders in 1994, but he is most remembered as the backup quarterback who filled in for an injured for Phil Simms in 1990 and led the New York Giants to a Super Bowl XXV victory. Hostetler, who spent the first seven years of his career with New York before joining the Raiders for four, retired in 1997 as a member of the Washington Redskins.

He currently lives in Morgantown, West Virginia (the site of West Virginia University, where he went to college), with his wife and three high-school-age sons, Jason, Justin, and Tyler. In an effort to spend time with his kids, Hostetler is the passing coordinator at University High, where Justin, a sophomore, is the starting quarterback and Jason, a senior, is a receiver/defensive back.

Hostetler also keeps busy in the business world. He owns Hostetler Bagels and does both retail and wholesale business. And though bagels can be exciting to some people, his greatest passion

is building houses. Hostetler owns a 40-acre tract in Morgantown and intends to build and sell eight spec homes on 3 of those acres. His interest in architecture has driven him to design and build his own home, as well as homes for his brother-in-law, sister-in-law, and father. Hostetler, of course, has some help with the construction, but he runs the equipment, ranging from bulldozers to backhoes.

Or So We Thought

The NFL is by far the most unpredictable league in all of sports. In late summer, the projecting of the league's outcome seems so simple. However, things never turn out as expected.

Here is a look back at last season, with a side-by-side comparison of what NFL experts and fans assumed the league would be like prior to the start of training camps and the shape into which the league actually wound up contorting by season's end.

NFC EAST

The Pregame Prognostication

The Eagles added Terrell Owens and Jevon Kearse, making them the clear-cut favorite in the NFC. The Cowboys had high expectations under Bill Parcells, particularly on offense, where quarterback Quincy Carter appeared to be settling in for another possible playoff season. Washington welcomed back Joe Gibbs, who was expected to bring about positive changes on offense. The defense, with a lone start in LaVar Arrington, was thought to hinder the team. In New York, the only big news was the arrival of rookie Eli Manning.

The Postgame Wrap-up

The Eagles do, in fact, live up to the hype, although their journey to the Super Bowl is not without some late-season bumps in the road.

Dallas shockingly cuts Carter shortly before training camp, citing unaccountability from their quarterback. Many believe Carter's drug problems are his ticket out of Valley Ranch. Nevertheless, the Cowboys attack the season with 40-year-old Vinny Testaverde at quarterback and sign longtime Titan Eddie George late in the summer as their new running back.

The Skins struggle mightily on offense, while Arrington and over half of the defense miss significant time with injuries. Somehow, Washington finds a load of hidden talent down in the depths of their roster, resulting in the third-ranked defense in yards.

Injuries, like the knee problem that Ravens tackle Jonathan Ogden experienced in 2004, can quickly shift the powers in the NFL.

The Giants begin the season 5-4 behind Kurt Warner, before placing the responsibility on Manning and finishing 6-10.

NFC NORTH

The Pregame Prognostication

The Packers and Vikings were to fight for the division, although the Lions, with their young receiving core, were viewed as a team that could find some unexpected success. Chicago had a new coach in Lovie Smith and, thus, new hope for '04.

The Postgame Wrap-up

The Packers and Vikings *do* slug it out to the end, although neither team becomes the Super Bowl contender as so many expected. Green Bay stuns the football world by starting 1-4, while Minnesota once again hits the wall late in the season.

The Lions look promising early on, but receiver Charles Rodgers suffers another season-ending injury, this time to the collarbone.

And those hopeful Bears? They lose their starting quarterback (Rex Grossman) to an ACL tear in week 3 and never establish an identity.

NFC SOUTH

The Pregame Prognostication

Both the Falcons and the Buccaneers had made significant changes over the offseason, while the Saints figured to at least have a chance at some wins. However, all three teams had to begin the year under the shadow of the defending NFC champion Panthers, a team that many saw as a lock for success, thanks to their defense, Stephen Davis and the ground game, and the emergence of the receiving attack, headed by the speedy Steve Smith.

The Postgame Wrap-up

The Panthers watch their season go up in flames as both Davis and Smith are injured and lost for the year well before November. Adding to the struggles, Carolina also loses star defensive tackle Kris Jenkins and backup running back DeShaun Foster. They start 1-7. The Falcons go from 5-11 in '03 to 11-5 in '04, thanks to not only Michael Vick but a suddenly potent defense under first-year head coach Jim Mora, Jr. Tampa Bay suffers ongoing changes at the quarterback, running back, and receiver positions, while New Orleans finishes their usual 8-8, despite an *unusual* late-season surge.

NFC WEST

The Pregame Prognostication

This division was Seattle's from the start, thanks to *their* talent, and the *lack* of talent in San Francisco and Arizona. The Niners spent all offseason negotiating with star linebacker Julian Peterson, Arizona banked on developing young players, and the Rams looked to rebound and make a Super Bowl run behind a hopefully resurgent Marshall Faulk.

The Postgame Wrap-up

The Seahawks start 3-0, but are inconsistent from there. At 8-8, they barely win the division and are immediately bounced from the playoffs by the Rams, who do just enough to finish 8-8 themselves. By the way, the man starting for the Hawks at receiver late in the year: Jerry Rice.

In St. Louis, Faulk is noticeably slower and all but replaced by Steven Jackson at season's end. The Niners wind up essentially losing the $6.1 million that they spent on Peterson, because he tears his left Achilles tendon in October. As for those "building for the future" plans in the desert, injuries strike at the running back and receiver positions, plus there is a quarterback controversy all year long. The result is an offense that is driven by 35-year-old Emmitt Smith.

AFC EAST

The Pregame Prognostication

The Patriots were set to defend their title, although there were questions about the acquisition of running back Corey Dillon. The team many thought would be New England's stiffest competition in the division was the Miami Dolphins, behind a solid defense and an offense that featured Ricky Williams with David Boston. Both the Bills and the Jets were thought to be little more than divisional sidebars in the minds of many.

The Postgame Wrap-up

The Pats forcefully defend their title and claim a third Super Bowl in four years. Dillon ends up being a huge factor on offense and a great presence in the locker room.

Miami, on the other hand, sees their season crumble in July, when Williams abruptly retires and Boston promptly hurts his knee and is put on injured reserve. Hurricanes reshape the team's schedule in September, plus head coach Dave Wannstedt eventually resigns midway through the season.

Both the Bills and the Jets are contenders late in the year, thanks to the unexpected contributions of running backs Willis McGahee and the resurgence of Curtis Martin, respectively. In fact, at 31, Martin, who is on the "downside" of his career, actually wins the NFL rushing title.

AFC NORTH

The Pregame Prognostication

The AFC North was thought to be a lackluster division that would easily be headed by Jamal Lewis and the Baltimore Ravens. Cleveland was a team that had head coach Butch Davis looking to rebound behind a new passing game that featured Jeff Garcia and Kellen Winslow. The Steelers were considered a long shot after a 6-10 season in 2003, and Cincinnati was a bit of a mystery.

The Postgame Wrap-up

The Ravens never gain their footing, thanks to injuries on offense. The most noteworthy surprise comes when Lewis pleads guilty to facilitating a cocaine deal in 2000. The plea earns him a two-game suspension in the middle of the season, which is to be followed by a sprained ankle.

In Cleveland, Winslow breaks his leg early in the year, Garcia alienates many in the organization and becomes the starter on the second string, while Davis ultimately resigns late in the season.

By the way, the hapless Steelers are led by rookie quarterback Ben Roethlisberger and finish 15-1, reaching the AFC title game. Cincy ends up being the only team that makes sense, posting an 8-8 record.

AFC SOUTH

The Pregame Prognostication

The Colts had the offense and, thus, the upper hand on the rest of the division. Both Houston and Jacksonville were thought to be lower-tier teams with potential, while the Titans, behind veteran leaders Steve McNair and Eddie George, were believed to be Indy's toughest competition.

The Postgame Wrap-up

Things go pretty much to plan in this division, although nobody can foresee the drama that goes into building the conclusion. MVP Peyton Manning and his three receivers, all of whom rewrite the record books, lead Indy's offense.

Houston is a very vanilla squad that finishes 7-9, while the Jaguars, falling just shy of the playoffs, become everybody's favorite underdog, thanks to their knack for winning tight games in dramatic fashion.

The Titans cut George before the season opens and go with rookie Chris Brown. Early on, McNair is mediocre at best, before missing most of the second half with an assortment of injuries. Things simply never get rolling in Tennessee.

AFC WEST

The Pregame Prognostication

The Kansas City Chiefs had a prolific offense and a new philosophy on defense, which meant that the expectations were for a Lombardi Trophy and nothing less. The Broncos had just lost Clinton Portis and were looking for one of their running backs to step up. Oakland was counting on resurgence from Rich Gannon and his receivers, Tim Brown and Jerry Rice. Perhaps the only guarantee in the entire league heading into training camp was that San Diego, behind rookie quarterback Phillip Rivers, would be the worst team in the AFC.

The Postgame Wrap-up

The Chiefs defense is still terrible, and the offense takes a small step backward. Denver makes the playoffs behind the running of . . . backup fullback and fifth-string tailback Ruben Droughns.

The Raiders wind up starting Kerry Collins after Gannon goes down in week 3. Brown ends up in Tampa Bay, and Rice finishes the year in the Pacific Northwest with the Seahawks.

The winner of the division turns out to be the pathetic Chargers, thanks to the Pro Bowl season of Drew Brees. Brees's chance to start comes about only because Rivers holds out throughout most of training camp.

Isn't it funny how things turn out sometimes?

Generation Gap

It is nearly impossible to be a true football purist these days, simply because the game is constantly renovating its rules, its business approach, and its presentation. To get a good handle on how the sport has evolved over the years, I sat down with former Green Bay Packer Jerry Kramer and his son, current Atlanta Falcon Jordan Kramer.

Together, the Kramers offer a unique illustration of the game of football. During his 11-year career in Green Bay (1958–68), Jerry, 69, became one of the most heralded guards in the game. He made the All-Pro Team five times, competed in five NFL championships, including the first two Super Bowls, and, of course, paved the way on the goal line for Bart Starr in the epic Ice Bowl against the Dallas Cowboys in 1967. With so many experiences to refer to, Jerry offers the "former star player" angle to a discussion about the sport.

Jordan, 25, represents a side of football that is so often overlooked. A linebacker out of the University of Idaho, he signed as an undrafted free agent rookie for the San Diego Chargers in 2003, before being cut prior to training camp. He soon joined the Tennessee Titans, where he spent two years alternating between serving on the practice squad and being on the active roster as a special-teams player. This past year, he signed a one-year deal with the Falcons, hoping for an opportunity not only to make his mark on special teams, but also to earn live game repetitions as a linebacker.

The Kramers are two athletes of the same bloodline, but they have more in common than DNA—they are great examples of the professional football player. Both men are extremely bright and judicious and each is well spoken, especially when it comes to discussing the game they love.

Upon sitting down with the Kramers, I anticipated asking a few general questions about football and fielding two distinct sets of answers. While this panned out to an extent, what I soon discovered was that the *game* of football has changed, but the *men who play the game* have not.

Money

Everyone, outside of the 300 inhabitants of the island Tristan da Cunha and those few individuals who still follow the teachings of Ralph Waldo Emerson in a literal sense, knows that the financial nature of the NFL has drastically altered over the past 40 years. Everybody knows about today's salary cap and signing bonuses, but Jordan points out that before all this, it starts with getting drafted or not getting drafted. There isn't a lot of bargaining in contracts for young players, because the system operates under a recognized status quo, which is based upon one's draft position. A player's salary is almost always determined by what the player who was drafted in the same spot the previous year made. Furthermore, contracts usually have a duration of three years, with a few minor exceptions here and there. Jordan points out that rookies drafted in the first three rounds have much more room for negotiating incentives in their deals, whereas lower-round players come away with very limited, or sometimes zero, incentives.

In 2003, Jordan's free agent salary was the league minimum: $225,000. This information can be obtained by simply signing on to USAToday.com and searching player salaries.

When Jerry entered the league, he brought in a total salary of $8,000 his first year. However, it is unknown how his figures compared to those of his teammates.

"We were not allowed to discuss contracts," Jerry says. "We were told by the powers that be that we couldn't talk to one another about how much we were making and most of the guys would not discuss contracts. Other players would not tell you what they were making, so there were no published figures. You had no agents and if the coach told you that you were the highest paid lineman in the league, you had to believe him." Jerry also says he believes that the money that drives today's game prevents players from forming the kind of close bond that he and his Packer teammates enjoyed. "We were [with the Packers] a short period of time and we knew we would have to go get a job and go to work and do something with the rest of our lives. [Today's players] can be set for life if they take care of their money. . . . They don't ever have to do anything. So they're a little more independent."

> "We were told by the powers that be that we couldn't talk to one another about how much we were making. . . . Other players would not tell you what they were making, so there were no published figures. You had no agents and if the coach told you that you were the highest paid lineman in the league, you had to believe him."
> —Jerry Kramer

Media

Jordan's former Titan team knows all about the media. In the most recent offseason, there was widespread coverage by the surfeit of newspapers, television stations, and radio stations in the Nashville area about the DUI arrest of safety Tank Williams. There was also plenty of coverage of the domestic assault arrest of the team's former cornerback and current Baltimore Raven, Samari Rolle, and the domestic assault arrest of offensive tackle Brad Hopkins. Not to mention that, thanks to outlets like ESPN, *Sports Illustrated*, and the bloggers' beloved World Wide Web, *national* attention was given to all three incidents, as well.

"In our day there were three media guys," says Jerry, emphasizing the sharp contrast to the era in which his son plays. "There was a Milwaukee newspaper guy, a Green Bay newspaper guy, and maybe a radio or television guy that traveled with the team. They ate with the team, drank with the team, and damn well better not *criticize* the team or anybody *on* the team." Jerry points out the special services that the journalists—who connected the players to the public—would provide. "You'd say all kinds of cuss words and they'd clean up your verbiage. They'd make it so it didn't sound bad and they didn't report things [such as] tickets or DUI's." Quite a stark contrast to today's world of athletes on Court TV and airwaves filled with bleeps on a regular basis.

Rules

We like to believe that football is football and nothing is going to alter that. However, the NFL is sailing on the same ship as midwestern weather, interest rates, and Michael Jackson's face: It is always changing. Both Jordan and Jerry have opinions for what they would like to see improved in the league.

"I would do away with the five-yard no-contact rule," says Jordan, without hesitation and perhaps showing some bias. After all, he's a linebacker and is most affected by the regulation. "The game is becoming faster and faster because the passing game has become much more through the rule changes. . . . [It] is becoming more high scoring."

Jordan believes the sport will ultimately see smaller and quicker players rise to the top, because of the numerous laws against contact in the league today.

Jerry notices a difference in play that is caused by today's rules, as well. "[The illegal contact rule] was an innovation to try to help the wide receivers and the passing game," he acknowledges. However, perhaps showing a little bias himself, he notices how much easier it is for an offensive lineman to pass-block in today's game. "The offensive linemen using their hands, they can hold on every play now as long as they don't get outside the player's body. That is a huge change to help the passing game," he says. Jerry goes on to asseverate, "They're screwing with a game that has had a long and illustrious history and I don't think they know what the hell they're doing." The smile on his face indicates that his anger may be in jesting exaggeration, but his opinion on the topic certainly is not.

Jerry Kramer played 11 seasons for Vince Lombardi and the Green Bay Packers, earning five All-Pro honors and a pair of Super Bowl titles.

Playbooks

In visiting with Jordan, one quickly picks up on how strongly he believes that a player's familiarity with his team's game plan is the most critical element for success. However, a player's knowledge of a team's offensive—or in Jordan's case, defensive—scheme isn't as simple as it appears in video games.

Jordan says that in reality a player's relationship with his team's playbook should be a short one. "You learn it during the offseason, you learn as much as you can, and then you move on because the season is full of adjustments. There are new schemes and new ideas, especially when you have injuries . . . so you have to be ready to move on." While with Tennessee, Jordan estimates that his playbook consisted of over 100 pages. All together, there were eight different defenses that he was obligated to learn.

Making matters even tougher was knowing that in all likelihood, he would not use the information come Sunday. He would either be watching the game in street clothes from the sideline or, if things went well, competing on special teams—a role that the speedy Jordan has proven to be very good at thus far. During the week, Jordan's familiarity with the Titan playbook was also mixed with his knowledge of the opposing team. Being on the practice squad often means that he would serve as the "opponent" in practice, mimicking the other team's style of play so his teammates could spend the week adjusting.

Jerry recalls the famous Lombardi playbook, which became known for, among other things, the power sweep. "We had a fairly limited set of plays and we really didn't change as much from year to year. We ran the same plays my first year with Coach Lombardi that we ran my ninth year with Coach Lombardi. We focused a lot more on execution and limiting our mistakes than

Jordan Kramer is in his third season in the NFL and his first with the Atlanta Falcons. He hopes to make the 53-man roster as a linebacker this fall.

"That whole moral victory thing, that doesn't mean [crap]."
—Jordan Kramer

we did on trying to outthink people and be cute."

The Packers had around 40 running plays and 12 variations of pass blocking, with other variations from week to week.

The Players

While much has changed from Jerry's days to Jordan's days, one thing that seems to have remained constant over the years is the attitude of the typical football player. "I think the most important element for winning would be basically for everyone to have a common understanding, to be on the same page," says Jordan.

"The most important element for winning is the attitude of the team, especially the players," adds Jerry. "Are they willing to subjugate their individual needs to win? Their individual egos to win? Put the team first?"

As with all football players, sacrifice is a common theme with the Kramers. Jordan speaks frequently of the importance of a player staying healthy—after all, this past season he, himself, suffered a hamstring injury and was ineffective for most of the early fall.

Jerry knows all about injuries, as well. He has had 22 operations in his life. He recalls a time when his teammate, defensive end Lionel Aldridge, broke a small bone in his leg. "He was out trying to run on it about 10 days later and Coach said, 'Aldridge, run on that leg! The bone you broke is not a weight bearing bone, you don't even need that damn bone in your leg!' "

Jordan is quick to react to this, saying, "The thing is, with my guys, they're so much more worried with potential down-the-road stuff, potential end-of-the-season stuff. At the beginning of the season, guys are real timid. If it's questionable, they'll probably put them out. There's just so much money wrapped up in so many players. There's a hell of a lot more concern for longevity," he says.

Although trainers and coaches may try to protect their million-dollar athletes, both Jerry and Jordan agree on one thing: Ultimately, it is the player's choice to play hurt.

"I didn't want to let the guys down," Jerry says. "I played with concussions, 103-degree temperatures, diarrhea, vomiting, busted ribs, busted thumb. They [the Packers staff] didn't make me play, I played because I wanted to play and I didn't want to let the guys

"You never accept a loss. Losing is very painful."
—Jerry Kramer

down." "There isn't a worse feeling than sitting there with an injury that feels like maybe you could go but you shouldn't . . . and the other guys are practicing and playing. . . . It's terrible," Jordan says, recalling his own frustrations.

The agony of defeat is another topic that all football players can relate to. Both Kramers agree that the effects of losing depend upon the game and the situation, but both also agree that losing is never all right.

"You never accept a loss. You're a competitor, you're trying to be a champion, trying to be a winner. Losing is very painful. You're gonna get beat once in a while, but you're never gonna like it," says Jerry, without blinking or wavering an ounce.

"That whole moral victory thing, that doesn't mean [crap]," Jordan states, looking at his father, who exhibits a tacit agreement.

This year, Jerry will continue to golf and make promotional appearances, serving as an icon of those great Lombardi teams. Jordan will be in Atlanta, working to make the 53-man roster and further his career. But wherever they go, both men's souls are tied to football. The game will continue to develop in the public setting, the rules will repeatedly be adjusted in future years, and many more advances that are yet to be fathomed will take place. But football players will always be football players.

Jordan's salary rookie year: $225,000
Jerry's salary rookie year: $8,000

1964
AFL—8 teams, 26 draft picks per team
NFL—14 teams, 20 draft picks per team
NFL—total games played: 98
   Average attendance: 46,562
Television revenue: $14 million

2004
NFL—32 teams, estimated 7 draft picks per team
   Total games played: 256
   Average attendance: 67,463
   Television revenue: $2.2 billion

Remembering Reggie

On December 26, 2004, the world lost a great man when Reggie White—aka "the Minister of Defense"—passed away at his home in Cornelius, North Carolina, at the age of 43. Doctors believe that White's years of suffering from sarcoidosis, a respiratory disease in which inflamed cells attack organs (namely, the lungs), was the cause of death.

On the field, White, who played 15 seasons in the NFL with the Philadelphia Eagles, Green Bay Packers, and Carolina Panthers, will be remembered most for being the greatest pass-rushing defensive lineman of all time. He is second on the career sacks list with 198, and he was the defensive captain on Green Bay's Super Bowl champion team in 1997.

So often when an athlete leaves this world, people are quick to say that he will be remembered much more for the person he was off the field than on the field, regardless of how valid the claim is. However, this could not be any truer than in White's case. In a lot of respects, White had the greatest social impact on the game of all of the players from his era. After spending the first eight years of his career as a key component of Philadelphia's "Gang Green Defense," White left and became the first major African American player to voluntarily join Green Bay. White's decision to move to the small Wisconsin town was a surprise to many. The town of Green Bay at that time was certainly not thought of as a haven for an African American athlete.

White's arrival soon proved this negative image of Green Bay to be false. His addition revived not just the Packers but the entire NFL. He was one of the first players to sign a major multi-million-dollar contract (four years, $17 million) as a free agent, and he showed other players in the league that it was all right to join small-market teams.

During the offseason, White expended a great deal of effort on mentoring inner-city youth. He also was known for being a very involved father to his son, Jeremy, and daughter, Jecolia.

White's most indelible mark on the league may very well stem from his oft-publicized religious faith. White, who was an ordained minister, spent much of his playing career preaching his belief in God. No person ever accused him of imposing his religious views on anyone, though it was White who helped broaden the acceptance of prayer on the field and in the locker room.

After his retirement from the NFL, White's life began to shift in a different direction. He became entangled in controversy after he made several derisive remarks regarding homosexuals. The problem kept him from being offered a job as an analyst with CBS. Ultimately, White opted to return to the NFL for a brief and fairly uneventful stint with the Carolina Panthers.

White's religious life took some little-known, yet dramatic, turns after his second and final retirement. Before his death, White became discontented with people asking him to preach because of who he was as a football player rather than what he was saying as a man of God. He became concerned that the message he had been preaching and following for so long was skewed through translation, and that he had not learned anything firsthand, accepting the teachings of Christianity without questioning. White therefore learned Hebrew and began to study the Torah. He did not convert to Judaism, although his quest for the truth led him to Israel, where he continued his study. At the time of his death, White was studying religion and reading from the Torah for up to 10 hours a day. His search brought him answers, and his wife has stated that her husband died with the religious affiliation of "believer."

With White's untimely passing, the football world is left to mourn a man who touched so many people, both directly and indirectly. Football fans will miss the calm and raspy voice of one of the greatest defensive players of all time. White's death should not be a threat to anyone, but rather a peaceful reminder of just how special the world is. It is fair to say this world is special because of individuals like Reggie White.

Far too often the public hears the negative stories about professional athletes, creating a skewed perception that all sports figures are simply overpaid, selfish, out-of-control, lawbreaking jerks. Nothing could be further from the truth. In searching for stories about the positive impacts that players make on their communities, one quickly realizes that the good far outweighs the bad in the NFL.

The Benoit Citizen Hall of Fame is a select class of professional football players who have gone the extra yard in making a difference in their community.

Players who are selected to the Citizen Hall of Fame participate in extensive charity work, contributing their money and, perhaps even more important, their time to noble causes. They are active and committed to bettering their society by staying involved in positive programs on a consistent basis and creating new ideas for helping others.

Not only do all members of the Citizen Hall of Fame commit acts of humanitarianism, they also commit the underrated act of living their lives as people of high character who operate with solid values and wholesomeness.

Joe Andruzzi, Cleveland Browns

Andruzzi's commitment to the community is beyond extensive. Overall, Andruzzi, a former Patriot, averages around 50 charitable appearances a year. After September 11, Andruzzi (whose brothers are firefighters in New York City) became extremely active in fund-raising efforts, highlighted by his duties as the spokesman for the New England Association of Fire Marshals.

What is unique about Andruzzi, 29, is that his involvement in helping his community is a family effort. His wife, Jen, is very active in her husband's causes. In 2002 they organized a trip for 200 inner-city children in the Boston area to visit Gillette Stadium and receive Christmas presents. Andruzzi's three young children (all under the age of six) have gained an early insight into the value of sharing by participating in a toy giveaway at a local homeless shelter where Jen volunteers.

In 2003 Andruzzi received the New England Patriots Ron Burton Community Service Award. The award recognized the $100,000-plus that he has raised for the C.J. Buckley Brain Cancer Research Fund at Children's Hospital in Boston. Every year, Andruzzi and his wife host Our Sailing Star Evening to benefit the cancer center. The fund was launched thanks to the Andruzzis' efforts. It is named in honor of C.J. Buckley, a teenager Andruzzi befriended back in 2001, who died of an inoperable brain tumor in December 2002. The Andruzzis reached out to the Buckley family during the young man's treatment.

If only Andruzzi could be so kind to opposing defensive tackles on Sundays.

Peyton Manning, Indianapolis Colts

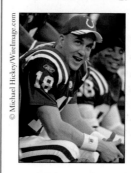

Manning, 29, has created the PeyBack Foundation, whose mission is to promote the future success of disadvantaged youth by assisting programs that provide leadership and growth opportunities to children at risk.

The PeyBack Foundation organizes countless charitable events each year. Some of the highlights include Manning's personal contributions to the PeyBack Classic, which gives high school football players an opportunity to play a charity game in the Louisiana Superdome. The event has raised over $120,000 for high school athletic programs in the New Orleans area, and last year the third annual PeyBack Classic had more than 8,000 participants.

During the Christmas season, Manning himself hosts Holiday Happenings, in which more than 700 needy kids from various Indianapolis agencies are invited to spend a day at the Children's Museum in Indianapolis, with live entertainment, food, and activities. Holiday Happenings also takes place in Knoxville (Manning's college town) and New Orleans (his hometown), touching more than 2,000 kids in all. Manning sponsors a similar event on Thanksgiving, as well.

Manning has also been very active in the Court Appointed Special Advocates (CASA) program, which strives to help neglected and abused children. Other contributions include Peyton's Pals, whereby he provides Colts tickets for underprivileged children; Play It Smart, which combines football and education; and Peyton's Rally at Gasoline Alley, which features a 2.5-mile walk around the Indianapolis Motor Speedway, benefiting the foundation.

This past December, Manning was the recipient of the NFL's Extra Effort Award, for his involvement in the community. Suddenly, 49 touchdown passes no longer seem like Manning's greatest accomplishment.

Class of 1999	*Class of 2000*	*Class of 2001*
Troy Aikman	Tim Brown	Jerome Bettis
Warrick Dunn	Ben Coleman	Derrick Brooks
Doug Flutie	Doug Pelfrey	Cris Carter
Darrell Green	Will Shields	Kurt Warner
Cortez Kennedy	Steve Young	Ted Washington

Class of 2002	*Class of 2003*	*Class of 2004*
Keith Brooking	Troy Vincent	Donnie Edwards
Wali Rainer	Donald Driver	Tony Richardson
New York Giants football team		
New York Jets football team		
Washington Redskins football team		

Acknowledgments

Ryan and John Brassey

When I watch the Academy Awards or the Grammy's, I tend to roll my eyes when I hear the honorees list a bounty of people they'd like to thank, then go on to exclaim that there are too many others, that it's hard to choose, and so on. However, my opinion always changes when the time comes for me to give *my* big thank-you's. It's true—there are too many to properly acknowledge, and someone important is always going to be left out.

With this in mind, let me first clarify that I am *very* thankful for my family—I have the greatest, most supportive parents in the world, I have the best little sister alive, and I am blessed with an outstanding extended family, to whom I am very close. I am also grateful for the countless people who have supported my goals and aspirations over the years, particularly my editor, Mark Tavani, and the people at Random House/Ballantine who have invested so much in *Touchdown* and given me the opportunity to do what I most love.

That said, I have to divert the attention this year to two specific individuals: Ryan and John Brassey. Ryan and John are twin brothers whom I've known well since junior high and who have been my best friends during my high school tenure. The Brassey twins are the most genuine, loyal, and caring friends I have ever had. So often the idea of "best high school buddy" is tossed around with a casual air and an "oh by the way" attitude, but the friendship that these guys provide is so much more than that to me.

The Brassey family has been incredibly supportive of my NFL project over the past couple of years. Not only does Ryan and John's immediate family own several copies of *Touchdown 2003* and *Touchdown 2004* (which were not published nationally), but their grandmother, aunts, uncles, and cousins all own copies as well. This year, the Brassey twins asked me if they could volunteer to help edit *Touchdown 2005*.

I had noticed before that, being the astute gentlemen that they are, Ryan and John had gone through all of *Touchdown 2004* and critiqued every single error that was printed. I figured I might as well have them find the errors *ahead* of time this year. After all, at least some of the embarrassing mistakes that I make would be caught by my close friends, rather than the dignified professionals at Random House.

But I soon realized just how dedicated they were to editing *Touchdown*. Ryan and John read every single page of the book, analyzed every single word that was written, and corrected every single error that they found. The Brasseys did not simply shuffle through pages like proofreaders—the mistakes they corrected and suggestions they offered were incredibly well thought out and helpful. In fact, their edits helped improve the overall quality of the book.

But it wasn't so much Ryan and John's dedication to getting their edits done (although they worked at all hours to accommodate my schedule, whether it was getting up early, doing them at 3:00 A.M., or substituting other assignments to help me out). What is more important to me about the Brasseys and their tie to this book is the genuine concern they had for seeing the project succeed.

They are thoughtfully anxious to see the book become a success. So often, high school kids have friends whom they hang out with and rely on for a good laugh, but the relationships extend little beyond that. Most high schoolers enjoy their friends, but a certain amount of jealousy rests underneath the surface. With the Brasseys, there is absolutely no jealousy—only sincerity. I know

this because I can feel myself lighten up when they ask every day, "How'd the book go?" "Did you get a lot done?" Or when they tell me how excited they are to "know one of the greatest sportswriters in the country." Back in March, when I was busy reviewing hundreds of hours of NFL game tapes to help refresh my memory for the upcoming writing process, the Brasseys would call up and volunteer to come sit with me, just because they know how boring watching the same games over and over can become.

At times, handling the responsibilities of writing a full-length book in about a six-week span while being a full-time high school student made me feel *close* to overwhelmed (never admit that you are overwhelmed, because then you're done for). However, it's nice to know that people care about what I'm doing with my life and are rooting for me to succeed.

Throughout this new book-writing process, from the day I agreed to a deal with Random House to the night in June when I wrote this page, the best single moment of the entire ordeal was seeing the excitement and joy of Ryan and John when they learned that *Touchdown 2005* had been signed by America's top publishing house and was going to be sold nationwide for the first time. Since then, they've continued to do all they can to help push me along. Once again, my family is incredible and I've been blessed with tremendous supporters. But I'm around my friends equally as much, and my life is greatly impacted by them. With this in mind, I am forever grateful to have a pair of friends as great as Ryan and John Brassey.

Judd Benedick

All of the art that you see in the *Painting a New Picture* section is the work of Judd Benedick. Judd is an art teacher at Centennial High School, in Boise, Idaho. He is one of my closest friends and also one of the key figures responsible for igniting my passion for football. I first met Judd when I was in second grade—he was my counselor at the YMCA. I quickly established him as a role model because he could draw anything, he loved football (Judd was a linebacker and two-time team captain at Pacific Lutheran University, in Tacoma, Washington), and, more important to an impressionable second-grader, he was able to be "cool" by being sincerely kind and caring for others. It was a thrill getting to work with Judd on a football book so many years later. Judd lives in Meridian, Idaho with his wife, Elessa, and $2\frac{1}{2}$-year-old daughter, Zoe.

The *Touchdown 2005* "Staff"

In addition to Mark Tavani and the Brasseys, my dad, Gary, helped edit the book. In fact, Dad suffered through editing *Touchdown 2003* and *Touchdown 2004* as well. Random House/Ballantine also had an amazing group of people contributing to *Touchdown*, including Publisher Gina Centrello, Editor-in-Chief Dan Menaker, Publicity Director Tom Perry, Publicist Lisa Barnes, Editorial Assistant Ingrid Powell, and production gurus Erich Schoeneweiss, Bradley Ross, and Penelope Haynes. Also, a big thank-you to the fine, talented, and hardworking folks at North Market Street Graphics.

About the Author

Since the fourth grade, Andy Benoit has been demonstrating his extraordinary knowledge and talent as one of America's bright young sportswriters. This year, as a graduating honor roll student at Boise High School, Andy completed his ninth annual NFL preview book, *Touchdown 2005*.

Touchdown was originally a summer hobby for Andy, a kid who has always been strapped with a need to constantly stay busy and take on new challenges. Each year, "The Book," as it has come to be known around the Benoit family household, has grown in detail and sophistication.

As a sophomore, Andy contacted a printing company in Pennsylvania and, without revealing his age, negotiated his own book deal over the phone. The book has since received recognition from numerous sports icons, including John Madden, Chris Berman, and Rick Reilly.

Andy's number one passion is the NFL, but he is well versed in basketball, baseball, and golf, as well. Admittedly a sports junkie, he still manages a wide range of other interests, too. This year Andy received the Gold Congressional Award, presented by the U.S. Congress, recognizing his years of diversified community service work, personal development activities, and commitment to physical fitness.

Andy has also taken early steps toward pursuing a broadcasting career. During his junior year of high school, he hosted his own weekly sports radio talk show, *Running Up the Score with Andy Benoit*, on a Sporting News Radio affiliate station. Last summer, Andy worked as a sports intern at KBCI Channel 2, a CBS affiliate station in Boise.

Andy currently lives in Boise, Idaho, with his family (father Gary, mother Janet, and younger sister Katy). This spring, he will attend the Honors College at Washington State University. Andy plans to major in broadcasting. The move will be a change for him, but the only catastrophic adjustment he foresees having to make is in his sophomore year, when he'll have to get used to watching *Monday Night Football* on Pacific time!